T0366704

Words derived from Old Norse in *Sir Gawain and the Green Knight*: An etymological survey

Publications of the Philological Society, 50

Words derived from Old Norse in *Sir Gawain and the Green Knight*: An etymological survey

Richard Dance

**Department of Anglo-Saxon, Norse and Celtic,
University of Cambridge**

Publications of the Philological Society, 50

WILEY
Blackwell

This edition first published 2018
© 2018 The Philological Society

Blackwell Publishing was acquired by John Wiley & Sons in February 2007. Blackwell's publishing program has been merged with Wiley's global Scientific, Technical, and Medical business to form Wiley-Blackwell.

Registered Office
John Wiley & Sons Ltd, The Atrium, Southern Gate, Chichester, West Sussex, PO19 8SQ, United Kingdom

Editorial Offices
350 Main Street, Malden, MA 02148-5020, USA
9600 Garsington Road, Oxford, OX4 2DQ, UK
The Atrium, Southern Gate, Chichester, West Sussex, PO19 8SQ, UK

For details of our global editorial offices, for customer services, and for information about how to apply for permission to reuse the copyright material in this book please see our website at www.wiley.com/wiley-blackwell.

The right of Richard Dance to be identified as the author of this work has been asserted in accordance with the UK Copyright, Designs and Patents Act 1988.

All rights reserved. No part of this publication may be reproduced, stored in a retrieval system, or transmitted, in any form or by any means, electronic, mechanical, photocopying, recording or otherwise, except as permitted by the UK Copyright, Designs and Patents Act 1988, without the prior permission of the publisher.

Wiley also publishes its books in a variety of electronic formats. Some content that appears in print may not be available in electronic books.

Designations used by companies to distinguish their products are often claimed as trademarks. All brand names and product names used in this book are trade names, service marks, trademarks or registered trademarks of their respective owners. The publisher is not associated with any product or vendor mentioned in this book. This publication is designed to provide accurate and authoritative information in regard to the subject matter covered. It is sold on the understanding that the publisher is not engaged in rendering professional services. If professional advice or other expert assistance is required, the services of a competent professional should be sought.

Library of Congress Cataloging-in-Publication Data
Library of Congress Cataloging-in-Publication Data is available for this work
ISBN 978-1-1195-8002-7
A catalogue record for this book is available from the British Library.

Set in Times by SPS (P) Ltd., Chennai, India

Printed in the UK

WORDS DERIVED FROM OLD NORSE IN *SIR GAWAIN AND THE GREEN KNIGHT*: AN ETYMOLOGICAL SURVEY

VOLUME 1

Richard Dance

Department of Anglo-Saxon,
Norse and Celtic,
University of Cambridge

For Sarah

TABLE OF CONTENTS

Volume 2 can be accessed on Wiley Online Library at https://onlinelibrary.wiley.com/toc/1467968x/2018/116/S2.

ACKNOWLEDGEMENTS

As with many of the best adventures, when I started out on this one I wasn't really sure where, or how long, it would take me. I have known all my life the North Staffordshire countryside around my mother's home town of Leek, often identified as 'the *Gawain* country'. But it was when I was a graduate student in Oxford, looking at the Old Norse influence on Middle English vocabulary, that I first started to think seriously about exploring the language of the *Gawain*-poet. I brought this idea with me to Cambridge, to a Research Fellowship at St Catharine's College in 1997 – an opportunity that I still feel incredibly lucky to have been given. I got some way into the lexical thickets at that time, including presenting some preliminary thoughts at conferences and seminars. But I was then distracted by other things, and it wasn't until the late 2000s that I picked up this research again in earnest, and started to develop the idea for the Survey as it appears in this book. I have been working more or less consistently on it over the last ten years, helped very much by a Fellowship from the Arts and Humanities Research Council (AHRC), which granted me an extra term's sabbatical in 2011, and immeasurably by the learning and patience of colleagues and students in the Department of Anglo-Saxon, Norse and Celtic.

I have learned an enormous amount by being able to discuss my work at seminars and conferences in Bergen, Bristol, Cambridge, Castellón, Dublin, Essen, Glasgow, Kalamazoo, Leeds, London, Manchester, Morella, Nottingham, Oxford, Prague, Santiago de Compostela, Seville and Stavanger. I am hugely grateful to everyone involved in these events for their kindnesses and their wisdom. Special thanks are due to the folk in Nottingham, for letting me come with them on a legendary trip to Lud's Church in 2006. Since 2016, I have benefited tremendously from being able to put the finishing touches to this book in the context of the larger '*Gersum* Project', also funded by the AHRC. I am enormously grateful to everyone involved in *Gersum*, but I owe a special debt to my collaborators Sara Pons-Sanz and Brittany Schorn, for their inspiration and their friendship. The completed Survey in this book is far better for the many discussions we have had. It has also been improved considerably by the input of Susan Fitzmaurice and the anonymous readers for the Philological Society.

I have built up many, many other debts of gratitude as I have worked on this book, and it is impossible to record them all here. But I would like to say thank you in particular to all of the following, for their help and expertise in pursuing etymological trails into many different languages, for giving my ideas an airing and talking about them with me, for generously sharing their knowledge, work, time, bookshelves, hospitality and sympathy, and for generally helping me tell the *blysse* from the *blunder*: Lesley Abrams, Rhona Alcorn, Matthias Ammon, Richard Beadle, Andrew Breeze, David Callander, Jayne Carroll, Jan Cermak,

Marcelle Cole, Helen Cooper, Paul Cullen, Roderick Dale, Hans-Jürgen Diller, Lucie Doležalová, Philip Durkin, Fiona Edmonds, Anthony Esposito, María José Esteve Ramos, Jonathan Grove, Nik Gunn, Simon Horobin, Carole Hough, Judith Jesch, Christian Kay, Jane Kershaw, Matti Kilpiö, Peter Kitson, Gillis Kristensson, Margaret Laing, Roger Lass, Chris Lewis, Katie Lowe, Peter Lucas, Manfred Markus, Richard Marsden, Simon Meecham-Jones, Máire Ní Mhaonaigh, D. Gary Miller, Axel Müller, Rory Naismith, Sam Newton, Andy Orchard, David Parsons, Lucy Perry, Mike Pidd, Ad Putter, Judy Quinn, Jane Roberts, Elizabeth Rowe, Paul Russell, Mercedes Salvador Bello, Don Scragg, John Simpson, Jeremy Smith, Eric Stanley, Merja Steenros, Gjertrud Stenbrenden, Patrick Stiles, Louise Sylvester, Marie-Luise Theuerkauf, Matthew Townend, Thorlac Turville-Petre, Clive Upton, Arjen Versloot, George Walkden, Anthony Warner, Sheila Watts, Edmund Weiner, David Willis, Laura Wright, Nicky Zeeman, and all the staff of Cambridge University Library (especially Colin Clarkson) and the librarians in the English Faculty and St Catharine's College. But above everything else I am grateful to and for my wife, Sarah Meer, to whom this book is dedicated, with love.

ABBREVIATIONS AND CONVENTIONS

LANGUAGES AND DIALECTS

dial = dialect
e = early
l = late
M = Middle
O = Old
Mn = Modern
P = Proto-
PD = Present-Day

Angl = Anglian
Anglo-Fr = Anglo-French
Brit = British
Burg = Burgundian
Corn = Cornish
Dan = Danish
Du = Dutch
E = English
EFris = East Frisian
EN = East Norse
Far = Faroese
Fr = French
Fris = Frisian
Gael = Gaelic
Ger = German
Gmc = Germanic
Gotl = Gotlandic
HG = High German
Icel = Icelandic
IE = Indo-European
Ir = Irish
Ital = Italian
Kt = Kentish
Lat = Latin
Latv = Latvian
Lith = Lithuanian
LF = Low Franconian
LG = Low German
Grk = Greek
Merc = Mercian
N = Norse

Nhb = Northumbrian
Norw = Norwegian (variety not specified)
NNo = Nynorsk
OCS = Old Church Slavonic
Orkn = Orkney
PGmc = Proto-Germanic
Port = Portuguese
PrN = Proto-Norse
Rom = Romance
S = Saxon
Scand = Scandinavian
Shetl = Shetland
Skt = Sanskrit
Span = Spanish
Sw = Swedish
VAN = Viking-Age Norse
VLat = Vulgar Latin
We = Welsh
WFris = West Frisian
WN = West Norse
WS = West Saxon

PLACES AND REGIONS

EM = East Midlands
N/EM = North and/or East Midlands (of England) (see Introductory Remarks p. 63)
NM = North Midlands
NW = North-West
NWM = North-West Midlands
SE = South-East
SW = South-West
SWM = South-West Midlands

Abbreviations for English counties are traditional. Regions of Britain and Ireland referred to in summaries of *EDD* entries may follow *EDD* conventions.

GRAMMATICAL ETC.

acc.	accusative
adj.	adjective
adv.	adverb
auxil.	auxiliary
comp.	comparative
cp.	compare

dat.	dative
demon.	demonstrative
fem.	feminine
gen.	genitive
imp.	imperative
inc.	including/includes
ind.	indicative
infin.	infinitive
interj.	interjection
intrans.	intransitive
lit.	literally
masc.	masculine
n.	noun
neut.	neuter
num.	numeral
perh.	perhaps
pers.	person(al)
pl.	plural
poss.	possessive
post-prep.	post-prepositional
pp.	past participle
prep.	preposition
pres.	present
pres. ptcp.	present participle
pret.	preterite
prob.	probably
reflex.	reflexive
sg.	singular
str.	strong
subj.	subjunctive
superl.	superlative
s.v.	*sub voce*
trans.	transitive
ult.	ultimate(ly)
v.	verb
vbl. n.	verbal noun
VL	Verner's Law
wk.	weak

NOTATION, SYMBOLS AND OTHER CONVENTIONS WHEN CITING FORMS

<   derives from
\>   develops into
[ ]   enclose phonetic notation (unless stated to the contrary, the system used is that of the International Phonetic Association)
/ /   enclose phonemic notation
< >   enclose attested spellings
Italics are used for general or hypothetical language states (e.g. OE, PGmc) during historical discussion and reconstruction
*   before a word: indicates a hypothetical form, dependent on reconstruction or emendation

Vowel length is marked conventionally with an acute accent when citing ON and Icel (e.g. *é*), but with a flat macron when citing other Gmc languages (e.g. *ē*).

Alphabetical order follows the normal conventions for each language. For ME words, including in the Survey, <y> is treated as equivalent to <i>; <ȝ> follows <g>; <þ> follows <t>.

TEXTS

Cl = Cleanness (a.k.a. *Purity*)
Erk = St Erkenwald
Gaw = Sir Gawain and the Green Knight
Pat = Patience
Pe = Pearl
WA = The Wars of Alexander

OE short titles normally follow those in *DOE*. In citations from *MED*, ME short titles normally follow those in *MED*.

BIBLIOGRAPHY (see References)

AEW	Holthausen, *Altenglisches etymologisches Wörterbuch*
AND	Gregory et al. (eds.), *Anglo-Norman Dictionary*
AW	Andrew & Waldron (eds.), *The Poems of the Pearl Manuscript*
Bammesberger	Bammesberger, *Die Morphologie des urgermanischen Nomens*
Barron	Barron (ed.), *Sir Gawain and the Green Knight*
Battles	Battles (ed.), *Sir Gawain and the Green Knight*
Bense	Bense, *A Dictionary of the Low-Dutch Element in the English Vocabulary*
Bj.	Björkman, *Scandinavian Loan-Words in Middle English*
Bj-L.	Bjorvand & Lindeman, *Våre Arveord: Etymologisk Ordbok*

Borroff	Borroff & Howes (eds.), *Sir Gawain and the Green Knight*
Boutkan-Siebinga	Boutkan and Siebinga, *Old Frisian Etymological Dictionary*
Br-N.	Brøndum-Nielsen, *Gammeldansk grammatik i sproghistorisk fremstilling*
BT	Toller (ed.), *An Anglo-Saxon Dictionary, based on the manuscript collections of the late Joseph Bosworth*
BTS	Toller (ed.), *An Anglo-Saxon Dictionary, based on the manuscript collections of the late Joseph Bosworth, Supplement*
BTSC	Campbell, *An Anglo-Saxon Dictionary, based on the manuscript collections of Joseph Bosworth, Enlarged Addenda and Corrigenda to the Supplement*
Burrow	Burrow (ed.), *Sir Gawain and the Green Knight*
CA	Cawley & Anderson (eds.), *Pearl, Cleanness, Patience and Sir Gawain and the Green Knight*
Campbell	Campbell, *Old English Grammar*
CONE	Lass et al., *A Corpus of Narrative Etymologies*
CV	Cleasby-Vigfusson, *An Icelandic-English Dictionary*
DEAF	Baldinger et al. (eds.), *Dictionnaire étymologique de l'ancien français*
DMF	*Dictionnaire de moyen français*, version 2015
DMLBS	Latham et al. (eds.), *Dictionary of Medieval Latin from British Sources*
DOE	Cameron et al. (eds.), *Dictionary of Old English*
DOST	Craigie & Aitken (eds.), *Dictionary of the Older Scottish Tongue*
DP (or Bj. DP)	Björkman, 'Zur dialektischen Provenienz der nordischen Lehnwörter im Englischen'
DSC	Macleod (ed.), *Dictionarium Scoto-Celticum*
eDIL	*Electronic Dictionary of the Irish Language*
EDD	Wright, *The English Dialect Dictionary*
EETS	Early English Text Society (o.s. = original series, s.s. = supplementary series)
eLALME	McIntosh et al., *An Electronic Version of a Linguistic Atlas of Late Mediaeval English*
Electronic Sawyer	Keynes et al. (eds.), *The Electronic Sawyer: Online Catalogue of Anglo-Saxon Charters*
EPNE	Smith, *English Place-Name Elements*
EPNS	English Place-Name Society
EWAhd	Lloyd et al. (eds.), *Etymologisches Wörterbuch des Althochdeutschen*

Falk-Torp	Falk & Torp, *Norwegisch-dänisches etymologisches Wörterbuch*
FEW	von Wartburg et al. (eds.), *Französisches etymologisches Wörterbuch* (where *FEW (Germanismes)* = appendix of words of Gmc origin)
Fritzner	Fritzner, *Ordbog over det gamle norske sprog*
GED	Lehmann, *A Gothic Etymological Dictionary*
GDS	Gollancz with Day & Serjeantson (eds.), *Sir Gawain and the Green Knight*
Godefroy	Godefroy, *Dictionnaire de l'ancienne langue française*
Gordon	Gordon, *An Introduction to Old Norse*, 2nd ed. rev. A. R. Taylor
GPC	Bevan et al. (eds.), *Geiriadur Prifysgol Cymru* (online ed.)
Hall	Hall, *A Concise Anglo-Saxon Dictionary*
Heid.	Heidermanns, *Etymologisches Wörterbuch der germanischen Primäradjektive*
Hellquist	Hellquist, *Svensk Etymologisk Ordbok*
Heusler	Heusler, *Altisländisches Elementarbuch*
Hofmann	Hofmann, *Nordisch-Englische Lehnbeziehungen der Wikingerzeit*
Hogg	Hogg, *A Grammar of Old English, Vol. 1*
Hogg-Fulk	Hogg & Fulk, *A Grammar of Old English, Vol. 2*
HTOED	Kay et al. (eds.), *The Historical Thesaurus of the Oxford English Dictionary*
Jakobsen	Jakobsen, *An Etymological Dictionary of the Norn Language in Shetland*
Jóh.	Alexander Jóhannesson, *Isländisches etymologisches Wörterbuch*
Jones	Jones (ed.), *Sir Gawain and the Grene Gome*
Jordan-Crook	Jordan, *Handbook of Middle English Grammar: Phonology*, trans. and rev. Crook
Ker	Ker, *Catalogue of Manuscripts Containing Anglo-Saxon*
Kluge-Seebold	Kluge, *Etymologisches Wörterbuch der deutschen Sprache*, 25th ed., ed. Seebold
Knigge	Knigge, *Die Sprache des Dichters von Sir Gawain and the Green Knight*
Krahe-Meid	Krahe, *Germanische Sprachwissenschaft*, rev. Meid
Kroonen	Kroonen, *Etymological Dictionary of Proto-Germanic*
Kullnick	Kullnick, *Studien über den Wortschatz in Sir Gawayne and the Grene Knyȝt*
LAEME	Laing, *A Linguistic Atlas of Early Middle English*
LALME	McIntosh et al., *A Linguistic Atlas of Late Mediaeval English*

LEIA	Vendryes et al. (eds.), *Lexique étymologique de l'irlandais ancien*
LexPoet	Sveinbjörn Egilsson, *Lexicon poeticum antiquæ linguæ septentrionalis*, rev. Finnur Jónsson
LIV	Rix (ed.), *Lexikon der indogermanischen Verben*
Luick	Luick, *Historische Grammatik der englischen Sprache*
MacBain	MacBain, *An Etymological Dictionary of the Gaelic Language*
Madden	Madden (ed.), *Sir Gawayne*
Matasović	Matasović, *Etymological Dictionary of Proto-Celtic*
Mätzner	Mätzner, *Altenglische Sprachproben*
Mag.	Ásgeir Blöndal Magnússon, *Íslensk Orðsifjabók*
McGee	McGee, 'The Geographical Distribution of Scandinavian Loan-Words in Middle English, with Special Reference to the Alliterative Poetry'
McGillivray	McGillivray (ed.), *Sir Gawain and the Green Knight*
McL	McLaughlin, *A Graphemic-Phonemic Study of a Middle English Manuscript*
MED	Kurath et al. (eds.), *Middle English Dictionary*
M(G)	Morris (ed.), *Sir Gawayne and the Green Knight*, rev. Gollancz (1897; rev. ed. 1912)
Moorman	Moorman (ed.), *The Works of the Gawain-poet*
Morris	Morris (ed.), *Sir Gawayne and the Green Knight* (1864; 2nd ed. 1869)
Nielsen	Nielsen, *Dansk Etymologisk Ordbog*
NIL	Wodtko et al., *Nomina im indogermanischen Lexikon*
Noreen	Noreen, *Altnordische Grammatik I: altisländische und altnorwegische Grammatik*
NOWELE	*North-Western European Language Evolution*
ODEE	Onions (ed.), *The Oxford Dictionary of English Etymology*
OEC	Healey et al, *Dictionary of Old English Web Corpus*
OED	*Oxford English Dictionary* (*OED2* = the 2nd ed.; *OED3* = the ongoing revised 3rd ed.)
ONP	Degnbol et al (eds.), *Ordbog over det norrøne prosasprog*
Orel	Orel, *A Handbook of Germanic Etymology*
PASE	*The Prosopography of Anglo-Saxon England*
Peters	Peters, 'Zum skandinavischen Lehngut im Altenglischen'
Pokorny	Pokorny, *Indogermanisches etymologisches Wörterbuch*
PS	Putter & Stokes (eds.), *The Works of the Gawain Poet*
Ringe-Taylor	Ringe & Taylor, *The Development of Old English*
Rynell	Rynell, *The Rivalry of Scandinavian and Native Synonyms in Middle English*

SAO	*Svenska Akademiens Ordbok*
Seebold	Seebold, *Vergleichendes und etymologisches Wörterbuch der germanischen starken Verben*
Silverstein	Silverstein (ed.), *Sir Gawain and the Green Knight*
SND	Grant & Murison (eds.), *The Scottish National Dictionary*
SPS	Pons-Sanz, *The Lexical Effects of Anglo-Scandinavian Linguistic Contact on Old English*
Stratmann	Stratmann, *Dictionary of the Old English Language*
Strat.-Brad.	Stratmann, *A Middle English Dictionary*, rev. Bradley
Tamm	Tamm, *Etymologisk Svensk Ordbok*
Thorson	Thorson, *Anglo-Norse Studies*
TG	Tolkien & Gordon (eds.), *Sir Gawain and the Green Knight*
TGD	Tolkien & Gordon (eds.), *Sir Gawain and the Green Knight*, rev. Davis
Torp-Falk	Torp, *Wortschatz der germanischen Spracheinheit, unter Mitwirkung von Hjalmar Falk*
Toll	Toll, *Niederländisches Lehngut im Mittelenglischen*
Torp	Torp, *Nynorsk Etymologisk Ordbok*
Vant	Vantuono (ed.), *The Pearl Poems*
VEPN	Parsons & Styles (eds.), *Vocabulary of English Place-Names*
de Vaan	de Vaan, *Etymological Dictionary of Latin and the Other Italic Languages*
de Vries	de Vries, *Altnordisches etymologisches Wörterbuch*
de Vries/de Tollenaere	de Vries, *Nederlands Etymologisch Woordenboek*, rev. de Tollenaere
Walde-Hoffmann	Walde, *Lateinisches etymologisches Wörterbuch*, rev. Hofmann
Waldron	Waldron (ed.), *Sir Gawain and the Green Knight*
WAWN	Holthausen, *Vergleichendes und etymologisches Wörterbuch des Altwestnordischen*
Wedgwood	Wedgwood, *A Dictionary of English Etymology*
Wright & Wright	Wright & Wright, *An Elementary Middle English Grammar*
Winny	Winny, *Sir Gawain and the Green Knight*

CATEGORY LABELS

(See the Introductory Remarks at pp. 39–65 and the Introductory Essays to Types A, B, C and D for further information.)

Structural categories

A Systematic, formal evidence for input from ON is available:
  A1 phonological criteria;
  A2 morphological criteria;
  A3 phonological *and* morphological criteria.

(Type A labels are suffixed with a * when a word's ON etymon has attested cognates in (pre-contact) OE.)

B Systematic, formal evidence for ON input is not available, but a readily identifiable form-source can be generally agreed. The Gmc root is not represented in early OE, but is represented in ON.
  B1 there is no clear evidence for forms derived on the same root anywhere else in Gmc;
  B2 forms derived on the same root are clearly identifiable in Go and/or the continental WGmc languages (but not in early OE).

C Systematic, formal evidence for ON input is not available, but a readily identifiable form-source can be generally agreed. The Gmc root is represented in early OE, or there is an unambiguous form-source in a third language. But some aspect(s) of the form, sense or usage of the ME word are rare or unparalleled in OE (or the third language), and better paralleled in the Scand languages. Loan or influence from ON has therefore been proposed in order to account for one or more of the following features:
  C1 derivational form;
  C2 orthographic (phonological) form;
  C3 sense;
  C4 formation of compound or phrase;
  C5 frequency.

(Type C labels are prefixed by an **F** when a word's form clearly cannot derive from OE, but when it belongs (ultimately or more recently) to a non-Gmc language, which could have been its direct source.)

D Etymology is 'obscure', i.e. a single, generally accepted form-source is not available. Input has been suggested from one or more comparable ON words, but these explanations have not met with general acceptance and they compete in each instance with one or more alternative derivations.

D1 the form and sense of the stem can be established (relatively) straightforwardly, and are usually agreed, but there is no generally accepted etymology;

D2 the interpretation in its *Gaw* context of the ME word, and hence its most plausible etymon, is debated.

Circumstantial categories

a a cognate is attested (in substantially the same form, sense or usage) in the continental West Germanic languages

b principally confined to the North or East in the toponymic record

c principally confined to the North or East in the lexical record

d early occurrences in English are strongly associated with Scand cultural influence

Probability markers

B or **C**
The case for ON input is very plausible. There is general agreement in the scholarship, often without exception.

BB or **CC**
The case for ON input is reasonable, but alternative explanations seem about equally plausible. There is usually some disagreement in the scholarship.

BBB or **CCC**
The case for ON input is not strong (though it still cannot be dismissed out of hand). The word's history can usually be explained more plausibly by other means. There is some history of attributing or at least suggesting ON input in the scholarly tradition, but the weight of (especially recent) argument is against it, and/or the case for it is problematic in some fairly fundamental way.

D
The case for ON input is reasonable, and (in most cases) has often been made in the scholarly tradition; but plausible alternative explanations are usually available.

DD
The case for ON input is not strong (though it still cannot be dismissed out of hand). The word can usually be explained more plausibly by other means. There is some history of attributing or at least suggesting ON input in the scholarly tradition, but the weight of (especially recent) argument is against it, and/or the case for it is problematic in some fairly fundamental way.

INTRODUCTORY ESSAYS

1

INTRODUCTORY REMARKS

This book presents a fully annotated analysis, word by word, of the etymologies of all the lexical items in *Sir Gawain and the Green Knight* which have been cited as borrowings, in whole or in part, from the medieval Scandinavian languages. The Old Norse influence on Middle English vocabulary has long been appreciated as very considerable, especially when it comes to the rich and diverse lexis of texts composed in the North and North Midlands of England, and the self-consciously showy and frequently obscure word-hoard of alliterative verse. Probably the best-known instance is *Sir Gawain*, which contains no fewer than 496 different words whose forms, meanings or usage have been explained as showing Old Norse input by one or more commentators – more or less confidently, in a plethora of editions, monographs, articles, notes, dissertations and historical dictionary entries – since the mid-nineteenth century. A large proportion of these words prove to be highly interesting, and variously problematic, whether etymologically or textually. But they have never been collected and considered in detail as a complete group before. The present survey is the first thoroughgoing analysis of this important body of words, conducted in accordance with a newly developed system of etymological classification, and with references to all relevant previous scholarship. It is the most detailed description ever undertaken of the Scandinavian influence on the vocabulary of a major Middle English text, and aims to provide a model for the collection and etymological investigation of Norse loans in any English source.

1.1. Backgrounds

The vocabulary of *Sir Gawain and the Green Knight* (hereafter *Gaw*) is famously capacious and expressive, and no less infamously difficult.[1] For modern editors, critics and linguists alike, interpreting it can at times feel like a quest into perilous and remote territory no less challenging than the hero's own. This is true not least when it comes to understanding the peculiarly diverse historical

---

[1] See the various remarks cited in the section '*Sir Gawain* and the "Scandinavian Element"' (1.3) below, e.g. at p. 11.

make-up of the poem's lexis, which plays host to many elements ultimately of non-native origin, amongst them the numerous words which have been ascribed a source in the early Scandinavian (hereafter Scand) languages. This 'Old Norse element' has often been trumpeted as a particularly distinctive ingredient, essential to characterizing the poet's language; and opening the glossaries to the standard editions of *Gaw* reveals an extraordinary variety of lexical items whose etymologies involve the citation of an Old Norse (ON) form. They include some very rarely attested words, unique to this manuscript (like **chymbled** 'bound, wrapped up', **gryndel** 'fierce' and **ruþes** 'bestirs'), some others associated especially with the alliterative poetic tradition in Middle English, in one or several dialects (e.g. **busk** 'to get ready', **kayre** 'to go, ride', **tulk** 'man, knight'), and some which were and remained typical mainly of the local vocabulary of the North and North Midlands (such as **bigge** 'to settle, found, build', **layt** 'to seek, wish to know', **mon** 'must'); next to many others which now strike us as far more run-of-the-mill, because they have become completely normal, everyday words to speakers of Present-Day English (everything from **hitte**, **take**, **skyl** and **wyndow** to **blaste** and **froþe**).

When I first started to investigate these words, I had intended to undertake a study primarily of a different kind from the etymological survey which is presented below. This is not to say that the etymological identification of ON borrowings in *Gaw* ever seemed likely to be a straightforward matter: working out which Middle English (ME) words really do show some kind of influence from the early Scand languages, so closely related and so similar as these were to the native vernacular, has always been appreciated as an especially difficult task, and I expected this part of my investigation to present some challenges.[2] Nonetheless, I assumed in the beginning that it ought to be possible to extract from the (extensive) previous scholarship on the *Gaw*-poet's lexis a list of fairly secure items of probable ON origin, on which most of the principal authorities would agree; and thence to progress to analysing the history and behaviour of these words, investigating how and why they are used in their particular lexical and stylistic contexts, how they came to be available to this poet, and how his usage compares to that of other late ME texts.[3] But as I worked my way through the ever-growing body of words which, I discovered, might be included in such a

---

[2] For detailed discussion of these matters see below, beginning with 'The identification of Old Norse input'.

[3] In other words, I had intended this study to follow the format of my earlier work on the Norse-derived lexis of early Middle English texts from the South-West Midlands (Dance 2003), in which a relatively brief account of etymological identification precedes a fuller survey of these words' semantic and stylistic functions. I have produced a preliminary analysis of this sort for *Gaw* (Dance 2013), which draws attention to some of the characteristics of a selection of words usually derived from ON. One of the focuses of that article is on the ways in which the vocabulary of ME alliterative verse cannot be regarded as a straightforward means of recovering 'local' usage; and that having regard to semantic and stylistic contexts highlights the fact that many items even at the 'basic' or 'grammatical' end of the *Gaw*-poet's lexicon seem to have been chosen because they filled a particular stylistic function.

study, I found myself increasingly sidetracked, and increasingly fascinated, by the sheer difficulties in identifying the items to which some ON influence really might be attributed. Far from being the occasional niggle, the problem of establishing a corpus of 'bona fide' ON loans became more and more apparent, and the differences of opinion more and more numerous and substantial, in proportion to the number of comments I found. Contrary to the assumptions expressed in some of the scholarly literature on this topic,[4] not only was there no full, etymologically-sensitive account of the words derived from ON in *Gaw* which actually set out the reasons for their inclusion, but such lists as one could extract from editions, dictionaries and studies dedicated to this topic disagreed with one another in far more extensive and unpredictable ways than could have been guessed at. And this is not to mention the vast array of other suggestions for ON input which one encounters across well over a century of philological, editorial and literary-critical scholarship, ranging from detailed, complex analyses of this or that word to the most casual of mentions. Many of these proposals are scattered in notes and articles, often with little or no explanation or discussion; some are claimed on much better grounds than others; and, what is more, they have only sometimes been noticed by lexicographers, editors and the authors of subsequent notes and articles.[5] Far from doing away with the requirement for further etymological investigation, then, the quantity and diversity of previous piecemeal attempts on this subject are precisely what necessitates it. I therefore came to the conclusion that collecting and collating existing opinions could be no mere preliminary to further analysis of the Norse-derived element in *Gaw*, but was the object of considerable interest, and would benefit from being the focus of a substantive study, in its own right.

Moreover, the situation we find with *Gaw* reflects, albeit in an extreme form, some significant issues in the study of ON loans in ME more generally. Scholarship on the broad subjects of Anglo-Norse contact and its linguistic consequences for English has of course been both extensive and profoundly important. The sociolinguistic contexts for the encounters of speakers of ON and Old English (OE) in Viking-Age England, and the mechanisms by which material was transferred from one language to the other, have in particular been the focus of crucial research in the last several decades, and we understand the linguistic nature of this contact better than we ever have.[6] But there remains a great deal to do to identify the full extent of the lexical material of possible ON origin in English – which is itself, of course, one of the major pieces of evidence for those interactions – and to evaluate its distribution and significance on a

---

[4] A notable case in point is Elliott's remark (1984: 73): 'Norse influence on the vocabulary of Middle English alliterative poetry has long been recognized and even calculated statistically, and there is no need to plough the same half-acre again'. Elliott cites the (relatively brief) discussion by Anderson (1969: 73–4) as an example.

[5] The relevant literature is reviewed in detail under '*Sir Gawain* and the "Scandinavian element"' below.

[6] See most importantly Townend (2002), and also the other work cited under note 95 below.

text-by-text basis. Many scholars have advocated the large-scale (re)assessment of ON influence on the medieval English lexicon, something which has long been regarded as a considerable desideratum.[7] There has been intensive work on the loaned vocabulary of some texts and traditions, especially in the period before *c.* 1300, including significant contributions by Pons-Sanz on the OE period, as well as my own earlier work on some twelfth- and thirteenth-century texts.[8] But the Scand input into the vocabulary of the great literary monuments of later ME, especially those composed in the North or North Midlands (where the effects of the ON spoken by Scand settlers are attested in their greatest range and complexity), has never seen sustained exploration. One of the main reasons for this, I suspect, resides precisely in those etymological difficulties so evident for *Gaw* – i.e. in the complexities and uncertainties that inevitably emerge when one tries to establish a set of words which really are, or might be, derived from or in some way influenced by ON. Agreeing on which lexical items we mean, or at least how we might go about identifying them, would seem to be foundational to any effort to collect and label them in a textual corpus. The criteria that underlie the attribution of Norse origin to ME words have seldom been delineated (and rarely if ever refined) since Björkman's magisterial *Scandinavian Loan-Words in Middle English* (Bj.), completed in 1902; this is still the only attempt to make a catalogue of ON loans in a considerable corpus of ME starting from etymological first principles, and remains essential reading for everyone working in the field. The identification of ON input is hardly mentioned in many recent handbook treatments of Norse loans, lists of which have tended to become conventionalized, with no indication that some are etymologically far more secure inclusions than others.[9] There are very many excellent accounts of individual words, pre-eminently in the great works of historical English lexicography (the etymological remarks in the revised *OED3* are models of careful, informed judgement), as well as in a panoply of other studies. But the purpose of such accounts cannot be, and is not, to consider and keep in mind aspects of argumentation which pertain to all words of one possible origin; and

[7] See most notably McIntosh (1978), and the remarks in Townend (2000: 92–3; 2002: 184).

[8] See esp. SPS, and on particular texts/authors see Pons-Sanz (2000; 2004; 2007; 2008; 2010); Dance (2003; 2011; 2012b). See also Skaffari (2009, inc. a case-study of *Vices and Virtues*). On the older Scots evidence see esp. Kries (2003; summarized 2007), and further Smith (1994; 1996: 177–86, with further references).

[9] There are honourable exceptions to this statement, inc. some discussions in general studies of loaned material in English which make valuable contributions to the subject in their own right; amongst recent work see most notably Miller (2012: 91–147) and Durkin (2014: 171–221). Otherwise, the fuller surveys and summaries of the last few decades include Rot (1991: 279–309), Kastovsky (1992: 320–36), Burnley (1992: 414–23), Wollmann (1996), Nielsen (1998: 165–88), Braunmüller (2002: 1029–34), Sandred (2005: esp. 2063–5), Townend (2006); and see further my discussions in Dance (2012a; 2018). But many introductory accounts in effect merely repeat and rearrange examples which go right back to the earliest summaries of ON loans in English. Symptomatic is Grant (2009a), which is still using, amongst others, Skeat (1882) in order to supply examples for a major project on the history of loanwords in English.

so there is an inevitable lack of consistency in the treatment of purported ON loans even within one and the same project.[10]

As I noticed above, nowhere are these issues more apparent than with a text like *Gaw*, whose very wide and often difficult vocabulary, and long editorial history, magnify the results of all the problems mentioned so far. If one gathers together all the claims for ON derivation, in all the relevant scholarship on this poem, there is a simply startling degree of variation. The possible corpus ranges from a minimum of no more than 200 words on which probably all commentators would agree,[11] to a maximum of nearly 500 total suggestions (496 lexical items, 399 stems) which cannot definitively be ruled out.[12] This last is a huge number which no single study gets anywhere near, but which exposes the enormous penumbra of speculative possibilities that have accumulated over the years. To give an idea of the difference between even the most commonly-cited authorities, the two great scholarly editions, those of Tolkien-Gordon-Davis (TGD) and Gollancz-Day-Serjeantson (GDS), say substantially different things about the etymologies of 83 (20.8%) of these stems; between *MED* and the various incarnations of *OED*, the discrepancy is greater still, at 108 stems (27.1%; and these are by no means always the same instances which split the editions). And it is an index of the enormous quantity of scholarship there has been since 1902 dealing with the OE, ME and ON lexicons, amongst many other relevant subjects, that 163 (40.9%) of the stems treated in the present survey are not even mentioned by Bj.[13] The scale of these discrepancies is ultimately so massive that it must have serious consequences for any study we might want to undertake of 'the ON element' in *Gaw* or any other comparable later ME text. It is clearly impossible to begin such a study by stating a simple list of 'bona fide' ON derivations, and at the very least it is ill-advised to assume that there is any such thing as a 'definitive' corpus of Scand loans which can attract even shaky consensus. Rather, if we hope to understand exactly what underlies the reasons for the differences in previous accounts – whether this has to do with the etymological evidence itself, or attitudes towards that evidence, or both – we must start by acknowledging that the grounds upon which ON input has been identified for each and every word need careful scrutiny and considered presentation.

In this book, I have set about to do precisely this work of collecting and examining, in what may be thought of as a kind of experiment in practical etymology. Taking *Gaw* as my case-study, my aim is to see what can be achieved by gathering and analysing all the many and various suggestions for Norse input which can be found in the scholarship on one major ME poem since the mid-nineteenth century (a body of work which has never been comprehensively reviewed like this), and trying to extract

---

[10] On this issue see also Hoad (1984: 38).

[11] See the summary discussion under Concluding Remarks below (section 6.2), where I suggest a set of 195 lexical items (134 stems) which would be generally accepted as showing some ON input.

[12] On my use of the term 'stem' in this study, see pp. 65–6 below.

[13] For detailed commentary on Bj.'s coverage, and on the differences between the major editions, see the Introductory Essays to each Type and the Concluding Remarks pp. 232–4 below.

the principles underlying those claims in a more rigorous way than has been attempted hitherto.[14] In doing this, I adopt first and foremost a lexicographical approach: the main mode of this book is to proceed word-by-word in a survey format, recording the crucial evidence and key opinions for each item in as much detail as seems helpful and possible in the space available. But analysing all these individual cases, and in particular going back to etymological first principles and paying close attention to the many and varied kinds of arguments for ON input which altogether they reveal, has enabled the development of a new, more refined way of classifying the evidence for Scand derivation, which can in turn be used to organize and interrogate the contents of the survey. This system categorizes putative Norse-derived words primarily according to the 'structural' evidence for ON influence that they present, i.e. what emerges when we compare the attested OE, ME and ON lexicons, and hence the problems that these words pose to the etymologist in the first instance. It therefore aims to clarify the etymological arguments involved in each case, and to promote a consistent approach to the treatment of each category of evidence, while acknowledging the elusiveness in most instances of a definitive identification (or rejection) of Norse input. This typological framework provides the structure for the Survey in this book, and is described and explained in detail below.

1.2. ABOUT THIS BOOK

The main component of this book is the Survey, which (with its Appendix) makes up the majority of Volume 2. It contains a numbered entry for each of the 496 words in *Gaw* for which ON input has been claimed by one or more authority. Bringing together lexical items which are or may be recent derivations on the same word base, this amounts to 399 different 'stems', according to which groups of entries are arranged. The Survey is organized into four sections, Types A to D, reflecting the principal categories of etymological evidence on the basis of which Scand input has been argued; see the discussion below. For reference, and as an aid to finding words in the Survey, I have appended an Alphabetical Word-List (the first section of the Index) giving each item with its summary category label and entry number.

The other elements of the book introduce and comment upon the Survey in various ways, in the form of a series of Introductory Essays. These have been gathered as Volume 1 for the pragmatic reason that they benefit from being read alongside the Survey, and it will often be helpful to have both volumes open at the same time; the Essays make constant reference to the words treated in the Survey (always cited in **bold**), and readers will need to turn to the relevant entry in Volume 2 in order to see details of each word's etymology and other features (meanings, occurrences, bibliographical references, etc.).

---

[14] On this sort of 'refurbishment' of linguistic narratives and of the methods underpinning them, see Lass (1997: 6–8).

The present Introductory Remarks discuss the backgrounds to this study and the methods employed. They continue with a review of previous scholarship on the lexis of *Gaw*, focusing on work which has collected and/or described words with a supposed Scand pedigree, and placing this in the context of other major books and articles dealing with the ON influence on English vocabulary. I then move on to a survey of the criteria which have been employed to identify ON input, assessing some of the attitudes and assumptions which, explicitly or implicitly, seem to me to underlie its attribution, and which can result in quite different interpretations of the same etymological evidence. Beginning from the principles here established, I divide this evidence into two broad classes, the structural and the circumstantial, and describe the characteristic features of each kind and the problems involved in assessing them. This serves to introduce the analytical methods and organization used in this book, in particular the new typology of evidence for ON input which generates my four main structural categories (and various sub-categories) and additional circumstantial flags, as well as the broad probability markers which signal the quality of the case for each item. The Introductory Remarks then close with a description of the Survey, what it includes and excludes, and a guide to the format and conventions of an entry.

The four introductory essays that follow deal specifically with the four main sections of the Survey, with one essay dedicated to each of Types A, B, C and D. Each essay begins with an account of the principles according to which items have been classed as belonging to this structural Type, and a summary list of words, sub-type by sub-type. These are accompanied by (brief) introductory discussions of the items, examining the characteristic profiles of evidence and argument which belong to each sub-type, and paying particular attention to aspects of etymology and distribution (in Germanic and English dialect contexts) which emerge as interesting. I also summarize the relative quality of the cases for claiming ON input, and the ways in which the principal scholarly authorities have differed in their assessment of these. The introduction to Type A also includes a 'handbook'-style guide to the formal criteria, phonological and morphological, which are (or may be) regarded as diagnostic of Scand input. Reference is made to these formal features (by § number) throughout the book, whenever one of them is relevant to the etymological evidence for an item under consideration. In the final essay (6. Concluding Remarks), I provide a (very brief) recap of my findings, collating some of the key figures and typical features established in the foregoing discussions. I also suggest some further ways of analysing the data, with some comments on the semantic and grammatical characteristics of what may be supposed to be the most secure items in the Survey. The essay ends by pointing the way to some possible directions in future research, including remarks on 'The *Gersum* Project', the broader, collaborative investigation of ON input in the lexis of late ME alliterative verse for which the present book is the foundation and precursor.[15]

---

[15] For '*Gersum*', see the project's website at <https://www.gersum.org>.

Some brief remarks on terminology may be helpful at this point. I have settled in this book for a fairly traditional use of terms, as also of conventions in the citation of (attested and reconstructed) linguistic forms (for more details on the latter, see below under 'The entries: format and conventions'). This includes employing 'Old Norse' (ON) in its habitual sense in Anglophone philology, i.e. to refer (collectively or non-specifically) to the Scandinavian languages in the period from about 700 AD to the close of the Middle Ages.[16] 'Norse' and 'Scandinavian' (Scand) may therefore be understood in this book as direct synonyms. ON words are cited first and foremost via their OIcel reflexes; but due attention is paid to the forms attested in the other Scand languages, medieval and modern, and to the reconstructed (and occasionally the attested runic) forms of 'Viking Age Norse' (VAN, which I take to refer to the ON of the period c. 700–1100) whenever these have a direct bearing on the etymon proposed for a ME word. I have also maintained the traditional labels 'Old West Norse' (OWN) and 'Old East Norse' (OEN) as the starting points for discussing geographical variation in the medieval Scand languages, simplistic and problematic though these terms must be recognized as being.[17] There is, moreover, no completely standard, conventional way of referring collectively to lexical material transmitted from ON into English, and/or to English words influenced in some way by contact with ON. This problem is to a large extent bound up with inconsistencies in the terminology used to deal with the lexical outcomes of language contact more generally.[18] 'Borrowing' or 'loan(word)' have been and may be used quite generically, as may 'interference', although each of these terms has also developed a narrower reference to a particular type of lexical transfer: so 'loanword' can specify that there has been a transfer of morphemic material from the source language (as opposed to a 'loan-shift' like a loan-translation or semantic loan, where this does not happen);[19] and 'borrowing' and 'interference' (esp. 'interference through shift') have sometimes been used to denote the products of recipient- and source-language agentivity respectively.[20] In an effort to find a term

---

[16] This is how the term has been used in major, recent treatments of the Scand influence on English, such as Townend (2002: see esp. xv). In practice, there has always been a moderate undertone of discomfort with this label in the scholarship, since 'Norse' originally referred specifically to things Norwegian (see e.g. *OED* s.v. *Norse* n. and adj.); and for some discussions of the periodization of the Scand languages and the terminology for them see further e.g. Birkmann (2002), Nielsen (2002b) and Ralph (2002). But attempts to introduce alternative labels (from Skeat's (1892a: 452–3) 'Scandian' and Flom's (1900) 'Old Northern' or 'Old Scandinavian', to the 'Old Nordic' used by Bandle et al. (2002–5), the 'Old Scandinavian' (again) in Faarlund (1994) and the 'early Scandinavian' preferred by *OED3* and Durkin (2014: 175)) have never really caught on, and – so long as we are careful to define what we mean by it – ON seems to me as good a shorthand as anything else.

[17] On Scand dial features and their development, beside the standard grammars (referred to under 'Formal Criteria' in the Introductory Essay to Type A below), see esp. the discussions in Andersson (2002), Barnes (2005), and further e.g. Nielsen (2002b), Birkmann (2002) and Ralph (2002).

[18] The most influential account is Haugen (1950). For recent discussions and further references see e.g. Fischer (2001), Winford (2005; 2010: 170–3), Haspelmath (2009: 36–40), Durkin (2009: 132–40; 2014: 8–11), and (with reference to ON input in English) see further Townend (2002: 202), Dance (2003: 71–4, 91–7) and SPS (4–5).

[19] See also Haspelmath (2009: 37 n.2) on the ambiguity of the phrase 'X loanword'.

[20] See e.g. Thomason & Kaufman (1988: 37–45) and Haspelmath (2009: 36–7).

which could act as an umbrella for all these kinds of transferred material, my solution in Dance (2003) was to employ what I hoped would be the unambiguous 'Norse-derived word'.[21] I still think that this label has certain benefits, even if it is something of a mouthful – and even though in itself it must, of course, be consciously defined as anything and everything transferred from or modelled on ON (including elements of form, meaning and usage, some of which are more naturally described as 'influence' rather than 'derivation' per se), plus later sub-derivations coined on that material within English.[22] Describing an ME word as *derived* from ON' is moreover advantageous in the context of the present study, given the focus that it implies on the act of etymological interpretation itself. I have therefore retained the phrase 'derived from ON' in the title of this book, intending this to encompass all the possible varieties of linguistic transfer and influence described above; but also so as to draw attention to the essential fact that the words that feature in the Survey are here ultimately because they have been derived from ON by some scholarly authority or other, and that the collecting and assessing of these claims are amongst the main aims of my work. In the course of the analysis in this book, nonetheless, and because the main viewpoint taken on the material is etymological, I have tended to prefer 'ON input' as a shorthand way of indicating some role played by the Scand languages in the development of a particular ME lexical item (the 'output', as it were).

1.3. *Sir Gawain* and the 'Scandinavian element'

If one seeks to understand scholarly approaches to the Scand influence on medieval English vocabulary, there are no better case studies than *Gaw*. The various investigations and discussions of this topic, and the plethora of other remarks that touch directly on it, constitute of course only a small sub-set of the vast array of scholarship on a poem whose longstanding celebrity as one of the great monuments of ME literature (and accompanying canonical status as a classroom text) have guaranteed it serious and sustained interest since the middle of the nineteenth century.[23] The fundamentals of the poem's composition and original context continue to be pursued with as much vim as ever. It is generally now accepted that *Gaw* shares an author with the other three pieces recorded with it in the single surviving manuscript, i.e. *Pearl, Cleanness* (or *Purity*) and *Patience*; *St Erkenwald* in London, British Library, Harley 2250 is sometimes,

---

[21] For discussion see Dance (2003: 72).

[22] See also Durkin (2009: 141). 'Norse-derived' is also taken up by Miller (2012: esp. 106).

[23] The best general guides to the mammoth bibliography are those by Andrew (1979) and Blanch (2000), and see further the annual round-up of scholarship on 'the *Gawain*-poet' (here including *Erk*) in the journal *The Year's Work in English Studies*. In the standard modern catalogues of ME, *Gaw* is no. 3144 in Boffey & Edwards (2005), and no. 4920 in *DIMEV* (Mooney et al. 1995); and see also the *Database of Middle English Romance* (MacDonald et al. 2012, at <http://www.middlee nglishromance.org.uk/mer/56>).

though now rarely, also attributed to the same poet.[24] I shall make no assumptions about authorship in this study. The manuscript witness itself – London, British Library, Cotton Nero A. x – is now usually dated to the last quarter of the fourteenth century.[25] The scribal dialect represented by this copy was localized to northern Staffordshire by McIntosh in 1963, supported by *LALME*;[26] but the most significant recent discussion of the language of the poems, by Putter & Stokes (2007), has cast doubt on the *LALME* findings, and prefers to put the scribe's orthography in Cheshire.[27] Since Morris (1864a), who rejected Madden's case for Scottish authorship,[28] it has been normal to assume that the author(s) of the poems also spoke and wrote in a dialect of the North-West Midlands, though this does not appear to have been identical in all details with that of the extant manuscript,[29] and indeed the texts occasionally differ amongst themselves (in particular, *Gaw* diverges from the other poems in 'minor but cumulatively significant ways').[30] For an excellent digest of earlier scholarship on the language of the texts, scc Duggan (1997: esp. 238–42).[31] There are important surveys in the major editions (especially Menner 1922: lviii–lxii; GDS xli–lxvi; Gordon 1953: xliv–liii, 91–116; TGD 132–47); otherwise the fullest and most influential studies are those by Knigge, Kullnick and McLaughlin (hereafter McL).[32] In what follows I shall focus on investigations

---

[24] Regarding these issues, and what can be deduced about the poet and his historical and cultural contexts, see the helpful recent accounts (with further references) in Putter (1996: 1–37), Andrew (1997), Schmidt (2010: 369–73), Bowers (2012: 2–13) and PS (ix–xvii). On these contexts see further esp. Bennett (1983; 1997), and also Barrett (2009: esp. 133–70).

[25] *Gaw* appears at ff. 91r–124v, copied by a single scribe with a few corrections in a second hand. See esp. Gollancz (1923: 1–11), Wright (1960: 15), Doyle (1982: 92–3), Edwards (1997), and also Guddat-Figge (1976: 177–8). A full digital facsimile has been produced as part of the Cotton Nero A. x Project (McGillivray 2012, with introductory essays forthcoming).

[26] See McIntosh (1963: 5), *LALME* (LP 26), and further Jones (1972: 214–16) and Duggan (1997: 240–2).

[27] See also the summary at PS (xvii–xxi).

[28] See Morris (1864a: v–ix, xviii–xxxvi). Madden (1839: 301) does appear to have recognized that the extant manuscript, at least, records the poems in a dialect from further south ('There is sufficient internal evidence of their being *Northern*, although the manuscript containing them appears to have been written by a scribe of the midland counties, which will account for the introduction of forms differing from those used by writers beyond the Tweed'). Morris (1864a: xxiv) looks to Lancashire (rather than, as he once thought, Cheshire or Staffordshire) on the basis of the 'large number of Norse terms employed'.

[29] See esp. Putter & Stokes (2007: 470–2), with references to previous discussions (notably Oakden 1930–5: I.84–5, 261–3).

[30] Putter & Stokes (2007: 489–90). Putter & Stokes attribute the features unique to *Gaw* to an intermediate stage in the copying of the poem, and regard them as closely comparable to the language of the commonplace book of Humfrey Newton of Pownall Hall (1466–1536) (*LALME* (LP 104), localized near Alderley Edge, Cheshire).

[31] The most influential previous accounts of the poet's dialect are Serjeantson (1927: 327–8) and Oakden (1930–5: I.73–87, 261–3).

[32] The most important general treatments of vocabulary are Kaiser (1937: 154–68) and Borroff (1962), and notice also e.g. Clark (1951), Aertsen (1987); and for some remarks on (probable or possible) lexical influence from other sources see also Clough (1985) and Meecham-Jones (2018).

of the vocabulary of *Gaw*, in particular when these have involved the establishing of etymologies or have otherwise given rise to discussions of ON input. This work will be considered next to developments in scholarship on the Norse influence on English at large, and in etymological resources more broadly, since all these things bear on ideas about which words in the poem can and should be labelled as Scand in origin (the principles behind which will be treated in greater depth in the next section). I shall restrict my attention by and large to *Gaw* itself, but will mention studies of the other poems in the manuscript when their remarks are especially noteworthy.[33]

Scholarship on *Gaw* realistically begins with the *editio princeps*, by Madden in 1839. It has relatively little to say about the characteristics of the poet's language, but the work it does to establish readings and sense (hesitant and improbable though a few of these may now appear) is gargantuan, and foundational to everything that follows. Its glossary very occasionally suggests etymological identifications in support of a particular translation. Madden's edition, and some of his readings, were superseded by Morris (in 1864, revised 1869), the standard text for the rest of the nineteenth century and that followed by most early studies of the poem's vocabulary. Morris conceived his work as a revision of Madden's, and his glossary is based closely on that of the earlier edition, though with a number of corrections and additions and more etymological labels, albeit still on a very occasional basis.[34] In these earliest attempts on the language of *Gaw*, when editors were grappling for the first time with the interpretation of its vocabulary, etymology is cited largely in the service of establishing sense, and the difficulties of this exercise are often foregrounded: the richness and concomitant slipperiness of the poet's diction are repeatedly alluded to in nineteenth- and early twentieth-century remarks on the language of the text, from Madden's self-deprecating comments on.[35] A case in point is Mätzner, who notices the 'mehrfach Schwierigkeit' (I. 313) of the poet's alliterative vocabulary in his important 1867 anthology of Old and Middle English texts, which contains an edition of lines 232–466 of *Gaw* with full and influential interpretive notes (I. 311–20). Mätzner's work is moreover notable for its accompanying dictionary of ME (begun in 1878, completed as far as *misbileven* in 1900), which was widely used and cited during this period, and which includes brief etymological head-notes in each entry.

More significant still in the development of lexicographical resources for ME is Stratmann's *Dictionary of the Old English Language*, whose first edition was

[33] The most important individual treatments of Norse-derived words in *Pe*, *Cl* and *Pat* are McGee (1940: 358–435), Gordon (1953: 97–101) and Anderson (1969: 73–4, 1977: 108). For comparative remarks see e.g. Oakden (1930–5: I.85–6), Vant I.373–4 and Duggan (1997: 238–9).

[34] There is no discussion of language in Morris's edition, but see his contemporary edition of the other poems in the manuscript (Morris 1864a), esp. pp. xviii–xxxvi; at pp. xxi–xxii he remarks on the 'large number of Norse terms employed', but offers no further details.

[35] 'The Glossary has cost considerable labor [sic], and will, I trust, be considered of value, but to those who know the difficulties which attend the explanation of the Northern alliterative poems, its imperfections will not prove matter of surprise' (xliv–xlv).

completed in 1867. Judged by later expectations, Stratmann's book can, as
Henry Bradley puts it in the introduction to his full revision in 1891, 'scarcely be
regarded as a dictionary at all',[36] in that it is often concerned more to elucidate
etymological connections than to gloss sense. These 'etymologies' are typically
no more than a list of cognates, and it is often difficult to tell whether Stratmann
regards a cited ON form simply as related to the ME word in question, or as a
direct source for it (a problem which sometimes persists in Bradley's revision).
But English etymology was in its infancy in the 1860s, and the foundational
work to differentiate cognates from loans was in large measure still to be carried
out.[37] This is apparent in the early work of Skeat, whose first attempt at
comparing English and the Scand languages was the similarly non-committal 'A
list of words the etymology of which is illustrated by comparison with Icelandic'
(1876), which offers cognates with minimum exegesis. The real watershed came
in 1882, with the first edition of Skeat's great *Etymological Dictionary*, notable
amongst other things for its list of words borrowed from the Scand languages
(750–1). This was not the earliest attempt at such a list,[38] but it was the first to be
drawn from an etymological study of such scale and philological rigour. It
disappeared from subsequent editions of the *Dictionary*, and Skeat himself
changed his mind about a number of the items in it as he revised his work.[39]
Nonetheless it is nicely representative of a growing confidence in the derivation
of ME words from ON as the nineteenth century grew to a close and the great
age of English etymology got into its stride, the other towering landmark being
the publication of the first fascicle of the *OED* in 1884.[40] The other generally-
recognized pioneers in the field are: Steenstrup, vol. 4 of whose *Normannerne*
(1882) includes in its final summary chapter a short list (at 389) of ON loans in
OE texts; Brate, whose study dedicated to the Norse-derived words in *The
Orrmulum* (1885) includes an important early treatment of the formal tests of
loan; Kluge, whose 1891 account in Paul's *Grundriss* (slightly expanded in

[36] Strat.-Brad (v).

[37] For some remarks on the history of etymological dictionaries of English, and further references,
see Liberman (1998; 2002a: 199–200), and on etymological scholarship during the nineteenth century
see more generally e.g. Malkiel (1993: 1–39) and Momma (2013: 95–136).

[38] There were some notable early efforts in the 1840s and 1850s, including the extensive sets of ME
and later English and Scots dialect words explained with comparison to their ON counterparts in
Hjort (1843: 77–121; and see Geipel 1971: 73), beside the lists of northern English dialect vocabulary
of supposed Scand origin offered by Garnett (1845: 78–9; followed by Latham 1855: 345–7) and
Worsaae (1851: 113–19). Some of the words they present would still be derived from ON today (e.g.
gar 'make', *big* 'build'), but for others we now recognize clear native sources (e.g. *bid* 'invite', *bide*
'stay'). Etymologically the most sensitive of these early studies is Coleridge (1859a), whose list
nonetheless contains several items which look eccentric by modern standards (e.g. *bray*, with which
he compares Sw *bräken*).

[39] On the evolution of Skeat's ideas, with reference to particular cases, see Hoad (1984: 27, 39, 46);
and for examples see the entries for **kylled** and **loupe** in the Survey (items 321. and 322.
respectively).

[40] Other influential work on English etymology during this period includes Wedgwood (1859–67),
Mueller (1865–7), Kluge & Lutz (1898); and notice also the first word-list in Sweet (1888: 279–372).

Kluge 1901a) contains massively influential lists of Norse loans, particularly for the OE period; and Wall (1898), which gives an extensive catalogue of Scand derivations in modern English dialects, prefaced by an unusually full account of the principles and problems in identifying them.[41] The culmination of this movement, and in some fundamental respects still the most significant work ever to appear on the subject, is Björkman's *Scandinavian Loan-Words in Middle English* (hereafter Bj.).[42] In the course of two volumes (1900, 1902), Björkman deals carefully and penetratingly with the criteria useful for identifying loans from ON, and presents a catalogue of lexical items divided according to the tests on whose basis they have been included; a brief note is given as to each word's attestation in the ME texts accessible to Björkman, which include *Gaw*.[43]

Very much in keeping with these scholarly trends, several early studies dedicated to the language of *Gaw* (and the other poems in the manuscript) treat the etymology of its words. Especially notable is Knigge's (1885) investigation, which is motivated by the common authorship question (and as such also treats *Pe, Cl, Pa* and *Erk*) but is dominated by a phonological study which arranges the texts' words by etymological origin. The section on loans from ON (71–89) is remarkable mainly for its introduction (71–4), in which Knigge sets out (apparently independently, and from first principles) the criteria by which he has attributed Scand origin. Some of these rules seem peculiar by later standards (in particular his differential treatment of vowels and consonants; see further below); a few of the items he includes are highly dubious and have not otherwise been derived from Norse, and he does not assign Scand input to a number of others whose status as loans would now usually be assumed.[44] But the majority of his corpus would still be regarded as uncontroversial, and it sets an important

---

[41] On scholarship in this period see further SPS (12–14), and notice in addition Egge (1887).

[42] This follows, and draws on, Björkman's briefer *Zur dialektischen Provenienz der nordischen Lehnwörter im Englischen* (1898–1901) (hereafter DP). As Luick (1901b: 413) puts it, 'Durch Björkmans Buch ist der Umfang des skandinavischen Lehnguts erst recht klar geworden' ('the extent of material loaned from Scandinavian has been made fully apparent for the first time by Björkman's book').

[43] I have found very few errors in Bj.'s attestation notes; but notice his mistaken claim that ME *basken* occurs in *Gaw* (136), and see also the entries below for **rawþe** (Survey item 165.) and **sware** (Appendix).

[44] For the dubious inclusions, see esp. some of the items I discuss in the Appendix (esp. **lykkerwys, mane, mote, rach, rehayte, sop, sprenged**), and also under 350. **byled** and 372. **neme** in the Survey. Note that Knigge works through his material sound by sound, and does not present a single, unified list of what he considers to be ON borrowings. At 72n he promises an alphabetical list of ON words at the conclusion of his study, but only this first part ('Lautlehre') was ever published, and no such list appeared. It is nonetheless clear from the words he treats at 74–89, and his comments elsewhere in the book, that he does not attribute ON input in a number of instances where it would now generally be accepted; hence thirty-six of the 134 stems that I class as belonging to Types A and to the highest probability levels of Types B and C (see note 11 above and the Concluding Remarks below) do not appear to be assigned ON etyma in Knigge's study. These stems are (in the order they appear in the Survey): **agayn, felle, gest, ǥete** (etc.), **gif, gifte, grayn, kyrk, lyþen, melle, sete, þoʒ, won** (1 and 2), **busk, wyʒt** (etc.); **kay, rotez, sparþe, ʒette, wale** (etc.); **bonk, calle, derf** (etc.), **or, spene, wykez, blaste, bruny, brusten, race** (etc.), **caryez, dreme, lawe, seme** v. (etc.), **cros, til** (etc.). (And **hundreth** does not figure in Knigge's ON section, but is derived from ON earlier at 56.)

benchmark; it was still being drawn upon well into the next century (e.g. by McGee). A similar sort of treatment, this time of *Gaw* alone (and only dealing with words which do not survive into MnE prose), is provided by Kullnick (1902). His study also breaks the poet's vocabulary down by etymological origin, including a section on ON derivations (14–18),[45] before moving on to a discussion of their distribution in various sorts of text elsewhere in ME. Kullnick is unfortunate to have been writing without access to Björkman's work: some of his etymologies contravene the principles established by Bj. as 'phonetic tests' (notably those regarding palatalization), and a few others would now generally be rejected on other grounds.[46] But despite its shortcomings, Kullnick's was one of the most detailed treatments of the Norse-derived element in *Gaw* that had been attempted thus far, and remains the most recent (albeit partial) list of such words in print; it was still being cited as the best available study by Borroff in 1962. It was drawn on by several subsequent scholars interested (in passing) in the etymological classification of the poet's language, at a period when categorizing words by their origin was the standard preliminary to phonological and morphological description. A notable case in point is Schmittbetz's (1909) enormous analysis of the adjectives in *Gaw*, which follows Kullnick's etymologies largely to the letter, although Schmittbetz is slightly warier and readier to declare derivations as 'uncertain' in a handful of instances.[47] In the same tradition is Brink's (1920) work *Stab und Wort im Gawain*, which offers brief etymological comments in the course of its word-by-word discussion of nouns and adjectives and their behaviour in the text's alliterative poetics.

Meanwhile, a great deal of scholarly industry was being devoted to the text of the poem. Morris's edition was revised for EETS by Gollancz in 1897 (hereafter M(G)), and again in 1912, but only the text appears, without notes or glossary (the long-anticipated full Gollancz edition would finally be published posthumously in 1940, as GDS; see below).[48] The gap left by this apparatus in philological and text-critical commentary was nonetheless filled by a myriad of published attempts to get to the bottom of difficult readings and enigmatic items of vocabulary. Amongst the most significant is Knott's article from 1915, which

---

[45] His separate (though ill-defined) list of 'sonstige germanische Wörter' (18–20) is frequently also of interest, and includes some comparisons to the Scand languages.

[46] On the one hand, for instance, he derives **skete** without comment from OE *scēot* (10); on the other see the entries in the Survey for e.g. **dare, glyfte, rokked** and **ruþes**. Kullnick's list of ON derivations amounts to 152 distinct ME lexical items in total. He omits any mention of sixty-eight of the 134 'most probable' stems referred to above. The majority of these equate to common MnE prose words (or could be understood as variants thereof, e.g. **hundreth, flat, renne, scaþe**), and so have perhaps been discounted for that reason; but this still leaves fifteen other notable stems which would now generally be accepted as showing ON input (viz. **grayn, kyrk, lyþen, melle, skere, skete, skyfted, wyȝt, ȝette, derf** (etc.), **or, spene, wykez, brusten, layne**).

[47] For his remarks on Norse-derived adjectives see esp. Schmittbetz (1909: 6, 12–13, 24).

[48] Following Morris (1864a), the first scholarly editions of (the whole of) the other poems in the manuscript were: Gollancz (1891) and Osgood (1906) for *Pe*; Menner (1920) and Gollancz (1921–33) for *Cl*; and Bateson (1912) and Gollancz (1913) for *Pat*.

includes readings recovered from the manuscript by an examination of the 'off-sets', and hence restores some passages previously considered illegible. Knott moreover compares the readings offered by the various editions of *Gaw* and supplies a very useful digest of editorial interventions, not all of which he finds necessary (he counts upwards of 125 emendations in Gollancz's second revision of Morris, 'rather more than half' of which 'are transparently justifiable'). For Knott (1915: 104), emendation can only be supported once one has exhausted the range of plausible interpretations of a passage as it stands, something which he describes as necessitating an 'Exhaustive search through dictionaries and glossaries, and extensive reading in works of the period for other cases of obscure words, parallel passages, and constructions that will throw light on the difficulties of the text at hand'. This quest for comparanda had already been taken up with gusto in contemporary scholarship, and Knott's remarks are emblematic of the apparently indefatigable and frequently ingenious lexical detective work of the very numerous articles and short notes clustering especially in the period from the turn of the twentieth century until the 1930s. At least as far as work on the *Gaw*-manuscript is concerned, these decades may be dubbed the great age of the etymological note; they coincide with the major groundswell of interest in English lexicology facilitated and inspired by the serial publication of the first edition of the *OED* (completed 1928, reissued with its first supplement in 1933). Armed with the lexicographical resources now to hand, including Bj., the *EDD*, and increasingly sophisticated dictionaries and grammars of the early Scand languages, a number of scholars in this period offer learned, detailed discussions of particular cruces in *Gaw* which include new (or more precise) proposed identifications of ON influences behind the poet's vocabulary. Amongst the most important of these, and dealing with dozens of words, are Wright (1906, 1935) and Emerson (1922a); Sundén's work is also noteworthy, including a 1920 article devoted to some new suggestions for Norse derivations in the text; but there are many others which will be cited in the course of the present study.[49] In many cases their opinions were absorbed by the editorial tradition and have become canonical; but a handful are rarely referred to again, and their conclusions have not been picked up by subsequent writers.

To this period of extraordinary critical and philological industry also belong the most influential modern editions of *Gaw*: that of Tolkien & Gordon (1925 (TG), reprinted with a few changes in 1930, and revised by Davis in 1967 (TGD); see below), and that of Gollancz, completed by Day & Serjeantson (GDS, 1940).[50]

---

[49] Those which I refer to most frequently include Holthausen (1923), Onions (1924), Menner (1926), Emerson (1927a), Magoun (1928), Gordon & Onions (1932; 1933), Savage (1931; 1944) and Wright (1939).

[50] Savage (1944: 342) indicates that Mabel Day was responsible for 'the lion's share of the work in getting out the present edition', but that the text stands essentially as Gollancz left it, and that the Notes and Glossary are moreover essentially Gollancz's. I count 306 distinct lexical items for which some ON input is claimed in the GDS glossary, or suggested in the Notes (compare the figure of 329 for TGD given below, note 67).

Crucially, both editions supply brief etymologies for every word in their glossaries, making them the most convenient sources of reference for those interested in building up a picture of Scand input, though these labels are (inevitably) somewhat deceptive in their simplicity. In many cases these attributions of (possible) Norse origin represent a synthesis of previous inquiry, and they set authoritative norms in treading by and large a moderate course between extremes of scepticism and enthusiasm in their identifications.[51] But only when the words in question are discussed in the Notes (or in the linguistic appendix in TG(D)) does the reader get a sense of the sometimes complex reasoning behind the cited etymologies, and of the competing theories; and in a perhaps surprising number of instances the two editions present quite different findings.[52] Both books contain descriptions of language and dialect, the survey in GDS by Serjeantson (which treats the whole manuscript) being especially full.[53] TG (125–8) is alone in offering a separate discussion of 'The Scandinavian Element', which is notable especially for its summary of the phonology of the Norse-derived material in the poem and its comments on a number of other matters, including developments of sense (especially in the context of alliterative poetry).

There were few other attempts during the 1930s and 40s to analyse the Scand loans in *Gaw* as a group. Oakden (1930–5) gives some figures for the four poems in the manuscript, reckoning 238 words in *Gaw* to be derived from Norse (this is 10.3% of the total vocabulary in the poem, according to his calculation). He regards the number of such words in the manuscript as remarkable, and as suggesting 'an area of composition in a dialectal region in which the Scandinavian element was very marked', probably Lancashire;[54] but there is no indication of which words he thinks these are, or how he has gone about counting them, and so any etymological reasoning is irrecoverable.[55] Similarly concerned with the value of lexis as a tool for dialectal localization is Kaiser (1937), in a foundational investigation of ME word geography. Kaiser treats a number of important texts (including the poems of the *Gaw*-manuscript and *Erk*) in the light of extensive lists of 'northern' and 'southern' vocabulary derived from a study of manuscripts of *Cursor Mundi*. He finds 131 of his 'northern'

---

[51] McGee (23–4) notably takes his lead from recent editions of the *Gaw*-manuscript poems like TG, describing them as occupying 'the sane middle ground'.

[52] See p. 5 above. I keep a running tally of the discrepancies between these editions in the Introductory Essays to Types A to D below, and they are revisited in the Concluding Remarks.

[53] TG (xxii–iv, 122–32) and GDS (xli–lxvi).

[54] See Oakden's various comments at I.85–6, II.190–1; the quotation here is from II.191. There is some indication that Oakden finds the extent of the Norse-derived items in the manuscript peculiar in (unspecified) ways, perhaps beyond what may be accounted for by a north-western localization: 'In the case of the "Gawain" poet, some fact, probably beyond our ascertaining, lies behind this remarkable number of Old Norse loan words' (II.190). In this connexion see further Dance (2013: 51–3).

[55] And note the appraisal of Oakden's work by McGee (22), who regards it as 'somewhat formless in its method and sometimes superficial', and who was not himself able to replicate Oakden's figures by any method of counting.

words in *Gaw*, and wants on that basis (like Oakden) to locate the author markedly further north than is now usual, i.e. the extreme north of Lancashire, or preferably Westmorland or south Cumberland.[56] By my count, 69 of the words in his 'northern' list for *Gaw* are derived by Kaiser unequivocally from ON, though his etymological labels are concise and there is no discussion of them.[57] There is a palpable sense in much of the philological scholarship of this period of a consensus having been reached, however rough, as to which ME words (frequently-occurring words, at any rate) can be listed as coming from ON; and, as in the case of Oakden, some studies no longer feel the need to provide a list at all, something that would have been unthinkable forty years earlier.[58] This is apparent not just in the handbooks, where examples have become typical and canonical,[59] but also seems to be the case in more specialist studies like Serjeantson's (1935) *A History of Foreign Words in English*, whose extensive tour of the medieval attestation of Norse loans cites OIcel reflexes as etyma but contains virtually no discussion at all of how these have been arrived at.[60] Dedicated treatments of the Scand influence on ME vocabulary are few, but there are some important exceptions. Foremost amongst the published accounts is Rynell's painstaking 1948 lexico-semantic analysis, which examines 102 pairs of Norse-derived and native synonyms and tracks their distribution (taking account of stylistic contexts like rhyme and alliteration) across a range of ME texts, including *Gaw*, paying special attention to the 'rivalry' of *taken* and *nimen*. Sixty-three of Rynell's word-fields appear in *Gaw*, forty-seven of which, according to him, contain Norse-derived words.[61] His etymological description is in the main brief, but he gives references to further discussion in the case of difficult items,[62] and takes helpful account of textual cruces. Extremely valuable moreover is the 1940 doctoral thesis by McGee, 'The geographical distribution of Scandinavian loan-words in Middle English, with special reference to the alliterative poetry' (hereafter McGee). This is a monumental study, which provides extensively-annotated lists of Norse derivations for *Cursor Mundi*, *The Siege of Jerusalem* and the *Gaw*-group (including *Erk*), and uses them as the basis for a careful and insightful investigation of dialectal distribution. McGee

---

[56] See Kaiser (1937: 154–6 on *Gaw*, 156–62 for the other poems in the group (inc. *Erk*), and 162–8 for conclusions).

[57] Kaiser's etymologies appear in his main lists of 'northern' (178–278) and 'southern' (279–91) words; he also gives an unannotated list of Norse loans in *Cursor Mundi* (39–65).

[58] As early as 1926, Ekwall was able to claim that 'the Scandinavian element in English has been so often and so well dealt with by previous scholars, that not much is to be done in the way of new etymologies' (Ekwall 1926: 165, cited by Rynell: 8).

[59] Particularly influential from this period is Jespersen (1982: 55–77; first edition 1938).

[60] Serjeantson (1935: 61–103); there are some very brief remarks on p. 63 about the problems posed by the similarities of OE and ON, and appendix C contains a short account of the fates of ON vowels in English. Serjeantson's treatment of the later ME period (1935: 94–102) tackles a number of texts as samples, not including the *Gaw*-manuscript.

[61] See esp. 186–8, with *taken* and *nimen* discussed at 188–93.

[62] See his general list of native and Norse-derived synonyms at 13–17.

mines a number of earlier discussions in order to compile his word lists, in the case of *Gaw* drawing principally on TG, Knigge, Kullnick, Wright (1906) and Emerson (1922a).[63] He is modest about his own contribution,[64] and in his main lists of words he does not offer etymologies except in cases of special difficulty; but in such instances his discussion is unusually full and sensitive, and synthesizes a great deal of previous work.[65] As well as the lists for each poem, what is more, McGee includes specimen entries (for a few letters of the alphabet only) from a much more ambitious 'Index' of Scand loan-words in ME, which includes etymological remarks on each word and notes its occurrences in a wider range of texts, and from his comments elsewhere it seems that he had collected much more material for this endeavour than appears in his dissertation.[66] But to my knowledge none of this material, nor any of the very valuable work from the dissertation itself, was ever published, and McGee's contribution to the subject has gone largely unnoticed by subsequent generations.

Since the middle of the twentieth century there have been, especially in comparison with what went before, relatively few new suggestions for reading the textual cruces in *Gaw*, or significantly different interpretations of particular lexical items; although this is often reflective of earlier scholarship merely having reached a (sometimes exhausted) consensus, or an impasse, rather than a solution. Norman Davis's (1967) revision of TG (= TGD) continues the format of its predecessor (including the glossary), and remains a useful digest of opinion for the vast majority of the poem's words.[67] In the chief critical editions published since (see esp. Silverstein, AW, Vant, PS, McGillivray) it is hard to find readings that are not also in either TGD or (when they differ, and to a lesser extent) GDS. The most radical of the recent editors is probably Vant, who has a penchant for defending the manuscript (in several instances implausibly) against established emendations,[68] but whose variorum *apparatus criticus* is a convenient starting point for

---

[63] McGee's list is at 321–57, introduced at 316–20. At p. 319 he supplies figures for the words he would identify as ON loans in the works of the *Gaw*-manuscript; he finds 303 in *Gaw* itself.

[64] 'The work which scholars have already done on the text and in examination of its vocabulary leaves little for the beginner but to summarize their achievement and to relate it to other poems which have not been so thoroughly examined'. (316)

[65] Note especially his treatment of **angardez, big (bigly), bullez, ferly** (etc.), **fest, festned, fyskez, fnast, glode, knot, lagmon, ronkled, runisch** (etc.), **samen, scrape, snyrt, snitered, spenne** (at *Gaw* 1074), **spenne-fote, sweȝe**, and (in the 'Index') **attle, bayþe, bene, blenk, boþe, brent, busk** (n.); though there is the odd case of a much-debated item being passed over without comment (e.g. **strothe**).

[66] The specimen Index is at 521–86, and see also the remarks at 7.

[67] The most important differences in etymological attribution next to TG are tracked in the Introductory Essays to Types A to D below, and summarized in the Concluding Remarks. The discussion of ON input in TGD's appendix (138–9, 140–1) covers the same general ground as in TG, sometimes carrying over the same remarks. Davis has added figures for the main foreign ingredients in the vocabulary, claiming that 'of those [i.e. words without OE ancestors] with identifiable etymology some 250 are Scandinavian and about 750 French (including those compounded with English suffixes)', out of a total lexicon of approximately 2,650 for the poem (p. 138). In fact I count 329 lexical items with some ON input cited or suggested in the TGD glossary and/or Notes.

[68] See notably the Type Ds *dyngez, *glopnyng, lenge, rykande, runischly.

investigating the editorial tradition.[69] This is categorically not to say that there has been no engagement with lexical detail during these decades. Important articles on particular words and cruces have continued to appear, especially notable for our purposes being Simpson 1981, which deftly tackles several purported Norse derivations in *Gaw*. These contributions must naturally be read against the background of the increasingly sophisticated lexicographical resources which have developed since the 1950s, pre-eminently the *Middle English Dictionary* (*MED*) and the revisions to *OED*.[70] *MED* (first fascicle 1956) is not an etymological dictionary, and its descriptions of word origins are usually minimalist and often tolerant of multiple possibilities without indicating a preference;[71] as the original *Plan and Bibliography* puts it, 'The historical notes, brief and conservative as they are, will raise as many questions as they will answer. That, indeed, is one of their functions' (7).[72] Given the scale on which it operates, moreover, the dictionary is rarely able to comment on the difficulties presented by particular readings in the texts it cites, and generally adopts silently the preference of one or other of the major editions of *Gaw*. Nonetheless the completed *MED* provides unparalleled access to the medieval lexicon, enabling the comparison of forms and senses on a scale and with a (relative) completeness unavailable to earlier studies. Alongside *MED* the full-scale revision to *OED* begun in 1993, and the completion of the associated *Historical Thesaurus* project (*HTOED*) in 2009, have put historical lexicology on a new footing; the etymological notes in the draft *OED3* entries are exceptionally full and well considered.[73]

Owing at least partly to the authoritative and massive nature of such resources, and in the context of the perceived consensus about ON loans noticed above, general discussions of the subject in recent decades have by and large drawn on the standard editions and the major reference works for their etymological information, rather than working out their own lists; and this to an ever greater

---

[69] As is the very helpful *apparatus* supplied by McGillivray, whose edition forms part of the Cotton Nero A. x project. McGillivray is interested mainly in establishing the text, and his Notes make several important new suggestions regarding readings and emendations (see esp. ***bulk, glaum, lenge, quethe**, and also e.g. **balȝ, draueled, dryȝe, teuelyng, tulk, twynnen** (v.), **þerwyth**). The other most significant new edition of recent years, PS, generally follows recent consensus as far as the items in the Survey are concerned, but it has interesting comments on e.g. ***bulk, gete** (v.), **glyȝt, glaum, grome, lyte, rasse, renk, ryd, rimed, spenne(-fote), stemmed, strothe, twynnen, þoȝ, *þwarte-knot, wylle** (adj.), and see also **list**.

[70] And notice also *ODEE*, first published in 1966.

[71] Occasionally a more detailed justification is given, and/or alternatives are rejected; note for instance its treatment of **bayþe** s.v. *baithen* v. What is more, practices and attitudes changed to some degree over the lifetime of the project; see the remarks on the citing of cognates at note 122 and in the Appendix (Section 2).

[72] For the editors' notes on etymologies, see Hans Kurath's *Plan and Bibliography* (1954: 7); the *Plan and Bibliography: Supplement I* (1984: 1) by Robert E. Lewis; and Lewis's *Plan and Bibliography: Second Edition* (2007: 12–14).

[73] At the time of writing the main tranche of revised entries available online, which began with *M*, has reached the start of *S*, and entries for common words elsewhere in the alphabet have also been produced (for our purposes most noteworthy are e.g. **big, boþe, dreme, gete, happe, scho, take, teuelyng, wont** (n. and v.)).

degree. This is true of the few analyses specifically devoted to the Norse influence on the lexis of *Gaw* which have appeared since the middle of the last century, and which are interested primarily in aspects of these words' usage and distribution, and sometimes in what they might tell us about the contact situation that produced them. A case in point is Harada (1961). This article makes a few etymological remarks in the course of a short survey of 'alliterative' and otherwise 'poetic' vocabulary in the poem, drawing closely on *OED* and Oakden (1961: 94–107). Harada (1961: 107) is especially interested in the Norse-derived element, and goes so far as to claim that 'The most important fact about *Sir Gawain* is the high proportion of ON words to be found in it'. His assessment of this material (1961: 107–13) appears to be a précis of a longer, unpublished survey comparing these words with their distribution in modern English, including dialectal, usage;[74] but as it stands it is limited to a short survey of Scand place-names in seven Lancashire hundreds, to one of the densest-settled of which Harada (like Oakden) would like to localize the poet.[75] Of somewhat more interest if similarly brief are the two articles published at around the same time by Nagano. His 1962 piece is made up mainly of comments on the formal and semantic features of Norse loans in *Gaw*, working through the fates of ON inflexions (1962: 61–3) and sounds (1962: 63–5); he refers to TG, and apparently uses it as the source of his etymologies. The 1966 sequel is fuller, and includes (1966: 54–70) a catalogue of 120 Norse-derived words in the poem arranged by part of speech, in which Nagano synthesizes a number of different remarks in his notes on etymology (principally *OED*, but reference is also made to Skeat 1882 and Wyld 1936 amongst others).[76] Nagano (1966: 51–3) also features a scheme for classifying loans according to their interaction with the native word-stock, that is their competition with native synonyms and some other effects on the lexicon, viz. the revival of native cognates from obsolescence, and their modification in terms of form or sense; but oddly this classification is not then applied to the loans Nagano lists from *Gaw*.[77]

There are some noteworthy approaches to the material from the 1970s and 1980s which achieve more sophisticated results by narrowing their focus and

[74] See his comments in the footnote to 1961: 107.

[75] Harada is keen to take ON influence in the area as evidence for its survival there as a spoken language much later than the twelfth century (1961: 110–11), and goes further still: 'The *Gawain*-poet himself may have been a descendant of a Scandinavian family, though no one has yet hazarded such a conjecture'. (113).

[76] He does not, however, seem to know the most important specialist treatments of Norse derivations, including Bj. Nagano's early statement (1962: 60) that he will confine himself to those words 'which have lived to be still in full activity in the present-day English' is difficult to reconcile with the words treated in either article, and his list here includes a number marked with a '†' indicating their obsolescence; it is hard therefore to judge his grounds for admitting and omitting words.

[77] A similar interest in the combination of originally English and Norse (and French) forms in the poet's language is pursued by Yamaguchi (1965), who gives some examples of affixation and collocation involving material from more than one source, and some synonyms for key conceptual fields. He cites GDS and presumably draws on it for his etymological information.

concentrating on words from particular conceptual areas. Especially significant is the series of case-studies of the vocabulary of *Gaw* by Elliott, mainly collected in *The Gawain Country* (1984); all of these articles contain some discussion of Norse input, and they are the main concern in his 1974 piece 'The Scandinavian influence: Some northern landscape features in "Sir Gawain and the Green Knight"'.[78] At one level Elliott's work represents a concerted effort to connect vocabulary and place, something we have seen tried before in attempted localizations of the poem, and in the vaguer invocations of regional affinity by those characterizing the poet's vocabulary, particularly its Norse-derived constituents (in respect of which 'local' is sometimes just a by-word for 'obscure'). But Elliott's approach should not be confused with the rather crude assumptions of some earlier scholars, for whom the procedure often seems to boil down to the simply quantitative (the greater the number of Norse loans in a text, the more it should be associated with areas of dense Scandinavian settlement; see especially Oakden and Harada). By examining just the topographical vocabulary used by the poet, and comparing this to specific place-name elements and later dialect currency, Elliott makes connections to particular landscapes which, he argues, were known to the poet, most strikingly the area in the Staffordshire moorlands around Leek.[79] As with toponyms of other origins, some of the Norse-derived terms he identifies are widespread and relatively colourless regionally, but he argues that several (e.g. **knot, ronez, strothe**) have been used by the poet in order to recall specific places ('when he describes a landscape apparently familiar to himself and to his audience he tended to use some uncommon topographical words which include a number of Scandinavian origin', Elliot 1974: 76). Elliott's treatment of these words is careful and he makes it clear that issues of etymological identification are not cut and dried, often citing and weighing up the evidence for Norse origin.[80] In this connexion it is also worth mentioning Hug's (1987) monograph, a lexico-semantic study of Norse-derived words in ME which focuses on landscape features. Hug examines thirty-six principal words in the broad fields of water, land and air, offering a conspectus of opinions on etymology in each case (*OED*, *ODEE* and Falk-Torp are cited routinely) and a detailed discussion of their synonyms from the point of view of semantics and distribution. The texts she routinely cites include *Gaw*, and she has a few comments on particular instances of the words in it. Of the main lexemes she analyses, those relevant to *Gaw* are *whirlwind, whirlpool* (see **whyrlande**), *bank, mire, fell, loft* and *sky*.[81]

---

[78] Reprinted in Elliott (1984); and see also Elliott (1989; 1997).

[79] Best-known is his association of the Green Chapel with the natural fissure in the moorland known as Lud's Church; see esp. Elliot (1984: 44–7).

[80] This is in spite of the protestations I cited above at note 4.

[81] Amongst the synonyms dealt with in subsidiary discussion are moreover *flash, ker, warþ, rasse, knarre, scowte, bur* and *blaste*; the possible Norse origin of many but not all of these is mentioned.

As far as I know, these are the most recent treatments of significant groups of Norse derivations in *Gaw* (or in sets of texts including *Gaw*) to make any serious effort to discuss etymology. The relative paucity of engagement with the grounds for identifying ON input into a word's history can no doubt be ascribed, at least partly, to the general decline in interest in etymology as a sub-discipline of linguistics in the later part of the twentieth century, with the exception of the major lexicographical projects as whose special province it has increasingly tended to be seen.[82] This idea that etymology is or should be someone else's problem can be understood as a reaction to information overload in the field – both for negative reasons (it is very difficult to keep track of the bibliography of scholarly writings on a given word),[83] and for positive ones (the completion of *MED* and the advent of large-scale, searchable electronic corpora mean that there is so much else out there which can be explored instead). Detailed discussion of the origins of individual word-forms is not a natural adjunct of corpus linguistics, which privileges investigation of distribution and usage, and therefore takes the identification of the features to be tagged as a preliminary; it is much more difficult to mark a word as only 'possibly' or 'probably' a member of a particular class.[84] Searches for Norse-derived lexis in large electronic corpora have therefore tended to take etymology for granted, and simply to follow one of the major authorities (generally *MED* or *OED*) in establishing a set of words that can be labelled as originally Scand.[85] The same is self-evidently true of studies of distribution which take one of the dictionaries as their starting point, such as Hinton's work on the language of the *Gaw*-group (1987).[86] Hinton (1987: 50) draws on an electronic database of random samples from *MED* A–M supplemented with material from other sources in order to analyse the 'etymological mix' of the poet's diction, and concludes that the *Gaw*-group poems are markedly different from the works of Chaucer in this respect (and representative of an 'older' stage of the language).[87]

Provided we bear in mind their inherent margins of error, corpus-based sweeps of where and when words occur can and do play an important role in the study of

---

[82] For some comments on this phenomenon see Malkiel (1993: xi–xii).

[83] For some remarks on this problem see e.g. Liberman (2002a: 200, 2010: ix–x); and note also Considine (2013: esp. 157–8).

[84] But see the *CONE* project for an important example of how etymology can be built into the labelling of a large corpus tagged with multiple types of information. For other experiments in the etymological tagging of electronic copies of medieval English texts, see Bianchi (2007) and Cuesta et al. (2012).

[85] For an important study based on the Helsinki Corpus, and a useful discussion of principles, see Skaffari (2001).

[86] Notable corpus and/or dictionary-based surveys of Norse loans include Moskowich-Spiegel Fandiño (1995; 1996), Moskowich (2012), Bator (2007; 2010).

[87] Hinton does not specify the sources of his etymologies, but he is presumably following *MED*. Duggan (1997: 238–9) cites a 1989 conference paper in which Hinton takes his analysis further, having expanded his sample from *MED* as far as *A–SIM*; Hinton there gives a figure for the Norse-derived component in the poet's vocabulary of 5.76%, which he reckons is not significantly different from the percentages for the *Morte Arthure*, *William of Palerne* and *Piers Plowman*.

borrowings; they give us a sense of the likely parameters of Norse influence on the grand scale of period and dialect, and allow us to compare a wide range of different sorts of material with increasing sophistication.[88] But while these panoramic surveys may build upon the focussed analysis of particular texts and authors, they are not a substitute for it. The etymological labels they begin by accepting represent the end-product of generations of minute, word-by-word inquiry, of just the sort reviewed in the last few pages; the arguments of this scholarship are foundational to the study of 'the Scand element' in medieval English lexis because they set out the actual evidence for it. As I underlined at the beginning of this book, it is therefore essential that we are prepared to re-examine these etymological attributions, not least because they so often turn out to be equivocal, and debatable. Most recent in-depth investigations of the Norse-derived lexis of particular periods, texts and traditions have stressed the difficulties involved in establishing a corpus of words, and thus the sheer slipperiness of the basic data.[89] Despite, or indeed because of, the number and variety of attempts that have been made on it from this point of view, *Gaw* is no different. The scope for disagreement is massive. Those who give figures for the amount (and/or proportion) of Norse-derived words in the poem tend not to be all that far apart: compare Davis (250 words, which is 9.4% of the figure he gives for the total vocabulary of the poem (2,650); TGD 138), Oakden (238 words, or 10.3%; 1930–5: I.86, II.190), McGee (303, or 11.16%; McGee 319). But when we come to examine lists of the words themselves we find that no two scholars ever agree entirely, not even when one claims to be basing his or her findings on a predecessor's work. There is, as we should expect, a fair degree of overlap when it comes to the 'core' of such lists, since there are some words which have always been derived from Norse since the earliest treatments of the subject, and which have never attracted serious controversy. In particular, most of the items grouped under Type A below, i.e. those for which formal, comparative 'tests' are available and which are accordingly considered the most secure, fall into this category, and are counted by all major discussions and reference authorities since Bj.; as are some of those of Types B and C, amongst them some very familiar examples in all surveys of ON loans.[90] But, beyond this consistent bedrock of items, the discrepancies between the etymologies given even by the historical dictionaries, and between the etymologies offered in the most influential scholarly editions of *Gaw*, are startling and multifarious; I gave some figures for *OED* vs. *MED*, and TG(D) vs. GDS, at the beginning of this chapter, and the details of these

---

[88] A good example of the possibilities opened up by the tagging of electronic corpora, and one with special relevance to the language of *Gaw*, is provided by Bianchi's (2007) survey of Norse and French loanwords in four late ME household treatises from north-east Cheshire. Bianchi's etymologies are taken from *OED* (supplemented by *MED* and *AND*), and she divides up the Norse-derived items according to Serjeantson's (1935) bands for period of first attestation.

[89] See for instance Dance (2003: esp. 68–97), Pons-Sanz (2007: 47–67), SPS (esp. 23, 25–122).

[90] Notice esp. the stems which I have assigned to the highest probability levels of Types B and C (i.e. single-letter B and C prefixes only); see further the Concluding Remarks (section 6.2) below.

differences will be explored further in these Introductory Essays. In a very few cases, especially (but not only) in the earliest scholarship, the suggestion of Norse input is demonstrably wrong, as for instance when it depends upon an erroneous assumption about early Scand or English phonology (e.g. **rach, þik** (etc.), **ver**; see Appendix section 1). In others, the grounds on which it was suggested have dissolved, and the argument would thus no longer be made; thus for example when a word was thought not to be recorded in (early) OE, but access to better lexicographical resources have shown that it is, and no one has subsequently tried to use this as evidence for Norse input (e.g. **belt, dit, lee, leke, stubbe**; see Appendix section 1). It is not surprising that such cases exist, but it is perhaps remarkable how few of them there are; I reckon that there are no more than twenty-five items of this sort, which can no longer be seen as meriting serious consideration under any interpretation of the evidence. They are not treated in the main Survey below, but have been listed in the Appendix section 1 as rejected items. Consensus has shifted away from a number of other early suggestions, which appear in lists of putative ON loans in the likes of Knigge and Kullnick, and not in subsequent accounts (amongst many others see e.g. **bene** (etc.), **blykke, fawne, gre-houndez, grome, ȝeȝe, hale (wel-haled), irked, kylled, nikked, rokked, samen, tryst (trystyly), warp, wast, wener**). But the changes of opinion that have hid these from view are as often a matter of the interpretation of textual cruces as they are of etymology *per se*, and one suspects that the silence of subsequent commentators is frequently because these older ideas have been forgotten, rather than that they have consciously been dismissed.[91] On the other hand, the sheer profusion of suggestions for Norse input that have seen print since the foundational scholarship on the subject means that there are many words not considered by early commentators and for which a Norse origin has since been posited, some of these now well established; see the remarks above about items not treated at all by Bj.

The main purpose of the present study is to collect and catalogue this wealth of material, i.e. to present and discuss in detail all the various words in *Gaw* which have been derived from ON. Doing this must, of course, be about more than just gathering and listing. Clearly, if we hope to understand why there can be such a wide range of different responses to an apparently basic question about one medieval text's etymological make-up, we must take the opportunity to assess these responses carefully; to uncover, as far as possible, the explicit and implicit arguments that have been adduced for the identification of Scand input, and thus the ways in which this input has been thought about, the principles by which it has been measured. Apart from anything else, this exercise is essential to navigating such a large body of suggested ON derivations, and will form the basis of how the material in this study is organized. The next section will therefore probe these issues, and their repercussions, in depth.

---

[91] And see the remarks by Liberman (2002a: 200; 2008: xxiii) on the merits of returning to older, since neglected theories, for example.

1.4. The identification of Old Norse input

Etymology is fundamentally an exercise in probabilities.[92] There are very many words whose development is less than completely transparent at one or more stages of their recorded histories, even if we regard our grasp of their essential 'stories' as secure, and this is still more apparent when we venture into their prehistories. Uncertainty is particularly rife given the sorts of conditions we are faced with when trying to isolate the Scand influence on early English, i.e. two very closely related sets of language varieties which were formally and lexically very similar, and a relative dearth of evidence for the vocabulary of either for the periods before and during which (and for some key parts of England for several centuries after which) contact between their speakers took place.[93]

The basic question that we ask is: for any given English word (or a given form, meaning or usage thereof), first recorded during or after the earliest period in which we assume significant contact with speakers of ON, what is the probability of Scand input into its development? Clearly, given the discrepancies between studies of *Gaw* that we have noticed so far, assessments of this probability can vary wildly in many cases, and it is worth trying to form a general idea of why this might be. Some differences of opinion will, naturally enough, have to do with matters specific to a particular word, and the quality of the information available about it. The etymological argumentation germane to some of the items treated in the Survey is unusually complex, and the outcome of discussion of it will depend on how *au fait* a scholar is with its various aspects, including the scope and accuracy of his/her information about the comparanda cited in a number of different languages, views on which are subject to changes and refinements; and our appreciation of the forms, usages and distributions of words in early English and the Scand languages, on whose evidence so much weight rests, is of course also open to improvement.[94] There is a whole legion of devils in these details. But a very great deal, it seems to me, is also bound up in the principles and assumptions, spoken and unspoken, that scholars bring to their assessment of this material; some of these are

---

[92] Notice the remarks by Liberman, cited at note 105 below. For an important discussion of the roles of probabilistic reasoning in philological argumentation more generally, see Fulk (1992: 6–24).

[93] A classic statement of the problems is at Bj. (8–13). The most important assessment of the formal closeness of OE and ON in the Viking Age is Townend (2002), who argues compellingly for the likelihood of adequate mutual intelligibility between the two; see esp. his conclusions (2002: 181–5), and further Townend (1998: 96–8; 2000). On the textual evidence for VAN, see generally Würth (2002); on Scand runic inscriptions in Britain, see the summary in Barnes (2004) and the surveys in Holman (1996) and Barnes & Page (2006). There is a convenient summary of OE Nhb and Merc dialect material in Hogg (§§1.7–8), and on the extant records of medieval Northern English see also Cuesta & Ledesma (2007: 117–18).

[94] For some notable examples of changes in knowledge and in the interpretation of the evidence, see the entries for **kylled**, **tryst** (**trystyly**), ***vntyl**. It should be remembered that the quality of the lexicographical information available to early scholars was sometimes relatively poor; compare the remarks of Durkin (2009: 172).

specific to the study of Norse influence on English, others are manifestations of attitudes which pertain to the interpretation of linguistic data much more generally. It seems best to establish some of these things first, since they help to make sense at a fundamental level of why different commentators can come to such different conclusions, even when the evidence they are looking at is exactly the same.

1.4.1. *Assumptions and interpretations*

A basic factor in how we are minded to read the evidence for Norse influence, in what we come to this particular data thinking, is our attitude towards language contact more generally. In recent decades studies of the mechanisms of contact, and theories about precisely how linguistic material is transferred between language varieties under a range of socio-cultural circumstances, have increased markedly in sophistication.[95] Nevertheless, predicting the kinds and extent of the linguistic developments that will result from contact, and (more to the point) telling contact-induced changes apart from those triggered independently of contact (endogenous changes), seems no easier a matter than it ever has.[96] This is so because, even though certain species of linguistic change (especially in combination) may be associated with particular contact scenarios,[97] and even though language varieties in contact are generally held to be more likely to undergo change than are isolated varieties,[98] it has been emphasized in a number of recent studies that the constraints on contact-induced developments are fairly minimal – i.e. there is no one sort of change which must have come about because of contact, any more than there is one which can only be endogenous, and the two processes are in fact fundamentally similar.[99] A major, cross-linguistic exploration of lexical borrowing, the *World Loanword Database* (see Haspelmath & Tadmoor 2009a, 2009b), has found that some conceptual areas

[95] The foundational modern accounts are Thomason & Kaufman (1988) and van Coetsem (1988). This is a fast developing and highly productive field, but for guides to the major recent thinking on the effects of contact see for instance Thomason (2001; 2003), Sankoff (2002), Kerswill (2002), Winford (2005), Matras (2009), Trudgill (2011), Millar (2016) and the essays in Hickey (2010); and there are good summaries of the key issues in e.g. Durkin (2009: 132–78), Miller (2010: 150–6), Schendl (2012). For a sensitive application of these models to the Anglo-Norse situation see pre-eminently Townend (2002; see also 2000, 2006); and for other recent accounts in the light of modern contact theories see e.g. Miller (2010: 157–61; 2012: esp. 145–7), Fischer (2013: esp. 31–7), Millar (2016: esp. 152–8), plus Lutz (2012; 2017), alongside the other studies cited under note 116 below.
[96] For general discussion see e.g. Romaine (1995), Lass (1997: 184–209; 2007: §8.9), Filppula (2003), Ross (2003), Thomason (2001: 91–5; 2003: esp. 708–10; 2010); and regarding lexis in particular see e.g. Haspelmath (2009: 43–5), Durkin (2009: 169–73; 2014: 13–15).
[97] For important discussions see Thomason (2001: 63–98; 2003: esp. 687–9, 708–10), Trudgill (2011), Millar (2016).
[98] This is a longstanding assumption; but for some recent discussion (and further references) see esp. Trudgill (2011: esp. 15–32), and further e.g. Smith (2007: esp. 22) and Millar (2016: chapter 5).
[99] For detailed discussions see notably Lass (1997: esp. 190, 209 for his key statements), Thomason (2001: esp. 63–5; 2003: 695; 2010: 39–45) and Matras (2009: esp. 218–21).

seem slightly more resistant to loan than others, but that universal contraints on the traffic of vocabulary are few, and that the loan even of 'core borrowings' is surprisingly pervasive.[100] Moreover, limits on the types and extent of material liable to be exchanged are particularly hard to set when the language varieties involved are very similar.[101]

Of course there are two possible responses to this state of affairs, and they neatly illustrate the role of underlying agendas in linguistic argumentation. One is to embrace positively the leeway implied by cross-linguistic precedent, to emphasize that the borrowing of linguistic features is a universal phenomenon and that (given the right conditions) almost anything can be borrowed. Hence borrowing is always available as a possible explanation for change, and when there is evidence of contact it can always be turned to as a plausible reason for the introduction of new features which otherwise may seem to be unmotivated. Borrowing therefore becomes a relatively powerful explanatory tool, and (especially) in the absence of positive evidence for other causes of change it may even be taken as the default hypothesis. This is the sort of reasoning that underlies statements like Thomason's (2001: 91), that 'a good solid contact explanation is preferable to a weak internal one';[102] the case for preferring contact-based explanations is championed notably by Smith (1996),[103] and has been taken up, often implicitly, in a number of studies which have promoted the idea of contact with ON as a prime factor in the actuation of changes in the history of English, especially when it comes to reductions in inflectional morphology and the establishment of new syntactic rules.[104] The other possible response to the apparent freedom with which borrowing can operate is to emphasize the absence of hard evidence that this presents us with: if, given the

---

[100] For a summary of the project's findings see esp. Tadmoor (2009).

[101] See in general terms e.g. Thomason (2003: 694), and Durkin's (2009: 164) proposed 'cline' of the difficulty of borrowing, which emphasizes the role played by the similarity of lects. For an important study of contact between closely related varieties, and the (distinctive) likely effects, see Millar (2016). For some other recent considerations of 'borrowability scales' and associated issues, and for further references, see e.g. Sankoff (2002: esp. 658), Thomason (2003: 691–4), Matras (2009: 166–221), Durkin (2009: 159–60), Tadmoor (2009) and Winford (2010: 175–9).

[102] See further Thomason (2003: 688): 'In my view, contact between languages (or dialects) is a source of linguistic change whenever a change occurs that would have been unlikely, or at least less likely, to occur outside a specific contact situation'. And notice also the remarks by Miller (2010: 150), who takes issue with Lass (1997) (see below) and claims that 'most changes are a combination of internal and external factors' (similarly Miller 2012: 145).

[103] An important statement of principles is at Smith (1996: 48): 'Contact is a crucial factor in linguistic change because no language or variety of language exists in a vacuum. Speech-communities come into contact with other speech-communities in all sorts of situations, and the subsequent interaction between these communities causes linguistic change. Some languages and varieties of language certainly change more slowly than others, and the reasons for the variable speeds of linguistic change are easy to determine, through the observation of extralinguistic correspondences'.

[104] For some recent examples and further discussion see e.g. Kroch & Taylor (1997), Millar (2000), Trips (2002), Hotta (2009), Miller (2012: 132–4), Fischer (2013: esp. 34–7) and Allen (2016), alongside the creolization debates cited at note 116 below.

right conditions, almost anything can be borrowed, then we are justified in regarding contact-induced change as nothing special, essentially no different from other (language-internal) sorts of change, which are also going on all the time in a wide variety of ways; and in that sense we do not need particularly to invoke borrowing as an explanation *unless* there is good reason to do so. An extended statement of this reasoning is supplied by Lass (1997: 209), who concludes:

> Change is simply change, as far as I can see, and there is no really solid and compelling evidence for types peculiar to (actively, mildly) contacting languages as opposed to totally or relatively isolated ones. Therefore, in the absence of evidence, an endogenous explanation of a phenomenon is more parsimonious, because endogenous change *must* occur in any case, whereas borrowing is never necessary.[105]

For Lass, then, there is always potentially a case to be made for language-internal causation, which by and large does not demand any special motivation. Those who persistently argue in favour of borrowing when the evidence for it is not compelling are dubbed 'contact romantics', and chided for 'making puzzles out of things that in wider perspective should not be all that problematic'.[106]

In practical terms, then, these positions on language contact essentially boil down to a methodological *shibboleth*: when faced with a linguistic feature which *could* conceivably be the result of borrowing, but for which the evidence either way is not very good, in which direction does one jump? For some people, an available and plausible explanation is better than none; for others, plausibility is not evidence, and there is nothing to be gained from groundless speculation. These are, of course, fundamental differences, and in this respect attitudes towards the explanatory value of borrowing are rooted in contrasting approaches to linguistic historiography much more generally. Jeremy Smith has written interestingly on this matter in a defence of speculative 'storytelling' in historical linguistics (which he calls an 'exercise in plausible argumentation'), and what he regards as the importance of the 'why' of linguistic enquiry.[107] For a reviewer of Smith's book, at stake here is 'the competition of basic scholarly epistemologies', which he encapsulates as follows:

> Is the point of scholarship in historical linguistics to reduce the interpretive possibilities through the application of a set of protocols

---

[105] And compare Romaine (1995: 481). From an explicitly etymological point of view, Liberman (2008: xxvi) expresses a similar preference: 'Tracing word origins is a game of probabilities. A language historian often reaches a stage when all the facts have been presented and it becomes necessary to weigh several hypotheses and choose the most probable or, to use a less charitable formation, the least improbable one. All other conditions being equal, tracing a word to a native root should be preferred to declaring it a borrowing'.

[106] Lass (1997: 201, 202).

[107] Smith (2007: esp. ix–x, 154–60).

designed to progressively narrow potential meanings, or is the point of scholarship in historical linguistics to discover new paths of interpretation by which potential meanings are multiplied?[108]

Casting these different mindsets as a straight fight between the rigorous but reductive and the creatively speculative perhaps risks oversimplifying the contest. But there is nevertheless a genuine and basic discrepancy between the two ways of looking at things which is inherently polarizing, and which cannot be resolved by argument – in much the same way that one person's good husbandry is another's stinginess.

In many ways the identification of ON influence on medieval English is the *locus classicus* of the consequences of epistemological orientation for the stories we tell about language history.[109] This is categorically not to say that there is any serious doubt about the existence of such influence; there are many very good instances of lexical borrowing from Norse which have never attracted controversy (as indicated by the broad zone of agreement in the etymological surveys of *Gaw*). But a very large number of suggested cases of Scand input, both lexical (as we shall see further below) and otherwise, are only supported (and can only ever be supportable) by slender or ambiguous evidence, and it is often impossible to be sure whether borrowing or endogenous change is at work; so that one's assumptions of the general likelihood of contact-based change, and specifically of Norse involvement, are vitally important in determining one's conclusions.[110] These assumptions have always played a particularly significant role, moreover, seeing that the *a priori* case for Scand influence is so massive. This is not the place to try to rehearse, or even to summarize at any length, the evidence for the presence of Norse speakers in Viking Age England; it is expansive, multifarious and complex.[111]

---

[108] Cain (2009: 30). Cain continues: 'This is the "postmodernist challenge" (157) that Smith outlines near the close of his book, and as a proponent of the latter point of view, he demonstrates that acceptance of alternative meanings is not a substitution for intellectual rigor, as those who hold the fomer point of view sometimes charge'.

[109] Smith and Lass both make case-studies of (possible) Norse influence on English high-profile parts of their arguments; see Smith (1996: 128–34, 139–40) and Lass (1997: 202–5). Closely comparable issues attend recent claims for Celtic structural borrowing into English (the so-called 'Celtic hypothesis'); for overviews see e.g. Filppula et al. (2008), Filppula (2010), Trudgill (2011: 50–5), Filppula & Klemola (2012), Miller (2012: 35–9), Durkin (2014: 87–90), Trudgill (2016: 323–4, 325–9), Millar (2016: 158–62), and for some attempts to link the consequences of Anglo-Celtic and Anglo-Scandinavian contact see further Miller (2012: 147; 2016: esp. 169–70) and Hornung (2017: 70–7).

[110] For an expression of this dilemma see Hoad (1984: 38), who refers to 'the two directions in which etymologists may be drawn in dealing with problems of this kind'; and compare Durkin (2014: 14).

[111] For some recent guides to the historical background, and convenient entry points to the vast bibliography on this subject, see e.g. Keynes (1997), Richards (2000), Dumville (2002), Hadley (2006), Downham (2007), Carroll et al. (2014), Townend (2014), and the essays in Graham-Campbell et al. (2001) and Hadley & Richards (2000). For Scandinavian activity in and around Cheshire, see esp. Cavill et al. (2000) and Edmonds (2009); and further Graham-Campbell (1992), Higham (1993: 104–14), Graham-Campbell & Philpott (2009), Griffiths (2010) and Harding et al. (2015).

Users of varieties of Norse and English were certainly in extensive spoken contact in the period between the major Scand settlements documented in northern and eastern England in the 870s and the end of Anglo-Danish rule in 1042, and there is good evidence for a form of ON being spoken as late as *c.* 1100 in the North-West of the country.[112] Estimates of the numbers of Scandinavians present in England at various periods have waxed and waned in the historical scholarship, but assessments of the subject by philologists have always tended to favour the idea of settlement by large numbers of Norse speakers: whatever be the complexities in interpreting the subsequent usage of Norse-derived place- and personal-name elements, their variety and the depth of their penetration are profoundly impressive;[113] and this is only one of the strands that justifies reference to a mixed, 'Anglo-Scandinavian' culture.[114] Given the scale and range of all this evidence for the interaction of English and Norse speakers, then, we should certainly expect to see some consequences of it in the form of influence on the English language, appearing from the late OE period onwards; if not, as Coleridge colourfully put it as early as 1859, then 'the Anglo-Saxon language must have been one of the most stubborn ever spoken by man' (1859a: 23).

In Smith's terms, therefore, here is our 'story', a very plausible rationale for language change in English at this time. Its attractions as an actuating force are obvious, even without considering the romantic pull of the Viking North consciously or otherwise embraced by much philological (and other) scholarship since the nineteenth century.[115] Such is its potential explanatory power, indeed, that a number of studies have pressed the fact of Anglo-Norse contact into service whenever they can, and have found its consequences (direct and indirect) in aspects of medieval English well beyond the lexical. The most vigorous have been the proponents of 'mixed-language' hypotheses, arguing that the sorts of change they identify as a result of the contact are tantamount to the creation of an inter-language or a creole. Unalloyed enthusiasm for what Barnes sardonically called 'the creolisation bandwagon' has ebbed in recent decades, but it represents

---

[112] See esp. Ekwall (1930), Page (1995), Parsons (2001), and also Townend (2007: 17–21), Fellows-Jensen (2013b: 61–7) and Dance (2003: 73 n.7 with further references).

[113] On Scand place-names in England, see notably the surveys of the evidence in Abrams & Parsons (2004) and of the field in Townend (2013), and other recent reviews of the subject like Fellows-Jensen (2004, 2013a), Sandred (2005: esp. 2065–71), Miller (2012: 102–6), all with further references. For Cheshire in particular, see the discussion and references in Dodgson (1997: 230–47), Coates (2011: 369–77, 380–3) and also Gelling (1995). For personal names, see notably Björkman (1910), Fellows-Jensen (1968; 2013b: 51–61), Insley (1994), Parsons (2002), Insley (2007: 11–12), Insley & Rollason (2007), and the insightful comments in Townend (2007: esp. 6–16).

[114] On possible evidence for cross-influences in literary culture, see Frank (1990), Bjork (2001), Dance (2016: 61–5), and references there cited.

[115] For nineteenth-century attitudes to the Vikings in scholarly as well as popular culture see esp. Wawn (2000) and Townend (2009). Notably, Wall (1898: 46) accuses some earlier dialect lexicographers of falling prey to 'the glamour of the Viking Age ... which has led them to refer to Scand originals many genuine English words'.

the epitome of the positive embracing of contact-based explanations for change.[116]

Etymological treatments of particular words have rarely professed a calculated favouritism for accounts involving Norse input, and indeed there is very little discussion about what we should do when, all things being equal, a given word may or may not be derived from Norse. There are nonetheless some interesting statments about policy in Kolb's 1965 article about Scand influence on modern northern English dialects, in which he edges in the direction of a (measured) preference for Norse derivation in ambiguous cases, arguing that we should not search too assiduously for unrecorded native cognates – this can be a useful corrective, he thinks, to an overzealous quest for Norse material, but he warns against an 'ultranationale oder auch ultravorsichtige' approach which 'übertreibt aber haüfig in der entgegengesetzen Richtung', and stresses his conviction of the importance of the Norse-derived element, of which there are many more examples to be found.[117] Knigge is also, under certain circumstances, willing to give the benefit of the doubt to derivation from Norse as a methodological principle.[118] In practice, very many of those who have aproached the subject would be in sympathy with this position. At any rate, the commonplace willingness we meet with in the scholarship to suggest a possible ON source for a difficult word cannot be ascribed merely to the perennial etymological tendency to abhor a vacuum, i.e. the preference for citing something rather than nothing, for giving a reference to a known comparandum in Norse rather than to a reconstructed English cognate; though this habit is surely far from negligible in boosting the numbers of suggestions.

In theory, it is possible to argue for routinely adducing at least some Norse input in a high proportion of medieval English etymologies. If we take our cue from the 'mixed language' hypotheses, in fact, then a case can be made for understanding the Gmc element of the (especially northern and eastern) ME lexicon not simply as continuing OE with the occasional addition of ON ingredients, but as a set of words with a dual inheritance; that is 'ME = OE + ON', since ME is then to be treated as a 'blend' of the two sources. Thus any ME word with cognates in OE and ON could, strictly, be read as the descendant of both, even where the two etyma are identical in form and sense and thus where

---

[116] Barnes (1993: 67–74, here at 71). The earlier (and most enthusiastic) accounts are typified by Domingue (1977) and Poussa (1982); the more recent work by Emonds & Faarlund (2014) on the Scand origins of English syntax is in many ways reminiscent of these earlier claims (but is apparently unaware of some later scholarship on the subject). For more considered, and generally less radical, treatments see e.g. Hansen (1984), Görlach (1986), Thomason & Kaufman (1988: esp. 275–304), Wallmannsberger (1988), Hines (1991), Allen (1997), and the reviews of the arguments in Mitchell (1994: 163–70), Danchev (1997), McWhorter (2002), Townend (2002: 196–9), Dance (2003: 295–8; 2016: 65–6), Dawson (2003) and Millar (2016: esp. 152–8). Of associated interest, mainly from the point of view of contact with (Anglo-)Fr, is Trotter (2012).

[117] Kolb (1965: 133, an 'ultranationalist or ultra-careful' approach which 'nonetheless frequently exaggerates in the opposite direction', 136).

[118] See Knigge (72).

the Norse word makes no palpable contribution; thus e.g. ME *hous* < OE *hūs* + ON *hús*. Very occasionally one meets statements of etymological principle which (seemingly) get quite close to this position, that is, putting the burden of proof on those who would like to exclude Norse input, rather than upon those who would include it. A recent formulation which at least tends in this direction is provided by Ringe (2004). Ringe argues in favour of regarding ON *mæla* 'to speak' as a source for late OE *mælan*, ME *melen*, despite the fact that there is an earlier OE *mǣlan* (at least in the pret. form *mǣlde*) in the same sense; and in so doing he takes issue with Gordon and Campbell, who saw no need to posit Norse input.

> But it appears that these authors are implicitly relying on a methodolog-ical principle which is indefensible. The idea seems to be that if we cannot *demonstrate* that an English word is a Scandinavian loan, we *must assume* that it is a native word; that is, descent from pre-invasion English is treated as a default, to be preferred in the absence of any evidence to the contrary. But argument by default is appropriate only when general principles are involved, or in cases in which a particular type of development is universal (or nearly so); for instance, we assume that a particular sound change is regular in the absence of evidence to the contrary because observation of linguistic change in progress and of the historical record shows that an overwhelming majority of sound changes are, in fact, regular. Such a line of argument cannot be applied to contingent events, which might have happened one way or another; and the possible borrowing of an ON word into OE is obviously such an event.[119]

These remarks return us to the epistemological binaries we considered above. There is, as Ringe has it, nothing to say that the ON word in question was not borrowed into English; there are no absolute constraints on this sort of linguistic development. It is therefore unnecessarily limiting to close down this avenue of explanation, and we are free to adduce Norse input in the case of ME *melen* if we wish. Though Ringe would presumably object that this does not mean that we should always claim Scand influence in such cases (for to do so would be to set up another default principle), there is a latitude implied by his dismissal of the need for positive evidence which tends precisely in that direction, i.e. it enshrines our ability to cite a Norse etymon whenever one is possible. But others are less coy, and there are some apparently unequivocal statements which expressly put the onus of proof on the rejection of Scand (and other foreign influence) on ME. Thus Price (1947: 38), whose breezily liberal invocation of Norse, French and Latin in the explanation of ME idioms is founded on the conviction that 'Middle English is not pure English. ... When, therefore, we see that a usage in Middle English can be found both in Old English and in any or all of these other languages, we are not entitled to exclude those languages from consideration'.

---

[119] Ringe (2004: 430), as against Gordon (1937: 43, note to l. 26) and Campbell (§421).

De Caluwé-Dor (1983: 212) seems to adopt the same approach with regard to what she calls 'etymological convergence', as in the case of ME *teuelin* 'to argue', which has possible sources in English and Norse (and French): 'Taken separately each of these sources is satisfactory but not enough since we have no sufficient reason to exclude any of them'.[120]

In practice, however, none of these scholars applies to individual etymologies quite the letter of the law that she or he formulates in the abstract. While in principle, that is, they seem prepared to admit multiple etyma on the simple grounds that these are possible *a priori*, in reality few if any of the words or usages they treat are of the *house* type, i.e. where the addition of Norse input makes no positive contribution at all to explaining the ME output. In the case of each of the etymologies probed by de Caluwé-Dor, for instance, the recorded OE word does not map completely onto its ME reflex. There is always something different about the later word, whether in terms of form (including derivational class), sense or usage (e.g. transitivity, idiom), in accounting for which some influence from the corresponding ON word could conceivably be helpful, even if the development in question is very plausibly endogenous. In other words, there is usually a positive trigger for considering Norse input, a reason for including it, as opposed to a reason for not excluding it, and the same is realistically true of the items considered by Ringe and even Price.[121] This is also the case, moreover, when it comes to all the English dictionaries I know of with an etymological component: even though the format of a dictionary entry allows for a range of possibilities to be considered, and does not demand a final decision be taken about exclusions, it is extremely rare to find descriptions of words of the *house* type which claim actual descent from anything other than the OE etymon.[122] All this is not of course to say that, at a basic level, the notion of the dual etymological inheritance of post-Viking Age English might not be meaningful; a few studies of Norse-derived words accept it in principle, but go on to acknowledge that it is impossible to find evidence for it in cases when a native and a Scand origin for a word would produce identical results, and therefore that this 'real extent' of Norse influence is best regarded as hidden.[123] Even for

---

[120] Emonds & Faarlund (2014: 47–58) take a similar position.

[121] Ringe introduces ON *mæla* to help account for the survival of the OE word outside of poetry (and see further Bj. 104), as also for what he argues is the extension of an originally pret. stem to the whole paradigm. Price (1947) starts from the idea of differences between ON and attested OE idioms: 'One is amazed at the wealth of phrases and uses common to ME and ON and OF which are not to be found in any OE dictionary' (Price 1947: 11).

[122] A possible exception might be the last few fascicles of *MED*, whose 'and cp.' label in entries like those for **piche, rome, ruche, slayn, tymed, waked, walke, wonde** seems to be proposing some ON input when it would make no obviously appreciable difference to a word's history (and, in earlier parts of the alphabet, notice also **draȝe**). See Appendix section 2.

[123] See e.g. Knigge (72), and notice also McGee's remarks (28): 'The identification of Scandinavian elements in Middle English must always be uncertain for a large number of words, since the two languages mingling in the Danelaw and the Norwegian kingdoms in the North-west were so much alike that many words must be due to both languages'.

avowed 'maximalists', then, i.e. those whose preference is to cite some putative Norse input into a word's history whenever it seems at all feasible, and thereby to get as close as possible to representing what they take to be the genuine scale of the contribution of Anglo-Norse contact to the history of English – even for these scholars, the attribution of Norse derivation depends on positive criteria, on some measurable characteristic of a post-contact word which marks it out in some way. Understanding these characteristics, and generalizing from them, is therefore fundamental to pursuing the Scand influence on the English lexicon, since they represent the actual evidence that is the basis for all interpretation, whatever one's epistemological inclination towards its admissability. These criteria have been discussed occasionally, and summarized repeatedly, since the earliest thoroughgoing treatments of the subject in the nineteenth century. In the next section I shall consider these grounds in some detail, asking how they have and can be used, as a basis for the presentation of the words in *Gaw* which arguments drawing on them have produced.

1.4.2. *On evidence*

This is not the place for anything approaching a complete history of attitudes towards ON loans in English.[124] In what follows I am concerned mainly with citing the fullest and most influential modern discussions of the evidence, many of which have already been referred to above, in particular Bj. and the tradition in whose line his work stands, pausing to note investigations specially concerned with *Gaw* when they make reference to principles and methods (viz. especially Knigge, McGee). My attempt to synthesize these principles draws, moreover, on the vast array of arguments about individual words embedded in the etymological scholarship surveyed above, in which approaches to methodology are rarely explicit. Distilling how these various contributions have established and utilized the criteria which they have regarded as pertinent in deriving words from ON is, at the same time, foundational to putting together the typology of features which will be used to organize the Survey in this book, and which I shall explain as I go along.[125]

There have been a number of detailed treatments of the identification of Norse lexical input, and it has been touched on obliquely many times. In the absence of an established framework, most of the pioneering studies tackle the problem directly, and to a large extent independently. There are cogent if often (relatively) brief attempts to establish ground rules in the likes of Brate (1885: 4–30), Knigge (71–2), Kluge (1891: 787, 791 (1901a: 935, 940–1)), Wall (1898:

---

[124] Such a commentary would need to go back at least as far as Higden and Trevisa; see e.g. Burnley (1992: 415) and Dance (2003: 4).

[125] The primary categories used in this expanded typology were introduced in Dance (2012a, 2013), and trialled in Dance (2011). But they are accounted for here at much greater length, and have been revised in a number of details in response to the full data from *Gaw*.

esp. 69–73) and Flom (1900: v, 22–3), before the magisterial survey in Bj. (1900–1902). Bj. makes reference to earlier scholarship, but his work puts the subject on a markedly sounder footing. His advance comes partly by virtue of considering so much material, which in itself is a major step forward; but the clarity with which he assesses it, and the incisiveness with which he sets out the phonological tests (in particular), remains a remarkable achievement. The broad consensus which emerged in the twentieth century derives largely from Bj.'s methodology, even if most subsequent discussions are much briefer and inevitably simplify his position. Amongst the specialist analyses of Norse-derived words, fullest attention to the principles of identification is to be found in Thorson (2–4), McGee (23–4, 28–9), Kisbye (1982: 37–42), Kries (2003: 87–9), Pons Sanz (2007: 47–67; 2015: 204–10), SPS (25–122) and Durkin (2014: 190–211);[126] and there are many other sensible summaries in articles (including Hoad 1984: esp. 30–40) and in a range of handbooks,[127] albeit that a surprising number of synopses of Norse influence mention this aspect of the subject hardly if at all, amongst them some otherwise detailed and sensitive treatments.[128]

If we examine the details of the criteria for Norse derivation cited in these discussions then we do meet some variation, and the earliest are most likely to appear idiosyncratic (just as they do in some of the loans they suppose as a result, as noticed above). But in broad terms the same types of evidence always appear. So in 1859, in one of the earliest etymologically cogent discussions of the subject, Coleridge (1859a: 26) proposes that a word's distribution across the Gmc languages (specifically if it is known in ON, but not in early OE or LG) is a test of its loan; as is its occurrence 'in different senses and under other forms' in Norse and early OE. Brate (1885: 4–30) focuses on the phonological tests of origin in OE vs. ON (and is the first to do so in detail),[129] but also refers to differences in sense and morphology, as well as to distribution (a word may be a loan if it is attested in ON and not in OE). Knigge (71–2) also gives most weight to phonological tests,[130] and does not mention sense or other aspects of a word's

---

[126] And see my own earlier attempt on the subject in Dance (2003: 74–97).

[127] There are far too many of these to list here, but notice the following (influential and/or esp. sensitive) remarks: Jespersen (1982: 60–2), Wright & Wright (§§163–77), Brunner (1950–1: 131–4), Kisbye (1982: 37–42), Barber (1993: 130–4; continued by Barber et al. 2009: 140–4) and Blake (1996: 78–81).

[128] There are very limited remarks on (selected) phonetic tests in Kastovsky (1992: 332), Toth (1995: 567–8), Miller (2012: 120–7); Burnley (1992: 414–23) and Grant (2009a) say virtually nothing about identification. Books targeted at a 'popular' readership inevitably have little or nothing to say on methodology, even when they are directly concerned with Norse loans; e.g. Geipel (1971; though notice his remarks at 69–70) and Ó Muirithe (2010; 2013).

[129] Most of Brate's tests would still be recognized as diagnostic, viz. (with § references to my Formal Criteria section below) the absence of palatalization of /k/, /g/, /sk/ (§8), typically ON developments of PGmc */ai/ and */au/ (§§1, 2), ON /ð/ rather than OE /d/ medially and finally (§7), ON consonant assimilation (§10.1). But his appeal to the quantity of a vowel in a (late OE) lengthening environment was abandoned as a criterion by subsequent scholars.

[130] Some of his claims are idiosyncratic, in particular that vowels are more diagnostic of ON input than are consonants.

usage, but does make use of Gmc distribution (a word is likely to be a loan if it is otherwise confined to ON, or at least is not attested in WGmc). Wall (1898: esp. 69–73) focuses on differences of form and sense, as well as Gmc distribution (a word is 'certainly' from ON if it occurs only in the Scand languages, or only there and in HG).[131] The idea that dialectal distribution within English might help us to assess the probability of Norse derivation is given surprisingly little airing in these early accounts: it is supported in principle by Kluge (1891: 787; 1901a: 935),[132] and discussed at greater length by Wall (1898: 81–8, who believes that it can be used only as negative evidence, however).[133] But thereafter the species of evidence referred to start to take on a conventional and familiar appearance, as in Flom (1900: 22–3), who cites form, meaning and distribution (in English dialects, and across Gmc) as useful discriminators (of which distribution is the 'final test').[134] These fundamentals are then firmly set in place by Bj., whose analysis sharply distinguishes between words amenable to formal tests ('phonetic criteria'), which he treats in his first volume, and those derivable from Norse by other means, which are dealt with in Volume 2; the tests available for identifying this second group are much less reliable than for the first, but Bj. favours English dialect distribution and (to a lesser extent) occurrence elsewhere in Gmc as providing helpful indications.

We might think about these various species of evidence in a number of different ways, but a primary categorical division seems to me to exist between what I shall call the 'structural' and the 'circumstantial'. Structural evidence is that which arises from a comparison of the OE (and ME) and ON linguistic systems themselves – i.e. taking a (late OE or ME) English word and examining it for tell-tale signs of input from Norse, for some features of form (phonological, morphological), sense or other aspects of usage which look more like those attested in one or more of the Scand languages than like those we find (or reconstruct) for a competing etymon in (early) OE. Circumstantial evidence, on the other hand, derives from patterns of occurrence, asking where a (late OE or ME) English word and/or its purported cognates are recorded.

---

[131] Wall (1898: 70–3) regards as *bona fide* tests only the ON reflex of PGmc */au/ (§2), /ð/ rather than OE /d/ (§7), and certain ON consonant assimilations (§10.1). He is unconvinced that the absence of palatalization/assibilation (§8) can be diagnostic in northern dialects, and also finds the Scand reflex of PGmc */ai/ (§1) difficult to detect with any certainty. See also (1898: 60–3) for some discussion of the VAN sound changes, and traces of Scand inflexional material, which he argues may be identified in loans into English.

[132] For Kluge (see esp. 1891: 787, 791; 1901a: 935, 940–1), phonetic and semantic differences are primary, followed by chronology and geography. His phonetic tests are limited to the reflexes of PGmc */ai/ and */au/ and the absence of palatalization.

[133] Remarkably, for Wall (1898: 81–2) the occurrence of a word only in the North or East is *not* proof of its ON origin, 'for very many English words are peculiar to those districts'; instead, he thinks, distribution can only be used to rule *against* the likelihood of Scand input, since words found in the South and West of England are more likely to be native (unless they show a formal feature diagnostic of ON derivation).

[134] For his tests of form, Flom focuses on ON developments of PGmc */ai/ and */au/, ON /ð/ rather than OE /d/ medially and finally, and ON consonant assimilation.

Symptoms of Scand input in this latter case depend (at least to begin with) on *a priori* asumptions: hence we look to Gmc distribution because we assume that the building blocks of the OE lexicon were more like those of WGmc than ON; and we are interested in a word's attestation in English dialects because we assume that Scand influence was stronger in the North and East (I shall return to these assumptions in more detail below). Establishing a plausible etymology for a given word is always, of course, about balancing probabilities. None of the available types of evidence for ON input is utterly unassailable (not even, as we shall see below, the best tests of form), and so a combination of factors in support of a claim is always at least reassuring. A good example is **wyndow**, for which the formal case is already very strong but can be reinforced by appealing to the fact that this compound, with its very particular metaphorical sense, is otherwise known only in ON.[135] Assessing the evidence in each instance certainly, therefore, means recording all potentially significant infomation; and I shall return below to considering how all the various available factors impact on our sense of the plausibility of attributing ON input. Nonetheless the distinct categories and sub-categories of evidence can be regarded as of quite different value. Hierarchies of reliability are explicitly applied by some commentators, most importantly Bj., to the different tests they espouse; and so in order to get to the bottom of scholarly epistemologies, as well as for the purposes of creating a typology of evidence, we must examine the categories separately.

Before going any further, we need to think about the role played by chronology. The date of a word's first attestation in English (or of its attestation in the requisite form, sense or usage) is rarely highlighted explicitly as a reason for attributing Scand input, and I did not cite it above as an example of either structural or circumstantial evidence. It is really, of course, the latter, and is underpinned by similar *a priori* assumptions about the nature of Anglo-Norse contact as is the case for geographical distribution, i.e. that speakers of OE and ON first met in substantial, and substantially language-changing, numbers in the late ninth century. But chronology is foundational to the evidence for Norse input in a way that other sorts of distribution are not normally taken to be. In most instances, that is, we need to establish the 'lateness' of a word (or some meaningful characteristic of it) before we consider it as potentially loaned. For practical purposes, 'late' equates to a first attestation after at least 900, the earliest point around which we might reasonably expect the effects of contact to become visible in the lexis of written OE; and in fact most scholars suspect native origin for words appearing in any text probably copied (and indeed composed, unless there are clear signs of updating in transmission to a later copy) before the tenth century, when

---

[135] This is Lass's example (2007: §8.9.2), and note further his remarks on 'reticulate' argumentation (1997: 53–6). Other similar examples from *Gaw* include **gifte**, **scaþe** and **þay** (see the Introductory Essay to Type A below).

uncontroversial Norse-derived words first begin to appear in the OE record.[136]
Words recorded earlier are generally regarded *prima facie* as cognate with their
counterparts in ON, not as loans; and, other than in exceptional cases, the
discovery of a significantly older OE witness to a suspect form or usage means
that the case for loan collapses.[137] Potentially significant differences between
(early) OE occurrences and post-contact ones can, on the other hand, be
accounted for by positing Norse influence. These differences may involve form
(including derivational form), sense or some other aspects of usage; and in a
few instances the only suspicious factor is a word's rarity and/or isolation pre-
contact (see the discussion of words of Type C below).

What we infer from chronology is therefore a fundamental preliminary to
further analysis, since it is an early step in establishing the data that we have to
work with.[138] It has to do with the basic comparative questions that we ask of the
English and Norse lexical systems, and helps us establish what there is to
compare: What words do the two languages have in common? How do they
differ before and after contact? These chronological issues can therefore be
thought of as a prolegomenon to the use of structural evidence, and *inter alia*
they are a useful reminder of how much of the etymologist's task is tied up in
putting the contents of languages next to one another and trying to account for
the differences. At a broader level, of course, any attempt to establish the
historical relationship(s) between two languages must begin by comparing their
contents. The definition of regular correspondence sets between the sounds of
words in one language and those in another, which allows us to reconstruct their
proto-language and thus to establish genetic filiation between them, is the best
known outcome of such activity, and the cornerstone of the comparative method;
these regular correspondences have particularly important consequences when it
comes to the evidence for Norse-derived words in English, as we shall see
further below. But, even when the results of individual acts of comparison are
ambiguous, and other sorts of evidence (including the circumstantial) are
required in order to help us assess the likelihood of the historical relationships
that we posit, the juxtaposition of forms and usages from one language with
those from another is always the first stage in the process, and in the

---

[136] For detailed discussion of the chronological distribution of Norse-derived words in OE texts, see
SPS (esp. 131–49), who also (Appendix II) provides a very useful digest of the evidence for dating
key texts. For important earlier analyses of the OE evidence see Peters and Hofmann.

[137] Notice for instance OE *wīcing*, whose status as a native word on account of its indisputably early
attestation (in the Épinal and Erfurt glossaries) was suggested as early as Kluge (1891: 787; expressed
with more certainty in 1901a: 935). For examples of *Gaw* items claimed as loans in some early
scholarship but rejected on this basis see e.g. **mane**, **sop**, **sprenged** in the Appendix.

[138] Because it is almost always a starting point, this may explain why chronological information is so
often taken for granted in the scholarship, and rarely cited explicitly as amongst the criteria for loan.
But notice Bj'.s careful statement (193–4): 'The question is, to decide in which cases the non-
existence of a word in English before the Danelag times is to be regarded as a loan-word test of any
importance and when not'. Chronology is also referred to in Kluge (1891: 787; 1901a: 935), and is
discussed in some detail in SPS (see esp. 131–49).

etymological description of a potential loan.[139] Structural evidence therefore forms the first layer in our classification of the grounds for attributing Norse input, and I shall introduce the possible uses of it in the next section.

1.5. TYPES AND USES OF STRUCTURAL EVIDENCE

Comparing the OE and ON lexicons seems to me to produce three essential, prototypical species of evidence that the forms and usages we see in Norse might have influenced those in post-contact English. I have designated these as Types A, B and C.

1.5.1. Systematic formal evidence: Type A

This category has long been recognized and distinguished in the scholarship. Items belonging to it are those for which there is reliable, formal evidence of Norse derivation based on regular, predictable correspondences between OE and ON phonology or/and morphology. It is not merely, that is, that we have a word in post-contact English which happens to be similar to an ON one, but that one or more features of that word's form are systematically characteristic of ON and uncharacteristic of OE. These features constitute what Lass terms 'regular correspondence sets', and their consistency is what allows comparative philologists to argue for English and Norse as distinct developments on the Gmc family tree in the first place.[140] Provided, therefore, that we understand these formal equations correctly, their presence in a late OE or ME word strongly indicates its descent from ON, and renders its descent from OE highly improbable. As an example, consider what in Lass's notation appears as 'C{OE ɑ:, ON ai}'. There are many unambiguous instantiations of this correspondence set, in which OE /ɑ:/ (ME /aː, ɔː/) answers to OIcel /ei/ (probably VAN /ɑi/ or /ɛi/), e.g. OE stān : OIcel steinn 'stone', OE hām : OIcel heimr 'home', OE bāt : OIcel beit 'bit' (pret. 3 sg. ind.); these descend regularly from, and contribute to the reconstruction of, PGmc ancestral forms in */ai/ (viz. *stainaz, *haimaz, *bait). Where this relationship breaks down, and a post-contact English form continues the ON rather than the OE reflex, we have solid evidence of loan, as in ME **layk**, with which compare OIcel leikr rather than OE lāc. Crucially, though in this case the OE cognate is

---

[139] This principle is implicit in the hierarchies of evidence expressed by the likes of Kluge (1891: 787; 1901a: 935) and Flom (1900: 22–3), both of whom regard phonetic and semantic criteria as primary in the search for Norse loans; it is also apparent in the etymological evidence for Norse derivation cited by Durkin (2009: 170), who privileges 'sound change' and 'semantic innovation'. And compare the principles set out in Bense (xv–xxxi) for identifying loans into English from LG/Du, which he divides into 'Internal Evidence' (form, pronunciation, sense) and 'External Evidence' (inc. distribution).

[140] 'In order to elevate intuitive similarities to the rank of correspondences or equivalences (i.e. evidence for cognateness), we have to establish that they are "lawful", statable in principle as particular instantiations of general rules' (Lass 1997: 126). And see Lass's extended discussion of the principles (1997: 123–39). For some general remarks on the use of sound correspondences to test for loans, see further Campbell (1986).

recorded and acts as a corroborative witness to the endogenous development, the regularity of these correspondence sets means that we do not actually require a native form to be attested in order to rule against descent from it; thus for instance ME **bayn**, which can be derived from the ON adj. represented by OIcel *beinn* but not its hypothetical OE cognate **bān*. The comparison we make between OE and ON in these circumstances is systematic rather than *ad hoc*, and hence its findings are replicable and (most importantly) predictive. A detailed discussion of the grounds for, and the validity of, each of these correspondences will follow as part of the Introductory Essay to Type A below. For the time being, notice that I have broken down this category into the following sub-types:[141]

> **A1** = phonological criteria
> **A2** = morphological criteria
> **A3** = phonological *and* morphological criteria

Its sheer reliability means that this type of formal evidence is very often distinguished from all other grounds for identifying Norse-derived words, and justifiably so. Bj.'s presentation of the divide between what he calls 'phonetic tests' and other criteria is especially sharp, and it has been reiterated in a number of subsequent discussions.[142] On occasion, these tests' efficacy is described as though it constituted absolute proof: for Kisbye (1992: 43), for instance, phonology provides 'the only absolutely reliable test'. But it is prudent to moderate one's choice of words slightly, even in the best cases. This is partly, once again, just to acknowledge the ways in which etymological reasoning must proceed, i.e. that it is inherently probabilistic, and therefore that the measure of a successful hypothesis is the gross improbability of other ones, not that they are absolutely impossible. For any pair of English and Norse types in a correspondence set, that is, it is always in theory possible to argue that there existed a native variant, unrecorded in OE texts, which had independently undergone changes (or failed to undergo changes) that left it looking much more like the form we associate with ON than those we otherwise know for OE. In the case of most of these pairs, however, the range of possible outcomes is large enough for us to regard it as highly improbable that an otherwise unknown English variant should have emerged which coincidentally took precisely the same path as the ON type, when the OE forms we do have all point to quite different results; and thus for the (relative) security that we associate with Type

---

[141] The sub-types I employ for each of Types A to D should not, incidentally, be thought of as a hierarchy arranged in order of 'strength', but (crudely) in descending order of intuitive 'significance' to the etymologist, with 'significance' meaning slightly different things in the case of each Type (since the nature of the evidence is different in each case). For Type A, I have put the words showing phonological criteria first (Type A1) simply because there are massively more instances where the evidence is of this sort (63 stems) than there are of morphological features (A2, 5 stems) or both (A3, 2 stems).

[142] Thus e.g. Luick (1901b: 413–14; §381 Anm. 1), Thorson (2–4,), Kisbye (1982: 37–42; 1992: 43–4), Dance (2003: 74–6), Pons-Sanz (2007: esp. 48; 2015: esp. 208), SPS (25–8), Lass (2007: §8.9.2) and Durkin (2014: esp. 201–2).

A evidence to appear unthreatened. Hence it is always possible to posit that there existed a variety of medieval English in which, say, the endogenous reflex of PGmc */au/ remained much more like this (for instance, that it retained a high back rounded second element) than like the sound suggested by attested late OE spellings (i.e. /æːɑ/), and thus that the ME /au/ of **lausen** owes itself to a survival of this native phoneme rather than to ON /ɑu/ (/ɔu/);[143] but all the evidence we actually have supports the alternative.[144]

However, the arguments that we are able to make on the basis of regular, formal correspondences between OE and ON are not, in practice, always quite as compelling as this, or as one another. Close examination of the grounds for the various 'tests', and moreover the process of applying them to the etymological information that we have for a particular lexical item, inevitably shows up complexities which are not apparent at first glance. For one thing, it is a fact of life that a PGmc root is much more securely reconstructible for some items than it is for others. When we have the wealth of cognate evidence that we do in the case of **layk**, for instance, we feel on rather safer ground in tracing a distinctively Scand pathway of transmission back to an ancestral form than we do in the case of words which have no, or no very plausible, cognates beyond Norse, and whose ulterior etymology is itself opaque, like **bayn**, even if its phonological features are distinctive in principle. In a surprisingly large number of instances, in fact, the items I have classified as Type A in the Survey have uncertain PGmc sources. Some are open to more than one quite plausible explanation, affecting the etymological correspondence sets to which their phonological features belong: see especially **lyþen** and **woþe**.[145] I have admitted

---

[143] Lass does indeed raise this possibility, very speculatively (see 2007: §8.7.2 n. 13); and for a suggestion that northern ME /aː/ (< OE /ɑː/) might have had diphthongal realizations independent of ON input, see now Cole (2018: 199–200). Sometimes the Norse-type reflex is not attested only in the Scand languages, of course, but is also that found in one or more other early Gmc languages (and/or in Gmc loan-words in Romance). PGmc */au/ is a case in point, non-native-seeming ME reflexes of which (/au, ou, oː/) can in principle be accounted for via loan from HG or Du. In such cases the declaration that a given form is *distinctive* of Norse can sometimes be shown to rely upon the *a priori* assumption that English is more likely to have obtained it from contact with speakers of ON than with speakers of one of these other languages, and in that case the claim should be treated with caution. (This happens especially often with words whose phonology can be accounted for by input from similar forms in Fr. See e.g. **wayue**, which I have included in Type A since its form and sense leave little doubt that some ON input is at work. But in most cases the possibility of Fr input is too palpable to allow an item to be securely included in Type A, and I have put items like **bruny**, **merk** (etc.), **messe** and **scrape** under C2; see the Introductory Essay to that section.) Nonetheless the relative claims of etyma in Norse and elsewhere can sometimes be tested; see Luick's discussion of ME *copen, coupen* 'to buy, exchange', some spellings of which indicate borrowing from ON *kaupa* (with /ɑu/ (/ɔu/)) rather than from the Du monophthong (which could only underlie ME forms in <o>) (Luick 1901a: 323–4).

[144] For one or two words it is possible to suggest specific reasons why a Norse-looking feature might have been developed endogenously (as e.g. **nay**; see that entry below), but the probability of these explanations is in itself relatively slight, and they do not upset the general principle on which the correspondence set is built.

[145] See the entries concerned, and on items with problematic ulterior etymologies see further the Introductory Essay to Type A (p. 80) below.

these items as Type A on the grounds that either of the proposed etymologies will do the trick as far as formal tests are concerned, but they are nicely indicative of the room for debate that exists in tracing the pre-histories of ON words, and of the significance that attaches to this. There are many more items that do not make it into Type A at all because they fall at this hurdle, i.e. not all of their several suggested PGmc sources would have given rise to distinctively ON formal features, and hence we have insufficient grounds for ruling firmly against endogenous origin (see e.g. Type D items like **mynne** (v.), **rake, rasse, ronez, rous**).

Potentially more troublingly, for tests of form to have (relatively) strong predictive value we need to be sure that we understand the early histories of the features in question properly in (all relevant varieties of) English and Norse, and there is often at least some space for doubt. There has naturally been a great deal of relevant discussion in the scholarship, both in the various grammar and handbook accounts of OE and ON and the very numerous specialist treatments of particular developments, and also (less frequently) in the form of detailed comparisons of the phonological and morphological systems of the two languages, undertaken in a bid to understand the effects of contact between them.[146] Still the fullest attempt to distil the probative differences is that by Bj., whose discussion is extremely careful in pointing out potential difficulties.[147] In some cases more recent scholarship has done nothing to assuage the doubts, and they are severe enough to rule out the features in question being used to establish regular correspondence sets. Thus, for instance, it is very difficult to say that the loss of /x/ in OIcel *rá* 'corner, nook' (< PGmc **wranhō*) is really distinctive as a Scand development, and could not have been a possible outcome in Old English too (see under **wro** and Formal Criteria §11.2); or that the assimilation of /ðl/ to /l/ which we assume for ON *mæla* could not have been independently replicated in OE (see under **mele** and Formal Criteria §10.4 (l)). Our uncertainty is partly a product of the paucity of evidence: there are just not very many parallels against which to compare the changes in these words, and on the basis of which a general 'rule' can be established. But our doubts also arise at least partly from what Lass (1997: 173) terms limitation in 'morphogenetic space', i.e. when the number of possible developments of a feature are so small that independent convergence is quite likely; it is no accident that changes like the loss of stem-final /x/ and the assimilation of consonant clusters like /ðl/ are cross-linguistically so common (contrast the change of PGmc **/au/ to OE /æːɑ/, which is much more difficult to predict, and

---

[146] For the major accounts of OE and ON phonology and morphology, including comparisons of the two languages and analyses of the fates of ON sounds in English, see my remarks at the head of the Formal Criteria section (Introductory Essay to Type A).

[147] Some of these have not tended to be picked up by subsequent treatments, e.g. the problems associated with ON /aː/ as a test of loan discussed by Bj. (81–2, 84–7). Detailed considerations also appear most notably in Wright & Wright (§§163–77), Dance (2003: 74–86), Pons-Sanz (2007: 48–58), SPS (28–76), Durkin (2014: 191–201).

in fact happens in no other early Gmc language). While in cases like these the difficulties may have remained insuperable, however, our grasp of certain early English and Norse phonological features has changed significantly since the late nineteenth century, and our appreciation of their roles as loan criteria has altered accordingly. The most important example is the extent of palatalization of PGmc */k, ɣ, sk/ in OE, and thus the degree to which its absence can be regarded as a marker of Scand influence. This is a famously knotty problem, and ideas about initial palatalization in particular are the source of some of the most obvious discrepancies between the earliest treatments of Norse loans and current attitudes;[148] the ramifications of palatalization were still being worked out as Björkman was writing, and indeed the report he offers of Morsbach's (1896) conclusions is itself often regarded as a major step forward (Bj. 147 n.2). There is still considerable room for debate with regard to some aspects of this topic, especially when it comes to the absence of palatalization in non-initial position in ME (and later); non-palatalized variants in this position are subject to a number of competing explanations, and as such cannot be treated as forms which are distinctively Norse for Type A purposes. Initial non-palatalization is now usually regarded, however, as a 'safe' test of loan, since it has long been accepted that (early) OE always palatalized the reflexes of PGmc initial */k, ɣ, sk/ in the appropriate environments, and that this happened in the North as well as in southern varieties.[149] While this is enough for us to set up OE : ON correspondence sets (palatalized : non-palatalized) and to regard the differences as distinctive according to the standard principle, doubts nonetheless linger about their reliability more than they do for most established sets. Again this is partly a symptom of the limited range of possible outcomes: crudely put, palatalization will either happen or else it won't, and it is accordingly hard to be sure that some of the instances of its absence in post-contact English are not due to transmission from some dialect (s) of OE where it had independently failed, rather than to loan from ON; and this suspicion is made to nag the more loudly in this case by the peculiar nature of the corpus of ME words which show the Norse-type feature, several of which have an initial velar alongside codas (in one or more attested ME forms) which possibly or certainly reflect native developments (thus notably **agayn**, **gayn** (etc.), **gest**, **gif**, and see under Formal Criteria §8 below). Provocative though this state of affairs is, the fact remains that, at least in the present state of our knowledge of early English and Norse phonology, the palatalization correspondence set is no less indexical of Scand input than are the others included as criteria for Type A. Numerous points of difficulty persist in this broad category, especially when it comes to applying the 'tests' in question to the lexical data, where each etymology must in the end be addressed separately. But the regular, formal criteria for loan which we

---

[148] For some examples see Formal Criteria §8 below (section 2.2.1.2, note 284).

[149] For a detailed discussion see under Formal Criteria §8 below.

deduce from the comparison of English and Norse systems have important things in common, certainly enough for them to be regarded as constituting a distinct category of evidence.[150]

1.5.2. *Other structural categories: Types B, C and D*

When no formal criteria of the sort described in the previous section are available, claims for ON input into a ME word's development are always, and inevitably, on a less solid footing. In important respects, the fault-line between Type A items and all others is therefore the most significant division in the structural evidence. Nonetheless, these remaining items (396 different lexical items in the Survey, arranged into 330 stems) are not all of a kind in structural terms, i.e. what we find when we compare the OE, ON and ME lexicons. They fall into three prototypically distinct groups, based on what we can say about their ultimate form-source (usually a Gmc root): sometimes this form-source is a root which is simply not attested in (early) OE (Type B); sometimes it is already found in (early) OE (Type C); and at other times it is not possible to identify an unambiguous form-source at all (Type D). Each of these three groups implies a different kind of case for ON input, with distinct underlying assumptions. I shall introduce them in turn here; for fuller discussions and detailed treatments of examples, see the Introductory Essay to each Type below.

For **Type B**, the absence of any closely related form in early OE means that it is the very existence of this root in post-contact English which ON input is being invoked in order to explain (and nothing more specific about the precise form, sense or usage which is at issue).[151] The basic assumption which underlies the case is that the absence of evidence for this whole word-family in early OE can be taken as an indication that the Gmc root in question had not survived into English long enough to be attested in writing, and hence that its appearance only during or after the period of Anglo-Norse contact is best accounted for by loan into English from ON. It hardly needs saying that absence of evidence is not the same as evidence of absence, and the plausibility of this argument inevitably varies wildly from ME word to ME word. The case is generally accepted for items like **ille** and **take**. It is not, of course, completely impossible that native reflexes of these forms did indeed exist, but were never recorded in writing (perhaps because they survived only in varieties of OE poorly or not at all reflected in the written record). But it seems inherently unlikely that words lexicalizing such very commonly occurring concepts existed without leaving any trace in early OE texts; and

---

[150] In asserting this I dissent from the views expressed by Luick (1901b: 413–14) and McGee (28–9), who regard Bj.'s 'phonetic tests' as extremely important in theory, but all in all as containing too many uncertainties and difficulties to stand as a separate category.

[151] For how I define 'closely related form' in practice in this book (i.e. 'the same Gmc root'), see further below.

moreover both **ille** and **take** are highly characteristic of the lexis only of the Scand branch of Gmc, and are either not found at all or are far less central to the relevant semantic fields in the other attested early Gmc languages. For words like these, the case for ON input is therefore hardly if ever questioned in etymological discussions. Some of these most plausible items are further supported by the circumstantial evidence of their regional distribution in English (discussed at greater length below). **Ille** is a good example, being most frequently attested in (albeit not totally confined to) northern and eastern ME texts; and another is **gate**, a word still recognizably characteristic of place- and street-names in the North and East of England. For the absence of an item in early OE writings to carry much evidential value, however, there has to be a reasonable chance of its being reflected in the textual record had it existed; and for words standing for some less mundane concepts, more peripheral to the lexicon, the probability of this is much less compelling. In particular, it is quite easy to imagine ultimately imitative (or 'ideophonic') words such as **cakled**, **ʒaule** and **wharred** escaping attestation in written OE; and in a few cases it is eminently possible that the item concerned was simply coined independently in OE (or in ME) and ON (e.g. **hoo**).[152]

Notice that is has seemed to me helpful to draw a broad distinction between Type **B1** (when there is no clear evidence for the existence of forms derived on the same root anywhere else in Gmc) and Type **B2** (when forms derived on the same root are clearly identifiable in Gothic and/or the continental WGmc languages, but not in early OE). In principle B1 provides a firmer foundation for positing Scand input than does B2, since for B1 stems the ON counterpart is then a word more or less 'characteristic' of the Scand group of languages, next to which there is nothing demonstrably related in other varieties of Gmc.[153] But this criterion must of course be applied alongside all the other grounds for arguing either way which pertain in the case of each individual item, and it by no means trumps them; there are certainly B2 items, that is, where the grounds for claiming ON input seem to me more compelling all in all than they do for some B1 items.

For **Type C**, the case for Scand input differs in ways that seem to me to be crucial. Here, the basic form-source of the word *is* already known in early OE, and so it is not its mere existence which is the focus of the argument. Rather, there must now be something about the item as it is attested in post-contact English, some aspect of form, or sense, or usage which cannot be paralleled in earlier occurrences (or at the very least is rare there), but which is supposed to be more reminiscent of a word in the Scand languages. The tell-tale feature, the

---

[152] On ideophonic ('sound-symbolic') words see further the Introductory Essay to Type B (section 3.2.3), esp. p. 124 below.

[153] And see Bj. (197): 'And we are no doubt entitled to look upon words only found in Scand. and M.E. as most certainly Scand., provided their distribution or other circumstances do not contradict such an assumption'.

'smoking gun', can have to do with one or more of the following, which I separate formally as sub-types:[154]

> **C1** = derivational form (e.g. **lofte**, apparently from a PGmc *luft-a-n* as represented by OIcel *loft* (*lopt*), rather than the *i*-stem *luft-i-z* known in OE *lyft*);
>
> **C2** = some other aspect of (supposed) phonology (which nonetheless falls short of the regular differences robustly diagnostic of Scand input treated under Type A; e.g. **brenne**, which looks more like the 'original' Gmc form of the root as in OIcel *brenna* than the metathesized variant seen in OE *beornan*, *biernan* etc.);
>
> **C3** = meaning (e.g. **dreme**, whose ME meaning 'dream' is found attached to OIcel *draumr* but not to the corresponding (though not necessarily related) OE *drēam*);
>
> **C4** = formation of a compound or phrase (e.g. **boþe**, perhaps < the extended (and originally compounded) ON form represented by OIcel *báðir* rather than a compound of OE *bā* + *þā*, which is not found as such in OE texts);
>
> **C5** = frequency (e.g. **til**, which is massively more frequent in ME than OE, where it is confined to a handful of early Nhb occurrences).

Notice that Type C is also where I have assigned words whose (more or less proximate) form-source may generally be agreed to belong to a third language, such as Fr or Lat; see e.g. **croun, breue, garysoun**. In all these cases the argument is fundamentally of exactly the same order: for all items of Type C, that is, it is possible to derive the basic form of the word from a source other than ON, i.e. from the Gmc root as it is known in (early) OE, or via direct loan from another language (Fr, Lat, etc.); but in each instance the claim for ON input is based on some difference, more or less subtle, between the form or function of the counterpart in OE or the third language and its form or function in one or more Scand varieties; and the argument then boils down to whether the feature in question could have come about without ON influence, i.e. as an unattested native survival in OE, as an endogenous development in English, or by direct loan into English from the other language concerned, rather than its having

---

[154] As for Type A above, my sub-divisions are arranged (more or less) in descending order of their general significance to the etymologist. It is most common for derivational features to be the crucial evidence in the case for ON input amongst this group (C1, 67 stems), followed by other formal differences (C2, 45 stems) and then semantic criteria (C3, 40 stems); C4 and C5 both have far fewer members (12 and 17 stems respectively). Since C5 is the heuristically 'left-over' sub-category, for which the only evidence for ON input is the relatively unspecific 'frequency' in English, it makes best sense for this to be treated last, even though there are slightly more stems belonging here than there are in C4. As it happens, the order of these C sub-types does also correspond roughly to the plausibility of the evidence amassed, since (in my judgement) C1 contains the most stems for which the argument for ON input is compelling (24 out of 67), next to fewer for C2 and C3 (8/45, 7/40 respectively), and fewer still for C4 and C5 (2/12, 2/17).

entered English through ON. Thus for **croun**, for example, it is an aspect of form (the loss of the pretonic vowel) which is held to be indicative of entry to English via ON, rather than direct from early (Anglo-)Fr; and hence this word is a Type C2, because the evidence precisely parallels that for a word like **brenne** (where the absence of metathesis is taken to be indicative of entry via ON, rather than direct native descent from Gmc).

Incidentally, this highlights a significant difference between the categorization I am advancing in this book and the 'morpho-etymological' typologies tradition-ally employed in discussions of the outcomes of language contact.[155] What the system being described here is designed to mark is not, first and foremost, the *outcome* of contact – at least in terms of the morphological structures of the source and recipient languages. I am not *primarily* concerned, that is, with understanding whether a loaned item is a loanword proper, where the form of the transferred morpheme is preserved more or less intact, or a loan-shift, i.e. a loan-translation or semantic loan, where native morphemic material is substituted for the formal constituents in the source language. Rather, my typology signals the *etymological evidence for* some (or any) kind of transfer of material from ON into English, however that transfer may ultimately have manifested itself. In many cases the labels from the two sorts of classification will overlap: i.e. a semantic loan will inevitably be categorized as my Type C3, since it is the difference of the meanings attaching to the basic form-source and the supposed ON etymon which is at issue; thus e.g. **dreme**, where the form of the word must be native, and so any Scand input is probably the result of 'semantic loan' as traditionally conceived. But Type C3 does not *only* include items which would always be classed as semantic loans, since there are some instances where the evidence for ON input consists mainly of a semantic difference but where we cannot necessarily say that only the meaning is what was transferred between the two languages. For a word like **layne**, for example, the sense of the ME output arguably owes something to ON, but the form could in fact derive from either ON or OE: so, while this could be a semantic loan *per se*, it could alternatively be explained as a full loanword, with both morphemic and semantic material taken into English from ON as a whole package. In the case of two very closely related language varieties like OE and ON, then, instances like this illustrate how the application of conventional morpho-etymological categories can sometimes be problematic; this fact is certainly not without interest, and I shall return to this issue in the Introductory Essay to Type C below. But from the point of view of attributing etymological input, making this kind of distinction is actually less vital than understanding the basic criteria according to which ON influence (of whatever kind) has been posited; and the goal of the system used in this book is to facilitate this understanding, by allowing us to consider together all the items for which the argument for Scand input involves *etymological* evidence of the same species.

---

[155] See in particular Fischer (2001: 98–101), and for recent discussions of terminology see note 18 above.

For Type C, the plausibility of the case for ON input varies from item to item to exactly the same degree, and for much the same reasons, as it does for Type B. In some instances, especially when a word lexicalizes a relatively common concept, the appearance of a key feature (of form, sense, etc.) in ON and in English only after contact with Scand speakers had begun is usually reckoned to be an unlikely coincidence; see the discussions of words like **bone** (C1), **mensk** (C2) and **lawe** (C3). But there are many others where alternative explanations – unattested survival into OE of a Gmc form or meaning, independent generation of that feature later in English, and so on – seem at least as credible; thus e.g. **blende** (C1), **askez** (C2), **borde** (C3).

Notice that the difference between Type B and Type C items is prototypically very clear: in one case, the root in question is not known in early OE; in the other, it is known (or else the form of the word can be unambiguously derived from some third language). As with many linguistic typologies, however, in practice there is something of a grey area in the middle,[156] and there are some items which could in reality have been argued into either category. This has to do with precisely how one defines the idea of 'the same Gmc root', and with the threshold of etymological evidence required for two words to count as formations on a given root. I have tried to be consistent in this book about where I have drawn this line, and have decided that 'the same root' has to involve a clear *derivational* relationship, and one that is generally agreed in the etymological scholarship. If we can define reasonably clearly how two words have been derived upon the same root, then the fact of their relationship can be stated at least relatively uncontroversially; whereas some less-well-understood potential connection is open to the charge that we do not really know for sure that the root is the same. A clear derivational relationship can include, in my view, derivation on one of the regular Ablaut grades of a known (or robustly hypothesized) Gmc root; thus e.g. **wykez**, which is apparently formed on the zero-grade of the root of the strong verb represented by OE *wīcan*, and so counts as a Type C. But this definition of 'the same root' does not normally extend to by-forms of roots whose connection cannot so transparently be explained; for example, **lowande** supposes a PGmc *lug- which seems to be represented with different vocalism in e.g. OE *līeg* (< PGmc *laug-), but these forms are not members of a strong verbal Ablaut series which can otherwise be securely reconstructed for Gmc, and so **lowande** is classed as a Type B.

The essential feature of **Type D**, finally, is that this time no readily identifiable form-source can generally be agreed. The whole basis from which the arguments for Types B and C have proceeded, i.e. an accepted starting point in Gmc or a third language, is therefore wanting; and so items in this category are those that the etymological authorities frequently label as 'difficult' or 'obscure', whether with respect to their careers in English at large or their occurrences specifically in the context of *Gaw*. The histories of their treatment by previous scholarship can

---

[156] For an enlightening discussion of the nature of taxonomic categories in linguistic argumentation, see Lass (2000).

be very varied and complex, several showing three or more quite different competing theories, and the entries in this section of the Survey accordingly tend to contain the lengthiest and most involved discussions of all those in this book. Generalization is peculiarly tricky for Type D items; but, broadly speaking, difficulties in the identification of a form-source can arise in two principal ways (sometimes in combination), and these constitute the main sub-categories I distinguish here. Type **D1** indicates that the form and sense of the stem in question can be established (relatively) straightforwardly, and are usually agreed, but that there is no generally accepted etymology. D1 items are therefore classically 'obscure', and they include well-known cruces like **big, kylled** and **scho**, alongside less infamous but still contested words like **enker-grene, gryndel** and **raþeled**. In Type **D2**, the interpretation in its *Gaw* context of the ME word, and hence its most plausible etymon, is argued about; see e.g. **glaum, lagmon** and **slokes**. It need not be hard to attribute a specific form-source to these items owing to etymological obscurity *per se*, therefore, but rather because it is difficult to know which word the *Gaw* form actually represents, and hence which stem found elsewhere in English (if any) we should identify it with. Having said this, there is a surprising number of D2 items where the etymology of one or more possible identifications in itself proves difficult, and so the kinds of problems involved may also incorporate those associated with D1 (as well as those associated with any of the preceding types and sub-types, of course).

1.6. Circumstantial evidence

All the items in the Survey fit into one of the four categories, Types A to D, described above. These categories represent the primary etymological charac-teristics of Norse-derived words based on the relationship between the OE (and ME) and ON lexical systems (or the absence of a properly definable relationship) in each case. The Survey is arranged into four main sections accordingly, each with its sub-types as explained above;[157] this facilitates the description and analysis of each category of evidence, and of the items belonging to it, in one place.[158] But there are, of course, other factors that can be brought to bear on the

---

[157] Each item is therefore treated in only one entry, and the vast majority have been assigned a single Type label. The only exceptions are a few items in Type C, where the primary structural criterion is accompanied by strong evidence of another C sub-type which is only slightly less germane, and hence where I have added a subsidiary Type label in brackets following the main category. But in each of these cases there remains one reason for adducing ON input which I have reckoned to be 'primary', and each item is still filed just by this main Type and sub-type. See the Introductory Essay to Type C for discussion and examples.

[158] An ancillary, practical benefit of ordering the items in the Survey according to these structural Types is that each item can be assigned to one and only one principal category; whereas an attempt to group primarily by the supporting, circumstantial evidence described in this section would result in many items being placed in more than one category (the implications of which might contradict one another), something that would heuristically alone be a less fruitful way to proceed.

problem, and thus additional ways of classifying the words in our list. This 'circumstantial' evidence is very often considered a useful, and sometimes a powerful, aid in assessing how probable it is that the hypotheses we have developed by structural comparison are correct. It has two main branches.

1.6.1. *Germanic distribution*

The identification of (possible) Gmc cognates and the delineation of their relationships are, as we have seen, fundamental to the comparative etymological work described above. Once we have pursued the historical ramifications of comparable forms, though, and analysed the basic correspondences between the English and Norse systems, there remains the circumstantial evidence of the exact distribution of cognates, and their usage, elsewhere in Gmc. It is usually felt to be especially useful to know whether the potentially Norse-derived element also occurs in one or more of the WGmc languages; this factor is mentioned in some form in most studies, including some of the earliest (see the remarks of Coleridge, Knigge, Wall and Flom, as noticed above).

The main reason this evidence is important is because of our very patchy first-hand knowledge of OE vocabulary, particularly when it comes to the early, pre-contact period, and to northern and Midland dialects. Though the attested OE lexicon is remarkably numerous and diverse (a recent estimate puts it at around 34,000 'separate word forms'),[159] the great bulk of textual evidence comes from the tenth and eleventh centuries, and from the South and West of England; and even this material must represent only a proportion of the words (and, moreover, of their senses and usages) which were actually known to its authors and scribes. This is an obvious enough point, but its significance is sometimes lost sight of when we refer to 'OE vocabulary', our idea of which, it can reasonably be argued, ought at the very least to take account of the wide range of potential sub-derivations, compounds and sense-extensions which are only *implied* by what is actually extant.[160] As a counter-balance to the inevitable gaps in attested OE, then, it is held to be useful to explore the vocabularies of its most closely related languages, which are usually taken to be the continental WGmc family (i.e., in their medieval stages, Old Frisian, Old Saxon and Middle Low German, Old and Middle High German, Old Low Franconian and Middle Dutch). If a word is found in one of these languages in a form, sense or usage identical or very similar to that of a suspect item in late OE or ME, then this is often taken to increase the probability that the latter is really the descendant of an unrecorded OE word (or usage thereof), and hence to reduce the need to appeal to input from ON in order to explain it. This argument is especially attractive to those scholars who are wary on principle of attributing linguistic change to the results of contact unless there is a strong reason actively to support it (the 'minimalists').

---

[159] See Kay (2012: 315).
[160] See Hoad (1985).

Thus Lass, for example, places considerable weight on the existence of WGmc cognates as evidence *against* Norse derivation.[161]

Attempting to gauge the likelihood of a previously unrecorded native survival or of an independent native development is, of course, an important part of assessing any case for borrowing, and pursuing the evidence of Gmc cognates is a sensible approach to take to it. It is not, needless to say, without its complications; one must as ever consider carefully the assumptions which underlie the use of Gmc distribution as evidence, and what precisely it is being supposed to demonstrate. The vocabularies of the WGmc languages do indeed have a great deal in common, and it is not difficult to substantiate the impression of them as a coherent group in terms of lexical developments from PGmc; there is a number of important examples in the Survey of divisions between these languages on the one hand, and ON on the other (note e.g. **ille**, **take**, **lawe**), and it would be easy to expand this list.[162] The overall picture, however, is much less clear-cut. There are plenty of exceptions to the idea of the WGmc languages consistently patterning with one another as against ON and/or Go, including some cases of a single WGmc tongue attesting a word otherwise only found outside the group, but where loan cannot be used as the explanation for this. Notable examples from the Survey, in which an OE form is paralleled only in Norse, are **glaum** (the only cognate of OIcel *glaumr* beyond the Scand languages is OE *glēam*) and **hap** (the only forms outside Norse related to OIcel *happ* are OE *gehæp*, *gehæplic* and their derivatives); a well-known instance of OE agreeing uniquely with Go is OE *ortgeard*, Go *aúrti-gards*. Sometimes there are words which are relatively widely attested, but whose precise sense developments are restricted to just two such languages, as is the case with OE *dragan* and ON *draga* (the only languages in which this verb has the sense 'to draw, pull'; the OE records of this sense start too early for us to entertain loan, at least in the Viking Age).[163] These minority patterns in the lexis are of course symptomatic of the complexities ingrained in the whole evidence for the early interrelations of the Gmc languages. Though for the most part we seem justified in treating WGmc as (in traditional terms) a 'branch' of the Gmc *Stammbaum* separate from NGmc (and still more so from EGmc), there are nonetheless some features, especially in the morphology, which suggest a more complex picture. The 'unity' of WGmc as an historical entity, something for which one could realistically reconstruct a proto-language, is an especially difficult proposition, given the early distinctiveness of OHG (which in some important respects looks

---

[161] See esp. Lass (1997: 203–5; 2007: §8.9.2).

[162] For recent discussion of the WGmc lexicon (esp. as against NGmc) see Seebold (2013), and for some shared WGmc lexical innovations see further Stiles (2013: 17), Ringe-Taylor (§4.3, inc. derivational features, and loanwords into Proto-WGmc), and also Euler (2013: 179–200). On the difficulties inherent in using lexis to determine early dialectal interrelations in Gmc, see Nielsen (1985: 73–4; 1989: 106 , n.22 to 96, 146; 2000: 148), with reference in particular to Arndt (1959), Lerchner (1965).

[163] See *DOE* s.v. *dragan* and *ONP* s.v. *draga* (2) (vb.).

different from the other languages) and the evidence for a North Sea (Ingvaeonic) sub-group in the West. This 'North Sea' group (OE, OFris, perhaps OS) problematizes still further our conceptions of Gmc sub-grouping, in as much as the languages in question share some (important) developments with ON not found elsewhere in WGmc. For many scholars, the presence of these features (sometimes conceptualized as 'areal changes') is evidence of ongoing contact between groups of speakers in North Sea coastal regions until at least the Anglo-Saxon migrations, and redolent of a NWGmc dialect continuum in which the nascent OE dialects and language varieties spoken in Scandinavia participated.[164] It is worth noticing in this connexion that the Anglian dialects of OE have sometimes been claimed to show particularly close affinities with ON not shared by other varieties of OE. Recent treatments of early Gmc language grouping tend to be sceptical about this idea, and it is difficult to accept without considerable qualification, even though it continues to be referred to in accounts of early English dialectology;[165] there are a couple of fairly high-profile lexical correspondences in its favour, viz. **til** and **ar**, both recorded early in Angl texts and basic to ON, but encountered hardly at all elsewhere in WGmc.

The relationships between OE and the other WGmc languages, and their connections with ON, are hardly as straightforward as is sometimes assumed, then; and this has repercussions when it comes to predicting how the cognates of a given lexical item will be distributed. As noted above, in the majority of cases OE patterns with continental WGmc, often against ON, and there is thus a greater probability that an inherited OE word will be shared with one or more other WGmc languages than there is of its being shared only with Norse; but there is plenty of evidence of other (minority) patterns, including lexical connections between OE and ON which are inherited from an earlier period rather than being the results of contact in the Viking Age. If, when we cite a

---

[164] For an important recent discussion see Stiles (2013: 13), who presents a careful account of 'Proto-WGmc' innovations (which were nonetheless preceded as well as followed by specifically Ingvaeonic changes); he calls WGmc 'a differentiated dialect continuum that could still undergo innovations that encompassed all members'. Ringe (2012: 33) also argues that Proto-WGmc was 'a single language (by some reasonable definition) for generations', but one with 'significant dialect differences ... well before it lost its linguistic unity'; and see further Ringe-Taylor (esp. §§3.1–4.3), and similarly the discussion in Euler (2013). The key review of earlier theories on the interrelations of the Gmc languages is Nielsen (1989: esp. 67–107). On WGmc, see further e.g. Lass (1997: 143–57), Nielsen (2000: esp. 241–7), Fulk (2018: §1.15); on NGmc see the recent surveys in Andersson (2002: 290–6), Fulk (2018: §1.14); and for discussions of a NWGmc continuum centred on the North Sea and the relevant shared features see e.g. Nielsen (1985: esp. 187–220), Hines (1998), Townend (2002: 25–6, 29), Nielsen (2002a), Quak (2002), Schulte (2002: 770–71), and further Nielsen (1975; 1976; 2000: 290–3), Fulk (2018: §1.10).

[165] For the case against, see esp. the conclusions in Nielsen (1985: 65–72, 248–59), and further Hines (1990: esp. 29–30; 1998), Townend (2002: 26–8), Dance (2003: 87–8), Stiles (2013: 30); as opposed to the earlier discussions in Skeat (1892a: 454–5), Jordan (1906: 112–24) and more recently the briefer mentions in e.g. de Caluwé-Dor (1983: 216–19), Smith (1996: 131; 2007: 120; 2009: 65–6), Miller (2012: 108 n. 19) and SPS (6). Contact with Norse speakers in some parts of England between the Anglo-Saxon settlement period and the onset of the Viking Age has also occasionally been mooted on non-linguistic grounds; for discussion and references see Townend (2002: 29–31).

WGmc cognate for a suspect word in late OE or ME, we are doing so in order to promote the possibility of an (unrecorded) shared retention in OE of a form or usage inherited from a WGmc parent language, we must therefore reckon with some of these doubts about the nature of early filiations within (and beyond) the group. At the least, the attestation of the same word in just one other WGmc language is not likely to be as meaningful as its occurrence right across the group, especially if the single language in question is one not especially closely associated with OE, like OHG. In practice, the occurrence of similar words in the most nearly related languages, especially OFris or OS, has always been regarded as more telling (and cp. Coleridge 1859a: 26). This kind of argument for unrecorded shared inheritance is liable to be shaky for other reasons, too, and these have a more general bearing on our assessment of similar-looking forms or usages in related languages. Especially when only one or two languages attest it, that is, what we take to be 'the same word' could always theoretically be an independent coinage, something coincidentally developed on the same deriva-tional base, and not really evidence of a form reconstructible for the proto-language at all. This is particularly likely, of course, when the feature in question could be derived by active word formation processes and/or commonplace semantic extension. In such circumstances, one should note, the evidence of comparable forms and usages elsewhere in Gmc is by no means useless to us in assessing the probability of loan: their existence can at least be taken as supporting the relative commonness of a particular development, and therefore the notion that it could have happened independently in English and Norse, as against the assumption that its being shared by these two languages is necessarily evidence of loan-traffic between them; a good (albeit particularly complex) example is **dreme**. But, taking all these uncertainties together, it is little wonder that some scholars have found the whole matter too close to call, and have shied away from placing too much faith in the Gmc distribution of a word as evidence for or against its having been derived from ON; they include Björkman.[166]

Nonetheless, the occurrence of a comparable form, sense or usage in continental WGmc is frequently enough invoked in discussions of ON input (at least by implication), and applies to so many items in the Survey, that it has seemed to me helpful to mark those words to which it pertains, and to comment further upon them in the Introductory Essays to each Type below. In the Survey, I have therefore labelled with 'a' those items which have an attested cognate in the continental WGmc languages with a closely comparable sense or usage. For those structural categories where the claim for ON input concerns the presence of a particular feature of form, sense or usage (Type C), this 'a' label has been reserved for those cases where one or more WGmc counterparts also show that same exact feature – and hence it is applied only when continental WGmc

---

[166] 'And in my opinion we must not attach any great importance to the existence or non-existence of the word in other Germanic languages' (Bj. 197).

reflexes provide potential supporting evidence for the argument that this feature might have developed independently of Scand input (which is of course the main purpose of the 'a' flag).[167] Some readers may object that this 'a' flag marks evidence *against* ON input, whereas circumstantial labels 'b', 'c' and 'd' (described below) indicate evidence *for* it. On the face of it this is a discrepancy, and counter-intuitive, and at an earlier stage of my work I did entertain using 'a' to indicate those instances where there is *not* evidence for a similar usage in continental WGmc. However, having considered all the etymological arguments that have been mounted for each word, it became clear to me that this is not, in fact, how analogues in other WGmc languages have tended to be used in the scholarship. Rather than invoking the *absence* of a feature in continental WGmc as evidence *in favour* of ON input, that is, commentators have more often tended to cite the *presence* of a WGmc cognate as part of an argument *against* Scand influence (as described in the foregoing discussion). As a general principle when dealing with 'circumstantial' factors, it also seems to me preferable where possible to cite positive evidence for the attestation of a feature, rather than negative evidence for its absence (especially given the inevitably very partial survival of forms and usages in the medieval record). The methodological corollary of this is that it is possible to use the 'a' label to refer to quite specific recorded features, marking a WGmc parallel to the precise aspect of form, sense or usage under investigation as the potential evidence for ON input, as noticed above. In this way, only ten (out of 40) Type C3 stems have the 'a' flag, for instance, providing (I think) a more specific and more helpful indication of their WGmc parallels than would have been the case had the reverse policy been adopted, and had the label been applied instead to the thirty out of forty stems where no such precise WGmc analogue is known.[168]

1.6.2. *Dialect distribution in England*

The other great strand of circumstantial evidence for ON input has to do with a word's distribution in English dialects. It looms very large in many recent

---

[167] For example, **dreme** (C3) is not marked 'a' simply because (perhaps) related forms *exist* in WGmc (this would often tell us relatively little for Type C words, in any case, since by definition there are formations on the same root for all of them in OE, except for those with a non-Gmc form-source), but because the OFris, OS and OHG counterparts have *the same sense* ('dream') as that which is being claimed as evidence for ON input into the development of the ME word. See further the remarks under 'Gmc distribution' in the Introductory Essay to Type C below. Notice that the 'a' flag cannot be applied to items of Type D, since (by definition) none of these words has a readily identifiable Gmc root.

[168] *Inter alia*, I hope that this explanation further clarifies the difference between Type B2 and the circumstantial 'a' flag. B2 is concerned with Gmc distribution at a broad, comparative level, incorporating all stems for which there are, somewhere else in the Gmc family (excluding OE), related forms derived on the same Gmc root (and notice that this can influde Go as well as the WGmc group). The 'a' label serves a more specific purpose, considering the evidence of distribution as part of the process of weighing the probability of the argument for ON input; it refers to the *precise* form, sense or usage that is being held up as a potential indicator of Scand derivation or influence. Hence there are many B2 items which are *not* also marked 'a', e.g. **dok, hitte, leggez**.

treatments of Scand influence on English, including those arguing for the effects of Anglo-Norse contact at various levels beyond the lexical, where other evidence is often thin on the ground. When the purported contact-induced changes are 'indirect' (such as simplifications of morphological and syntactic structures attributed to the intensity of the contact situation, as opposed to the direct importation of Norse morphemic and syntactic features), the case is based in the first instance upon the supposed typicality of these changes as contact phenomena; but its primary support tends to be circumstantial, and it is usual in such instances to rely quite heavily upon the features in question being first attested in northern or eastern dialects.[169] The commonness of this argument can foster the impression that dialect distribution is essential to demonstrating Norse influence *per se*, including at the lexical level, and it is perhaps this that lies behind Miller's (2012: 99) surprising assertion that 'It is generally agreed that the safest way to recognize a Scandinavian loan is introduction in one or more northerly texts and/or restriction in Middle English to Danelaw territory, even better if it remains so restricted in Modern English'.[170] But when it comes to lexical borrowing this is not 'generally agreed' at all. As we noticed above, some (especially early) remarks on the criteria for establishing loan do not mention this one at all (e.g. Coleridge 1859a; Brate 1885), and Wall (1898: 81–2) actually discounts it. Though Bj. favours it as an ancillary test (see below), some subsequent studies have hesitated over applying it (so e.g. McGee 11–13), and Lass is avowedly sceptical.[171]

It is easy to see why dialect distribution generates such interest. I referred above to the massive *a priori* case for Scand influence on English in the wake of the late ninth-century settlements of ON speakers, and if we are to expect this influence anywhere then it should be in the regions where settlement was demonstrably strongest, i.e. the North and East of England and certain parts of Scotland. On the basis of onomastic evidence the most densely affected areas are usually reckoned to be Cumberland and Westmorland, the North and East Ridings of Yorkshire, and parts of the North-East Midlands, esp. Lincolnshire.[172] But staples of the scholarship, like Smith's famous 1956 map plotting parish names of Norse origin against the boundary of the Danelaw (*EPNE* map 10), present a formidable impression of the impact of settlement across the whole region, and raise concomitant expectations about the levels of

---

[169] For some examples see the studies cited at notes 104 and 116 above.

[170] This comes in the course of an otherwise careful treatment of Norse influence (Miller 2012: 97–9) which is mainly concerned with the differences between the two languages in contact and their 'convergence'.

[171] See Lass (2007: §8.9.2): 'The general principle is: regardless of history and attestation, looking for Scandinavian sources, where the phonology or morphology do not specifically demand them, is non-parsimonious, and does not serve as evidence for borrowing'. For a careful statement about the difficulties of the evidence see also Durkin (2014: 202).

[172] For the key scholarship on place-names see note 113 above, and on the 'density' of settlement see further the comments esp. in Kolb (1965), Samuels (1985: esp. 271–2) and Townend (2002: 47–8).

Scand influence on English in that same broad area. We are therefore entitled to assume that Norse input into English lexical development was greater in the North and East of England than it was in the South and West. And this is not just an assumption: it can be and has been tested. Thus Bj. bases his use of dialect distribution as a subsidiary criterion on the finding that a significant proportion of the 'phonetically testable' words in his first volume occur only, or more often, in northern or eastern texts. This conclusion is supported by a number of major studies of medieval vocabulary, including Kaiser's groundbreaking investigation of ME word geography, 251 (36%) of the 'northern' words in which are derived by Kaiser from ON (see Kaiser 1937: 178–278); and it is borne out by detailed accounts of the distribution of Norse-derived words in medieval texts.[173] The evidence of modern English and Scots dialects has, moreover, been extensively tackled, beginning with Wall (1898) and Flom (1900), and in a more thoroughgoing way by Xandry (1914) and Thorson (1936) (drawing on the materials in *EDD*).[174] The area known as the 'Great Scandinavian Belt', in which Norse influence on English can be demonstrated to have been especially strong, has been the subject of important studies by Kolb (1965) and Samuels (1985).[175] The outcome of all this scholarship, therefore, is the broad but powerful claim that there is a *relatively* greater number of different Norse-derived words in the dialects of the North and East than in those of the South and West; and moreover that there is a qualitative as well as a quantitative difference, with northern/eastern dialects showing a greater penetration of loaned items into the closed-class, 'grammatical' portion of the lexis.[176]

The finer details of this case are always, naturally enough, open to objections. For one thing, several of the words habitually cited as evidence of ON influence are debatable as loans. This objection can be countered by testing the claim for northern/eastern distribution against only the most secure items, as Bj. does for his 'phonetically testable' group, and there are enough universally agreed instances of ON input in the studies cited above for the case to stand up robustly

---

[173] For the more detailed accounts see McGee (chapters V, VI and VII), SPS (131–49, 245–72), Kries (2003: esp. 404–30 for conclusions), Dance (2003: esp. 187–9, 197–200, 270–84, 285–330), and for a variety of remarks and further references see e.g. Oakden (1930–5: II.190–1), Rynell (357–63), McIntosh (1973), Samuels (1985: esp. 274–9), Miller (2012: esp. 118–20), Durkin (2014: 211–13).

[174] There is a valuable summary table in Thorson (5), which presents (what Thorson identifies as) ON loans by county, reckoning the number of loans per 100,000 acres. Yorkshire heads the list (with 443 words), followed by Cumberland and Northumberland, and then Lancashire, Westmorland, Durham, Lincolnshire, Derbyshire and Cheshire (all with 100+ words), with Nottinghamshire, Northampton-shire and Norfolk next (all in the 80s); all the remaining counties trail these significantly (Shropshire is next, with 50 words). For some other interesting early accounts of dialect usage (with thanks to Dr Matthew Townend), see esp. Atkinson (1868: esp. x–xxxix), Streatfeild (1884: esp. 258–75), Ellwood (1895), Skeat (1911: 88–93), Cowling (1915: 55–65), Haigh (1928: xxi, xxii); and notice also the comments in Geipel (1971: 73–9) and Townend (2009: 184–90). More recently, see esp. Kolb (1965, 1989) and Orton & Wright (1974: 14–17) on the distribution of some ON loans in the *Survey of English Dialects* material, with maps.

[175] See also Kries (2003: esp. 404–13; 2007: 117–20), who would include parts of SW Scotland.

[176] See e.g. Samuels (1985: 274–5) and Dance (2003: 289–91).

in this respect. The other principal grounds for concern relate to the state of our knowledge about ME word geography, and hence what it means to say that some word is more or less restricted to northern or eastern dialects in the period. Early studies like Bj.'s had access to relatively limited material (whether edited texts or dictionaries) on which to base their claims;[177] Bj.'s assessment of his words' dialectal distribution is accordingly rather crude by modern standards, as for that matter is Kaiser's, and in some instances their findings can be questioned.[178] Armed as we are with *MED*, electronically searchable corpora and decades of detailed work by the linguistic atlases (*LALME* and *LAEME*), the information potentially available to us now about lexical distribution is of a completely different order, even if the task of interpreting this information has hardly diminished in its complexity. The problems involved, particularly that of disentangling diatopic variation from the results of textual transmission, have been discussed sensitively by a number of scholars.[179] They are exacerbated amongst other things by both diachronic and stylistic factors. On the one hand, that is, words often turn out to have become more or less geographically restricted when we compare different periods in their histories; this is no less evident when we put the evidence for early and later ME next to one another than it is when we move from Middle to Modern English.[180] On the other hand, the occurrence of a word in a 'literary' text, especially in a marked stylistic environment and/or as part of the lexis of an influential literary tradition, cannot simplistically be equated with its usage by all speakers of the author's local dialect; it is well known that words can travel far and fast in such circumstances, and this accounts *inter alia* for why attempts to localize a poem like *Gaw* on the basis of (an uncritical assessment of) its vocabulary produce such unreliable results.[181] All these things are, of course, central in their turn to approaching the very complex matter of how each Norse-derived word was diffused from whichever speech community and dialect area first adopted it. In the great

---

[177] The inadequacy of the lexicographical resources available to them is remarked upon explicitly by Kluge (1891: 787; 1901a: 935) and Wall (1898: 46).

[178] Where Kaiser is concerned, notice the remarks in the entries below for e.g. **mensked, race**. It is telling that, for McGee (11), 'No adequate study of the localization of this influence has ever been made'.

[179] The classic modern accounts of the principles and problems of ME word geography are McIntosh (1973, 1977); amongst recent work notice esp. the project of Carrillo-Linares and Garrido-Anes, which has produced a series of important articles on this subject (see e.g. Carrillo-Linares & Garrido-Anes 2012). For further discussions and references see e.g. Aertsen (1987), Peters (1988), Laing (1992), Hoad (1994), Dance (2003: 270–84), Williamson (2012: 501–2).

[180] For some discussion of particular instances of Norse-derived words, see McGee (497–9), and the detailed work undertaken by Kolb (1965) (though his use of place-names as indicators of the original distribution of loaned elements in the lexicon is open to question).

[181] On the 'literary' expansion of Norse-derived words, see the examples in McGee (494–6), and (for *Gaw*) my remarks in Dance (2013: 51–6). I have treated this matter at length in my study of the early ME SWM evidence (Dance 2003: esp. 185–284). On the Norse-derived element in the vocabulary of the Alliterative Revival, see e.g. Oakden (1930–5: II.190–1), McGee (chapters V, VI, VII) and Turville-Petre (1977: 69–83).

majority of instances we can know very little directly about these processes, and can only surmise the unpredictable, chaotic interaction of variables (semantic, stylistic, social) which eventually led to the state of affairs we are able to pick out with such difficulty from the medieval and modern evidence of attestation.[182] But given the complexities both of the nature of this diffusion and of the evidence for its results, it is hardly surprising that the identification of a word as 'northern or eastern' in character rarely amounts to its having been entirely or almost entirely confined to the region throughout its known history. There are a few cases amongst the Type A words in *Gaw* of such 'stable' distributions (e.g. **layt, melle, snayped**), but they contrast with many others, such as **ay, fro, gifte, skete** (which start off as northern/eastern in early ME, but show signs of wider distribution by the fifteenth century) or **attle, grayþe** (etc.), **lyþen** (for which the reverse is true); a number seem to be mainly characteristic of northern and eastern texts, but with a smattering of occurrences elsewhere throughout their histories (thus **bigge, neuen, tayt, wro**); and some others are classic examples of apparently northern/eastern words more widely attested in alliterative poetry (thus **carp, kayre, layk, busk**). Nonetheless, rolling all these items together for the sake of argument, the evidence of the Survey in this book strongly sustains Bj.'s case: fifty-five of the sixty-nine stems listed under Type A can be characterized in this way as 'predominantly northern or eastern' to a greater or lesser extent.

The broad claims about dialect distribution made in the scholarship cited above therefore seem to me unassailable, and they can be used to construct a very crude statement of probability which we can apply to items of other than Type A. Namely: a word which shows some signs of having been restricted (wholly or mainly) to northern or eastern English dialects can be derived from ON with more likelihood than can one which is attested with no such restrictions. But this statement is not necessarily as powerful as it appears; we must, at any rate, be extremely careful about the work we make it do, and about the further assumptions to which it leads us. For one thing, we must not take it absolutely, i.e. we must not fall into the trap of assuming that, because Norse-derived words are especially common in the North and East, they are simply absent or very thin on the ground in the South and West. This is demonstrably not the case. All careful discussions of the subject have been quick to notice the fact that, though they may be fewer in relative terms, loans are nonetheless plentiful in southern and western texts from as early as the thirteenth century; and even in the southern OE of the tenth and eleventh centuries the list of plausible Norse derivations is considerable, extending to words for commonplace concepts with no automatic overtones of Anglo-Norse cultural interaction.[183] Hence McGee can refer to the

---

[182] Occasionally a word's geographical progress can be posited on the basis of its phonology in modern dialects. Thus Kolb (1989: 287–8) finds that the modern pronunciation of *gaumless* is at odds with the usual dialectal reflexes of VAN /ɑu/ (/ɔu/) in English, and shows a form regularly to be expected only in the south-west of Yorkshire and parts of Lancashire. Such cases are few, but more can perhaps be done with modern dialect materials in order to explore routes of diffusion.

[183] See SPS (esp. 133–49).

'astonishing variety in Middle English distribution' of ON loans, many of which must have been 'adopted into general English at a very early time', and Hoad concludes 'that there was no absolute boundary beyond which Scandinavian influence could not, by the early Middle English period, have extended'.[184] Nevertheless, it is surprising how often this fact has been overlooked in favour of the supposition that Norse influence on the English lexicon should be straightforwardly coterminous with the evidence for Scand settlement, perhaps because the impression fostered by the likes of Smith's map has become so ingrained in our basic reactions to the subject. Time and again one meets the assumption that the numbers of *bona fide* Norse-derived words in the South and West are negligible, and hence the willingness to believe that the etymologies of the items recorded in these regions are positively *unlikely* to show ON input. There is a particularly forceful articulation of this viewpoint in Flom,[185] but it is by no means restricted to the earliest scholarship, and similar sentiments have been expressed many times.[186] One of the knock-on effects is the propensity for special pleading one encounters in etymological remarks like those in (the original) *OED* s.v. *rife* (adj.) and *MED* s.v. *bōn* (n. 2), where a word is regarded as perhaps having been influenced by ON, but only in its northern/eastern occurrences, even though it appears with identical form and usage in the South and West, too.[187] The starting point for my doctoral research on the South-West Midlands (published as Dance 2003) was a reaction against assumptions like this. I began from the position that the use of dialect distribution as a 'test' for identifying Norse derivation, however valid for words found predominantly in the North and East, was not of much help when one is looking at texts from other parts of the country; i.e. it could sensibly be used as a positive criterion for suggesting a word's inclusion in a corpus of probable Norse loans, but not as a negative one for rejecting it.[188] In framing this argument, I did not intend to imply that distributional evidence should be regarded as inapplicable *per se* to our etymological deliberations. And, indeed, establishing a corpus of likely South-West Midland Norse-derived words without regard to their distribution, ruling out no items simply because they are recorded in these texts, led ultimately to my reinforcing orthodox views of the dissemination of Scand lexical influence: I found that there was very little evidence for the introduction of

---

[184] McGee (465) and Hoad (1984: 33). For similar remarks see e.g. Burnley (1992: 420–2) who however greatly underestimates the numbers of loans in *Ancrene Wisse* and Laȝamon's *Brut*.

[185] 'The distribution of a word in South England diall [sic] . . . indicates that the word is not a Scand. loanword' (Flom 1900: 23); and compare the similar remarks in Wall (1898: 82).

[186] And notice that Braunmüller (2002: 1029) seems to suggest that Norse-derived words did not start to diffuse more widely in England until the fourteenth century.

[187] There is an especially convoluted example in Diensberg's (1997: 459–61) treatment of **cros**, which he insists cannot be Norse-derived in the South-West Midlands (where there are few such loans, he claims); he accordingly derives southern ME *cros* from Fr, northern ME *cros* from ON, and (on the grounds that neither is a good source of loans in the OE period) OE *cros* direct from Ir.

[188] See esp. my remarks in Dance (2003: 10–12).

loaned material directly into the South-West Midlands, independently or differently from what is found in the North and East; but that some lexical classes, notably closed-class, 'grammatical' words like *til* and *froward*, were very sparsely represented in my data (except, tellingly in these two cases, in a manuscript copied in the north-eastern corner of the region). This supports the long-established idea that the great majority of Norse-derived items were first adopted by English speakers in northern and eastern dialects, and then diffused south-westwards, some (open-class words) more quickly than others.[189] The corollary of this is that it does not seem to me sustainable to argue that a word's occurrence in southern and western dialects of early ME *reduces* the probability of its derivation from Norse, with the important exception of lexemes with basic 'grammatical' functions, which as a group are markedly less likely to be found in the South and West at this period; it is also relatively unlikely that a Norse-derived word, of any class, would be recorded *only* in the South and West.[190]

However, as well as being wary of the use of dialect distribution as negative evidence, as grounds to rule against Norse input, it is also worth injecting some caution as to how far it is safe to pursue it as a positive criterion. When we say, that is, that a word which shows some signs of having been restricted to northern or eastern dialects can be derived from Norse *with more likelihood* than one that is more widely attested, what exactly do we mean? Just how likely is 'more likely'? Here, naturally enough, there is a great deal of disagreement, and one's answer to this question will depend to a large extent upon one's general attitude towards the desirability of trying out a Scand etymon, i.e. upon the epistemological positions discussed above. As we have seen, it is easy to see the attractions of a contact-based explanation in the face of so much *a priori* evidence for ON influence in northern and eastern dialects, and Scand input is demonstrable in a good many cases. It is, therefore, very often *plausible* as a way of accounting for an innovation whose origin is not transparent, and it has been used in the scholarship to explain a wide range of characteristically northern/eastern forms and usages. But, equally, plausibility is not the same thing as

---

[189] See Dance (2003: 279–80, 287–91, 305–16), and the references cited under 'Attestation' in the entry for þay (þayr, þayres) in the Survey.

[190] There have been very occasional attempts to demonstrate significant independent loan traffic in the South and West, and even to overturn altogether the idea that there is a greater number of Norse-derived words in northern and eastern dialects; but these claims seem to me to depend upon incautious readings which simplify or misrepresent the data. Thus Moskowich-Spiegel Fandiño's (1996: 156) survey of the loans in a sample of *MED* A–C finds that the 'dialects of the Danelaw area' do not show a 'higher number of loans' than do other dialects; but by 'number of loans' she means *tokens*, not *types*, and she counts these without adjusting for the fact that the textual witnesses to southern and western ME amount to a massively larger corpus of words than exists for the North and East. Bator (2007) finds some potentially interesting differences in usage between the northern/eastern and southern/western attestations of selected Norse-derived words, but she does not explain the basis for her conclusion that *graith* and *busk* were first borrowed outside the Danelaw, unless she is equating date of borrowing with date of first attestation; if so, she has not taken account of the extent to which the earliest ME writings are dominated by material from the South and West, and thus that there is (once again) simply far less opportunity to observe northern/eastern usage at this stage.

demonstrability. It can reasonably be objected that Anglo-Norse contact was not the *only* source of linguistic change in medieval northern and eastern varieties, and it is not the only cause of isoglosses separating north-eastern from south-western dialects.[191] In particular, though words of (likely) Norse derivation make up a significant proportion of the set of vocabulary characteristic of northern usage, it is a mistake to assume that they are the only things we find in it. As Kaiser puts it: 'Diese Gliederung widerlegt die Vermutung, daß sich der nördliche Wortschatz lediglich durch seinen Gehalt an skandinavischem Lehngut auszeichne'.[192]

As ever, these competing perspectives underlie the different levels of confidence with which scholars have employed dialect distribution in order to diagnose ON input. Some have manifestly (and in some cases avowedly) been impressed by the existing claims for Scand influence in the North and East, and have wanted to identify other possible examples of it; this in turn has knock-on effects, in that the more candidates for ON loans that there are in a particular dialect (or text), the more plausible it seems to be to add new ones, according to the well-known (and in itself reasonably robust) principle of the hermeneutic circle. A number of the many piecemeal claims that have built up since Bj. for deriving individual lexical items from Norse seem to me to depend upon this 'vogue' for finding loans in the North and East. Other commentators, however, are perturbed by the tendency to equate characteristically northern/eastern features with Scand influence as an explanation of first resort, and prefer to take stock of the other possibilities. For some well-known and oft-discussed cases this leads to competing orthodoxies in the scholarship. Good examples are verbal -*s* (as the ending of the pres. 3 sg. ind., and of other pres. forms) and the pronoun *she*. The evolution of both of these forms has regularly, and sometimes forcefully, been attributed to the output of Anglo-Norse contact. These explanations are plausible enough, and have been repeated uncritically in some handbooks and popular accounts; but they draw for much if not most of their credibility on the fact that the two forms are first attested in northern/eastern English, and there have been some lucid recent arguments for alternative origins which have stressed that the circumstantial evidence of early distribution is not

---

[191] In the course of an article which emphasizes the importance of Norse influence on northern English, Kolb (1965: esp. 152–3) nevertheless stresses the likelihood that some significant features separating northern from Midland usage (part of the bundle of isoglosses that make up the so-called 'Humber-Lune belt') pre-date the Viking Age. For recent suggestions that some northern English dialect features owe their development to the effects of Anglo-Celtic (perhaps in combination with Anglo-Scand) contact, see Miller (2012: 147; 2016: esp. 169–70), Trudgill (2016: 329), Hornung (2017: 70–7), and the references cited at note 109 above. And for some further comments on changes which seem to have diffused south-westwards during the Middle Ages, not all of which can be attributed to Scand influence, see Thomason & Kaufman (1988: 274, cited by Hotta 2009: 174–5).
[192] 'This classification refutes the assumption that the northern vocabulary is simply distinguished by its containing material loaned from Scandinavian' (Kaiser 1937: 15). For an interesting indication of the English words derived from varieties of Fr and confined to particular dialect areas (inc. a relatively large number in parts of Yorkshire), see the *AND* website at <http://www.anglo-norman.ne t/dissem/data/page3.htm>.

the end of the story.[193] Another good example of dialect distribution perhaps having led etymologists by the nose, when closer inspection suggests a different explanation, is PDE *plough*. This word has frequently been supposed to be derived from ON, principally on the grounds that its earliest occurrences are in the North and East of England; but the evidence for a Norse origin is otherwise relatively poor, and their complex relationships with a range of Latin and Romance analogues suggest instead that both English and Scand reflexes might have been loaned from continental WGmc.[194] In short, just as one scholar's stinginess is another's parsimony, so what from one perspective can be defended as a hermeneutic circle (building reasoned case upon reasoned case) from another starts to look like a hermeneutic snowball (whose main justification is in danger of being its own momentum).

Nevertheless, and notwithstanding these substantial caveats, regional distribution within English remains a potentially significant piece of circumstantial evidence in support of claims for ON input, and it is one which figures (implicitly or explicitly) in the cases that scholars have made for a large number of the items in the Survey. Once again, it has therefore seemed to me helpful to label those words concerned, and to discuss the nature and ramifications of their distribution further in the Introductory Essays to each Type. The flags that I have used to indicate attestation mainly in the North or East of England are twofold, and distinguish the evidence of the toponymic record ('b') from that of the general ME lexicon ('c'). This distinction is imperative, not only because the lexicon and the onomasticon can never be straightforwardly equated as reflecting the same system of vocabulary;[195] but, in this case, because English place-names containing ON material were quite possibly coined not by speakers of English (who had adopted originally ON words) but by speakers of ON who had settled in Viking Age England, and hence the presence of a Scand word-form in a toponym need not mean that that element was ever borrowed into English and used as an English word.[196] In the case of the ME lexicon in particular ('c'), and as noticed above, stating that an item occurs mainly 'in the North or East' may include several possible distributional patterns: some words are entirely or almost entirely confined to this region, or to a particular area or group of texts within it, for their whole recorded history; some are restricted only in their earliest attested usage, some later in ME; and so on. But, given the imperfect ways in which an item's 'real' distribution in spoken ME might be reflected in the textual record, and moreover in order to capture any and all potentially relevant evidence of regional occurrence for

---

[193] Both are cited as unproblematic instances of contact-induced change by e.g. Ó Muirithe (2010: xviii). On verbal -*s* see esp. Miller (2002; also Miller 2004: 10; 2012: 128), and also Dance (2003: 292–4), with further references. For *she* see most notably Britton (1991), and the discussion and references under **scho** in the Survey.

[194] See the discussion at Durkin (2009: 261–3), and *OED* s.v. *plough, plow* n. 1 [Sep06].

[195] For an important discussion see Hough (2010).

[196] But this is, of course, very complex territory. For sensitive treatments of the ON elements in English place-names, and guides to further reading, see the references cited at note 113 above.

consideration in this study, it has seemed to me advisable to err on the side of inclusiveness and provisionally to count all such words as 'marked' dialectally, including those which are found only in *Gaw* or the other poems in the same manuscript. I have therefore labelled with a 'c' all items which are, for some or all of their medieval attestation, and to a greater or lesser degree, restricted to the North or East of England, as very broadly conceived. My (admittedly crude) shorthand for this is 'N/EM', which can be taken to incorporate essentially the whole of the area of the North and East of England in which Scand settlement and its immediate concomitant influence may be regarded as having been significant, including the North-West Midlands and East Anglia.[197] This label should always be taken in conjunction with the summary discussion given in the 'Attestation' section at the end of each entry in the Survey, where further (brief) details may be found.

1.7. CATEGORIES AND PROBABILITIES: OTHER LABELS IN THE SURVEY

The items in the Survey are therefore arranged by primary structural Type, A to D (and in turn by sub-category, viz. A1–3, B1–2, C1–5, D1–2), and labelled with one or more circumstantial flags. Of these latter, 'a', 'b' and 'c' have been described above.[198] There is also the label 'd', which is used to indicate that early occurrences of an item in English are strongly associated with Scand cultural influence. This is potentially a very powerful kind of supporting evidence. It applies most often to ON loans found already in late OE, and which attach in their first instances to recognizably Scand artefacts and cultural phenomena; examples include OE *cnearr* 'warship (of Scand type)', *hūsting* 'indoors assembly (of a Scand kind)' (see SPS 76–88). Few such words survive into the lexis of late ME texts like *Gaw*. I have nevertheless decided to retain the label here, for the purposes of comparison with other similar studies, even though it applies to just a single item in the present Survey, viz. **lawe** (C3).[199]

It would be possible to do no more labelling than this, and to signal only these main structural Types and the supporting circumstantial flags. But to do so would be to leave an important characteristic under-represented, namely my impression of the relative quality of the case for ON input in each instance. It is true that one of the starting points for this book is the impossibility of producing a 'definitive' list of words which show some kind of derivation or influence from ON; hence my decision to present and analyse all the items for which some Scand input has been claimed with at least some degree of plausibility. But it is also an inescapable fact that the argument for Scand input is not equally strong

[197] An idea of which ME texts I have routinely regarded as belonging to this broad region may be gained by examining the comments in the 'Attestation' section of each entry.

[198] Note that I have dispensed with the 'derivational class difference' flag which I employed once in an early experiment with this typology (Dance 2011), since this is not a species of evidence that belongs to the circumstantial level of analysis.

[199] See the Attestation summary for this item in the Survey, and references there cited.

for all items. That much is implicit in any attempt to sort the words by the nature of the evidence involved, whether structural or circumstantial. We have seen that Type A words by definition present the best case, with the basis being less solid for all of Types B, C and D, since these lack the evidence of formal features systematically characteristic of Scand input. Prototypically at least, the quality of the argument is then liable to decline as we move through the remaining Types: other things being equal, that is, Type B items (where the Gmc form-source is not known at all in early OE) may be more securely linked to Norse than may those of Type C (where the form-source exists in early OE, or in a third language, and such items are therefore in principle open to explanation by endogenous processes of phonological, semantic or other change); and Type C more securely than Type D (where the starting point is by definition unclear, and hence any connection with an ON etymon is not a given).[200] But in practice, and as the discussion of Types B, C and D above should have made plain, each of these Type categories encompasses a very wide spectrum of probabilities attaching to the argument for ON input, from the apparently uncontroversial to the highly contentious, depending on a word's individual circumstances and the quality of the etymological and supporting evidence involved. As a result, there are certainly items of Type D for which the case appears to me (much) stronger than it does for some of those of Type B; compare e.g. D1 **neked** with B2 **hoo**. It therefore seemed to me irresponsible not to attempt to signal, at least roughly, these differences in the relative quality of the argument for ON input – since not to do so would be to risk leaving users of the Survey with the impression that all the items in it may be admitted to a canon of Norse derivations with equal validity, and this is very far from true. And, whilst a view on the probability of Scand input can only ultimately be formed on a case-by-case basis, by examining the unique evidence which bears on each item, nonetheless it seems to me that there are some useful generalizations to be made by analysing together as a group those items belonging to each structural Type for which the plausibility of the case appears approximately the same.

This, then (at the risk of complicating my etymological formalism still further), is the aim of the loose 'probability marker' which I have added to the summary category label for each item. These markers are (necessarily impressionistic) efforts at encapsulating the likelihood of ON input in each case, drawing on my sense of the quality of the evidence and the opinions of the authorities discussed in the entries. They consist of additional Type letters prefixed to the label, with the more iterations signalling the lesser plausibility. There is a maximum of three letters for Types B and C, and of just two for Type D (since by definition no D

---

[200] This progressive decline in generic plausibility is in fact demonstrable from a comparison of the proportions of the probability levels (described below) marked for each Type: so the ratio of B:BB:BBB is 22:17:10, with the most secure level being dominant numerically, compared to that for C:CC:CCC of 43:66:72, where the reverse is true; and the ratio for D:DD (where the single D corresponds in probability to the double-letter levels in B and C) is then 37:63, with the least plausible cases more frequent to a still higher degree.

items show a *very* strong case for ON input, and all attract at least some disagreement in the scholarship). These labels are defined and discussed further in the Introductory Essays to each Type below. But to give an idea of their function, here are the probability categories for Type B:

B
The case for ON input is very plausible. There is general agreement in the scholarship, often without exception.

BB
The case for ON input is reasonable, but alternative explanations seem about equally plausible. There is usually some disagreement in the scholarship.

BBB
The case for ON input is not strong (though it still cannot be dismissed out of hand). The word's history can usually be explained more plausibly by other means. There is some history in the scholarly tradition of attributing or at least suggesting ON input, but the weight of (especially recent) argument is against it, and/or the case for it is problematic in some fairly fundamental way.

Needless to say, this is the element of the typology employed in this book which is most likely to provoke disagreement. It should be stressed that these labels are inevitably crude, and are simply a way of reflecting my own impressions at the time of writing, based purely on the evidence described in each entry. Other commentators may very well reach different conclusions, and might wish to argue the probability of certain items either up or down accordingly.

1.8. The Survey: inclusions and exclusions

With certain exceptions (detailed below), the Survey contains an entry for every lexical item in *Gaw* for which some ON etymological input has been claimed by at least one scholarly source commenting on its vocabulary (since the beginning of serious editorial and linguistic study of the poem).[201]

Entries are arranged into groups by structural Type (see above); hence the Survey is divided into sections for Types A, B, C and D, with sub-sections (A1, A2, A3 and so on). Moreover, entries for words which I have judged to belong to the same 'stem' have been gathered together: these are those word-forms which are, or which could feasibly be, recently related derivationally, i.e. derivations on the same OE or ME word-base, and/or on the same ON stem; hence e.g. 7a. **broþe** and 7b. **broþely**; 8a. **carp** (v.) and 8b. **carp** (n.); 13a. **gart**, 13b. **gere** (v.),

---

[201] For a potted history of this scholarship and the milestones in it, see the section '*Sir Gawain* and the "Scandinavian element"' above.

13c. **gere** (n.) and 13d. **stel-gere**. The principal argument for Scand input is fundamentally the same for all sub-entries belonging to a particular stem, and it therefore seemed to me sensible to treat such 'related' forms together, wherever possible. Each stem is numbered, sequentially from 1 (A1 **agayn**) to 399 (D2 **wylyde**), and sub-entries are distinguished with an alphabetical suffix ('a.', 'b.', 'c.' ...). It is not necessarily possible to establish, of course, whether these affixed and compounded forms were created within English, perhaps long after the original period of Anglo-Norse contact, using native word-formation processes to derive a new word on a stem (arguably) loaned from ON (i.e. they are instances of the phenomenon sometimes called 'hybrid creations'); or whether they were modelled directly on a Scand formation extant in ON, as 'loan blends'.[202] Where a corresponding derived form or compound is attested in OIcel, this is always cited as a comparison in the entry; but it should not, of course, be inferred from this that the ME outcome was necessarily constructed on the direct pattern of this form at the time of contact.

Notice, however, that items where there seems to me *no* realistic case to be made for ON input, i.e. when it has been argued on the basis of what are (now) demonstrably false principles or faulty assumptions, are not included in the main Survey. Instead these words will be found treated briefly in the Appendix, section 1. Section 2 of the Appendix is then reserved for a slightly different class of material, viz. when an ON word has been referred to by one or more authorities as some kind of comparandum for the ME item, and when it seemed helpful to notice this. This is usually because it is not immediately clear (in the context of a short etymological gloss) what the commentator concerned means the reader to make of this reference, even if it appears unlikely that the ON form in question is being cited as an etymon; and a short remark clarifying what I understand to be intended has seemed useful.

There are some other important exclusions. By 'lexical item', I mean only a word-form which can appear as a free morpheme (including in compounds), and – following Bj.'s lead – *not* a bound morpheme which is being employed as an affix or an inflexional ending. Naturally, distinguishing these two categories (free vs. bound morphemes) involves a series of potentially complex issues, including that of the 'fuzzy' boundary between 'grammatical', closed-class lexis and inflexional morphology.[203] What is more, some forms which are bound morphemes in ME, especially certain productive prefixes and suffixes, are of course closely related historically to free morphemes (in particular to prepositions/adverbs and nouns, respectively). But to have incorporated all lexical items containing only bound morphemes of arguably ON origin would have meant a considerable increase in the number of entries in the Survey, since a variety of important derivational and inflexional elements has been claimed (with greater or

---

[202] For remarks on these categories see e.g. Haugen (1950: 218–19, 220–1), Dance (2003: 94–7), and the discussions of terminology cited at note 18 above; and the comments at Durkin (2014: 217–18).

[203] For some discussion see e.g. Smith (1996: 199), Dance (2003: 155–6).

lesser plausibility) to show Scand input. They include not only the prefix *vmbe-* and the noun-forming suffix *-leik*,[204] and the verb-forming suffixes *-n-* and *-l-*,[205] but also the extremely commonplace adv.-forming *-ly*;[206] and then there is the pres. ptcp. ending *-ande*,[207] and even the pres. verbal ending *-s*,[208] which certainly belong to analyses of the purported morphosyntactic outcomes of Anglo-Norse contact rather than to a lexical study like this one. For the same reasons, I make no attempt in this book to discuss the ON influence on ME syntax, a very complex topic which extends from specific syntactic patterns like 'phrasal verbs' to much broader potential effects on the evolution of English grammatical categories and word order.[209]

I have also decided to omit from the Survey words whose spellings are ambiguous, and hence where some letter forms could conceivably stand for sounds which potentially show ON input, but which no one has suggested actually represent those sounds in *Gaw*. This is true, for example, of the word *bryg(g)e* 'drawbridge' (<bryge>, *Gaw* 779, 781, <brygge> 821, 2069). The <g(g)> here could in principle indicate /g/, in which case some input from the ON n. represented by OIcel *bryggja* would be a possible explanation for the lack of palatalization and assibilation. But, so far as I can see, *Gaw* editors and commentators have always

---

[204] I have included **vmbe** in the Survey only when it is used as an independent prep.; see that entry (226.), and further *OED* s.v. *umbe-* prefix. For *-leik*, see *OED* s.v. *-laik* suffix, Dance (2003: 429–32, with further references) and Durkin (2014: 218).

[205] On *-n-* (with further references) see e.g. Bj. (15–16), OED s.v. *-en* suffix 5, Marchand (1969: 272–3), Koziol (1972: §633), Miller (2004: 11–12; 2012: 128). Examples in *Gaw* inc. *harden* 'to encourage, make bold', for which TGD in fact offers ON *harðna* as etymon (and see further Magoun 1928: 80; McGee 335–6); but the evidence for ON input resides essentially in the *-en* suffix, and so I have not treated this word in the Survey. On *-l-* see e.g. Bj. (15), *OED* s.v. *-le* suffix (3), Marchand (1969: 322–3), Koziol (1972: §635), Miller (2004: 11–12; 2012: 128) and Durkin (2014: 218 n. 38).

[206] Most commentators derive ME (PDE) *-ly* straightforwardly from OE *-līce*; but for the argument for some ON input (cp. OIcel *-liga*) see Bj. (158–9n), *OED* (s.vv. *-ly* suffix 2, *-ly* suffix 1), Jordan-Crook (§§21, 179 Anm.4), Luick (§655), Durkin (2014: 218), and further Knigge (89, who refers to ON input only with respect to the ending of *Gaw* 42 *iolilé* 'gallantly').

[207] See e.g. Bj. (17 n.1), Gordon (1953: 99 n. 1), Dance (2003: 292), Miller (2004: 13; 2012: 130–1), Budna (2010: esp. 81–4), Durkin (2014: 218), *OED* s.v. *-and* suffix 1.

[208] See note 193 above.

[209] For general surveys of the supposed ON influences on early English morphology and syntax, see esp. Miller (2004; 2012: 127–45 and the references cited), and further the remarks and references in e.g. Kirch (1959), Kisbye (1982: 79–83), Rot (1991: 302–9), McWhorter (2002), Dance (2003: 292–5; 2012a: 1734–5), Cuesta & Ledesma (2007: 125–31), Grant (2009a: 375), Lutz (2012: 31–4), Fischer (2013: esp. 31–7), Durkin (2014: 217–19), Hornung (2017: 26–51), plus the (provocatively maximalist) Emonds & Faarlund (2014, followed in Trudgill 2016: 330–1, and reviewed by e.g. Bech & Walkden 2016; Stenbrenden 2016b). I shall also not deal here with the few supposed instances of Scand influence on English which have been argued to be primarily phonological in character; for some suggestions and references see e.g. Sundby (1956), Samuels (1985: 277–9), Danchev (1986), Lutz (1991: 50–4), Fellows-Jensen (1994: 256), Smith (2007: 123, 138, 144, 149). But notice, of course, that the adoption of so many ON loans inevitably affected at least the distribution of phonemes in ME, and the boundary between lexical borrowing *per se* and interference at the phonological level can be a tricky one to negotiate; see the discussion under Formal Criteria §8 in particular.

assumed that the <g(g)> spelling of the word in this manuscript stands for /dʒ/, and hence derive it straightforwardly from OE *brycg*.[210]

MED often (though without explanation) cites an ON cognate as possible input alongside the more obvious native etymon in those cases when *EPNE* suggests that originally English and Scand place-name elements are difficult to distinguish in the toponymic record, and therefore that a particular name-form could in principle have been coined by either OE or ON speakers. I have decided only to include such words in the Survey if they are used in *Gaw* to refer to places or to features of the landscape – since in that case the form and/or usage found in *Gaw* potentially reflects back-derivation from a place-name of ON origin. See my discussions under **berʒ** and **clyff**.[211] Another toponym, which this time I have excluded, is *cragge* 'crag' (*Gaw* 1430, 2183, 2221). This word seems to be of Celtic origin; thus TG(D) derive it from a MWe '**crag*' (cp. medieval Breton *cragg*), GDS compares Gael *creag*, We *craig*, and it is usually regarded as a loan direct from a Celtic language.[212] Elliott (1984: 77, 91–2) cites *EPNE* s.v. *cragge*, and follows it in deriving probably from Ir *creag* 'introduced by Norwegian Vikings'. But I can find no evidence that this word-form was ever present in the lexis of a Scand language, and so this claim for entry into English via ON, while plausible enough historically, is purely hypothetical; I have therefore not included *cragge* in the Survey in this book.[213]

1.9. THE ENTRIES: FORMAT AND CONVENTIONS

For Types A, B, C and D1, each entry in the Survey contains the following elements:[214]

---

[210] See further *VEPN* s.vv. *brycg, bryggja*. The same is true of *rygge* 'back' (cp. OE *hrycg*, OIcel *hryggr*). TGD makes brief reference to this issue in its appendix ('But since the spelling *gge* could represent either the stop or the affricate . . ., it is not certain whether forms like *brygge, rygge* denote one or the other', 141), but its glossary offers only the OE etyma. See further under §8 under Formal Criteria below.

[211] But I have *not* included the *Gaw* instances of the words treated by *MED* s.vv. *hat* n., *helm* n., *rigge* n., *rīs* n.1 or *sāl(e* n.1, since these do not refer to places or landscape features in *Gaw*. See in each case the *MED* entry and the corresponding account in *EPNE*, which sometimes gives a more precise indication of the particular ME form or sense which is at issue; thus e.g. *helm*, where the meaning in question is *MED*'s sense (2), not found in *Gaw*.

[212] See similarly *OED* s.v. *crag* n.1, *MED* s.v. *crag* n., and the comments in e.g. Ekwall (1918a: 73), Förster (1921: 126–8), Coates (2007: 178), Durkin (2014: 78), Meecham-Jones (2018: 112–13); and further *GPC* s.v. *craig*, MacBain s.v. *creag*; ult. < PIE **kar-* 'hard, rough', as Pokorny (I.532).

[213] I have also made no attempt to deal with the more fanciful suggestions for ON lexical influence introduced by Beekman Taylor in the course of his pursuit of Scand mythological backgrounds to the story of *Gaw* (1970; 1989; 1998: 225–32).

[214] Notice that, for Type D2 only, because the meaning (and sometimes the grammar) of the item is usually a matter of debate, and its occurrences and possible referents in context in *Gaw* are central to the discussion, the format of the opening of each entry is slightly different from those in previous sections of the Survey. Each D2 headword is followed, in the next line, by a set of numbered alternative meanings (and where necessary different proposed readings and grammatical analyses); and the Text section gives a quotation of the immediate *Gaw* context(s) as well as the standard reference to the line numbers where the word occurs.

item number. **headword**; part of speech (etc.); 'sense' [summary category label]

Text: (occurrences in *Gaw*; discussion of any textual issues)

Etymology: (etymological discussion)

Attestation: (attestation summary)

Bibliography line 1

Bibliography line 2

(sometimes followed by a cross-reference ('See also . . .') to other related entries)

Headword

As far as possible this is given in a form actually recorded in *Gaw*. Where there is more than one instance of the word in the poem, I have preferred as headword a singular, non-oblique form for nouns, adjectives etc., and an infin. for verbs. When there is no infin. attested, but various other parts of the verbal paradigm, I have usually given a hypothetical infin. form (ending in *-e*). Usually the headword is the same as that used by the glossary in TGD.[215] Headwords are in bold face, and wherever a word which has an entry in the Survey is cited, throughout the book, it is referred to by this headword form, also in bold; reference to a headword should be understood as shorthand for the lexical item whose entry it denotes, in any and all of its relevant forms and usages.

Part of speech (etc.)

I have tried to keep this label as brief and straightforward as possible (generally following TGD), though in a few cases some additional description has been necessary (in brackets; e.g. **stad** 'adj. (pp.)').

Sense

Unless there is debate (this usually only applies to Type D items), this is a summary based on the senses given in the glossary in TGD, separated by semi-colons if TGD identifies more than one sub-sense.

Summary category label

See the discussion above of the criteria for claiming ON input (which are also schematized under Abbreviations and Conventions at pp. xiv–xv above).

Text

A list of the item's occurrences in *Gaw*, primarily following TGD. If there are more than four occurrences, only the first three have been listed, followed by an 'etc.'.

Forms ordinarily follow those printed by TGD, unless there is good reason not to. Notice that I have followed TGD in printing MS <ȝ> as a *z* when it is

---

[215] TGD is my preferred model, since it is the most recent, authoritative full critical edition of *Gaw* as a single text. I have also followed it, where possible, for its glosses on sense and its list and parsing of occurrences in the poem. But where other editions and commentators differ significantly from TGD, this is always noticed.

generally agreed to represent the sound [z], and as ʒ when it represents a *yogh*.[216] (Some editions print <ʒ> for both, notably GDS.) I have indicated significant variant forms in brackets. In practice, 'significant' means any spellings other than regular and predictable inflected parts of the paradigm, though I have also tried to show what the plurals and preterites look like even where these are regular, to give an idea of the class of n., v. etc. to which the word belongs. Usually these variants are given in brackets at the end of the list of occurrences, where helpful with an indication of their frequency.

Remarks on disagreements over readings or senses by editors or other commentators follow here. Notice that where there is at least one genuine, i.e. unambiguous or uncontroversially identified, instance of the word in question in *Gaw*, that word has usually been given a straightforward entry in the Survey (under Types A, B, C or D1), and I have discussed any additional contested occurrences here in the 'Text' section. When, however, there are no such 'safe' instances of the item under consideration (i.e. they are all subject to another possible identification, or identifications), then the item has been treated as the distinct Type D2, where its interpretation as this or that lexeme has become a main part of what is being discussed under 'Etymology'.[217] I have generally been interested in the interpretations of the three most important, full scholarly editions of *Gaw*, viz. TG, GDS, TGD; but I have tried to take account of, and to cite, other editions when they offer substantially different readings.[218] The most interesting editions for these purposes are usually the earliest (Madden and Morris, and occasionally its revision M(G)), and later on AW (the most influential edition of the whole manuscript),[219] Vant (with its tendency to defend the manuscript reading, even when this is implausible) and the most recent editions by PS and McGillivray (which sometimes have innovative interpretations). The other editions almost always follow one or the other of these, and I tend to cite them only in the case of a significant 'fault-line' in the scholarship, when I have felt it interesting to notice which editor falls into which camp. Notice that, here and elsewhere, 'TG(D)' means both TG *and* TGD (i.e. TGD has retained the reading of TG).

Etymology

The discussion under this head is as full as seems to me to be helpful in each case. For items of Type A, where the argument for ON input is based on clear phonological or morphological criteria, the remarks may be relatively brief; but they are generally longer for words of subsequent Types, especially the complex Type D (where by definition two or more competing theories have been

---

[216] An important exception is **forʒ** (D2), where the signification of <ʒ> is not agreed.

[217] See further under the Introductory Essay to Type D.

[218] But notice that this does not include occasions when these editions' readings differ simply because they have 'normalized' the spelling, as most notably does PS with its semi-modernized forms.

[219] AW may be assumed to continue the interpretation of Waldron unless otherwise indicated.

proposed). Note that formal 'tests' of loan are always signalled by a § number in brackets, which refers the reader to the fuller discussion and references for each feature found in the Formal Criteria section of the Introductory Essay to Type A below; the feature in question is not usually described further in the course of an entry, unless there is a specific issue to be dealt with.

In each instance I have cited a (proposed) ON etymon, in comparison with an OE cognate (or hypothetical form) where possible, alongside a set of cognates or near-cognates in the other early Gmc languages. Following etymological convention, ON forms are taken to be represented primarily by an OIcel reflex, wherever one is attested.[220] If forms or meanings in another Scand language are significantly different from those attested in OIcel, and if these will help illuminate the ME reflex, then they are also cited (sometimes also with a reconstructed VAN form); but otherwise I have not usually given the cognates to the OIcel word in Norw, Sw, Dan etc., since to do so would rarely clarify matters and would add an unnecessary degree of extra complexity.[221] Definitions of OIcel words summarize *ONP* when it has a completed entry which includes a definition, and otherwise follow CV; for other Scand languages, I have generally translated into English the definitions given in the handbooks/dictionaries (preferably Mag.).

OE words are normally cited in a standard (late) WS form if one is attested.[222] Nonetheless, it is often helpful to refer in addition to forms (recorded or hypothetical) from other dialects and/or periods, and in that case I specify the dialect/period concerned; and I have always done this when a *Gaw* reflex (or potential reflex) of the OE form in question descends from a dialect variant significantly different from that known in WS. Definitions for OE summarize *DOE* when it has reached that entry, and otherwise Hall. Other Gmc cognates are

---

[220] Coates (2006) argues against the routine use of OIcel forms to stand for the VAN etyma of English words, given the distance in time and place between OIcel and the ON actually spoken in Viking Age England; he prefers to cite reconstructed 'Anglo-Scandinavian' word-forms. However, reasonable though Coates' case is in itself, I have decided against following his lead. It is an excellent idea in principle to give transparently early Scand forms as the proposed sources of ON input, but in many cases it is hard to agree (and in several it is hard to tell) what the precise VAN forms concerned would have been; and any such reconstructed forms would therefore have to be hedged about with caveats very similar to those which attend the citation of OIcel reflexes. As long as OIcel forms are understood to be only a way of *representing* the VAN etyma in question, then it seems to me that they remain one of the least problematic ways of referring to those etyma – and the most convenient, seeing as it is OIcel forms which are conventionally referred to in other etymological authorities, including the Gmc and IE handbooks. These OIcel reflexes are, moreover, important evidence in themselves: it is the very occurrence of these forms in the OIcel corpus, of course, which is generally the main basis on which we assume the existence of such words earlier in the history of the Scand languages, and their attestation and usage in OIcel is therefore frequently an object of discussion in and of itself.

[221] Reflexes in the other Scand languages can generally be found by consulting the entry for the OIcel word in de Vries or Mag., and will also be cited in the *Gersum* catalogue.

[222] Again, this is largely for pragmatic reasons: the majority of OE words are recorded only in West Saxon forms, and in consequence this is how all standard dictionaries of the language present their headwords.

usually cited in the order Go, OFris, OS, OHG.[223] I have not generally given MLG, MDu or MHG cognates, or their modern descendants, unless it seemed helpful to do so (usually when a reflex in the Old phase of the language is not recorded). I have tried to be consistent about how I have cited reconstructed PGmc forms, adopting a fairly conservative model and eschewing further mark-up where possible: so adjectives are given ending in *-a-, not assuming a gendered inflexional ending; infinitives are given in *-an-, without specifying what could have been in the next syllable at the PGmc stage; wk. 2 infinitives are given in *-ō(j)an-; voiced stops/fricatives are given as b, d, g; and so forth.[224] Reconstructing a hypothetical PGmc form is the most convenient way of envisaging how a given word might have appeared in the prehistoric stages of the Gmc group, and this is my main aim in citing PGmc reflexes; it should not be assumed that I think that this precise derivational form certainly existed at the common ancestral stage of all Gmc languages, merely that this is how it may plausibly be imagined if it had. On the principle that 'a cobbler should stick to his last',[225] I have not generally attempted to pursue ulterior etymologies beyond PGmc unless this has a material bearing on the relationships being posited between the Gmc words, and the citation of forms in other IE languages (and in PIE) is kept to a minimum; further discussion may be sought in the standard etymological authorities referred to at the foot of the entry.

For Type A items, where there is generally little disagreement between the etymological authorities, I have not normally referred to these by name in the body of the entry; unless otherwise noted, it can be assumed that all those cited in the references at the immediate foot of the entry ('Bibliography line 1'), and also the glossaries in TG(D) and GDS, agree on derivation from ON. For Types B, C and (especially) D there is often much less consensus, and in such cases I have noticed who thinks what; in that event, I have paid most attention to *OED*, *MED*, Bj., TG(D) and GDS, and the other important authorities which express an opinion (most often the likes of McGee, SPS, etc.), and also individual articles or notes where they deal especially with the word in question. (These authorities are assumed to be representative of scholarly views, and I have not attempted to pursue words which survive into PDE into all the modern etymological dictionaries, or all general discussions of loans into ME.) *OED* means the original entry as found in *OED2*; *OED3* means a revised entry in the ongoing third edition. Where it is helpful to discuss OE phonology and morphology, I refer as standard to Campbell, Hogg and Hogg-Fulk, and sometimes to others (esp. Luick, Ringe-Taylor); for ON, I turn first to Noreen and Br-N., and sometimes to Heusler and Gordon; for ME, mainly to Jordan-Crook and Luick.

---

[223] I follow the forms and definitions (translated into English where necessary) in the more recent and/or detailed authorities, preferably *OED3*, Seebold, Heid., Mag., *EWAhd*.

[224] Even the recent handbooks may differ considerably in their practices; compare e.g. Orel and Kroonen (and see Orel xi–xiii for a few remarks on the conventions he follows).

[225] See Liberman (2002a: 207).

Attestation

The focus here is on ME distribution, with a (very) brief summary based on the relevant *MED* entry. For a few items there is also information in *LAEME* and/or *LALME*, and occasionally full enough discussion elsewhere in the scholarship that it has seemed worth citing (usually for very common and important words, like **þay**). Any (late) OE occurrences are also noted (summarizing mainly SPS and (where running) *DOE*), as is place-name evidence (drawing on *EPNE* and (where running) *VEPN*). Especially for rare words, or when dialect distribution is hard to establish in ME, I have also included some reference to distribution in later English, drawing on *OED*, *EDD* and sometimes others, esp. Thorson.

Notice that, where several related words are treated together under the umbrella of a single 'stem', I have usually given a collective Attestation summary at the end of the group, below the final sub-entry.

Bibliography

Key works of reference are cited here. In order to be featured, a dictionary or handbook entry must deal directly with the stem under discussion (its Scand reflex(es), its Gmc source, its OE cognate, etc.); i.e. these are what I take to be the key reference points for elucidating the particular form(s) being treated, and for looking up further discussions, cognates and so on. In the body of the Etymology discussion, a reference to one of the authorities listed in the Bibliography section (e.g. 'see de Vries') can be assumed to be to the entry cited here, unless specified otherwise. Authorities are cited either by headword entry or by page number, whichever seems the easiest to use in finding a reference in each case. Words cited are not given in italics or preceded by 's.v.' here (as they normally are when being referred to in the body of one of the entries), since this seems otiose in a short-title citation format like this.[226]

Bibliography line 1

The principal works of English lexicography, and the key catalogues of ON influence on English, are cited here, in the following order:

MED

Cited by entry, part of speech and any entry number.[227]

OED

Cited by entry, part of speech and any entry number. This is always *OED2*, i.e. the original entry, as presented in the combined 1989 edition and as 'unrevised'

---

[226] Note that, in sub-entries in a multi-part entry (a set of items grouped by stem), I do not normally repeat for each subsequent sub-entry the full Bibliography given under the first item, but I only give references where these actually deal with the new sub-form in question and its immediate comparanda.

[227] Notice that I have adopted a simplified version of *MED*'s phonological mark-up, which can be hard to replicate typographically. So I have marked long vowels, but have not attempted to reproduce some of the dictionary's diacritics, e.g. the under-dotting of a close vowel; vowels which *MED* prints as either short or long are not marked here (and the same is true for head-words in other authorities, such as *AEW* and Orel).

on the *OED* website, unless indicated otherwise.[228] Entries followed by a date in square brackets (e.g. '[Sep16]') are the new, revised *OED3* entries, where these have been posted online.[229]

ODEE
Cited by entry, part of speech and any entry number. But note that *ODEE* is cited *only* on the rare occasions when its summary disagrees with (or adds an important suggestion to) that in the original *OED*.

Bj.
Cited by page. Sometimes Björkman's other main book on ON influence, his DP, gives a fuller discussion, in which case that is also cited here.

SPS
Cited by page.

Bibliography line 2
I cite here the other major etymological or lexicographical authorities, as relevant. This section ordinarily begins with the Scand authorities, then moves on to the general Gmc handbooks and the dictionaries of OE and of place-names, followed by other pertinent references (with other things, e.g. Fr and Ger dictionaries or those of the Celtic languages, added when necessary). Of the Scand authorities, I have cited *ONP*, de Vries and Mag. whenever they have a relevant entry (these being the major references to OIcel lexis and etymology), as also Bj-L. (being a particularly full, and particularly recent, Scand etymological dictionary). Other Scand dictionaries are cited only when I have referred to them, or to the languages that they cover, in the Etymology section above; or, in the case of CV, *LexPoet* and Fritzner, when *ONP* does not (fully) treat the form(s) in question.[230] In these citations, I have tried to be consistent in separating multiple headwords in a single dictionary entry with commas, and distinct entries with semi-colons.[231] Where a particular word-form is given as a sub-entry within a larger entry, I have noticed this by putting the sub-entry in brackets.[232]

---

[228] For all entries, headwords and grammatical identifiers follow the online *OED* (hence 'adj.' rather than the original 'a.', and so on).

[229] At the time of writing, the full, rolling revision of *OED* has gone from *M* to the beginning of *S*, but new entries for a number of important words elsewhere in the alphabet have also been released.

[230] I have not routinely cited Jóh. (by page number) or *WAWN* (by entry), whose opinions do not in most cases differ significantly from those of the more influential and/or recent OIcel etymological dictionaries; but I refer to them occasionally, esp. when the ulterior etymology of an ON word is obscure or debated.

[231] So e.g. under **melle**, 'de Vries meðal; milli, millim, millum' refers to two de Vries entries, viz. s.v. *meðal* and s.v. *milli, millim, millum*.

[232] E.g. under **wayth**, 'de Vries veiða (veiði, veiðr)' refers to the discussions of *veiði* and *veiðr* within the de Vries entry for *veiða*.

ONP
Cited by entry, part of speech and any entry number. I always give an *ONP* headword if one exists, whether or not there is a full entry in the online resource as it exists at the time of writing (i.e. even if *ONP* provides merely a headword and access to the attestation slips). If not, or if the *ONP* entry is in some way problematic, then I have used CV, *LexPoet* and/or Fritzner instead.

de Vries
Cited by entry.

Mag.
Cited by entry. Mag.'s entries often have multiple headwords, giving (Mn)Icel and older/rare/other spellings; in such cases, I have cited only the first headword.

Other authorities are cited in the following order, by entry unless otherwise specified: Bj-L., Nielsen, Hellquist, Torp, Falk-Torp, *EWAhd*, Kluge-Seebold, Heid., Seebold, Bammesberger (cited by page), Orel, Kroonen, *AEW*,[233] DOE, *EPNE* or *VEPN*,[234] AND, DEAF,[235] FEW, Matasović, GPC, eDIL, LEIA, MacBain.

---

[233] *AEW* is cited by entry, but sometimes with a clarifying page number (if the entry is not where one would expect it to be alphabetically).

[234] Depending whether an entry has been released in *VEPN*. So far it has been published as far as *cockpit*, with advance access to some entries for the letter M available online.

[235] Including reference to stub entries, which are as yet incomplete.

TYPE A AND FORMAL CRITERIA

2.1. TYPE A

Type A contains all words for which there is systematic, formal evidence for input from ON: that is, each item shows the reflex(es) of one or more regular and predictable ON developments in phonology (A1), morphology (A2) or both (A3) which cannot reasonably be explained as having taken place in OE.[236] For this group of words, Scand input may therefore be assumed with a uniquely high degree of probability. Included as Type A are some cases where the form of the ON etymon is clear enough, even if its Gmc root is debatable (e.g. **woþe**), or if the exact identity of the ON etymon/etyma can be argued about (e.g. **þro**) – so long as a test or tests of form are still clearly applicable.

These 'tests' themselves are set out and discussed in the Formal Criteria section below. Before that, I give for convenience a summary list of Type A words, arranged by 'stem', showing their category labels and circumstantial flags. This is followed by a short introductory discussion of these items, paying particular attention to aspects of their etymology and distribution which emerge as interesting.

2.1.1. *Summary lists*

Sixty-nine stems belong to Type A, seventeen of which contain one or more sub-entries, giving a total of 100 different lexical items.

Category A1 (phonological criteria) comprises sixty-two stems, fourteen with sub-entries; there are eighty-eight distinct lexical items.

1. **agayn**; adv.; 'in return' [A1*c]
2. **ay**; adv.; 'always, ever, in each case' [A1*c]
3. **attle**; v.; 'to intend' [A1*c]
4. **bayn**; adj.; 'obedient' [A1bc]
5. **bayþe**; v.; 'to grant, agree, consent' [A1*c]
6. **bigge**; v.; 'to settle, found, build' [A1*bc]
7a. **broþe**; adj.; 'fierce, grim' [A1c]
7b. **broþely**; adv.; 'fiercely' [A1c]
8a. **carp**; v.; 'to speak, say, converse' [A1c]
8b. **carp**; n.; 'talk, conversation; mention' [A1c]
9. **felle**; n; 'fell, precipitous rock' [A1bc]

---

[236] On the nature of this evidence, see the discussion in the Introductory Remarks at pp. 39–44 above.

10. **frayst**; v.; 'to ask (for), seek, make trial of, test' [A1ac]
11a. **fro**; prep.; 'away from, from' [A1*c]
11b. **fro**; conj.; '(after the time) when, after' [A1*c]
12a. **gayn**; adj.; 'ready, prompt, obedient, direct' [A1*bc]
12b. **gayn**; ?adv.; ?'promptly' [A1*c]
12c. **gaynly**; adv.; 'appropriately, appositely, fitly, rightly' [A1*c]
12d. **gayn**; v.; 'to profit, be of use' [A1*]
13a. **gart**; v.; 'made, caused (pp.)' [A1*c]
13b. **gere**; v.; 'to clothe, attire; fashion, construct' [A1*c]
13c. **gere**; n.; 'gear, armour; bedclothes; ?doings, behaviour' [A1*]
13d. **stel-gere**; n.; 'armour' [A1*]
14. **gest**; n.; 'guest' [A1*]
15a. **gete**; v.; 'to get, seize, fetch' [A1*c]
15b. **get**; n.; 'thing obtained, something one has got' [A1*]
15c. **forgat**; v. (pret. sg.); 'forgot' [A1*c]
16. **gif**; v.; 'to give, grant; surrender; wish' [A1*c]
17. **gifte**; n; 'gift' [A1*c]
18. **grayn**; n.; 'blade (of axe)/spike?' [A1b]
19a. **grayþe**; adj.; 'ready' [A1*c]
19b. **grayþely**; adv.; 'readily, promptly, at once; duly, as was right; pleasantly' [A1*c]
19c. **grayþe**; v.; 'get ready (reflex.); arrayed, prepared, set (pp.)' [A1*c]
20. **haylse**; v.; 'to greet' [A1*c]
21. **hundreth**; num. (adj. and n.); 'hundred' [A1*c]
22. **kayre**; v.; 'to go, ride' [A1c]
23. **ker**; n.; 'thicket on marshy ground' [A1bc]
24a. **kest**; v.; 'to throw, put; lift; offer, make; utter; aim; ponder; speak' [A1]
24b. **kest**; n.; 'stroke; trick; ?fastening; (pl.) speech, utterances' [A1]
24c. **vmbe-kesten**; v.; 'cast about, searched all around' [A1c]
25. **kyrk**; n; 'church' [A1*bc]
26a. **layk**; n.; 'sport, entertainment' [A1*bc]
26b. **layke**; v.; 'to play, amuse oneself' [A1*c]
26c. **laykyng**; vbl. n.; 'playing' [A1*c]
27. **layt**; v.; 'seek, wish to know' [A1*c]
28. **lausen**; v.; 'to loosen, undo, break' [A1*]
29. **lyþen**; v.; 'to hear' [A1c]
30a. **loȝe**; adj.; 'low, low-lying' [A1*]
30b. **lowe**; adv.; 'low' [A1*]
30c. **loȝly**; adv.; 'humbly, with deference' [A1*]
31. **lote**; n.; 'sound, noise; noise of talking; word, saying, speech' [A1ac]
32. **melle**; n.; 'middle, midst' [A1*c]
33. **myre**; n.; 'mire, swamp' [A1*b]
34. **nay**; interj.; 'no' [A1*]
35. **nayted**; v.; 'named, mentioned (pp.)' [A1ac]

36. **neuen**; v.; 'to name, call, mention' [A1*c]
37. **rayke**; v.; 'to wander, depart, go' [A1c]
38. **raysed**; v. (pret. sg./pp.); 'raised, bid rise' [A1*c]
39. **scaþe**; n.; 'injury' [A1*c]
40. **scowtes**; n.; 'jutting rocks' [A1bc]
41. **sete**; n.; 'seat, place at table' [A1*]
42. **sister-sunes**; n. (pl.); 'sister's sons, nephews' [A1*c]
43. **skere**; adj.; 'pure' [A1]
44. **skete**; adv.; 'quickly' [A1*c]
45. **skyfted**; v.; 'shifted, alternated' [A1ac]
46. **skyl**; n.; 'reason' [A1a]
47. **skyrtez**; n. (pl.); 'skirts, lower part of flowing garment or covering; flaps of a saddle, saddle-skirts' [A1*c]
48. **snayped**; v. (pret. sg.); 'nipped cruelly' [A1c]
49. **stad**; adj. (pp.); 'placed; put down (in writing); present; standing there' [A1*c]
50. **tayt**; adj.; 'merry; vigorous, well-grown' [A1*c]
51. **trayst**; adj.; 'sure' [A1c]
52a. **þay**; pron., 3 pl. subject; 'they' [A1*c]
52b. **þayr**; pron., 3 pl. poss. (poss. adj.); 'their' [A1*c]
52c. **þayres**; pron., 3 pl. poss. (predicative); 'theirs, their affairs' [A1*c]
53. **þoȝ**; conj.; 'even though' [A1*c]
54a. **þro**; adj.; 'intense, steadfast; oppressive; fierce' [A1c]
54b. **þro**; adv.; 'earnestly, heartily' [A1c]
54c. **þroly**; adv.; 'heartily' [A1c]
55. **wayke**; adj.; 'weak' [A1*]
56. **wayth**; n.; '(meat gained in) hunting' [A1*bc]
57. **wayue**; v.; 'to wave, swing; sweep from side to side; offer, show (trans.)' [A1*c]
58a. **wylle**; adj.; 'wandering, perplexing' [A1*c]
58b. **wylsum**; adj.; 'bewildering, leading one astray' [A1*c]
58c. **wylt**; v. (pp.); 'strayed, escaped' [A1*c]
59. **wyndow**; n.; 'window' [A1*]
60a. **won (1)**; n.; 'dwelling, abode' [A1*]
60b. **won (2)**; n.; 'course (of action); multitude, host' [A1*]
61. **woþe**; n.; 'danger' [A1c]
62. **wro**; n.; 'nook' [A1bc]

Category A2 (morphological criteria) is made up of five stems (two with sub-entries), giving nine different lexical items.

63. **busk**; v.; 'to get ready, array, dress, make haste (intrans.); make (trans.)' [A2*c]
64. **haȝer**; adj.; 'skilful, well-wrought, fit, ready' [A2*c]
65a. **sere**; adv.; 'in each case, severally' [A2c]

65b. **sere**; adj.; 'separate, individual; various, several' [A2c]

65c. **serlepes**; adv.; 'separately, in turn' [A2c]

66. **snart**; adv.; 'bitterly' [A2*c]

67a. **wyȝt**; adj.; 'lively, loud, valiant, fierce' [A2*c]

67b. **wiȝt**; ?adv./adj.; 'ardently' [A2*c]

67c. **wyȝtly**; adv.; 'swiftly' [A2*c]

Category A3 (both phonological and morphological criteria) comprises two stems, and three distinct lexical items.

68. **ouerþwert**; prep.; 'through (a line of)' [A3*b]

69a. **tite**; adv.; 'quickly' [A3*c]

69b. **as-tit**; adv.; 'at once; in a moment' [A3*c]

Items listed as sub-entries of Type A stems could all in principle have been created in English via native derivational processes. But notice that exact Scand counterparts are attested for the following words, and any VAN reflexes might therefore have served as direct models for them:[237] **broþely, carp** (n.), **gaynly** (adv.), **gayn** (v.), **gere** (v.), **gere** (n.), **get** (n.), **grayþely, grayþe** (v.), **kest** (n.), **layke** (v.), **loȝly, þayr, þroly, wylsum, wylt**.

2.1.2. *Further remarks*

As one would expect for items with strong formal evidence in their favour, most of the Type A *Gaw* words are very well established as Norse derivations in the scholarly literature. All the stems are already treated to some extent by Bj.,[238] and there are no serious discrepancies between the etymologies offered by the major commentators.[239]

Eight stems show reliable formal evidence of more than one kind:[240] **bayþe, grayþe** (adj., v., **grayþely**), **kayre, layt, melle, stad, (ouer)þwert, tite (as-tit)**.

In some cases, structural features other than form (potentially) play a role in supporting the case for ON input. Thus, the sense development of **gifte** (the

---

[237] This is esp. likely in the case of **þayr**, though it has sometimes been suggested that ME oblique forms in *þ-* were created in English on the model of **þay**; see the entry for **þayr** in the Survey (note 126). Notice also **sister-sunes**, where the same combination is known in ON (as well as in OE and elsewhere in WGmc).

[238] Bj. does not have an entry for **trayst** (adj.) *per se*, but he has an entry for other formations on the stem *traist-*, inc. the adv. *traistly* (Bj. 65), so this looks like a simple oversight. His entry for words of the **wylle** family (Bj. 170) is moreover missing **wylt** (58c.); and for **sere** he includes only the adj. itself, not **sere** (adv.) or **serlepes** (Bj. 167–8).

[239] Relatively minor differences include the following (see discussion at the entries). For **agayn**, both *OED* (original entry) and Bj. allow for the possibility of a native route for velar /g/ (though this is at odds with what we now understand about the operation of palatalization in OE). For **gart**, only TG (D) (helpfully) refer to input from ON *gǫrr* as well as the v. *gera, gør(v)a*. For **tayt**, only GDS (implausibly) posits some connection with ME *toȝt*.

[240] Three distinct criteria apply in the case of **grayþe** (etc.) and **tite** (etc.).

meaning 'gift' is relatively infrequent for the OE cognate) and **scaþe** (the sense 'harm' is rare for the OE cognate); the use of the originally demonstrative **þay** (**þayr**, **þayres**) as pers. pronouns (though this role has been claimed for their OE cognates, too); and the compounding of the elements of **wyndow** in this way is otherwise unique to the Scand languages (see these entries).

But a few items present etymological complications of one sort or another. These are discussed in the entries, but the following may be noted here:

> **bayn, carp** (v., n.), **grayn, kayre, rayke**: the ulterior etymology is obscure in each case;
>
> **bayþe**: the older theory connecting this with ON *beina* has now generally been abandoned;
>
> **felle**: similarly, an earlier suggestion that this is related to OE *feld* has now been given up;
>
> **fro** (prep., conj.): there were some early attempts to explain this form via a native sound change, but this idea is no longer current;
>
> **grayn**: perh. not to be derived < *greiðn*, as has sometimes been supposed;
>
> **kyrk, skyrtez**: the immediate origin of the ON etyma of these has been debated (they have sometimes been explained as loans from OE in the first place);
>
> **lyþe, woþe**: in both these cases, there are two possible ulterior etymologies for the ON source;
>
> **þro** (adj., adv., **þroly**): there is possible input from two originally distinct (but homophonous) ON adjectives, with different formal profiles;
>
> **wayue**: despite *OED*'s earlier doubts, recent authorities regard OE *wæfan* as cognate with the ON etymon of this v. (and note also the possibility of input from early Fr behind some senses in ME);
>
> **won (1)** and **(2)**: it is conventional to treat these as two distinct lexemes in ME, although it is not clear whether their source(s) in ON would have been regarded as two separate words or just one (and note also the possibility of influence from the reflex of OE *wunian*).

Related but more minor issues of form, or sense, or interpretation in context in *Gaw* are various. But notice for instance: **bayþe** (the sense development in ME), **kest** (the origin of the <e> spellings), **lausen** (several other possible instances, depending on how the manuscript is read), **melle** (the earliest editors did not recognize this word at all), **wayue** (can be read as a form of **wayne** in some instances), **won (2)** (the interpretation of both instances has caused argument at one time or another). I have made new suggestions, or highlighted rarely cited observations, in particular for: **bayþe** (the development of the sense 'to grant' in ME), **gart** (that an ON source in etymological /ɑ/ is to be preferred), **gest** (the possible relevance of OE <gæst> 'guest'), **gifte** (that OE *gift* is attested in the sense 'gift'), **sete** (that ME spelling and rhyme evidence in general strongly point to derivation from ON), **sister(-sunes)** (a consideration of the phonology strengthens the case for ON input), **snart** (the PGmc *sner-root is known with a *-t* extension, but this is not sufficient to cast doubt on ON input).

2.1.2.1. Germanic distribution

Forty-six of the Type A stems have ON etyma with attested cognates in (pre-contact) OE, and are therefore marked with an asterisk (*).[241] Note that I understand 'cognate' here fairly generously, as including any similar formations demonstrably on the same Gmc root; several are not *exactly* cognate, i.e. there are no OE equivalents of precisely the same derivational form in a very similar sense.[242]

Five stems do not have (clear) cognates in OE, but have them elsewhere in WGmc; these (**frayst, lote, nayted, skyfted, skyl**) are marked with an 'a'.

Five stems (**broþe, ker, kest, skere, snayped**) have no closely related forms in Gmc at all beyond the Scand languages. In the case of six more (**bayn, carp, grayn, kayre, rayke, woþe**) it is difficult to tell Gmc cognates because their ulterior etymology is obscure.

Within ON, four stems have been claimed with more or less plausibility to have etyma restricted to OWN (**bayn, grayþe, tayt, busk**), and four to OEN (**attle, gif, melle, wro**).[243]

2.1.2.2. Distribution in England

There are thirteen stems in Type A where at least one of the sub-entries is more or less confined to the N/EM in the toponymic record; these items are marked with a 'b'.[244] The majority of these stems are also principally attested in the N/EM in the ME lexicon (on which see below); but notice that **grayn**, **myre** and **(ouer)þwert** are widespread in general lexical use in the surviving texts even though they are mainly northern or eastern in place names.

---

[241] Note that I have accepted the current assumption that OE *wǣfan* 'to wrap, clothe' is cognate with OIcel *veifa* 'to wave, vibrate, pull', despite *OED*'s hesitation (**wayue**). I have also followed the majority view in taking OE *-sciftan* as a native cognate to OIcel *skifta, skipta*, though there have been occasional attempts to treat the OE word as a loan from ON (**skyfted**).

[242] I count fifteen out of the forty-seven stems for which *exact* cognates in OE are not attested, viz. **attle, bigge, grayþe** (etc.), **melle, myre, raysed, scaþe, sete, skete, stad, wayth, won** (1 and 2), **snart, wyʒt** (etc.), **tite** (etc.).

[243] All are noticed as such by Bj., with the exception of **attle** (cited by McGee).

[244] Notice that for the **gayn** word-group there is toponymic evidence only for the adj. itself (12a.), and for the **layk** group only for the n. (26a.). The place-name material cited by *MED* for **wayth** suggests that it may be more widely distributed than *EPNE* indicates.

Fifty-six Type A stems are marked with a 'c' in at least one sub-entry, i.e. they are principally attested to a greater or lesser extent in the N/EM in the lexical record (with all the caveats which must apply to this statement; see the Introductory Remarks at pp. 56–8 above).[245] Twenty of them appear in Kaiser's (1937) list of 'northern' words.[246] However, on closer inspection many of these fifty-six have more complex profiles. Only twelve are unambiguously northern/ eastern words or word groups which are entirely or almost entirely confined to this region throughout their recorded history, viz.:[247] **broþe (broþely), frayst, ker, kyrk, layt, melle, nayted, scowtes, snayped, trayst, wylle** (and **wylt** v. [only]), **snart**. Of the remainder, **bayþe, get** (n.) and **haȝer** are attested only rarely, and it is difficult to say much about their distribution. A relatively large number of stems (fourteen) seem to be restricted to the N/EM in their earliest recorded appearances, but have become more or less widespread by the end of the ME period:[248] **agayn, ay, bayn, carp** (v., n.), **fro** (prep., conj.), **gayn** (adj., ? adv., and **gaynly** [only]), **gete** v. (and **forgat** [only]), **giftc, rayscd, skctc, skyrtez, þay (þayr, þayres), þoȝ, wayue.** Conversely, five stems or sub-entries begin life with a wider distribution (or, at least, they are attested in areas other than the N/EM), but have become more restricted to northern or eastern areas by late ME: **attle, gere** v. [only], **grayþe** (adj., v., **grayþely), lyþen, lote.** Twelve are more or less limited to the N/EM, at least by later ME, but are more widespread in alliterative verse: **attle, carp** (v., n.), **gart** (v. pp.) [only], **grayþe** (adj., v., **grayþely), haylse, kayre, vmbe-kesten** [only], **layk (layke, laykyng), lyþen, stad, þro (þroly), busk.** And fourteen are generally N/EM words throughout the ME period, but not entirely, having some attestations further afield which hint at wider usage: **bigge, felle, hundreth, neuen, rayke, scaþe, skyfted, tayt, wylsum** [only], **woþe, wro, sere** (adv., adj., **serlepes), wyȝt (wiȝt, wyȝtly), tite (as-tit).**

2.2. FORMAL CRITERIA

This section describes those formal features of ME words in *Gaw* which have been regarded as diagnostic of ON input: phonological, followed by morphological.[249] I include all features clearly applicable to the *Gaw* material, as well as

[245] Stems for which regional restriction is not true of all sub-entries are: the **gayn** word family, where it does not apply to **gayn** v.; the **gart** group, where it does not apply to **gere** n. or **stel-gere**; the **gete** family, where it does not apply to **get** n.; and the **kest** group, where it applies to **vmbe-kesten** only.
[246] These are **attle, bayn, carp** (v., n.), **gayn** (adj., ?adv., **gaynly** [only]), **grayþely** [adv. only], **vmbe-kesten** [only], **layk (layke, laykyng), lote, nayted, rayke, snayped, tayt, trayst, þro (þroly), wayth, wylle** [adj. only], **woþe, wro, busk, sere** (adv., adj., **serlepes).**
[247] **Scowtes** is recorded only from *Gaw* in ME, but has other (all N/EM) attestations later on. **Snart** is known only from *Gaw* as an adv., but occurs elsewhere (but only in the N/EM) as an adj.
[248] The possessives **þayr** and **þayres** are still slower to spread than is the subject form **þay**; see entry.
[249] On the general principles of these comparative 'tests', see the Introductory Remarks at pp. 39–44 above.

those which have been suggested but which in practice prove less secure as evidence (whether in general, or with respect to the *Gaw* words supposed to show them; see esp. §§6.4, 10.4, 12).

The discussion of most criteria follows a common format. In each case I begin with a short summary of the feature concerned, where: (i) is the characteristically Scand development in question; and (ii) sets out the contrasting native form(s) which descend from the same Gmc source. This is followed by a set of references to the key handbook accounts. In the phonology section, references in the first line are to previous detailed treatments of sound-based 'tests' of loan from ON, on which I draw; routinely cited (as representative) are Bj. (32–185), Wright & Wright (§§163–77), SPS (28–67) and Durkin 2014 (§§10.2–10.5).[250] Morphological criteria have in general seen less discussion (though see SPS 67–76);[251] the treatment of each feature in the morphology section is therefore prefaced with references to representative discussions of PGmc grammar (Prokosch 1939; Voyles 1992; Ringe 2006; Fulk 2018). For both phonology and morphology, references are then given for each of: (i) the ON development and the ME reflex(es) of this feature; and (ii) the OE reflex and its ME descendant(s). For ON, I cite routinely (as representative authorities, and as useful sources of further references) Noreen, Heusler, Br-N. and the summary in Gordon, besides the accounts in Voyles 1992 where relevant; for OE, Campbell, Luick, Hogg (and/or Hogg-Fulk), Ringe-Taylor; and for ME, Wright & Wright, Luick, Jordan-Crook, CONE and (for reflexes in the *Gaw*-manuscript in particular) GDS (xli–lxvi, cited by § number), TGD (133–8, 141).[252] The further discussion of each feature that follows deals not only with *Gaw* words of Type A, for which the criterion in question can be identified (relatively) straightforwardly as a marker of ON input, but also notices those words of Types B, C or D for which it might apply (and has sometimes in the past been assumed to do so), but which are more or less problematic. Reference will therefore be made back to this Formal Criteria section (by § number) throughout this book.

---

[250] For further discusssion see also Blake (1996: 78–81), Dance (2003: 74–86), Pons-Sanz (2007: 48–58). For an important phonological comparison of OE and ON see Townend (2002: 31–40).

[251] Bj. does not treat morphological features in detail as 'tests' alongside the phonetic criteria in his first volume, and simply deals with the relevant ME words under his 'tolerably certain' section in Volume 2.

[252] Also referred to in the discussions that follow are the helpful (generally briefer/summary) accounts in Faarlund (1994), Nielsen (2000: 255–65), Ralph (2002), Andersson (2002), Barnes (2005), Lass (1992), Fulk (2012), Minkova (2014), Fulk (2018), and the treatment of the orthography of the *Gaw*-manuscript by McL; for ME long vowels I also cite the valuable recent accounts in Stenbrenden (2016a). For remarks on the fates of ON sounds in English (and Scots), see further Kluge (1891: 788–9, 791; 1901a: 936–7, 940–1), Skeat (1892a: 456–66), Wall (1898: 73–81), Flom (1900: 76–82), Luick (§§381–4, 700–1), Serjeantson (1935: 293–4), Thorson (8–15), Kries (2003: 84–7), Dance (2003: 104–55).

2.2.1. *Phonological features*

2.2.1.1. *Vowels*

§1.   PGmc */ai/ > VAN /ɑi/, /ɛi/

(i) PGmc */ai/ > VAN /ɑi/, later /ɛi/, giving late ME /ai/ (<ay> in the *Gaw*-manuscript); (ii) but monophthongizes to OE /ɑ:/, giving late ME /ɔ:/ (usual in the South and Midlands) or /a:/ (usual in the North), or /a/ when shortened (usually <o> in *Gaw*, occasionally <a>).

Bj. (36–63), Wright & Wright (§168), SPS (§2.2.1.1) and Durkin (2014: §§10.2.4, 10.4.2).

(i) Noreen (§§54, 97), Br-N. (§§104–6); Wright & Wright (§§106–7), Luick (§§372–3, 384.1, 408.1), Jordan-Crook (§§93–5, 130.1, 284), Fulk (2012: §25.2) and GDS (§§32–3).

(ii) Campbell (§134), Luick (§§121–2), Hogg (§§5.7–9), Ringe-Taylor (§6.1.2), CONE ((AIM)); Wright & Wright (§§51), Luick (§§369–70), Jordan-Crook (§§44–6), Lass (1992: 46–7), CONE ((ARR)), ((NLAF)), Stenbrenden (2016a: 37–77), GDS (§8) and TGD (135, 141).

Remarks

SPS follows Ralph (2002: 705) in giving the VAN reflex of this diphthong as /ɑi/, though it is usual to assume a raising of the first element phonetically to [ɛ] during the Viking Age.[253] In words borrowed into English, it appears to have merged with the reflexes of late OE /æj/ and /ej/;[254] in early ME it is normally spelt <ei>, but <ai> in final position.[255] As noted by Bj. (42 n. 1), in some (esp. late) northern ME scribal dialects <ai> (<ay>) was an ambiguous spelling which could also stand for the reflexes of OE /ɑ:/.[256] But in the *Gaw*-manuscript the spellings of these two sounds are normally kept distinct, and hence the consistent <ay> here can be taken to represent etymological /ai/.[257]

---

[253] The resultant diphthong is traditionally expressed as *æi* (thus by Noreen and Br-N.), and [ɛi] by Ralph (2002: 710).

[254] On these new diphthongs see e.g. Hogg (§7.69), Lass (1992: 49–52), Minkova (2014: 177).

[255] See Luick (§384.1), Dance (2003: 127); and further Luick (1901a) on the fate of this ON diphthong in ME.

[256] On the monophthongization of late ME /ai/ in the North, and its merger with the reflex of OE /ɑ:/, see Luick (§§434, 515), Jordan-Crook (§19), Dobson (1968: §98), CONE ((ILD))), and further the discussions in Kniezsa (1983), Williamson (2002: 258, 265, 283–4), Minkova (2014: 202–3), Cole (2018: 197–9), and references there cited.

[257] See GDS (§§8, 32–3), and McL esp. 81–3. McL concludes that a phonemic distinction of /a:/ and /ai/ operated for the poet of *Pe*, at least, as demonstrated by the rhyme evidence. He suggests that merger of the two sounds for the scribe of the present manuscript is perh. indicated by a handful of spellings, but the evidence does not seem to me very robust; see further under **daylyeden** (D2).

(Relatively) unproblematic instances of ME /ai/ < VAN /ɑi/ in *Gaw* classified under Type A are as follows. Native cognates are attested and may be compared with the stems of those items marked with a *.[258]

> **ay** A1*
> **bayþe** A1*
> **bayn** A1
> **frayst** A1
> **grayn** A1
> **grayþe** (adj., v.), **grayþely** A1*
> **haylse** A1*
> **layk, layke, laykyng** A1*
> **layt** A1*
> **nay** A1*
> **rayke** A1
> **raysed** A1
> **tayt** A1*
> **þay, þayr, þayres** A1*
> **wayke** A1*
> **wayth** A1*
> **wayue** A1*

Another Type A item likely to exhibit a reflex of PGmc */ai/ is **woþe** (A1), in which case its vocalism is similarly incompatible with a native origin; but an alternative etymon has been suggested, which would be open to a different formal test (see §6.1 below).

Input from ON words in VAN /ɑi/ has also variously been suggested for the following items. But all are in some way problematic, and cannot be treated as Type A; see the entries for further discussion.[259]

> **are** CC1
> **ayquere** CC5
> **bene** (adj., adv.), **vnbene** DD1
> **daylyeden** DD2
> **enker(-grene)** D1
> **heme** DD2
> **hemely** CCC1
> **hete, hetes** CCC2

---

[258] The etymologies of some of these items present difficulties, but not in such a way as to cast serious doubt on the diagnostic value of their forms. See the entries for discussion of: the sense development of **bayþe**; the ulterior etymology of the ON source of **grayn**; the possibility of native input into the development of the diphthong in **nay**; the difficult ulterior etymology of **rayke**; the relationship of OE *wǣfan* and ON *veifa* (**wayue**).

[259] Notice nonetheless that both of the alternative interpretations proposed for **skayned** produce a derivation from an ON word containing this diphthong.

kay B1
lante CCC1
or C1
skayned D2
stayned D1
sweʒe DD1
taysed D1
waytez DD2

Note that **are, or** and **lante** might all show VAN /aː/ < /ɑi/ with monophthon-gization (see Noreen §54, Br-N. §104), but in all three cases it is difficult to rule out late OE /ɑ(ː)/ from native (near-)cognates. It has been suggested that **bene (vnbene), heme, hemely** and **hete (hetes)** contain /eː/ < late VAN /eː/ via OEN monophthongization of /ɛi/;[260] but probable reflexes of this change in Norse loans in ME are very few, and generally open to debate (see esp. Bj. 60–3, DP 11–21 and Luick 1901a; Luick §384 Anm. 1, and further Dance 2003: 151–2).

§2.   PGmc */au/ > VAN /ɑu/, /ɔu/

(i) PGmc */au/ > VAN /ɑu/, later /ɔu/, generally giving late ME /au/ or /oː/ (<au> and <o> in the *Gaw*-manuscript); (ii) but changes to OE /æː:ɑ/, giving ME /ɛː/ (or /e/, sometimes /a/ when shortened) (<e>, <a> in *Gaw*).

Bj. (68–81), Wright & Wright (§169), SPS (§2.2.1.2) and Durkin (2014: §10.2.5).
(i) Noreen (§§55, 98), Br-N. (§§107–8), Luick (§§384.2, 408.2), Jordan-Crook (§130.3), Fulk (2012: §25.1) and TGD (141).
(ii) Campbell (§135,) Luick (§119), Hogg (§§5.13, 5.41–6), Ringe-Taylor (§6.1.2), CONE ((AUF)), ((DHH)); Wright & Wright (§63), Luick (§§352–4, 356.2), Jordan-Crook (§§23, 81–2), CONE ((EAM)) and GDS (§27).

Remarks

The first element of the VAN diphthong /ɑu/ seems to have rounded during the Viking Age, giving a pronunciation [ɔu].[261] The general outcome in ON words borrowed into English and first attested during the OE period seems to have been /oː/, consistently spelt <o>;[262] but there is a greater variety of reflexes in ME, where (alongside /oː/) there are spellings which indicate the diphthongs /ou/ and

---

[260] On this change, which seems to have begun in parts of Denmark *c.* 900, see Noreen (1904: §§123–4), Br-N. (§§172–5), Haugen (1970: 49–52), Barnes (1997: 35), Andersson (2002: §3), Faarlund (1994: 41) and further Dance (2003: 151–2).

[261] See Ralph (2002: 710), SPS and the standard authorities. Rounding is dated to *c.* 900 (Noreen §55). On OEN monophthongization, in this case to /øː/, see the references under §1 above and in the preceding note (and Bj. DP 21–2). Andersson (2002: §3) notices that, in parts of Sweden, the resultant monophthong seems to have been an unrounded *o* sound, as in OS.

[262] See SPS, and further Kolb (1989: 286); and also Bj. DP (22) for an unusual explanation.

/au/, with the latter apparently being the normal output in the language of the *Gaw*-scribe.[263]

These are the uncontroversial instances of items containing VAN /ɑu/ in *Gaw*:

lausen A1*
þoȝ A1*
wyndow A1*

The unmarked tendency in *Gaw* is towards a diphthong spelt <au>. **Þoȝ** probably shows VAN /ɑu/, /ɔu/ > /oː/ before a /x/ (see Noreen §98.2; Br-N. §107; Gordon §50); and in **wyndow** the /o(ː)/ perh. shows the effects of light stress in the second element of a compound (see Dance 2003: 128; cp. Br-N. §108).

Problematic items which might derive from words containing VAN /ɑu/ but which must be assigned to other categories are:

glaum D2
ȝaule BB2
laucying D2
loupe DD1
ronez D1
rous D1
bost DD1

§3.   PGmc */au/ + front mutation > VAN /ɛy/, /øy/

(i) When front mutated, PGmc */au/ > VAN /ɛy/, later /øy/, giving late ME /ai/ (<ai, ay> in the *Gaw*-manuscript) (as with §1 above); (ii) but the expected *i*-mutated product in Angl OE is /eː/ (*Gaw* <e>).

Bj. (63–7), Wright & Wright (§170) and SPS (§2.2.13).
(i) Noreen (§§63, 69, 99), Heusler (§§56–61), Br-N. (§78), Gordon (§34); Wright & Wright (§§106–7), Luick (§§384.4, 408.1), Jordan-Crook (§§93–5, 130.2, 284), Fulk (2012: §25.2), CONE ((EYU)) and GDS (§§32–3).
(ii) Campbell (§200), Luick (§194), Hogg (§5.82), Ringe-Taylor (§6.6.3); Wright & Wright (§53), Jordan-Crook (§83) and GDS (§28).

Remarks

The ON front mutation product of PGmc */au/ was originally probably /ɛy/ (sometimes described as /æy/), with the first element labialized to /ø/ later in the Viking Age.[264] The outcomes of this sound in ME are identical with those of VAN /ɑi/; see §1 above.

---

[263] Jordan-Crook (§130.3) explains 'almost all *au* forms' by the NWM change of /ou/ > /au/ (§105 Rem.). On the fates of VAN /ɑu/ in English, see further the discussions in Thorson (10), Dance (2003: 128–9) and esp. Luick (1901a: 322–5) and Kolb (1989).

[264] See e.g. Faarlund (1994: 41) and SPS.

Relatively straightforward instances of this diphthong in *Gaw* are the following. Notice that none of these happens to have an attested OE cognate for comparison.[265]

kayre A1
nayted A1
snayped A1
trayst A1

More difficult cases, where the presence of VAN /ɛy/ is harder to demonstrate, are these:[266]

deʒe C1
layne C3
tryst, trystyly BBB2

§4.   PGmc /eː/[1] > VAN /ɑː/

(i) PGmc /eː/[1] > VAN /ɑː/, giving late ME /ɔː/ (usual in the South and Midlands) or /ɑː/ (usual in the North), or /a/ when shortened (usually <o> in the *Gaw*-manuscript, occasionally <a>); (ii) but > OE Angl (and later Kt) /eː/, WS /æː/ (OE *ǣ¹*), /e/ or /a/ when shortened (*Gaw* usually <e>, sometimes <a>), and > /oː/ before nasals (*Gaw* <o>).

Bj. (81–98), Wright & Wright (§166), SPS (§2.2.1.4) and Durkin (2014: §10.4.4).
(i) Noreen (§53), Br-N. (§71); Wright & Wright (§51), Luick (§§369–70), Jordan-Crook (§§44–6), Lass (1992: 46–7), CONE ((ARR)), ((NLAF)), Stenbrenden (2016a: 37–77), GDS (§8) and TGD (135, 141).
(ii) Campbell (§§127–9), Luick (§§111, 117), Hogg (§§3.22–5), Ringe-Taylor (§§5.1.2, 6.1.1), CONE ((AÆ1R)), ((AFR)); Wright & Wright (§52.1), Luick (§§361–2), Jordan-Crook (§§49–50, 53–4), Stenbrenden (2016a: 78–102), GDS (§§12, 19) and TGD (135).

Remarks

The Norse-derived vs. native reflexes of PGmc /eː/[1] are generally distinctive in most ME dialects,[267] though shortening to /a/ is possible for both (see below).

---

[265] The etymon of **kayre**, ON *keyra*, is usually explained as containing a reflex of VAN /ɛy/ (/øy/) by front mutation of PGmc */au/ (< a PGmc **kaurjan-* or **kauzjan-*); but see the entry for a recently suggested alternative derivation from PGmc **kaizwjan-*, in which case the diphthong in ON *keyra* would be the result of *w*-mutation of /ɑi/ (/ɛi/) (see e.g. Noreen §82.13).

[266] Note that **deʒe** has sometimes been derived from an OEN form with monophthongizaton to /øː/, but the form of the ME v. does not require this (and the change in OEN may be too late to lie behind a loan). See Dance (2000: 373), and on OEN monophthongization see the references cited under note 260 above.

[267] Though notice that OE /æː/ (of whatever origin) seems to have retracted to /ɑː/ in a small part of the SEM. On this 'East Saxon' development see e.g. Bj (85 n.1, reporting the findings of Morsbach 1896), Ringe-Taylor (§6.1.1), Jordan-Crook (§50) and CONE ((ELÆR)). And the OE development was to /ɑː/ in all dialects before /w/ (as in OE *blāwan*, *cnāwan* etc.; see Bj. 82 and n.1, Hogg §§3.22 n.1, 5.21), but there are no potential Norse loans in *Gaw* with this environment.

The presence of VAN /ɑː/ is uncontroversial for *Gaw* forms spelt <o> (i.e. southern and Midland ME /ɔː/), as in the following:[268]

broþe, broþely A1
loʒe, lowe, loʒly A1*
lote A1

The root vowel in **sete** (A1*) must descend from VAN /æː/, the front-mutated form of /ɑː/ (since ME spelling and rhyme evidence indicates open /ɛː/, rather than OE Angl close /eː/ by native descent from PGmc /eː/[1]).[269] And **won (1)** and **(2)** may also be labelled A1*, since ME spellings of these words in <a> as well as <o> indicate ME /ɔː/ < ON /ɑː/ (rather than an unrecorded native ō-stem *wōn with OE /oː/ < PGmc /eː/[1] before a nasal).

More problematic items, whose vocalism cannot clearly be demonstrated to go back to VAN /ɑː/, are:[270]

blaste C2
race, rasez CC2
rad B2
rake DD1
rak DD2
rasse D2
sate CCC2
scholes DD2

Spellings in <a> are potentially ambiguous where shortening is likely (most notably in **blaste** and **rad**), since there is some slight evidence in the *Gaw*-manuscript for /a/ (<a>) as the shortened form of the native reflex of PGmc /eː/[1], alongside the regular (and overwhelmingly more frequent) /e/ (<e>) by shortening of Angl /eː/.[271]

§5.   PGmc */iu/ + front mutation > VAN /yː/

(i) When front mutated, PGmc */iu/ > VAN /yː/, borrowed as late OE /yː/ which generally gives ME /iː/ in the North, NM and EM and /y/ and /e/ elsewhere (usually <i, y> in the *Gaw*-manuscript, with occasional <u> and rare <e>); (ii) but the expected *i*-mutated product in Angl OE is (/iːo/ >) /eːo/, generally giving late ME /eː/ but with some spellings reflecting rounded reflexes (*Gaw* <e>, more rarely <u> or <eu>).

---

[268] OE *gelǣte* 'manners, bearing' has sometimes been taken as a native cognate for the ON etymon of **lote**, but see that entry.

[269] For the ON mutation see Noreen (§§63.2, 68.2) and Br-N. (§78).

[270] Alongside **sate**, notice also the pret. sg. variant <gafe> discussed under **gif**.

[271] See GDS (§12), which cites <a> forms in *ar(e)nde*, *radde* and *stratez* (the latter in rhyme at *Pe* 1043), and TGD (135), which adds *brad* (< OE *brǣdan* 'to grill'). On the ME reflexes of OE *rǣdan* see further my remarks in Millett (2007: note to 1.398). The handbook accounts present <e> forms as the norm in the N/NM; see Jordan-Crook (§49), and further Kristensson (1987: 47–52).

Bj. (114–17) and Durkin (2014: §10.4.3).
(i) Noreen (§§63, 68), Heusler (§57), Br-N. (§78), Gordon (§34); Wright &
Wright (§57), Luick (§287), Jordan-Crook (§§39–43), Lass (1992: 53–5),
Stenbrenden (2016a: 262–97), GDS (§§22–3) and TGD (134).
(ii) Campbell (§§201–2), Luick (§§191–3), Hogg (§§5.83–4), Ringe-Taylor
(§6.6.3), Wright & Wright (§§65, 67), Luick (§§357–8), Jordan-Crook (§86),
Lass (1992: 53–5), CONE ((EOM)), ((EOR)), Stenbrenden (2016a: 103–37),
GDS (§30), TGD (134) and McL (85–7).

Remarks

There is a single unambiguous case of this VAN /y:/ in the *Gaw* data, viz. **myre**
(A1*). The conventional (and most plausible) etymology for ON *hlýða* means
that **lyþen** (A1) should most likely also be included here, though an alternative
source (in PGmc */u:/) cannot be ruled out; see the entry.
   More problematic potential instances are:

> **lyre** CC2
> **lyte** D2

§6.   Other vocalic changes
§6.1.   PGmc */an/ before /x/ > VAN /ɑ:/

(i) /n/ is lost in (later) PGmc before /x/, causing nasalization and lengthening of
the preceding vowel,[272] resulting in PGmc */anx/ > VAN /ɑ:(h)/ (with
subsequent loss of /h/, see §11.3 below), giving late ME /ɔ:/ (usual in the
South and Midlands) or /a:/ (usual in the North), or /a/ when shortened (usually
<o> in the *Gaw*-manuscript, occasionally <a>); (ii) but PGmc */an/ in this
position > OE /o:/, ME /o:/ (*Gaw* <o>).

Bj. (98–100) and SPS (§2.2.1.5).
(i) Noreen (§175.4), Wright & Wright (§51), Luick (§§369–70), Jordan-Crook
(§§44–6), Lass (1992: 46–7), CONE ((ARR)), ((NLAF)), Stenbrenden (2016a:
37–77), GDS (§8) and TGD (135, 141).
(ii) Campbell (§§119), Luick (§§85, 111), Hogg (§3.13, 22), Ringe-Taylor
(§5.1.2), Wright & Wright (§55), Jordan-Crook (§§53–4), Stenbrenden (2016a:
197–238) and GDS (§19).

Remarks

The only clear-cut descendant of this VAN sound in *Gaw* is **wro** (A1)
(and see also §11.3 below). There is no known OE cognate, but derivation <
PGmc *wranhō is the etymological consensus, and moreover ME spellings

[272] See e.g. Prokosch (1939: §29.2.f), Voyles (1992: §3.1.15), Ringe (2006: §327(ii)).

in <a> as well as <o> demonstrate early ME /a:/ (later southern/Midland ME /ɔ:/) < ON /ɑ:/, rather than the /o:/ which would have developed in a native word.

Þro (adj., adv.), þroly (A1) might also be included under this head, if we accept that some input is possible from the ON adj. represented by OIcel þrár 'decomposed, stale', prob. < PGmc *þranha- (and contrast OE þrōh 'rancid'); but we need not do so (see the entry, and further §12.3 below). And it is conceivable that woþe (A1) contains PGmc */anx/, if we derive it < PGmc *wanh-; but the majority of etymologists prefer a different etymon (see the entry, and also §7 below).

§6.2.   ON syncope (and associated changes)

(i) There was extensive syncope (and apocope) of lightly-stressed vowels in (pre-) VAN; (ii) in the same positions, vowels in OE often remained.

(i) Noreen (§§153–60), Br-N. (§§121–3), Gordon (§§56–7) and Voyles (1992: §5.1.18).
(ii) Campbell (§§341–54, 388–93), Luick (§§303–10, 334–46), Hogg (§§6.13–25, 66–71) and Ringe-Taylor (§§6.7–8).

Remarks

Syncope is one of the most characteristic developments of ON, and its effects are clearly evident by the time of seventh- and eighth-century inscriptions.[273]

The clearest instances in the *Gaw* material of words showing syncope which is diagnostic of ON (rather than native) derivation are:

> **grayþe** (adj., v.), **grayþely** A1*
> **melle** A1*
> **stad** A1*

Compare in each case the ON and related OE forms with their PGmc ancestors, viz. OIcel *greiðr*, OE *geræde* < PGmc *ga-raid-* (ON loss of vowel in *ga-* prefix); ODan *mellæ* < PGmc *medal-*, cp. OE *middel* < PGmc *midil-* (ON loss of medial vowel); OIcel *staddr*, OE (Angl) *steded* < PGmc *stadada-*. **Stad** moreover shows the failure of *i*-mutation typical of the past tenses of ON verbs of this type, since front mutation characteristically failed in ON after a light root syllable, perh. a side-effect of syncope.[274] All three stems are guaranteed as ON

---

[273] See further Nielsen (2000: 259–61), Andersson (2002: §3), Faarlund (1994: 40), Ralph (2002: 711–12) and Barnes (2005: 176).
[274] For ON front mutation see generally Noreen (§§63–9), Br-N. (§§78–81), Gordon (§§33–8), and further Voyles (1992: §5.1.14), Faarlund (1994: 40), Andersson (2002: §3), Ralph (2002: 706–8) and Barnes (2005: 176), and references there cited. Note that Bj. (21) treats the absence of *i*-mutation in light-stemmed wk. 1 preterites as a morphological feature, but I have preferred to include it here as basically phonological.

derivations by other formal features, to boot; see respectively §§1, 7, §§7, 10.1, §10.3.

§6.3.   PGmc *swestēr > ON systir

For the specific combination of likely ON vowel changes which produced ON *systir*, see the discussion and references at **sister-sunes**. The /i/ (< VAN /y/) in ME, PDE *sister* is not a plausible outcome of OE *sweostor*. The <u> spelling in the *Gaw* variant **(half-)suster** (CC2) is, on the other hand, not a secure indicator of ON derivation.

§6.4.   Other vowel changes, of uncertain relevance

A range of other vocalic features has been used to argue for ON input into the development of *Gaw* words, but none can be used securely as a diagnostic 'test' of loan in the instances adduced. They are noticed here for convenience; in each case, see the entries concerned for references and discussion.

(a) VAN /i/ (> ME /i/) rather than OE /io/ (> /eo/) with back mutation (> ME /e/)
     silk, sylkyn CC2
     syluerin CC2

(b) 'stress-shift' in (late) VAN diphthongs
     ȝol CC2
     scho DD1

(c) (late) VAN *u*-mutation of /ɑ/ > /ɔ/
     knot DD2

(d) VAN front mutation of */ɑst/ > /ɛst/
     fest, festned CC2

2.2.1.2. Consonants

§7.   PGmc */ð/ > VAN /ð/ medially and finally

(i) Except after /n/ or /l/,[275] non-initial PGmc */ð/ > the VAN fricative /ð/, giving ME /ð/ (spelt <þ> or <th> in the *Gaw*-manuscript); (ii) but it becomes a stop /d/ in OE, giving ME /d/ (*Gaw* <d>).

Bj. (159–67), Wright & Wright (§173) and SPS (§2.2.2.3).

---

[275] And when two /ð/ came to stand next to one another because of syncope; see Noreen (§238.1).

(i) Noreen (§§35, 44.2, 219, 223, 238.1), Heusler (§§170–1, 173), Br-N. (§§47, 243); Wright & Wright (§§271, 74), Luick (§700.3), Jordan-Crook (§§200 Rem. 4, 203, 206, 207 Rem. 3) and TGD (136).

(ii) Campbell (§409), Luick (§632), Hogg (§§4.17–18), CONE ((VFH)); Wright & Wright (§270) and Jordan-Crook (§200)

Remarks

The *Gaw* items for which the presence of /ð/ may most securely be treated as diagnostic of ON input are:

> **bayþe** A1*
> **grayþe** (adj., v.), **grayþely** A1*
> **hundreth** A1*

I also include **melle** (A1*) under this head, since the VAN medial cluster /ll/ results from assimilation of earlier */ðl/, the first element of which would have been /d/ in OE; and **tite (as-tit)** (A3*) likewise shows assimilation of */ðt/ > /tt/; see the discussion at those entries.

Bayþe, **grayþe** (etc.) and **melle** seem to descend from roots containing PIE */dh/, in which case PGmc */ð/ is the only possible outcome. But PGmc */ð/ may also reflect PIE */t/ with the operation of Verner's Law (VL),[276] meaning that by-forms of the same root (or suffix) in PGmc */ð/ (with VL) and */θ/ (without VL) are possible, and sometimes attested; and in that case ME /ð/ is less secure as a test of loan, since it could in principle descend from a voiced native reflex of the non-VL variant (OE [ð] < PGmc */θ/). I have listed **hundreth** as a Type A1* since, though it contains PIE */t/, no Gmc language attests a cognate showing an outcome other than PGmc */ð/ with VL. But there are other possible instances of ON input in *Gaw* for which the evidence is more equivocal, and for which the presence of ME */ð/ is not a secure test; see below (esp. **burþe, ruþes**).

Amongst Type A items, **lyþen** (A1) might also be grouped here, but only if we follow the minority derivation of ON *hlýða* < PGmc **hlūdjan-* (cp. OE *hlȳdan*). It is more likely that the ON v. derives < PGmc **hleuþ-* instead, in which case an OE cognate would also have had [ð]; but in that event **lyþen** is guaranteed as a Type A on the basis of its vocalism (see the entry, and §5 above). Similar things may be said of **grayn** (A1), whose ON etymon *grein* in the requisite sense is now usually derived from a PGmc **grainō* rather than the **ga-raidni-* asssumed by Bj. (see entry); but the diphthong in any case is diagnostic of Norse derivation (§1). And **broþe, broþely** (A1) and **woþe** (A1) are also guaranteed by their vocalism, whichever of two possible derivations one adopts for **woþe** (see entry and §§6.1, 7), but the source of the medial /ð/ in both cases is uncertain.

---

[276] For representative discussions of VL see e.g. Prokosch (1939: §20), Voyles (1992: §3.1.3), Ringe (2006: §3.2.4(ii)), Fulk (2018: §6.6), next to the accounts in Br-N. (§227), Gordon (§71).

Other *Gaw* items for which the presence of PGmc */ð/ has been suggested in one or more possible etyma, but which present problems of one sort or another, are the following:

burþe CC2
forth CC2
glode DD1
heþen B1
quethe DD2
raþeled DD1
ruþes D1
soþen CCC2
sparþe B1
strothe D1
stryþþe CC2
warþe CC3
wheþen B1

Notice that **heþen** and **wheþen** have traditionally been explained otherwise, i.e. as showing ON **hiðan-* < **hinan-* and **hvaðan-* < **hvanan-* by consonant cluster dissimilation (§10.2); but other etymologies have been proposed, inc. derivation from PGmc forms with a medial fricative, whose origin is not entirely clear (see the discussion at **heþen**).

Burþe and **ruþes** both (probably) descend from forms in PIE */t/, and are open to the doubts noticed above about PGmc variants with and without VL: in the case of **burþe**, there is some evidence for the existence of Gmc cognates without VL in the suffix; and for **ruþes**, though OE *hryd-* may indeed be cognate with the supposed etymon ON *hryðja*, there are also potentially formations on the same root in OE with [ð] < PGmc */θ/ (see the respective entries for further discussion).[277] **Soþen** is a str. pp. and therefore certainly ought to have had VL, but in this case there is a distinct likelihood of levelling across the paradigm (see the entry).

Another source of difficulty here is the tendency for late ME /d/ to vary with /ð/ in the vicinity of liquids and nasals, something which seems to have led both to etymological /ð/ > /d/ (as in OE *byrðen* > PDE *burden*, OE *fiðele* > PDE *fiddle*) and to the reverse, a 'spirantization' of etymological /d/ > /ð/ (e.g. OE *fæder* > PDE *father*, OE *gadrian* > PDE *gather*).[278] The latter change is not well attested in the *Gaw*-manuscript, but it probably lies behind the

---

[277] Similar uncertainties apply to **broþe, broþely** (A1) and **woþe** (A1).

[278] On these changes see esp. Luick (§§638, 751–2), Jordan-Crook (§§206, 298), Wełna (2004), Lass & Laing (2009), CONE ((LDS)), ((LDH)), and further Dobson (1968: §§383–4). There was already a tendency in late OE for [ð] > [d] before an immediately following (non-syllabic) /n/, /m/ or /r/; see further Campbell (§424), Hogg (§714). Wełna (2004) thinks that there is some evidence for /d/ > /ð/ as early as the eleventh century, but the change is usually dated *c.* 1400.

variant *alþer* of the intensive *alder* (as in *alþer grattest* 'greatest of all' at *Gaw* 1441),[279] and it is a possible alternative or additional source for <th, þ> in **burþe, forth, raþeled** and **strothe**.

§8.	Absence of palatalization of velar consonants in VAN

§8.1.	PGmc */k/

(i) PGmc */k/ remains in VAN, giving ME /k/ (spelt <k, c> in the *Gaw*-manuscript); (ii) but palatalizes in front environments in OE, giving ME /tʃ/ (*Gaw* <ch>).[280]

Bj. (139–47), Wright & Wright (§174), SPS (§2.2.2.1), Miller (2012: 120–3, 124–5) and Durkin (2014: §§10.2.2., 10.4.1).
(i) Noreen (§39), Br-N. (§29); Wright & Wright (§281), Luick (§§700.1, 701), Jordan-Crook (§178) and TGD (137, 141).
(ii) Campbell (§§426–39), Luick (§§637, 685–90, 696), Hogg (§§7.15–43), Ringe-Taylor (§6.4.1), CONE ((VP)); Wright & Wright (§282–8) and Jordan-Crook (§§177, 179–80).

§8.2.	PGmc */g/

(i) PGmc */g/ remains in VAN ([g], [ɣ]), giving ME /g/ and /ɣ/ > /w/ (spelt <g> and <ʒ, w> in *Gaw*); (ii) but palatalizes in front environments in OE, giving ME /j/ and (after nasals and when geminated) /dʒ/ (*Gaw* <ʒ> and <gg>).[281]

Bj. (148–57), Wright & Wright (§§176–7), SPS (§2.2.2.1), Miller (2012: 123–5) and Durkin (2014: §§10.2.3, 10.4.1).
(i) Noreen (§37), Br-N. (§§33–4); Wright & Wright (§§291, 296, 298), Luick (§§700.1, 701), Jordan-Crook (§§184–6) and TGD (136–7, 141).
(ii) Campbell (§§426–39), Luick (§§633, 637, 685–90), Hogg (§§7.15–43), Ringe-Taylor (§6.4.1), CONE ((VP)); Wright & Wright (§§292–6, 299) and Jordan-Crook (§§189–94).

§8.3.	PGmc */sk/

(i) PGmc */sk/ remains in VAN, giving ME /sk/ (spelt <sk, sc> in *Gaw*); (ii) but palatalizes (in most environments) in OE, giving ME /ʃ/ (*Gaw* <sch>).

---

[279] See McL (110–11), who argues for a neutralization of the /ð/ ~ /d/ distinction in the neighbourhood of liquids.
[280] It is debated whether assibilation to /tʃ/ occurred during the OE period, or whether the completion of this change took place in ME. For discussion and references see Minkova (2016) who argues for an eleventh-century date at the earliest.
[281] The same issues pertain to the date of assibilation to /dʒ/ as they do for /tʃ/; see the preceding note, and further Stenbrenden (forthcoming).

Bj. (119–39), Wright & Wright (§175), West (1936: 118–26), SPS (§2.2.2.2),
Miller (2012: 125–7) and Durkin (2014: §§10.2.1, 10.4.1).
(i) Luick (§700.1) and Jordan-Crook (§182).
(ii) Campbell (§§440–1), Luick (§§691–2), Hogg (§§7.37–43), Ringe-Taylor
(§6.4.1), CONE ((SKP)); Wright & Wright (§289), Jordan-Crook (§§181, 183)
and TGD (137).

Remarks

The palatalization (and eventually assibilation) of /k/, /g/ and /sk/ is one of the
most characteristic features of the OE/ME consonant system,[282] and its absence
in some ME words is probably the best known, and at the same time (esp. in
non-initial position) the most contested, piece of evidence for ON input.

Initial position
At the turn of the twentieth century, the details of OE palatalization had yet to be
fully worked out by scholars. In particular, it was often assumed (largely on the
basis of its frequent absence in ME words in northern texts) that it had not
operated fully in Nhb OE – or at least that fronted /k/ (the main object of this
discussion) had never developed assibilation in that region.[283] This belief is
reflected in Bj.'s tentative use of the absence of palatalization as a test of loan
from ON (see e.g. Bj. 140–1), and apparently in some of the etymological labels
in Gollancz (1921).[284] It is symptomatic of how closely entwined scholarship on
palatalization has been with that on the ON influence on English that what is
recognized as the first generally accurate formulation of the principles of OE
palatalization as they are now understood comes in Bj.'s book, in a footnote (Bj.
147 n.2) in which Bj. communicates a schema supplied to him by Morsbach.[285]
But this note continues to assume that developments in the North were different.
The extent of palatalization and assibilation in Nhb was first established by
Gevenich in 1918, demonstrating the ubiquity with which /k/ > /tʃ/ in fronting
environments in (native) northern place-names;[286] and since then it has largely

---

[282] For further discussion of the operation and timing of these changes, inc. the environments in
which fronting took place, and the phonemicization of their outputs, see notably Kluge (1887: 113–
14), Weyhe (1908), Luick (1935), West (1936), Penzl (1947), Watson (1947), Kristensson (1976),
Hogg (1979), Cercignani (1983), Minkova (2003: esp. 72–7, 90–133, 193–202; 2014: 84–8; 2016),
and more broadly Liberman (2007), and references cited there.

[283] For this view see e.g. Wall (1898: 70–2), Flom (1900: 10–11), Bülbring (1902: §493). The idea
persists into Prokosch (1939: §31) and, as Hoad (1984: 36 n. 40) notices, as late as Strang (1970:
292).

[284] Gollancz gives OE etyma for ME words with initial velars s.vv. *gayn*, *geste*, *gyue*; see the entries
for **gayn** (adj.), **gest**, **gif** below. The same assumptions are, less surprisingly, reflected in earlier
treatments of ON loans such as those by Knigge (who does not give ON etyma for such items as
agayn, gest, gete, gif, gifte and **kyrk**).

[285] On the significance of this note see e.g. Gevenich (1918: 1), Kristensson (1976: 321 n.3) and Hogg (§7.16
n. 2).

[286] Though notice Chadwick (1902: 24) for an earlier objection to the idea (as stated in Bülbring
1902: §493) that Nhb /k/ had not assibilated, again on the grounds of place-name evidence.

been accepted that these changes occurred to the same extent in the North as elsewhere in England.[287]

Seeing that palatalization (and eventually assibilation) can be demonstrated for northern OE, and their absence – at least in initial position – does not seem to be the regular native development, then the obvious alternative explanation for velars in palatalization environments is to invoke ON input. This is the approach taken (albeit nervously) by Bj., and it is supported by Gevenich (1918), who shows that the distribution of the /k/-forms of place names is densest in precisely the same northern areas as are most marked (according to Lindkvist 1912) by the presence of Norse-derived toponyms (and moreover that elements in /k/ all have plausible ON etyma). Since Gevenich's work, initial velars have been generally admitted as a reliable test of loan from ON.[288]

Word-forms falling unambiguously into this category in *Gaw* are as follows.[289]

With /k/:
carp (v., n.) A1
kayre A1
ker A1
kest (v., n.), **vmbe-kesten** A1
kyrk A1*

With /g/:
agayn A1*
gart, gere (v., n.), **stel-gere** A1*

---

[287] The most persistent bone of contention has been /k/ before OE /æ/. Gevenich (1918: 84) claimed that assibilation had taken place in this environment, but some of the handbooks (notably Wright & Wright §284; Luick §685.1) state that this was not true of the North; and the same argument is made by Kristensson (1967: 201) on the basis of consistent *-caster* names in many northern and NM areas (inc. Lincolnshire). But the reflexes of OE *ceaster* have long been a source of difficulty (for an even-handed discussion, see *VEPN* s.v. *cæster*), and more recent grammars assume assibilation before OE /æ/ in all regions (thus Campbell §427; Hogg §7.16; Ringe-Taylor §6.4.1). For objections to Kristensson's case, see also Miller (2012: 121). Doubts as to the ubiquity of OE palatalization/ assibilation are still occasionally met with, however: notice for instance Blake (1996: 78), who insists that, since it is only really by the presence of palatal diphthongization that we can tell when palatalization had occurred in OE texts, 'it remains possible that the palatalisation of these initial consonants did not take place in all Old English dialects'. For the initial cluster /skr/, see below.

[288] See the references at the head of this section, and notice also Thorson (2) and Townend (2002: 39). On orthographic difficulties in (esp. early) ME which can make the identification of velars as opposed to palatalized/assibilated sounds difficult, see further e.g. CONE ((EOCG)), ((OR3)), ((ORG)), ((ORPC)), ((ORPSC)), West (1936: 94), McL (122) and Dance (2003: 141–2). For palatalization of /g/ and /k/ in the Scand languages at a later period, see e.g. Haugen (1976: §11.3.18, cited by Townend 2002: 39).

[289] See the entries for discussion of: possible influence from Lat *carpere* 'to pluck, gather' on **carp**; early suggestions that a native etymon might stand behind **agayn**; the problem of whether late OE *sciftan* and *-scylian* are cognate with or early instances of borrowings of ON words (**skyfted, skyl**); and the possibility that the (usually supposed) ON etyma of **kyrk** and **skyrtez** might themselves derive from OE.

gest A1*
gete (v., n.), **forgat** A1*
gif A1*
gifte A1*

With /sk/:
scaþe A1*
scowtes A1
skere A1
skete A1*
skyfted A1
skyl A1
skyrtez A1*

It is worth remarking here that, though several of these items (**agayn**, **gayn** (etc.), **gest**, **gif**) show clear ON input in their initial velars, the coda (esp. the vocalism) of one or more of their attested ME forms possibly or certainly reflects that of their native cognates (see the discussion at these entries). This raises the interesting possibility that ON influence on these words (or at least on some variants) was effectively confined to the initial consonant, replacing a palatalized sound with a velar one. The same phenomenon has been proposed for both /k/ sounds in **kyrk**,[290] and could also lie behind several of the other items listed above (i.e. **gete** (etc.), **gifte**, **scaþe**, **skete**, **skyfted**, **skyrtez**).[291] The idea of 'sound substitution' in products of the Anglo-Norse contact process has often been proposed, especially to explain ME and later dial words with an initial velar for which there is no known ON cognate,[292] and indeed *vice versa*, to account for English words with a palatalized/assibilated consonant but whose etymology otherwise points to an origin in ON.[293] There is a key early discussion of 'sound substitution' (for initial palatals/velars and other OE-ON sound equivalences) at Bj. (9–12, see also 13 n. 2); and it has been claimed by one or more etymological commentators as a factor in various of the *Gaw* words treated in this book (see esp. the remarks in the

---

[290] See that entry for the notion that **kyrk** represents a Scandinavianized form of OE *cyrice* created by ON speakers in Viking Age England, which was subsequently borrowed into ON (cp. OIcel *kirkja*).

[291] For some cautious remarks on words of this type see Lass (2007: §8.9.3), who is 'agnostic' about the possibility of ON input being the cause of loss of palatalization.

[292] See the discussion in Hoad (1984: 37–8). The classic supposed example is PDE *scatter* (next to *shatter*); see Bj. (10), and further e.g. *OED* s.v. *scatter* v., Serjeantson (1935: 76), Miller (2012: 127 and n. 490) and Durkin (2014: 208). For some possible instances in MnE dialects, see Thorson (2 n.1), who suggests e.g. *skippon* 'shippen, cow-house'.

[293] Thorson (2 n. 1, 43 n.2) argues that *shorpen* 'to shrivel leather or other substance by heat' (cp. OIcel *skorpinn* 'shrivelled') is an example of this type. PDE *shift* has sometimes been claimed to be another; see the discussion at **skyfted** and ***schifted**.

entries for **kyrk, skyfted, skyrtez, ȝaule, chymbled, *schifted, flosche, schunt** and also **dreme**).[294]

The following items with initial velars (or supposed input from ON words with initial velars) are more problematic, and cannot be treated as Type A, since the sound in question, or the word as a whole, has other possible explanations:[295]

> **cakled** BBB2
> **kay** B1
>
> **angardez** FCCC3
> **gayne** D2
> **gate, algate** B2
> **garysoun** FCC3
>
> ***schifted** DD2
> **schunt** (v., n.) DD1
> **scrape** CC2
> **skayned** D2
> **skwez** D2

Notice in particular the issues surrounding the initial cluster /skr/. It has sometimes been suggested that /sk/ developed endogenously (or was retained) in English in this combination. This possibility is not often alluded to in recent scholarship,[296] but *OED3* s.v. *S* n.1[297] highlights the unusually wide range of English *scr-* forms, inc. variants of *shr-* words for which there is no corresponding stem in ON (e.g. PDE *screed* next to *shred*, < OE *scrēade*); and it is treated at greatest length by West (1936: 63–102), who notices that the cluster /skr/ often persists unpalatalized not only in the North and Scotland (where he is content to allow for input from ON) but

---

[294] For further discussion of sound substitution, see variously e.g. Skeat (1892a: 469–71; Skeat is a particular enthusiast for substitution as an explanation in English etymology), Kluge (1901a: 935), Luick (1901b: 414), Serjeantson (1935: 76), Thorson (2 n.1), Jordan-Crook (§§179, 192), Hoad (1984: 37–8), Dance (2003: 101–2), Miller (2012: 121, 127) and Durkin (2014: 208). For the operation of the 'switching code' during contact which plausibly underlies the phenomenon, see in particular Townend (2002: esp. 85–7) for a list of the many likely instances of what he calls 'cognate phonemic substitution' ('usually where an Old English word is recorded without an Old Norse cognate' (Townend 2002: 85); and for the idea of phonological substratum interference, i.e. pronouncing OE 'with a Norse accent', see Townend (2002: esp. 205–10). In this connexion, notice also the converse process, i.e. the regular depalatalization of WGmc loans into ON highlighted by Gammeltoft & Holck (2007: 144).

[295] Notice the further discussion in the following entries in particular: **gate** (etc.), where the initial /g/ has often been regarded as securely diagnostic of ON input, but which I argue cannot be assumed; **garysoun**, where the form is overwhelmingly likely to derive from Fr; **skayned**, which is nonetheless formally guaranteed to derive from ON whichever of the two possible interpretations we accept.

[296] There is no mention of it in Campbell (§440) or Hogg (§§7.17(4), 7.37); though notice Ringe-Taylor (§6.4.1: 204).

[297] In a note on 'the combination *scr*' in the etymology section. And see also the original *OED* s.v. *scr-* (1).

also in the NWM and in the SW.[298] In the *Gaw* material, see the entry for **scrape** (where Fr input is also possible).

Medial and final position

The remarks above hold for the absence of palatalization/assibilation in initial position, where it is now usually accepted that it was regular in all OE dialects in the appropriate environments. But explanations for its absence non-initially are more contested.

That medial and final velars could not be afforded the same weight as a test of loan was realised relatively early, inc. by Bj. (e.g. 144). The origin of velars in these positions is discussed in detail by Luick (1935, followed in Luick §§688–90, 701), in what became a very influential treatment. Luick is prepared to accept ON influence in the N and NM (1935: 285), but otherwise he finds the degree of variation between velars and palatals non-initially to be too extensive for this to be the only factor, and he prefers levelling across paradigms within OE as the explanation. This argument was already well understood before Luick's work,[299] and it has often been used to account for velars in words like PDE *seek*, some of whose OE reflexes would regularly have had palatalization (e.g. infin. *sēcan*) and others of which would not (e.g. syncopated pres. 3 sg. ind. *sēcð*). But Luick's case is particularly cogent,[300] and gained widespread acceptance.[301] But even though levelling is often an adequate explanation for non-initial /k/, /g/ and /sk/, it is hard to rule out other possible influences on the development of these sounds, whether separately or as a reinforcing factor; and more recent scholarship has increasingly tended to return to the likelihood of ON input as at least a possible ingredient, and to highlight the essential intransigence of the issues, more strongly than did Luick. In the final reckoning, it is often very difficult to say that Scand influence is improbable, esp. when ON cognates are attested for the English words in question.[302]

These arguments apply to some extent to all the following *Gaw* items (or have been claimed for at least one of their possible etymologies). ON input is in all

---

[298] See also Bj. (132 n.1), Thorson (2–3) and Jordan-Crook (§181 Rem), and references cited there.

[299] See e.g. Bj. (inc. 147 n.2, Morsbach's 1896 formulation of the rules of palatalization), Wright & Wright (esp. §282), and the references in Hoad (1984: 34 n. 29).

[300] Amongst other findings, Luick presents good evidence via words like PDE *bellows* < OE *belgas* (an original *i*-stem transferred to the *a*-stem pl. type) that consonants which would originally have been palatalized could be replaced with velars once they came into contact again with a back vowel (Luick 1935: 276).

[301] Luick's thinking continues to be reflected, to a greater or lesser extent, in the likes of Penzl (1947: 39–40), Campbell (§437–41), Jordan-Crook (§179), Cercignani (1983: 320) and Hogg (§7.40–42). (See esp. Hogg §7.16 on the ambisyllabicity of medial consonants in OE, which explains why priority often seems to have been given to the following vowel in determining the presence or absence of palatalization.) There are nonetheless dissenters, such as Watson (1947), who admits Luick's reasoning for most of England but argues that palatalization of /k/ never took place finally (and in some areas medially) in Nhb.

[302] See esp. the discussion in Hoad (1984: 34–6 with further references), Penzl (1947: 39–40), Campbell (§438), Jordan-Crook (§192), McL (113, 117), Hogg (esp. §7.43), Miller (2012: 120–7) and also Ramisch 1997. Particular enthusiasm for ON input here is expressed by Krygier (2000) Bibire (2001: 99–100), and Kocel (2009; 2010).

cases possible, and often on other grounds very probable; but lack of palatalization/assibilation non-initially cannot be regarded as a sufficient 'test' in its own right to qualify these items as Type A.[303]

> **blenk** CC2
> **gyng** CC1
> **irked** DD1
> **lyke, lyk, vnlyke** CCC2
> **merk, merkkez** CC2
> **muckel** CC2
> **nikked** CCC2
> **rykande** DD2
> **þenk** CCC2
> **þynke** CCC2
> **wykez** C1
>
> **big, bigly** D1
> ***dyngez** D2
> **fawne** CCC2
> **haȝer** A2*
> **henge** CC1
> **lygez** C2
> **loȝe, lowe, loȝly** A1*
> **raged** D2
>
> **askez** CC2
> **busk** n. CC2
> **mensk, menske, mensked, menskful, menskly** C2

The first item in this list, **blenk**, is a typical example of the kinds (and range) of issues which become relevant: OE *blencan* (< PGmc **blankjan-*) ought to have shown palatalization in many parts of the paradigm; but as well as possible input from the ON cognate with /k/ (cp. OIcel *blekkja* < **blenkja*), and/or levelling across the OE paradigm of a form which retained the velar, there is also the likelihood of influence from an etymologically related v. with /k/ like ME *blinken* (see the entry). On the OE suffix *-isc* and its possible pronunciations, see the references and discussion under **mensk** adj. Note further that I have not included in this study *Gaw* forms whose spellings are ambiguous, esp. *brygge* 'drawbridge', *rygge* 'back' (for which MnE dial forms in /g/ are also attested), since these words have always in practice been taken to represent native-derived

---

[303] Notice that Bj. (112) takes the failure of OE first fronting (of PGmc **a/* > */æ/*), which would in turn have led to palatalization, as the test of loan for **fawne** and **haȝer**; but the direct diagnostic criterion in most ME forms of these words is the presence of the medial velar. **Haȝer** is nonetheless guaranteed as a Type A by its final *-r* (§12). **Loȝe** (etc.) also remains as a Type A, on account of its vocalism (§4).

forms containing assibilated /dʒ/, and no commentators have attempted to argue otherwise (see also the Introductory Remarks at pp. 67–8 above).[304]

Other *Gaw* items which arguably descend from ON words with a non-initial velar, where the problems are various but generally of other sorts, are:[305]

> **aghlich, aʒlez** C1
> **lagmon** D2
>
> **busk** v. A2*
> **flosche** DD1

Notice in particular **lagmon**, for which an *ad hoc* native development of 'expressive' /gg/ has sometimes been supposed, as it has for one of the possible etymologies for **big** (etc.) in the list above.[306]

§9.   VAN /gg/ by 'sharpening'

(i) PGmc */jj/ and */ww/ > VAN /ggj/ and /ggw/, giving ME /g/ (*Gaw* <g(g)>); (ii) but this change does not occur in OE, leading to OE and ME forms in vowels/diphthongs or semi-vowels.

Bj. (32–5), SPS (407–8) and Durkin (2014: §10.2.6).
(i) Noreen (§227), Heusler (§185), Br-N. (§233), Voyles (1992: §5.1.5), Fulk (2018: §6.10), Luick (§§626, 700), Jordan-Crook (§§188, 190 Rem. 2) and TGD (137).
(ii) Campbell (§120(1)), Hogg (§3.17) and Ringe-Taylor (§3.1.5).

Gmc 'sharpening', a.ka. *Verschärfung* or Holtzmann's Law, is a change attested regularly in ON and Go, albeit in a small number of word-forms. Its operation remains somewhat obscure, but in the clearest instances it is a very robust marker of ON or Go as opposed to WGmc descent from PGmc; cp. OIcel *tveggja*, Go *twaddjē* with OHG *zweiio*, OE *twēg(e)a* (*twēgra*) 'of two' (gen.) containing PGmc */jj/, and OIcel *tryggvar* (pl.) 'trust', Go *triggwa* 'alliance' with OHG *triuwa*, OE *trēow* 'faith' containing PGmc */ww/.[307] The best known example of this test in a Norse loanword in English is ME *egg(e)*, PDE *egg* < the ON n. represented by OIcel *egg*, < PGmc *ajjaz* (cp. OE *ǣg*).

---

[304] TGD (141) carefully notices the ambiguity of the spellings, but does not pursue the possibility of ON input; and McL 117 explicitly assumes the assibilated pronunciation. On **henge** see that entry.

[305] I have included **busk** here, since the presence of *-sk* is a diagnostically ON morphological feature (§15) even if the sound combination /sk/ cannot be used in itself as a test of loan.

[306] See the discussion at these entries, and notably Coates (1982) as well as Thorson (3).

[307] See the handbook accounts listed above for discussion and further references, and also in particular Prokosch (1939: §33(c)), Collinge (1985: 93–8), Smith (1997; 1999), Rasmussen (1999), Rowe (2003) and Pons-Sanz (2006a), and further Bammesberger (2004: 93, 96). In her detailed treatments of the change, Smith (1997) (summarized in Smith 1999) accounts for the geminate stops as developing from laryngeals which were subject to VL and strengthened at a syllable onset; and notices some possible reflexes in WGmc, such as OE *brycg* 'bridge' (on which see Pons-Sanz 2006a: 147).

There is only one *Gaw* item which clearly shows a reflex of this change, viz. **bigge** (A1*). Its ON etymon (cp. OIcel *byggva* (*byggja*)) is always derived from a PGmc **bewwjan-* or **buwwjan-* with sharpening, even though there is no attested Go cognate which would prove this etymology beyond doubt.[308]

The presence of *Verschärfung* has also been proposed for (one or more suggested etyma of) the following words, but all present more serious problems:

> **big, bigly** D1
> **raged** D2

§10. Changes affecting VAN consonant clusters
§10.1. Assimilation

(i) VAN consonant clusters (sometimes created by syncope; see §6.2 above) underwent a wide range of assimilatory changes; (ii) these changes did not occur in OE.

Bj. (168–76).
(i) Noreen (§§266–78), Br-N. (§§249–59) and Gordon (§§76–7).

The following cluster assimilations are all characteristic of ON,[309] and cannot be safely paralleled in OE.[310]

§10.1.1. Regressive assimilation

(a) VAN /ðt/ > /tt/

This ON assimilation clearly lies behind **tite** (**as-tit**) (A3*) (and for the presence of VAN /ð/ here see also §7 above).[311]

(b) VAN /ht/ > /t(t)/

This change is indisputably present in **attle** (A1*).[312]

It also perh. occurred in one of the two possible ON etyma of **ʒette** (B2) (cp. OIcel *játta*), whose history presents various difficulties, however; see that entry.

(c) VAN /ðl/ > /ll/

---

[308] And for possible evidence of OE (and hence WGmc) forms in /g/ see the discussion at the entry.

[309] See also Ralph (2002: 714, 715–16).

[310] For general accounts of OE consonant assimilation, see Campbell (§§480–5) and Hogg (§§7.88–92).

[311] For the ON change see Noreen (§268.2) and Br-N. (§253).

[312] On this assimilation see Bj. (173–4), Noreen (§267; 1904: §233 Anm. 2), Br-N. (§255), Ralph (14), and further Kolb (1962), Roe (1967). Kolb argues that ME forms which preserve [xt], such as the *-ght-* by-forms of **attle**, reflect loans made from ON earlier than those in [t], before the assimilation had taken place; thus also Bj. (173–4), and similarly Gordon (§233), McGee (521–2), who think that ME *aghtel-* represents an OEN form as opposed to an OWN variant with assimilation). But Roe suggests that ON assimilated [t(t)] was a pre-aspirated cluster, which would still have been perceptible as [xt] by English speakers (and see also the discussion at Dance 2003: 153–4).

This assimilation must be assumed behind **melle** (A1*) (and for the presence of VAN /ð/ here see also §7 above).[313]

§10.1.2. Progressive assimilation

(a) VAN /lR/ > /ll/

This change, in which the VAN reflex of PGmc */z/ by VL assimilates to preceding /l/, is now agreed as present in the etymon of **felle** (A1).[314]

(b) VAN /lθ/ > /ll/

This assimilation lies behind ME /l/ in **wylle** (**wylsum, wylt**) (A1*).[315]

For the wide range of other ON assimilatory changes posited in supposed etyma for *Gaw* items, see further §10.4 below.

§10.2. Dissimilation

The only clear example of ON dissimilation in the *Gaw* material is the change /mn/ > /fn/ which lies behind **neuen** (A1*).[316]

A dissimilatory change /n ... n/ > /ð ... n/ is often assumed to have occurred in the ON etyma of **heþen** (B1) and **wheþen** (B1), but there are other possible sources for the ON words; see the entry at **heþen**.

§10.3. Other changes to consonant clusters

§10.3.1. VAN /ðð/ > /dd/

This characteristically ON change must be understood in conjunction with syncope, which caused two /ð/ to stand next to one another, and with the absence of *i*-mutation in a wk. 1 v. with a light root syllable in the case of **stad** (A1*) (see §§6.2, 7 above).[317] An ON /dd/ cluster < /ðð/ also occurs in the likely ON etymon of **rad** (B2), but in this case ME /d/ is not a secure test of loan; see the entry.

§10.3.2. VAN initial /wl/ > /l/ (and /wr/ > /r/)

(i) PGmc */w/ is lost in VAN before /l/ (and sometimes before /r/), giving ME /l/ (and /r/) (spelt <l>, <r>); (ii) but remains in OE, giving ME /wl/ (and /wr/) (spelt <wl>, <wr>).

---

[313] See Noreen (§268.4), Br-N. (§252). This is also one of the several possible assimilatory changes suggested for the ON etymon of **ille** (B1).

[314] See Noreen (§277), Br-N. (§258) and the discussion at the entry. Notice that I employ the (non-IPA) symbol '/R/' here as a convenient way of representing the VAN reflex of PGmc */z/.

[315] See Noreen (§275), Br-N. (§257), Ralph (2002: 714); and on the OE development of PGmc */lθ/ > /ld/ (as in the cognate *wilde*) see Campbell (§414), Luick (§635.2) and Hogg (§4.18).

[316] On this change see Bj. (176), Noreen (§225), Heusler §154, Br-N. (§241) and Ralph (2002: 716).

[317] See Noreen (§23.1(a)), Br-N. (§234(a)) and Gordon (§66).

Bj. (177–80), Wright & Wright (§172) and SPS (§2.2.2.5).
(i) Noreen (§§235.1(b, c), 288), Heusler (§§138.1, 138.3), Br-N. (§§264.2), Gordon (§63), Voyles (1992: §5.1.6); Luick (§700.7(b)) and Jordan-Crook (§162 Rem. 1).

Remarks

The change /wl/ > /l/ seems to have taken place across ON during the Viking Age. It is generally agreed to lie behind the etymon of **layt** (A1*).

   The equivalent loss of /w/ before /r/ was more restricted, occurring in all ON dialects only when a rounded vowel followed; later in the Viking Age it was extended to all instances of /wr/, but mainly in OWN dialects only.[318] There are no indisputable instances in the *Gaw* material. Most frequently claimed in recent scholarship is **rotez** (B1), but there remain grounds for uncertainty. Etyma in PGmc */wr/ have also been suggested for one or more possible sources of the following words, but all present difficulties of one sort or another:[319]

   rak DD2
   rake DD1
   rayke A1
   ronkled B1

§10.4.   Other changes to consonant clusters, of uncertain relevance

A number of other changes to consonant clusters, usually assimilations and similar articulatory simplifications, appear in ON etyma suggested for items in the *Gaw* material; but the etymologies concerned are all problematic, and none of these changes can be used as a test of loan. These words are noted here for convenience; in each case, see the entries concerned for references and discussion.

(a) ON (usually OWN) assimilation of /nt/ > /tt/

   hitte B2
   sprit D1

(b) ON (usually OWN) assimilation of /nk/ > /kk/

   rokked D1

---

[318] See further Kluge (1891: 790; 1901a: 939), citing Jessen (1871: 27), who notices that initial /v/ is retained before /r/ in the modern Scand languages in Denmark, Sweden and much of southern Norway, but was lost in Iceland and western Norway (prob. during the ninth and tenth centuries); and also Bj. DP (22–3) and Ralph (2002: 716). Smith's claim in *EPNE* s.v. *vrá, rá* that initial /w/ 'is always retained in ME in the Danelaw' is overly confident.

[319] **Rayke** is nonetheless guaranteed as a Type A by its vocalism (§1).

(c) ON (usually OWN) assimilation of /mp/ > /pp/

staf(-ful) D1

(d) ON assimilation of /nθ/ > /nn/

mynne (v.) D1

(e) ON loss of /ð/ before /n/[320]

grayn A1

(f) ON assimilation of /nð/ > /nn/

spenne(-fote) D2

(g) ON assimilation of /nnR/ > /nn/

mynne (adj.) C1

(h) ON assimilation of /rn/ > /nn/

spenne(-fote) D2

(i) ON assimilation of PGmc */zn/ (> /Rn/) > /nn/[321]

twynne (adj., v.) C1
twynnen D2
þrynne B1

(j) ON /ft/ > /pt/

happe D1

(k) ON assimilation of /θs/ (> /ss/) > /s/

rous D1

(l) ON /θl/ > /l/ (with compensatory lengthening of preceding vowel)

mele C2

(m) ON /hl/ > /l/ (with compensatory lengthening of preceding vowel)

wyles, wyly, biwyled D1
wylyde D2

(n) ON /rf/ > /rr/

wharred B1

(o) ON (esp. OEN?) /rfl/ > /rl/

whyrlande C2

---

[320] **Grayn** is nonetheless guaranteed as a Type A by its vocalism (§1).

[321] An (implausible) change of ON /hn/ > /nn/ has also been suggested for **þrynne**; see the entry.

(p) Other (lexically specific) cluster simplifications

neked D1

And notice also **ille** (adv., n.) (B1), the /ll/ cluster in the ON etymon of which has been explained by recourse to a variety of different assimilatory changes (see the entry).

§11.   Other losses of consonants in VAN

§11.1.   VAN final /m/

(i) PGmc */m/ which had come to stand in final position was lost in VAN (perh. via /n/), with compensatory lengthening of the preceding vowel; (ii) but was (usually) retained in OE, giving ME /m/ (spelt <m>).

Bj. (100–1), SPS (§2.2.2.6) and Durkin (§10.2.8).
(i) Noreen (§§122, 298.1), Heusler (§§89, 152), Br-N. (§§111.1, 268 Anm. 5, 321), Gordon (§69) and Jordan-Crook (§169 Rem).
(ii) Wright & Wright (§§258–9) and Jordan-Crook (§169)

Remarks

The loss of /m/ in **fro** (prep., conj.) (A1*) is generally regarded as diagnostic of borrowing from ON. (The native loss of nasals in final, unstressed position has sometimes been regarded as a possible source of doubt, here, but an endogenous change is very unlikely to lie behind this word.)[322]

§11.2.   VAN medial /h/

(i) PGmc */x/ was lost in VAN in medial position (inc. stem-finally) in most environments, inc. before most consonants (except before /s/, and between a vowel and /t/); (ii) but it was retained more widely in OE (being lost medially only between voiced sounds), giving ME [x] (spelt <ȝ> in the *Gaw*-manuscript).

Bj. (181).
(i) Noreen (§230), Br-N. (§273), Gordon (§64) and Voyles (1992: §5.1.4).
(ii) Campbell (§§461–6), Luick (§§656–7), Hogg (§§7.45–51), Ringe-Taylor (§§6.9.1, 6.9.3), Wright & Wright (§307), Jordan-Crook (§§196–8), GDS (§54 (a)) and TGD (136).

Remarks

Loss of PGmc */x/ can only be accounted for by loan from ON in **(ouer)þwert** (A3*); cp. OE *þweorh* with OIcel *þver-r*.

---

[322] See the discussion at the entry. On final nasal loss in OE, esp. Nhb, see e.g. Campbell (§§472–3), Hogg (§§7.98–100) and further CONE ((FND)).

The same ON etymon has also been suggested for *þwarte(-knot) (D2), but in this case its presence is debatable.

VAN loss of /h/ stem-finally (prob. not word-finally until later)[323] is also present in the ON etymon of **wro** (A1), and in one of two possible ON sources of **þro** (adj., adv., **þroly**) (A1). Loss of /h/ can prob. be treated as a secure test of loan only in the case of **þro, þroly**; see the discussions at these entries. Both items are nonetheless guaranteed by other features (see §§6.1, 12.3).

§12.   Other consonant changes, of uncertain relevance

§12.1.   Metathesis, esp. of /r/ plus vowel

(i) A PGmc sequence (usually /r/ + vowel) generally remains in ON; (ii) but there is a tendency for metathesis (esp. > vowel + /r/) in OE.

Bj. (181–5) and SPS (§2.2.2.4).
(i) Noreen (§315; 1904: §§337.12, 339.2), Br-N. (§346); Luick (§700.5).
(ii) Campbell (§§155, 193, 459), Luick (§693), Hogg (§§7.93–7), Ringe-Taylor (§6.10.2), CONE ((RM)), Wright & Wright (§244) and Jordan-Crook (§165).

Remarks

Metathesis of /r/ + vowel is unusual in the Scand languages (though is occasionally to be found, esp. in unstressed positions).[324] It is much more common in OE, esp. when the following consonant is a dental (inc. /n/), but far from systematic; by-forms of the same root are frequently found with and without metathesis in OE.[325] Accordingly, the absence of metathesis of /r/ + vowel can never be regarded as a secure test of loan, even if it is often highly suggestive of ON input.[326]

It is a factor in the following *Gaw* items:

brenne C2
bruny C2
brusten C2
gres C1
renne C2

Other types of metathesis are still more sporadic in OE, but the absence of a change /sp/ > /ps/ has been suggested as evidence for ON input in the case of **haspe** (n., v.) (C2).

---

[323] See Bj. (181) and the discussion at **þoȝ**.
[324] And see also the discussion at **rasse**.
[325] See also esp. Stanley (1952–3) and Hogg (1977).
[326] See also Dance (2003: 84).

§12.2.   Loss of VAN /w/ before rounded vowels

(i) PGmc /w/ was lost before rounded vowels in VAN; (ii) but it was retained in OE, giving ME /w/ (*Gaw* <w>).

Bj. (177–80), Wright & Wright (§172) and SPS (§2.2.2.5).
(i) Noreen (§235.1(a)), Heusler (§138.2), Br-N. (§264.1), Gordon (§63), Voyles (1992: §5.1.6) and Luick (§700.7(b)).
(ii) Jordan-Crook (§§162–3).

Remarks

VAN /w/ was regularly lost in this position, and hence its absence in ME words which should show PGmc /w/ is in principle a good test of loan from ON.[327] It is potentially applicable, however, only in the two following *Gaw* items, neither of which can be conclusively demonstrated to show input from an etymon in /w/:

> **irked** D1
> **sete** (adj.) C3

§12.3.   Loss of VAN /w/ in medial position (with compensatory lengthening of preceding vowel)

(i) PGmc /w/ was often lost medially in VAN; (ii) but it was retained in OE, or retained long enough to affect the preceding sound in (then) vowel-final stems in distinctive ways.

(i) Noreen (§§80.2, 123), Br-N. (§§70.1, 111.2, 264.6) and Gordon (§63).
(ii) Campbell (§653.1), Hogg (§§3.19(2), 7.72–3) and Jordan-Crook (§162).

The majority of etymological authorities derive **þro** (adj., adv., **þroly**) (A1) from PGmc **þrawa-*, and in that case the fate of /w/ is a decisive test of ON input: in OE adjectives of this shape, we should expect PGmc */aw/ to develop into a stem-final diphthong (eventually > /æːɑ/), giving OE **þrēa* or **þrēaw* (with restored /w/; cp. PGmc **hrawa-* > OE *hrēaw* 'raw').[328] In the case of **þro** there is the possibility of input from a different ON etymon, however, meaning that this criterion cannot be used definitively to argue for a Scand origin; but the alternative etymology is also guaranteed by formal tests (see entry, and §§6.1, 11.2 above).

Medial loss of /w/ also probably occurred in a suggested (but not very compelling) ON source for **glyʒt** (D1).

---

[327] And see further Nielsen (2000: 257).

[328] See further esp. Campbell (§653.1), Hogg-Fulk (§4.40) and Ringe-Taylor (§6.1.2 at 172–3).

§12.4.   Absence of WGmc consonant gemination in VAN

(i) PGmc single consonants (other than /g/ and /k/) remained single in VAN when following a short vowel and preceding a /j/; (ii) but (with the exception of /r/) these consonants were geminated in WGmc (inc. OE) in this environment.

(i) Noreen (§279.1), Br-N. (§274.1) and Gordon (§74).
(ii) Campbell (§§407–8), Luick (§631), Hogg (§§4.11–14) and CONE ((WGG)).

The only possible item in the *Gaw* corpus where this criterion might apply is **byled** (D2), if < ON *bylja* (contrast hypothetical OE *byllan, < PGmc *buljan-), and provided we assume that the vowel of the *Gaw* form has been lengthened (in an open syllable in ME); but it is open to a number of other explanations.

2.2.2.   *Morphological features*

§13.   VAN inflexional -*r*

§13.1.   VAN nom. sg. -*r* < PGmc *-*z*

(i) VAN retained -*r* (i.e. -*R*, rhotacized < PGmc *-*z*) as the nom. sg. ending of masc. *a*-stem (*wa*-, *ja*-stem), *i*-stem and *u*-stem nouns and str. adjectives, giving ME /(ə)r/ (spelt <-(e)r> in *Gaw*); (ii) but OE had lost this ending.

Prokosch (1939: §§79b, 80, 90a), Voyles (1992: 228–9, 239–40), Ringe (2006: 269–80, 281–3) and Fulk (2018: §§7.7–12, 7.19–21, 7.24–5, 9.2–6).
(i) Noreen (§§356–8, 364–5, 367–8, 370–1, 385–9, 393–7, 425–7, 430–1), Heusler (§§198–200, 202–7, 216, 221–2, 270), Br-N. (§§429.1, 430.1, 432–5, 454.1, 460.1, 461.1, 512.1, 516.1) and Gordon (§§80–2, 87–9, 96).
(ii) Campbell (§§571, 640), Hogg-Fulk (§§2.6, 2.8, 2.13–14, 4.10, 4.13), Ringe-Taylor (§3.1.1) and CONE ((FZD)).

Remarks

Despite the doubts raised by Bj. (see the entry), the -*er* ending of **haȝer** (A2*) can safely be treated as diagnostic of ON input.
   But the endings of the following are not reliable evidence on their own for loan from ON, for the reasons discussed in the entries:

> **anger** C1
> **weterly** C1

§13.2.   VAN gen. sg. *-r* < PGmc *-z

(i) VAN retained *-r* (i.e. *-R*, rhotacized < PGmc *-z*) as the gen. sg. ending of *ō*-stem (*jō-* and *wō*-stem), many *i-* and *u*-stem and (esp. fem.) athematic nouns and several *a*-stem (*ja-* and *wa*-stem) nouns, and the gen. sg. fem. of str. adjectives, giving ME /(ə)r/ (spelt <-(e)r> in *Gaw*); (ii) but this ending did not occur in OE.

Prokosch (1939: §§79d, 80–3), Voyles (1992: 228–33), Ringe (2006: 269–80) and Fulk (2018: §§7.7–25, 7.27–8, 9.2–6).
(i) Noreen (§§358.2, 365, 367, 373–98, 412–14, 416–18, 425–7, 430–1), Heusler (§§201, 209, 213, 216, 217a, 219, 221–2, 243–5, 269–70, 272), Br-N. (§§445.4, 446.4, 454.4, 455.4, 457.4, 458.4, 460.4, 461.4, 465.4, 513.4, 517.4) and Gordon (§§83–9, 96)
(ii) Campbell (§571), Hogg-Fulk (§§2.6 (esp. n. 4), 2.8, 2.13–14) and Ringe-Taylor (§3.1.1).

Remarks

There are no unimpeachable examples of this feature in the *Gaw* material. But, if it shows input from the ON adv. represented by OIcel *einkar*, then **enker(-grene)** (D1) contains ON gen. sg. *-r*.

§13.3.   VAN dat. sg. pron. *-r* < PGmc *-z*

(i) VAN retained *-r* (i.e. *-R*, rhotacized < PGmc *-z*) as the dat. sg. of the 1, 2 and reflex. pers. pron., giving ME /(ə)r/ (spelt <-(e)r> in *Gaw*); (ii) but OE had lost this ending.

Prokosch (1939: §98), Voyles (1992: 252), Ringe (2006: 290–1), Fulk (2018: §§8.2–4).
(i) Noreen (§§464–5), Heusler (§249), Br-N. (§565) and Gordon (§§108–9).
(ii) Campbell (§701), Hogg-Fulk (§§5.23–5, 5.39) and Ringe-Taylor (§3.3.1).

Remarks

ON pronominal dat. sg. *-r* clearly lies behind the *-r* of **sere** (adv., adj., **serlepes**) (A2).

§13.4.   VAN adv. comp. *-r* < PGmc *-z*

(i) VAN retained *-r* (i.e. *-R*, rhotacized < PGmc *-z*) as the comp. ending on some adverbs (< PGmc *-iz*), giving ME /(ə)r/ (spelt <-(e)r> in *Gaw*); (ii) but OE had lost this ending.

Fulk (2018: §11.3).
(i) Noreen (§442), Heusler (§289) and Br-N. (§§536, 538).
(ii) Campbell (§673) and Hogg-Fulk (§4.78).

This adv. comp. ending, inherited from PGmc *-iz, is in principle char-acteristic of ON,[329] and thus **helder** (C1) is very likely to show ON input. But it is in practice difficult to rule out the presence of native morphemic material in this word (inc. ME comp. -er), and so it cannot strictly be treated as a Type A.

§14.   VAN inflexional -t

(i) VAN had -t as the nom. and acc. str. neut. adj. ending, and this was also used to form adverbs on adjectives, giving ME /t/ (spelt <t>); (ii) but this ending did not occur (on adjectives and adverbs) in OE.

Prokosch (1939: §90(a)), Voyles (1992: 239–40), Ringe (2006: 281–3) and Fulk (2018: §§9.2–6).
(i) Noreen (§425), Heusler (§§269–72), Br-N. (§§514, 518) and Gordon (§96, 149(iii).
(ii) Campbell (§640), Hogg-Fulk (§§4.10, 4.13) and Ringe-Taylor (§4.2.3).

Remarks

The presence of a /t/ in each of the following seems to reflect ON neut./adv. -t, and cannot reasonably be explained in any other way.[330] All have therefore been accepted as Type A.

> **(ouer)þwert** A3*
> **snart** A2*
> **tite (as-tit)** A3*
> **wyȝt** (adj., ?adv./adj., **wyȝtly**) A2*

Another very plausible instance is **wont** (n.); but I have recorded this word as a Type C1 rather than a Type A owing to the possibility of derivation (or influence) from the related v. (as in **wont** v.), where the -t has a different source.[331]
Notice also **gart** (A1*), whose -t could conceivably represent ON neut. -t but cannot in this case be distinguished from the normal ME wk. pp. ending -t.
*Þwarte(-knot) (D2) is altogether more problematic.

§15.   VAN middle voice -sk

(i) VAN developed a middle voice ending in -sk in the 2 and 3 sg. and 3 pl. (< the PGmc acc. sg. reflex. pron., with contraction via syncope),[332] giving ME /sk/

---

[329] And see further Sturtevant (1931).

[330] In spite of Lass's concerns (1997: 203; 2007: 18), neut. -t is not known in WGmc (except as part of the stem of the demonstrative and interrogative pronouns, as in OE hwæ-t, þæ-t, from which it seems extremely unlikely to have been transferred to the adj. and adv. forms here).

[331] For derivations on PGmc *sner- with -t suffix, where the case seems to me to be slightly different, see **snart** and the discussion there.

[332] Notice that some dialects of ON grammaticalized a variant in -s formed with the dat. sg. sér.

(spelt <sk>); (ii) but this ending, and the medio-passive category which it marked, did not appear in OE.

(i) Noreen (§§542–6), Heusler (§§356–63), Br-N. (§§911–43) and Gordon (§§125, 170).

This feature lies behind the -*sk* of **busk** (v.) (A2*). It has also been proposed to account for the form of **fyskez** (D1), but there are several alternative etymologies for this word.

3

TYPE B

Words classified under this head and in the following section (Type C) are those for which systematic, formal evidence of the sort that distinguishes Type A is not available (or, at least, cannot definitively be demonstrated); but for which a readily identifiable form-source, usually in Gmc, can be generally agreed.[333] For items in **Type B**, the Gmc root is *not* represented in (early) OE,[334] but *is* represented in ON (and neither is there any unambiguous form-source in a third language, like Anglo-Fr).[335] ON input has therefore been proposed to account for the ME word.

It seems helpful to distinguish two sub-types:

> **B1**, when there is no clear evidence for forms derived on the same root anywhere else in Gmc;

> **B2**, when forms derived on the same root are clearly identifiable in Go and/or the continental WGmc languages (but not in early OE).

On the notion of 'the same root' adopted in this book, see the Introductory Remarks (at p. 48) above. In summary, for a word to qualify as derived on 'the same root' as another given Gmc word, there needs to be a clear derivational relationship between the two; this can include derivation on one of the regular Ablaut grades of a known (or robustly hypothesized) PGmc str. v. (but does not usually extend to by-forms of roots whose relationship cannot so clearly be posited).

In practice, many of the stems grouped under **B1** have obscure or difficult ulterior etymologies (see under 'Further remarks' below). In several cases, the proposed ON etymon has been connected to words in other Gmc languages, but this relationship is not clearly demonstrable or generally accepted; see the discussions under **craue**, **glam**, **gre-houndez**, **heþen**, **ille**, **kay**, **nirt**, **rotez**, **sparþe**, **þrynne**, **þryue**, **vgly**, **wharred** and **wheþen**. In

---

[333] In the case of words with obscure or debated ulterior etymologies (see under Further Remarks below), we cannot necessarily identify precisely how that source would have looked. But we can always, at least, talk in terms of 'the PGmc etymon of ON *x*' and its attested Gmc cognates – e.g. the PGmc etymon of ON *illr*, whatever that might have been. Contrast items of Type D, where a (generally agreed) specifiable form-source like this is not available.

[334] For what counts in practice as 'early OE', see the Introductory Remarks at pp. 37–8 above. There is, naturally, considerable room for disagreement as to whether forms attested in later OE represent native cognates of the potential ON loan, or early instances of such a loan itself. Such cases will always be discussed in the Etymology and/or Attestation sections of my entries. In Type B, notice in particular the remarks for **bole**, **droupyng**, **croked**, **ȝette**.

[335] I have included **hale (wel-haled)** under B2, even though it is likely that **hale** was loaned into ME via Fr, since Fr is not the ulterior or unambiguous source.

some cases, several possible origins and therefore known relatives for the ON word have been theorized (the most debated is probably **ille**); in others, there may be a near-consensus as to ulterior etymology in recent work, but problems remain with demonstrating the link to other branches of Gmc (e.g. **rotez**).[336] In addition, there is a handful of items which do seem to be *related* to similar roots known in Go and/or WGmc, but where the derivational relationship between the two is not clear enough to meet the definition of 'the same root' given above. For the sake of consistency, I have therefore filed **croked, mekely, muged, rad** and **swange** under B1.[337]

The broader etymology of some of the words in **B2** can also be hard to make out. In some cases (e.g. **hitte**), there is nonetheless a clear relationship with cognate forms in other Gmc languages (even if not in early OE). A few items, viz. **droupyng, hale (wel-haled)** and **lowande**, may be connected to roots attested in OE, but are not clearly related derivationally; by the same principles adhered to above, these have therefore been classed as B2 (rather than under Type C).[338] The various problems posed by the etymology of **ӡette** mean that it, too, is best treated under B2.

3.1. SUMMARY LISTS

Forty-nine stems belong to Type B, nine of which contain one or more sub-entries, giving a total of sixty-two different lexical items.

Category B1 comprises twenty-one stems, two with sub-entries; there are twenty-six distinct lexical items.

70. **craue**; v.; 'to claim, ask for, crave, beg' [BB1]
71. **croked**; adj.; 'crooked, astray' [BB1b]
72. **donkande**; v. (pres. ptcp.); 'moistening' [BB1c]
73. **glam**; n.; 'din, noise of merrymaking' [BB1c]
74. **gre-houndez**; n. (pl.); 'greyhounds' [BBB1]
75. **heþen**; adv.; 'hence, away' [B1c]
76a. **ille**; n.; 'harm, ill-treatment' (in *tas to ille* 'take amiss') [B1c]
76b. **ille**; adv.; 'ill, badly' [B1c]

---

[336] See also the remarks under 'Germanic distribution' below.

[337] For **croked**, there is a likely connection by Ablaut to OHG *kracko*, and perh. also (though this is not generally assumed) to OE *crycc*. The root of **mekely** seems to be in Ablaut relationship with PGmc *mūk-* as in LG *muck*, etc. OFris *smūgen* apparently shows a by-form in *s-* of the root of **muged**. The likely ON etymon of **rad** seems ult. to be an Ablaut variant of PGmc *hrad-* as in OE *hræd*, etc. And the root of **swange** looks like a by-form of PGmc *swank-*, as in MLG *swank*, OE *swancor*. See the entries concerned for further discussion.

[338] The source of **droupyng** seems to be a root-variant of PGmc *dreup-*, as in OE *drēopan*. Similarly, **hale (wel-haled)** is prob. related by Ablaut to the root of OE *geholian*; and **lowande** to OE *līeg*. See the entries for details.

77. **kay**; adj.; 'left' [B1c]
78. **mekely**; adv.; 'humbly' [B1]
79. **muged**; v. (pret. sg.); 'drizzled, was damp' [BB1c]
80. **nirt**; n.; 'slight cut' [BB1c]
81. **rad**; adj.; 'afraid' [B1c]
82. **ronkled**; v. (pp.)/adj.; 'wrinkled' [BB1c]
83. **rotez**; n. (pl.); 'roots' [B1]
84. **sparþe**; n.; 'battle-axe' [B1]
85. **swange**; n.; 'middle, waist' [B1c]
86. **þrynne**; adj.; 'three(fold)' [B1c]
87a. **þryue**; v.; 'to thrive' [B1]
87b. **þryuande**; adj. (pres. ptcp.); 'abundant, hearty' [B1c]
87c. **þryuandely**; adv.; 'abundantly, heartily' [B1c]
87d. **vnþryuande**; adj. (pres. ptcp.); 'unworthy, ignoble' [B1c]
87e. **þryuen**; adj./v. (pp.); 'fair' [B1c]
88. **vgly**; adj.; 'gruesome, threatening, evil-looking' [B1c]
89. **wharred**; v. (pret. sg.); 'whirred' [BBB1c]
90. **wheþen**; adv.; 'whence; from wherever' [B1c]

Category B2 consists of twenty-eight stems, seven of which have sub-entries; there are thirty-six lexical items altogether.

91. **bole**; n.; 'tree trunk' [BB2ac]
92. **cakled**; v. (pp.); 'cackled' [BBB2a]
93. **dok**; n.; 'tail' or perh. 'trimmed hair (of tail, etc.)' [B2]
94. **droupyng**; vbl. n.; 'torpor, troubled sleep' [BBB2ac]
95a. **gate**; n.; 'way, road' [B2abc]
95b. **algate**; adv.; 'at any rate' [B2]
96a. **glent**; v. (pret.); 'glanced, flinched, sprang; glinted; looked' [BB2ac]
96b. **glent**; n.; 'glance' [BB2c]
97. **ȝaule**; v.; 'to yowl, howl' [BB2ac]
98. **ȝette**; v.; 'to grant' [B2ac]
99a. **hale**; v.; 'to draw; loose (from bow); rise, come, go, pass' [BBB2a]
99b. **wel-haled**; v. (pp.)/adj.; 'pulled up properly, drawn tight' [BBB2a]
100. **hitte**; v.; 'to hit, smite; fall, drop to' [B2]
101. **hoo**; interj.; 'stop!' [BBB2a]
102. **knaged**; v. (pp.); 'fastened' [BBB2ac]
103. **knyf**; n.; 'knife' [BB2a]
104. **knorned**; adj./v. (pp.); 'rough, craggy' [BBB2a]
105. **lakked**; v. (pret. sg.); 'found fault with; (impers.) were at fault' [BBB2a]
106. **leggez**; n. (pl.); 'legs' [B2]
107. **lowande**; v. (pres. ptcp.); 'shining, brilliant' [B2ac]
108. **lurke**; v.; 'to lurk, lie low, ?lie snug' [BB2a]
109. **norne**; v.; 'to announce, propose; offer; urge, press' [BB2ac]

110a. **rapes**; v.; 'hastens, hurries (reflex.)' [B2a]
110b. **rapely**; adv.; 'hastily, quickly' [B2a]
111. **ryue**; v.; 'to rip, cut (open)' [B2a]
112. **slentyng**; vbl. n.; 'slanting flight, shooting', or perh. 'sleet'? [BB2]
113. **snyrt**; v. (pret. sg.); 'snicked, cut lightly' [BB2c]
114. **sprent**; v. (pret. sg.); 'leapt' [BB2c]
115. **stor**; adj.; 'mighty; strong, severe' [BB2abc]
116a. **take**; v.; 'to take, accept, receive; capture; detect; acquire; assign; commit' (and various idiomatic phrases) [B2]
116b. **ouertake**; v.; ?'to regain' [B2]
116c. **vndertake**; v.; 'to take in, perceive' [B2]
117a. **tryst**; v.; 'to believe, be sure' [BBB2]
117b. **trystyly**; adv.; 'faithfully' [BBB2]
118a. **wale**; v.; 'to choose; take; find' [B2ac]
118b. **wale**; adj.; 'choice, excellent, fair' [B2ac]

As ever, items presented as sub-entries for Type B stems represent forms which could have been created in English via native derivational processes. But those for which exact Scand counterparts are attested, and which therefore might in principle have been modelled directly on ON forms, are: (B1) **ille** (adv.), **þryuen**; (B2) **glent** (n.), **rapely**, **vndertake**.[339]

3.2. FURTHER REMARKS

The ulterior etymology is more or less obscure for several Type B items, meaning that the tracking of filiations for these within the Gmc family and/or more broadly is difficult. Notice in particular: (B1) **craue**, **donkande**, **glam**, **grehoundez**, **ille** (n., adv.), **swange**, **þryue** (**þryuande**, **þryuandely**, **vnþryuande**, **þryuen**), **vgly**, **wharred**; (B2) **bole**, **gate** (**algate**), **ȝaule**, **hitte**, **leggez**, **lurke** (see the entries concerned, and the introductory comments above). The ON etymon proposed for **sparþe** is usually assumed to be a loan from Ir (perh. itself in turn < ON), but on the basis of rather weak evidence.

In a few instances, etymological uncertainties bear directly on the nature of the (possible) evidence for ON input in ME. Note especially the following:

> **heþen, wheþen** (B1): only if ON *heðan* and *hvaðan* are directly cognate with the WGmc forms as in OE *heonan*, *hwanon* is formal evidence applicable (§10.2), but other etymologies have been suggested (and see also §7);
> **rotez** (B1): most modern authorities tend to present ON *rót* as unproblematically connected to PGmc **wurt-iz* (as in OE *wyrt*) (§10.3.2), but it is difficult in fact to be sure about this relationship;

---

[339] Notice also **vgly**, for which a corresponding OIcel adv. form is attested; **ouertake** (OIcel has an equivalent nominal compound, and the v. phrase *taka yfir*); and **algate** (cp. the OIcel phrase *alla gǫtu*).

ӡette (B2): there are two possible ON inputs at issue here (viz. the near-homonyms *játa* and *játta*), the etymology of one of which is itself uncertain, meaning that formal tests are hard to apply (§10.1);

tryst (trystyly) (B2): a well-known crux, which looks very much as though it should be derived from ON, but the vocalism of known Scand words does not support this (§3).

Other items for which formal tests have been suggested, but where they are not clearly applicable or cannot be shown to be diagnostic (see Formal Criteria above under the §§ cited), are:

(B1)
ille (§10.4)
kay (§§1, 8.1)
rad (§§4, 10.3.1)
ronkled (§10.3.2)
sparþe (§7)
þrynne (§10.4)
wharred (§10.4)

(B2)
cakled (§8.1)
gate (algate) (§8.2)
ӡaule (§2)
hitte (§10.4)

Related but more minor issues of form, or sense, or interpretation in context in *Gaw* are various. But notice for instance: **kay** (the exact shape of the supposed ON etymon);[340] **muged** (the interpretation of the sense in context); **nirt** (the exact ON vocalism that lies behind the ME word); **ronkled** (*OED*'s suggestion of possible influence from OE *gewrinclod*); **dok** (the precise referent in context); **lurke** (the sense in context); **slentyng** (the meaning in context, which may favour derivation on an ON vbl. n. rather than simply from the ON v.); **snyrt** (the parsing of the word in context); **sprent** (*MED*'s suggestion of input also from the pret. of ME *sprengen*); **take** (various issues of textual interpretation, the explanation of some variant forms (esp. *tone*), and whether the phrase *tan on honde* might have come direct from ON); **wale** (v., adj.) (the exact ON etymon, whether an ON v. or n.). I have drawn attention to rarely cited issues in the case of **sparþe** (the dubious supposed origin in or via Ir), **swange** (that the connection often supposed with PGmc **swengwan-* cannot be taken for granted) and **dok** (*DOE* rightly problematizes the assumed OE cognate *-docce*), and mounted a new argument esp. for **gate (algate)** (that the initial velar in ME cannot in fact be taken as a secure test of loan).

---

[340] Note also that Bj. (mistakenly) took this word in *Gaw* to be a *hapax legomenon*, and tried to emend it away.

3.2.1. *Germanic distribution*

By definition, stems of Type B1 have no clearly demonstrable close Gmc relatives beyond the Scand languages (though in several cases some have been suggested).[341]

There are unambiguous cognates or near-cognates in continental WGmc in a recognizably similar sense for twenty stems of Type B2, which have been marked with an 'a'.[342] In some cases, the WGmc form is not precisely cognate, but it is clearly derived on the same root and I have judged it close enough to provide a good parallel to the ME word(s).[343] For some stems OE (near-)cognates have also been suggested, but these cannot be regarded as secure.[344]

Only **kay** has been supposed (by Gordon §233) to represent a borrowing of a form specific to a particular branch of ON (in this case OEN), but this claim is problematic (see the discussion at that entry).[345]

3.2.2. *Distribution in England*

There are only three stems in Type B where at least one of the sub-entries is more or less confined to the N/EM in the toponymic record; these items are

[341] Notice the following: **donkande**, where the sense 'marsh' of Du *donk* could conceivably show the influence of a form of the **dank-* root; **kay**, where an apparent Fris cognate *kei* is more usually assumed to be a loan from Dan; **nirt**, where again there is a possible Fris cognate, but this may be a loan from Scand; **ronkled**, where a relationship to Ger *Runkel-* has been proposed; **þrynne**, for which there may be WGmc cognates derived < PGmc **þrizn-*, but these (OE *ðrīn-* etc.) are usually explained as < **þrīhn-*; **þryue** (etc.), which is conceivably related to MnWFris *triuwe*; and **wharred**, where WGmc cognates exist if one accepts the theory that Dan *hvirre*, Sw *hvirra* are related to ON *hverfa*. See also the remarks on obscure or difficult etymologies of Type B in the headnote to this section.

[342] Note that this applies to **gate** but not its sub-derivation **algate**, for which there is no corresponding WGmc compound form; and to **glent** (v.) but not the related n., since no nominal derivation is attested in WGmc. For **ʒette**, both possible ON etyma (see the entry) have WGmc cognates.

[343] Thus **knaged, knorned, lowande, rapes (rapely), wale** (v., adj.), where the attested WGmc forms are cognate with the related n. or adj. (but where the latter could in any case be the ulterior etymon of the ME word(s)), and also **bole** (where the cognate WGmc n. is a different stem-derivation from that known in ON, but where either stem-type could in principle lie behind the ME word equally well). There are some other instances where there is a plausible etymological relationship to a recorded WGmc word, but where the sense or form of the WGmc (near-)cognate is somewhat more remote; thus **dok, hitte, slentyng, snyrt, sprent, take** (etc.), **tryst (trystyly)**. In these cases, the WGmc usage does not seem to me near enough to that known in Scand and English to provide a very close parallel, and I have therefore not labelled these words with an 'a'. There is also **leggez**, whose only known cognate is in Langobardic, a language which is often classed as WGmc but which is poorly attested and whose precise filiations remain debatable; see e.g. Hutterer (1999: 336–41), Falluomini (2015), with further references, and the remarks in Stiles (2013: 10) ('Langobardic may have been a West Germanic language, but it is too fragmentarily attested to play a part in these discussions'.). (And notice that Langobardic *lagi* exemplifies some of these difficulties, since it appears to show neither the *i*-mutation nor the consonant gemination one would expect in WGmc.) I have not regarded this as sufficient basis for an 'a' label.

[344] See esp. the entries for **dok, ʒette, lakked, rapes (rapely), ryue** (v.), **sprent, wale** (v., adj.). For late OE forms which have often been explained as early attestations of the (supposed) loan from ON, but which could in reality be native cognates, see also **bole, droupyng**.

[345] Notice also **ronkled**, which (if derived from ON) represents a form without OWN assimilation (but could therefore derive either from OEN, or from a variety of OWN before the assimilation took place there). And note that the closest Scand forms which have been compared to **wharred** (with medial cluster assimilation) are in Dan and Sw; and the only Scand analogues cited for **knorned** and **norne** are in Sw.

marked with a 'b'.[346] Two of these are also principally attested in the N/EM in the ME lexicon (on which see below), but **croked** is more widespread in general lexical use.

Twenty-eight Type B stems (15 B1, 13 B2) are marked with a 'c' in at least one sub-entry, i.e. they are principally attested to a greater or lesser extent in the N/EM in the lexical record.[347] 10 of these feature in Kaiser's (1937) list of 'northern' words.[348] Only six are unambiguously northern/eastern words or word groups which are entirely or almost entirely confined to this region throughout their recorded history: (B1) **rad, swange, þrynne**; (B2) **glent** (n.) [only], **sprent, wale** (v., adj.).[349] Of the remainder, **nirt** (B1) and **snyrt** (B2) are *hapax legomena* in *Gaw*,[350] and **norne** is found only in the *Gaw*-manuscript and *Erk*. **Muged** (B1) is recorded only here in ME, but attested again later mainly (but not solely) from the N/EM.[351] **Glam** and **knaged** are attested only rarely, and it is difficult to say much about their distributions.[352] **Heþen** (B1), **wheþen** (B1) and **ȝette** (B2) seem to have become restricted to the N/EM by late ME, but to have been more widely used earlier in their recorded histories.[353] **Gate** (B2; simplex n. only) is recorded mainly from N/EM texts, but is found more widely in the vocabulary of alliterative verse.[354] And ten stems have one or more sub-entries which are generally N/EM words throughout the ME period, but not entirely, having some attestations further afield which hint at wider usage: (B1) **ille** (n., adv.), **ronkled, þryuande/þryuandely/vnþryuande/þryuen** [only], **vgly**; (B2) **bole, droupyng, glent** (v.) [only], **ȝaule, lowande, stor**.[355]

---

[346] For the **gate** word-group there is toponymic evidence only for the simplex itself (95a.), and not for the compound **algate** (95b.). Notice also **bole**, where the picture of mainly N/EM distribution given by *EPNE* is complicated by *VEPN* (see the entry).

[347] Stems for which regional restriction is not true of all sub-entries are: the **þryue** word-group, where the v. **þryue** itself is widespread in ME, but the other members (the **þryuande**- words and **þryuen**) are more restricted; and the **gate** group, where the simplex n. is characteristically N/EM but the compound **algate** is widespread. Notice also that **glent** v. is more widely attested (though still favouring the N/EM) than **glent** n.

[348] These are: (B1) **heþen, ronkled, þrynne, vgly**; (B2) **droupyng, ȝette, rad, sprent, swange, wale** (v., adj.).

[349] Though notice the earliest (and the only OE) occurrence of **þrynne** in *LawIIIAtr*; that there is modern dial evidence for **sprent** also from Shropshire; and that **swange** is quite rarely attested throughout its history.

[350] Though cp. later Scots *nirt* and Northumberland dial *snirt*, which have somewhat different senses but which are plausibly reflexes of the same words as ME **nirt** and **snyrt** respectively (see entries). **Slentyng** (B2) is also recorded only from *Gaw* as a vbl. n., but the related v. is more widespread, and so I have not classed it as a 'c'.

[351] Notice also **dok** (B2), which is recorded only in *Gaw* in ME but is widespread in later English, and I have therefore not labelled it as 'c'.

[352] Though there are hints of wider distribution for **glam** in modern dial usage; see the entry.

[353] The same is perh. true of **kay** (B1), though its ME attestation history is not extensive. Notice also **slentyng** (B2), which is apparently restricted in modern dial usage but not before (and which I have therefore not classed as a 'c').

[354] **Donkande** is also primarily an alliterative poetic word in ME, albeit found in verse of N/EM origin only.

[355] The v. **þryue** itself is not regionally restricted in ME. **Droupyng** has been placed in this list on the basis of the distribution of the related v.; the vbl. n. itself is infrequently attested. Notice also **donkande**, and (esp.) its related adj. *dank*, which become more widespread after the ME period.

3.2.3. *Probability of ON input*

As will be evident from the above, the items grouped under Type B present a range of etymological characteristics and complications, which have a bearing on the argument for ON input into their development. When weighing the probability of that input, each word must of course be examined separately, and assessed based on all the evidence for Scandinavian origin summarized above and described in the entries. But there are some useful generalizations to be made by considering these items together as a group, and it is the aim of my loose 'probability markers' (B, BB, BBB) to facilitate this. These markers are (necessarily impressionistic) attempts to encapsulate the likelihood of ON input in each case, drawing on the quality of the evidence and the opinions of the authorities discussed in the entries. They may be defined as follows:

> B (22 stems)
> The case for ON input is very plausible. There is general agreement in the scholarship, often without exception.

> BB (17 stems)
> The case for ON input is reasonable, but alternative explanations seem about equally plausible. There is usually some disagreement in the scholarship.

> BBB (10 stems)
> The case for ON input is not strong (though it still cannot be dismissed out of hand). The word's history can usually be explained more plausibly by other means. There is some history in the scholarly tradition of attributing or at least suggesting ON input, but the weight of (especially recent) argument is against it, and/or the case for it is problematic in some fairly fundamental way.

As these figures show, the great majority of stems in Type B may (in my judgement) be argued to show some ON input with high or at least reasonable plausibility. But fewer than half have a *very* robust case. *Inter alia*, this reflects the fact that the absence of a Gmc root in (early) OE and its presence in ON is not necessarily enough in and of itself to provide a firm basis for argument for ON derivation, and to rule against other possible explanations – usually a native development which happens to be unattested in early OE.

The most plausible items, marked B1 or B2, are:

> B1
> **heþen**
> **ille** (n., adv.)
> **kay**
> **mekely**
> **rad**

rotez
sparþe
swange
þrynne
þryue (**þryuande, þryuandely, vnþryuande, þryuen**)
vgly
wheþen

B2
dok
gate (**algate**)
ʒette
hitte
leggez
lowande
rapes (**rapely**)
ryue
take (**ouertake, vndertake**)
wale (v., adj.)

The case for ON input is strongest, and almost always accepted, for those items whose supposed ON etymon is frequently attested and lexicalizes a commonly occurring concept. In these instances, the standard counter-argument (that the same root did in fact survive into OE, but that it failed to be attested in the surviving textual corpus) seems improbable. The evidence tends to be especially compelling for the B1 stems – since the ON counterpart is then a word characteristic of the Scand group, next to which there is nothing closely related in the other Gmc languages (which contrast obviously by lexicalizing the same field with a word certainly or possibly formed on a different root altogether). Twelve of the twenty-two stems in Type B1 belong here, and are marked with a single 'B'. The clearest instances are very distinctively Scand words for fundamental concepts, such as directional adverbs (**heþen, wheþen**; contrast WGmc forms with medial /n/ as in OE *heonan, hwanon*) and a core evaluative adj. (**ille** (n., adv.); contrast the typical WGmc root as in OE *yfel*). Several other B1s are characteristically Scand words for common ideas, i.e. **mekely, rad, rotez, swange, þryue** (etc.), **vgly**, and their ON origin attracts little or no disagreement in the etymological authorities. The case for **kay** also seems to me relatively robust, even if its exact ON etymon is uncertain; as does that for **sparþe**, which is best accounted for as a Hiberno-Norse development. The majority of these stems (nine out of twelve) are labelled with a 'c', and their regionally-restricted distribution in ME may be taken as supporting circumstantial evidence in favour of ON input.

By their nature, stems of Type B2 (where a formation on the same root is known elsewhere in Gmc) provide slightly fewer words quite so obviously 'typical' of the Scand languages. But there are still a number of important examples here (I have assigned a single 'B' marker to ten of the twenty-seven Type B2 stems). Several of these lexicalize very basic ideas, esp. the body-part word **leggez** (contrast OE *scanc*) and the basic action v. **take** (contrast OE *niman*); and the case also seems to me relatively strong for **gate (algate)**, **hitte**, **rapes (rapely)**, **ryue**, **wale** (v., adj.). I have also included in this set words for some less commonly occurring concepts, but where the ME and ON sense or usage are distinctively similar (more so than their recorded counterparts in the other WGmc languages); thus **dok, snyrt**. Again, all these items have long been treated as secure instances of ON input in the etymological authorities (though **dok** was not noticed by Bj.). Notice that six of these stems (**gate** [only], **ʒette**, **lowande**, **rapes (rapely)**, **ryue**, **wale** (v., adj.)) contain items labelled with an 'a' (see the discussion under 'Germanic distribution' above); but I have not taken the mere existence of a closely similar formation in WGmc as a barrier to accepting the likelihood of ON input in these cases, since it is otherwise so plausible. Four of the ten B2 stems are labelled 'c', and their distribution sometimes adds helpful additional weight to the claim of ON input; this is most notably true of **gate**, which was (and is) characteristic of the N/EM in place- and esp. street-names as well as in lexical usage.

The less and least plausible stems, marked BB1, BBB1 and BB2, BBB2, are these:

BB1
craue
croked
donkande
glam
muged
nirt
ronkled

BB2
bole
glent (v., n.)
ʒaule
knyf
lurke
norne
slentyng
snyrt
sprent
stor

BBB1
gre-houndez
wharred

BBB2
cakled
droupyng
hale (wel-haled)
hoo
knaged
knorned
lakked
tryst (trystyly)

As these lists show, the less compelling items are spread across Types B1 and B2, but are slightly more plentiful in B2 (ten and eight of the total of twenty-eight B2 stems are marked 'BB' and 'BBB' respectively, next to seven and two out of twenty-one B1 stems).

In general, the case for ON input tends to be less strong for items which lexicalize relatively uncommon concepts, and whose failure to be attested in (earlier) OE texts would, if they were really native words, occasion less surprise than those treated under the single 'B' category above. Stems with an arguably 'expressive' origin (i.e. 'sound-symbolic' or 'ideophonic' forma-tions) are very typical of this group, since it is especially easy to envisage them having been current in (colloquial) speech but escaping record in writing until ME.[356] **Wharred** and perhaps **glam** (which may at least ultimately be sound-symbolic in origin) are examples of Type B1, and an unattested native etymon seems especially likely when WGmc cognates are known, as they are for the B2s **cakled**, **ȝaule**, **hoo**, **knorned** and **norne**. **Hoo** (B2), an emphatic interj. which one can imagine being coined independently in ME and ON, is an especially unconvincing candidate for ON input. Words for very specific climatic conditions like **donkande** (B1), **muged** (B1) and **slentyng** (B2) have a similar profile.

In a few instances, the shapes of the ME stems make input from ON relatively implausible. In the case of **gre(-houndez)** (B1), **ȝaule** (B2) and **tryst (trystyly)** (B2), the phonology of one or more of the attested English forms does not correspond well to that of their supposed ON etyma (though sound-substitution has been invoked for **ȝaule**); and **craue** (B1) and its ON counterpart are different derivations on their Gmc root. The alternative to proposing ON input is usually an endogenous origin, but **hale (wel-haled)** (B2) is better explained as a loan via Fr (with the ON cognate apparently having been borrowed from MLG),[357] and **lakked** has sometimes been regarded as a loan from MLG.

---

[356] The classic account with reference to ME words is Smithers (1954), and for remarks on ME vocabulary see also Frankis (1991) and Smith (2000: 94–8). Notice Smithers's (1954: 91) suggestion that 'unrecorded OE antecedents may less dubiously be posited for ideophones than for most other types of word'. For fuller discussions (with references) see e.g. Marchand (1969: 397–428), Hock (1991: 287–92), Reay (2006) and Durkin (2009: 124–31).

[357] Fr input is also possible for **hoo** (B2).

When it comes to circumstantial evidence, the profiles of the 'BB' words are comparable to those marked with a single 'B'. Seven of the ten BB2 stems have an 'a' label (compare six out of ten B2s); and twelve out of seventeen 'BB' stems are flagged with a 'c' (five of seven BB1s, seven of ten BB2s; cp. thirteen out of twenty-two 'B' stems altogether). The existence of similar, cognate forms in the WGmc languages might be (and sometimes has explicitly been) taken to lower the probability of ON, as opposed to native, origin for these items; whereas a largely N/EM attestation in the medieval record could be (and, again, sometimes has been) assumed to raise the probability of ON input. (But notice that five BB2 stems have both 'a' and 'c' labels, contributing to the overall impression that the likelihood for this group is rather betwixt and between.) For the 'BBB' stems, however, the relative implausibility of the case is accompanied by an increased proportion of those labelled 'a' (seven out of eight BBB2 stems), and a decreased proportion of 'c' flags (three out of ten 'BBB' stems in total).

A few of the Type B items are generally derived from ON by the standard authorities, but have nonetheless seemed to me problematic enough to merit a 'BB' label (thus **glam**, **muged** (B1)). The vast majority of 'BB' and 'BBB' items, however, have been subject to at least some disagreement in the scholarship. A good index of this is difference of opinion between *OED* and *MED*, which is significant in the case of two B1 stems (**croked**, **donkande**) and nine B2s (**ȝaule**, **hoo**, **knyf**, **lakked**, **lurke**, **norne**, **sprent**, **stor**, **tryst** (**trystyly**)). In these cases, *MED* is somewhat more likely to favour ON input (for seven stems, next to just four where *OED* champions a Scand origin).[358] TG (D) and GDS also disagree in their summary labels for a number of stems: (B1) **wharred**, (B2) **cakled**, **hoo**, **norne**, **tryst** (**trystyly**).[359] Eight stems are not treated at all by Bj.: (B1) **nirt**; (B2) **hale**, **hoo**, **knorned**, **lakked**, **lurke**, **norne**, **sprent**. Six were often regarded as Norse derivations early in the scholarly

---

[358] For **croked**, *MED* goes no further than late OE; *OED* derives from ON. *OED* is not sure about the source of **donkande**, but *MED* (and most other authorities) look to ON. For **ȝaule**, *MED* derives from ON, whereas *OED* does not, and the same is true for **knyf** and **lurke**. *OED* regards **hoo** as native, but *MED* cites possible ON and Fr etyma. *MED* regards **lakked** as most likely to be native, but *OED* entertains ON input. *OED* labels **norne** as simply obscure, but *MED* follows subsequent orthodoxy by deriving from ON. In the case of both **sprent** and **stor**, *OED* derives from ON, but *MED* is more equivocal. For **tryst** (**trystyly**), *OED* prefers a native origin, but *MED* still seems to be holding out for at least some ON input. And note that there is more minor disagreement also regarding **nirt** (where the doubts expressed in the original *OED* entry have given way to more certainty about ON derivation in *MED* and *OED3*), **cakled** (where *OED* is not sure, but suggests native origin, and this is clearer in *MED*) and **knorned** (where the comparanda cited are different: *OED* refers to WGmc *knor*- words, but *MED* to ME *knarre*).

[359] Honours are about equal when it comes to preferring ON input: TG(D) do so on two occasions, GDS three times. TG(D) label **wharred** as native, but GDS compares Scand words. For **cakled**, TG (D) compare a Dan word, but GDS only Dutch. GDS derives **hoo** from ON, but TG(D) prefer a native origin. GDS follows *OED* in labelling **norne** as obscure, but TG(D) (like *MED*) derive from ON. GDS looks only to ON for the origin of **tryst** (**trystyly**), whereas TG(D) cite both OE and ON forms. Notice also the more minor differences in the case of **gre-houndez** (where only GDS gives the ON word as a comparison), **lakked** (TG(D) derive from LG, GDS offers a comparison only to LG) and **wale** (v.) (GDS derives via the ON n. *val*, TG(D) prefer to see the ON v. (pret. *valdi*) as the source).

tradition, but are now generally explained as native: (B1) **craue**, **gre-houndez**; (B2) **hale** (**wel-haled**), **knaged**, **knorned**, **tryst** (**trystyly**). Other items concerning whose ON pedigree doubts are often, but not always, expressed include (all B2s) **bole**, **droupyng**, **glent** (v., n.), **knyf**.[360]

---

[360] Concerns have been raised quite recently regarding **bole** by *VEPN* (on the basis of a late OE form not widely noticed). The English etymological tradition seems content with an ON origin for **droupyng**, but examination of late OE *drūpung* makes the case for a native etymon much stronger. Similarly, the English etymological authorities derive **glent** (v., n.) relatively unproblematically from ON, but Bj. is less convinced and the Scand etymologists tend to see the ME forms as cognate with rather than loans from ON. **Knyf** is a standard example of a Norse loan in the handbooks, but etymological discussions regard it as less secure (esp. on the basis of its plentiful WGmc cognates).

4

TYPE C

As for Type B above, items of Type C lack systematic, formal evidence of the sort that distinguishes Type A; but a readily identifiable form-source, usually in Gmc, can be generally agreed. For **Type C**, the Gmc root *is* already represented in (early) OE,[361] or alternatively (in a handful of instances) there is an unambiguous form-source in a third language, such as (Anglo-)Fr. But some aspect(s) of the form, sense or usage of the ME word in question are rare or unparalleled in OE (or the third language), and better paralleled in the Scand languages. Loan or influence from ON has therefore been proposed, more or less convincingly, to account for one or more of the following key features, which I distinguish as five sub-types:

C1 derivational form
C2 orthographic (phonological) form
C3 sense
C4 formation of compound or phrase
C5 frequency

Further discussion and exemplification of these categories will be found in the sections introducing each below. But they may be illustrated by some prototypical examples:

C1
Lofte (alofte): OE had the *i*-mutated *lyft* (prob. originally a fem. *i*-stem < PGmc **luft-i-z*); but ME *lofte* corresponds better to the derivational form shown by the ON n. represented by OIcel *loft* (*lopt*) (< a neut. *a*-stem PGmc **luft-a-n*).
Leme: OE had a n. *lēoma*, but no derived v. is attested; and so the occurrence of such a v. in ME has been attributed to input from ON, as in OIcel *ljóma*.

C2
Brenne: the metathesized OE forms descending from PGmc **brenn-*, **brann-* (OE *beornan, biernan, byrnan* (str.), *bærnan* (wk.)) are often regarded as less plausible sources for the ME *br-* variants than are the ON verbs represented by OIcel *brenna* (but the operation of metathesis in OE is not so regular that it can be regarded as a formal 'test' of loan of the kind treated under Type A1).

---

[361] For the definition of 'Gmc root' in use here, see the Introductory Remarks (at p. 48) above and the preliminary remarks to Type B. With regard to **busk** (n.), notice that an OE *busc* is not attested as such in texts from the (early) OE period, but its existence is normally assumed on the grounds of the place-name evidence; and I have followed that assumption here.

C3

Dreme: OE *drēam* is recorded only in the senses 'joy, bliss; sound, music', and so the meaning 'dream' in ME is usually explained as the result of influence from the ON n. represented by OIcel *draumr*.

C4

Boþe: an OE compound of *bā* + *þā* perhaps existed, but it is not attested as such in OE texts; and so ME *boþe* is often accounted for as a loan of, or a new compound created on the model of, the ON compounded form as seen in OIcel *báðir*.

Sake: the phrase *for . . . sake* 'for (someone's) sake' is not known in OE, and has often been explained as a loan-translation of the ON phrase represented by OIcel *fyrir (. . .) sakir*.

C5

Til: an early OE prep *til* is recorded, but it is confined to a handful of occurrences in early Nhb texts; it is therefore usual to interpret the rise of *til* in ME, where it appears with much greater frequency, with reference to at least some input (or 'reinforcement') from ON *til*.

Note that all items where the evidence for ON input depends upon derivational affixation have been treated together under sub-type C1, whether that affixation has to do with stem-formatives producing a different declensional or conjugational type (e.g. **bone, lofte, blende** (v.)) or with the presence (or occasionally absence) of affixes of other kinds (e.g. **draȝt, sware**), since it did not seem to me helpful to try to distinguish these categories taxonomically. Some scholars have attempted to differentiate between affixes proper (which clearly belong to derivational morphology) and 'affixoids', i.e. elements like PDE *over* which can function as either free morphemes or affixes (and which may therefore be classifiable as an aspect of compounding). But most recent work finds this distinction problematic, and tends to treat all affixation as a part of derivational morphology.[362]

The category label is prefixed by an 'F' to distinguish those instances where a word's form clearly cannot derive from OE, but when it belongs (ultimately or more recently) to a non-Gmc language, which could have been its direct source. This is the case for only ten items, viz. **(vmbe-)torne** (C1), **croun, tulk** (C2), **angardez, baret, breue, caryez, garysoun** (C3), **caple, cros** (C5).[363]

---

[362] For discussion, see e.g. Bauer et al. (2013: 340, 440–1) and Olsen (2014: 30–2, 36–7). But notice that I have assigned to **forlondez** the secondary label CC4 (as opposed to CC1) since, although OE *fore-* can function as a prefix when it is joined to verbs and (with an intensifying function) to adjectives, with nouns it seems to have its full lexical sense of 'before'; this construction is best understood as a compound, therefore.

[363] Note that this label is strictly reserved for items whose form-source is *not* represented in (early) OE. Words attested in early OE, even if they are not ultimately of Gmc origin, are not marked with an 'F' prefix; thus **silk**, for example, which is labelled simply CC2, and which could have developed from an OE starting-point without further external influence.

181 stems altogether belong to Type C, twenty-eight of which contain one or more sub-entries, giving a total of 219 different lexical items – so this is by some distance the most populous structural category in the present study. For all Type C items, a form-source in Gmc (or a third language) can be identified with reasonable security,[364] and the argument then concerns whether we need to adduce ON input in order to explain the particular development found in ME. When the form-source is Gmc, the proposed ON etymon is most often a Scand derivation on that same Gmc root; and the discussion therefore generally turns on whether the ME outcome could be the result of endogenous changes (to form, sense or whatever), or whether some influence has occurred from developments of the same root in the Scand branch of Gmc. But the putative ON etymon is not necessarily related to the main form-source in this way. This is most often to be expected with items of Type C3, where semantic influence may have occurred from an etymologically unconnected (but formally similar) ON word (see e.g. **sete, þrast, warþe**); but it is also found with the other sub-types (see e.g. **twynne** (etc.) (C1), **stryþþe, wela** (C2), **may** (C5)). It may also be noticed here that, ordinarily (for types C1 – C4), the ME form or sense or usage under discussion is simply unknown in early OE. But in a handful of cases it is (or might be) attested, but rarely; and the argument then is over whether that specific feature might have been reinforced by ON input. Thus for instance **lyndes** (C1; there is an apparent OE by-form without -*n*), **mele** (C2; OE forms in *mæl*- are attested in the pres. stem) and **(ȝeres-)ȝiftes** (C3; there is some evidence for the sense 'gift' in early OE).[365] In general terms, it is worth emphasizing the sheer variety in the evidence and arguments for ON input which feature even amongst items of the same sub-type, and one of the main purposes of the preambles to each section below is to illustrate and catalogue this.

Moreover, there is a handful of Type C items which I have marked with two category types, since in these cases both kinds of structural evidence make a significant contribution to the argument for ON input. There are nineteen of these stems, where one or more of the sub-entries has been given an additional summary label in brackets following the main category – e.g. 'C1 (C3)'. All these items appear only once in the catalogue in the usual way, being entered under the sub-type which in my view reflects the evidence for ON input which may be regarded as dominant (or, in some instances, which has been explicitly claimed by scholars as dominant), but with an 'extra' indicator showing the feature type which plays a

[364] Inevitably, several Type C items do give room for debate, including over how they should be interpreted in their *Gaw* contexts; but this disagreement is not so fundamental as to cast doubt on the identity of a basic form-source, which is generally agreed (and hence these items are not classified as Type D2; see the introductory remarks to Type D below). See for instance **forlondez, forne, sete, warþe**, where the case for ON input depends upon reading a particular (debatable) sense in *Gaw*, but where there is no serious problem in identifying the origin of the form (for **sete**, notice that the ME rhyme evidence strongly indicates a word containing PGmc $*/e:/^1$, as in the generally cited OE etymon). Sometimes the possible sources of additional input are themselves complex and debated (see e.g. **angardez**), but there remains a single form-source which most modern commentators agree on as the basis for the word.

[365] For some other items, the evidence that the required feature existed in OE is ambiguous; see e.g. **blende, bonk** (C1).

meaningful but more subsidiary role in the argument. Thus for instance **helder, dryftes, hapnest** and **wener**, which are all grouped under C1 with an additional (C3) label, because the primary evidence for Scand input comes from their derivational forms, but their meanings also figure significantly in the case;[366] or **dryȝe** (etc.), where the sense is the main criterion and the derivational form is a less striking part of the argument (given the probable existence of an OE *gedrēog*), and which is therefore a C3 (C1); or **forlondez**, which is filed under type C3 but with an additional C4 label, since the principal argument rests on the sense of the ON word, but the creation of the ME compound could itself have come about under Scand influence. I have tried to keep the application of these double labels to a minimum, and to restrict them to those items where both the marked features play a substantial and definable role in the etymological evidence.[367] Hence the mere attestation in OIcel of a phrase which is similar to one of the collocations recorded for an item in ME has not in itself been regarded as grounds to add an extra (C4) label, since there are in practice too many examples of these relatively minor pieces of supporting data to make it useful to signal them formally in this way.[368]

Because the nature of the case for ON input, and hence the characteristic arguments and issues involved, differ from sub-type to sub-type, the introduction to Type C which follows begins with separate sections for each of groups C1 to C5. These sections give lists and discussions of the typical profiles and further etymological difficulties which pertain in the case of each group, before turning to a summary of the probability with which ON input has been identified for members of this sub-type, and the ways in which the principal scholarly authorities have differed in their assessment of it. I then survey the circumstantial evidence of Gmc and English dialect distribution for Type C as a whole.

4.1. TYPE C1

4.1.1. *Summary list*

Category C1 comprises sixty-seven stems, nine with sub-entries; there are eighty distinct lexical items.

119a. **aghlich**; adj.; 'terrible' [C1]
119b. **aȝlez**; adj.; 'without fear' [C1]

---

[366] **Derf (deruely)** (C1) has the additional label (C3) because sense is a factor in *some* of the meanings recorded in *Gaw* ('doughty', etc.), but not in all.

[367] Note that **mon** has been recorded only as a Type C3. The spelling <mon> is in principle ambiguous, because the <o> could in theory be a spelling for ME /o/ (< the ON variant *man* which corresponds in form to the attested OE pres. 1/3 sg. *man* of *(ge)munan*); I have therefore avoided adding a (C2) sub-label, although there is no other clear evidence for a reflex of ON *man* in ME, and the *Gaw* spelling most probably does indicate the (distinctively ON) by-form in /u/.

[368] But notice that I have made an exception for **garysoun** (FCC3 (FCC4)), where the collocation with *golde* is one of the substantial pieces of evidence in favour of making the connection with ME *gersum* < ON.

120. **anger**; n.; 'harm' [C1]
121. **are**; adv.; 'before' [CC1]
122. **arwes**; n. (pl.); 'arrows' [CC1]
123. **blande**; v. (pp.); 'adorned' [CCC1c]
124. **blende**; v. (pret./pp.); 'mingled; streamed together' [CCC1c]
125. **blykke**; v.; 'to shine, gleam' [CCC1a]
126. **bolne**; v. (pres. pl.); 'to swell' [CC1c]
127. **bone**; n.; 'request, boon' [C1]
128. **bonk**; n.; 'hillside, slope; shore, bank' [C1abc]
129. **brent**; adj.; 'steep' [CC1c]
130. **calle**; v.; 'to call, shout, cry out (intrans.), crave, beg; call, name, summon (trans.)' [C1a (C5)]
131. **chymbled**; v. (pp.); 'bound, wrapped up' [CCC1c]
132. **cost**; n.; 'nature, quality; terms; manners, ways, disposition; condition, plight' [C1ac]
133. **deȝe**; v.; 'to die' [C1a]
134a. **derf**; adj.; 'doughty, stout; grievous, severe' [C1ac (C3)]
134b. **deruely**; adv.; 'boldly' [C1ac (C3)]
135. **draȝt**; n.; 'drawbridge' [CCC1a]
136. **dryftes**; n. (pl.); '(snow)drifts' [CC1a (CC3)]
137. **flat**; n.; 'plain' [C1bc]
138. **fonge**; v.; 'to take, receive, get; welcome, entertain; derive' [CCC1ac]
139. **frayn**; v.; 'to ask, inquire (of); make trial of' [CCC1c]
140. **froþe**; n.; 'froth' [C1]
141. **gyng**; n.; 'company' [CC1c]
142. **glemered**; v. (pret. pl.); 'gleamed' [CC1a]
143. **glyter**; v.; 'to glitter' [CC1a]
144. **gloue**; n.; 'gauntlet, glove' [CCC1]
145. **greme**; n.; 'wrath; grief; mortification; hurt' [CC1ac]
146. **gres**; n.; 'grass' [CC1ac]
147. **ȝeȝe**; v.; 'cry (as wares), cry (for)' [CCC1a]
148a. **hap**; n.; 'happiness' [C1]
148b. **vnhap**; n.; 'mishap' [C1]
149. **hapnest**; adj. (superl.); 'most fortunate' [CC1c (CC3)]
150. **helder**; adv. (comp.); 'rather, more' [C1c (C3)]
151. **hemely**; adv.; 'suitably, neatly' [CCC1a]
152. **henge**; v.; 'to hang (trans. and intrans.)' [CC1ac]
153. **heterly**; adv.; 'fiercely, vigorously, suddenly' [CCC1ac]
154. **holsumly**; adv.; 'healthfully' [CCC1a]
155. **lante**; v. (pret.); 'gave' [CCC1a]
156. **leme**; v.; 'to shine' [CC1c]
157a. **lyfte**; v.; 'to lift, raise; build; extol' [C1ac]
157b. **vplyften**; v. (pres. pl.); 'to lift, rise' [C1a]

158. **lyndes**; n. (pl.); 'loins' [CCC1a]
159a. **lofte**; n.; 'upper room; high place' [C1b (CC3ab)]
159b. **alofte**; adv./prep.; 'up, above, at the top, on; on horseback' [C1]
160. **mayn**; adj.; 'great, strong' [CC1a]
161. **mynne**; adj.; 'less' [C1ac]
162. **mysses**; n. (pl.); 'faults' [CC1a]
163. **or**; conj.; 'than' [C1]
164. **piked**; v. (pp.); 'polished' [CCC1a]
165. **rawþe**; n.; 'ruth, grief' [CCC1]
166. **same**; adj. (pron.); 'same' [C1ac]
167. **samen**; adv.; 'together' [CCC1ac]
168a. **seme**; adj.; 'seemly, fair, excellent' [C1ac (C3)]
168b. **semly**; adj.; 'seemly, fitting; comely, fair' [C1a (C3)]
168c. **semly**; adv.; 'becomingly, excellently; pleasantly, sweetly' [C1a (C3)]
168d. **semlyly**; adv.; 'becomingly' [C1ac (C3)]
169. **sene**; v. (pp.)/adj.; 'visible, plain, clear; seen' [CCC1a]
170a. **sleȝe**; adj.; 'skilfully made' [C1]
170b. **sleȝly**; adv.; '(made) warily' [C1]
170c. **sleȝt**; n.; 'skill; device; act of practised skill' [C1]
170d. **vnslyȝe**; adj.; 'unwary' [C1]
171. **spene**; v.; 'to be fastened, cling' [C1ac]
172. **stange**; n.; 'pole' [CC1abc]
173. **sware**; v.; 'to answer' [CC1c]
174a. **twynne**; adj. (as n.); 'two, double' [CC1c]
174b. **twynne**; v.; 'to be separated, depart' [CC1]
175. **vmbe-torne**; pp. as adv.; 'all around' [FCCC1c]
176. **waltered**; v. (pret. sg.); 'weltered, rolled in streams' [CCC1a]
177. **wandez**; n. (gen. sg.); 'stave's' [C1c]
178. **warp**; v.; 'to cast; utter; put' [CC1c]
179. **wast**; n.; 'waist' [CCC1a]
180. **wener**; adj. (comp.); 'more lovely' [CCC1 (CCC3)]
181. **weterly**; adv.; 'clearly' [CC1]
182. **wykez**; n. (pl.); 'corners (of the mouth)' [C1c (C3)]
183a. **wont**; n.; 'lack (of good things)' [C1]
183b. **wont**; v.; 'to want, lack, fall short of (impers.)' [C1]
184. **wouen**; v. (pp.); 'woven' [CCC1]
185. **wrang**; adj.; '(in the) wrong' [C1]

4.1.2. *Further remarks*

For all items of Type C1, the case for ON input rests ultimately on derivational form. This includes any kind of affixation, and the transfer from one grammatical category (part of speech) to another; it also includes derivation on a different Ablaut grade of a known Gmc str. v. root.[369] Essentially, I have considered items under this head if the crucial difference between the forms attested in OE (or a third language) and the proposed ON etymon arises from derivational factors (even if there are other possible explanations, for instance via endogenous phonological developments alone, for the formal outcome we find in ME); see e.g. **are**, **lante**.[370]

As usual, all the sub-entries listed for Type C1 stems represent forms which could have been created in English via native derivational processes. But those for which exact Scand counterparts are attested, and which therefore could in principle have been modelled directly on VAN words, are: **aȝlez**, **deruely**, **vnhap**, **vplyften**, **semly** (168b. adj. and 168c. adv.), **sleȝly/sleȝt/vnslyȝe**.[371]

Items labelled with additional, subsidiary structural criteria but mainly classed as C1 are: **calle**, **derf** (etc.), **dryftes**, **hapnest**, **helder**, **lofte** (159a. only), **seme** (etc.), **wener**, **wykez**. Of these, **calle** has extra evidence of Type C5; for all the others it is C3.

The only C1 item labelled 'F', whose basic form-source (for its second element) is non-Gmc, is **(vmbe-)torne**; and in this case, notice that the supposed ON input source has itself often been accounted for as a loan from LG. The ON etyma proposed for **hemely** and **piked** are also frequently regarded as borrowings from LG;[372] and that of **gloue** has in the past sometimes been explained as entering Scand via English (but this is not now generally thought plausible). Otherwise, few of the stems treated here have problematic or controversial ulterior etymologies. Only the following tend to be regarded as more or less obscure or have attracted different theories: **calle**, **froþe**, **gloue**, **hap** (etc.) and **hapnest**, **helder**, **lofte** (etc.) (as ever, see the entries for details). Etymological uncertainties which bear directly on the evidence for ON input in ME involve:

---

[369] I.e. following the understanding of derivation on 'the same root' used elsewhere in this book; see the Introductory Remarks (p. 48) and the Introduction to Type B above. For general guides to the morphology of OE and ON, see esp. the standard grammars at Campbell (§§568–768), Hogg-Fulk, Ringe-Taylor (§7), Noreen (§§356–546), Br-N. (§§424–950), Heusler (§§197–363); there are useful introductory surveys of ME in Wełna (1996: 80–148) and Fulk (2012: §§42–89). For helpful descriptions and discussions of word-formation in the early Gmc languages and English (esp. OE/ME) see further e.g. Kluge (1926), Krahe-Meid (III), Marchand (1969), Koziol (1972), Bammes-berger, Kastovsky (1992: 355–400; 2012), Faiss (1992: esp. 54–81), Lass (1994: esp. 105–119, 190–205), Ringe (2006: §4.4), Fulk (2018: chapters 7–12); and for recent accounts of the broader principles and issues see e.g. Minkova & Stockwell (2009), Bauer et al. (2013) and the essays in Lieber & Štekauer (2014).

[370] For **are**, the argument for ON input is based on the idea of derivation from the positive ON *ár*, rather than the comp. grade *ǽr* which is the only form clearly attested in OE; but ME *are* need not descend from a form of the Gmc positive, and can be explained in other ways (viz. as an unstressed OE variant of *ǽr* with shortening). Similarly, **lante** can be accounted for as a form of the OE v. *lǽnan* with shortening, but may show influence from the vocalism of the related n. ME *lōn(e)*, the case for Scand input into which depends upon the difference between the ON *lán* < PGmc **laihwn-az* vs. OE *lǽn* < **laihwn-iz*.

[371] Notice too **flat**, **hemely**, **heterly**, **holsumly** and **weterly**, where Scand analogues are also available for the precise derivatives found in *Gaw*.

[372] **Piked** has also sometimes been claimed to be ultimately of VLat origin, but the relationship between Gmc and Rom forms seems to be more complex.

lofte (etc.): if the original Gmc sense of **luft-* were indeed 'upper room' (though this is not generally agreed), then this arguably strengthens the case for ON involvement behind the ME word;

wont (v. and n.): if the ON v. *vanta* is originally a derivation on the neut. adj. *van-t* (though this explanation is not generally favoured now), then this renders still more secure the idea that both ME v. and n. were loaned from ON;

wrang: if late OE *wrang* 'rough' is indeed a native cognate of ON *vrangr*, then the case for ON input here is arguably weakened.

Notice also the following issues:

arwes: many discussions treat OE *earh* as if it is a *wō*-stem (directly cognate with ON *ǫr*), but this cannot in fact be the case;

bone: ON *bón* is perh. not an original *ō*-stem, as is usually assumed;

bonk: OE *-banca* could be a direct cognate of the supposed ON etymon, or a more recent reworking of OE *benc*;

chymbled: ON *kimbla* is prob., but not necessarily, cognate with OE *cimbing*;

glemered: OE *gleomu* is often understood as cognate with the proposed ON etymon (< the **glim-* root), but other explanations have also been adduced;

mynne: a supposed OE adj. *min* is sometimes cited, but this form is usually now accounted for in other ways;

sene: ON *sýnn* and OE (Angl) *sēne* are prob. not directly cognate;

twynne (adj., v.): it is probable that the OE n. *(ge)twinn* and the ON adj. *tvennr, tvinnr* go back to distinct PGmc forms;

wandez: OHG, MLG, MDu *want* 'wall' are sometimes but not universally identified as cognate with the putative ON etymon.

In the following cases, tests of phonological and/or morphological form have been proposed, but they are not clearly applicable or cannot be shown to be diagnostic (see the Formal Criteria above under the §§ cited, and the entries for further discussion):[373]

aghlich (etc.) (§8.2)
anger (§13.1)
froþe (§2)
helder (§13.4)
henge (§8.2)
mynne (§10.4)
wykez (§8.1)
wont (n.) (§14)

---

[373] In the case of **wont** (n.) the morphological criterion is especially plausible, and almost always assumed; but the possibility of input from **wont** v. (which may have a slightly different source) means that the 'test' cannot be regarded as definitive here. Two other items which might be listed here are **gres** (§12.1, although I have not seen absence of metathesis articulated as a factor in this case) and **gyng** (§8.2, but again this feature is not usually cited in arguments).

Related but more minor issues of form, or sense, or interpretation in context in *Gaw* are numerous and various. But notice the following in particular: **anger** (the possible influence of Lat *angor*); **blande** (v.) (is this a wk. or a str. pp. in *Gaw*?); **chymbled** (if derived from ON, sound substitution is required); **cost** (the identity of <costes> at *Gaw* 750); **derf** (etc.) (the reading of some possible instances, as <deru-> or <dern->); **flat** (is this formed in ME on the Gmc adj., prob. from ON, or direct from an ON n.?); **hapnest** (the vocalism is awkward if derived from ON *heppinn*, and is perh. influenced by **hap** or OE *gehæp*); **piked** (the identity of <piked> at *Gaw* 769); **sene** (editors' different division of instances between entries for the adj. and the pp.; early misinterpretations of *Gaw* 148 and 341); **vmbe-torne** (Morris's suggested emendation, never taken up by others); **weterly** (the interpretation of the sense in context). I have drawn attention to rarely cited issues and/or mounted new arguments in a few cases. Notice in particular: **blende** (there is plausible if ambiguous evidence for an OE wk. v. *blendan*, something often apparently assumed but rarely argued out); **ʒeʒe** (some OE spellings could in principle reflect a native cognate of the proposed ON etymon); **seme** (etc.) (the ME adj. is always derived from the simplex adj. represented by OIcel *sæmr*, but both ME and ON adjectives are rare, and I suggest borrowing via a derived from like **semly** (adj. or adv.) in the first instance).

4.1.2.1. Types of structural evidence at issue

Here is a summary classification of Type C1 stems according to the derivational features upon which the attribution of ON input depends.[374]

1. Nouns

The crucial distinction between OE and ON nouns often involves a different Gmc nominal stem-formative, i.e. a distinct declensional suffix type. This is most apparent when one language shows a variant which produced *i*-mutation, and the other does not, as with: **bone** (perh. an original ON *ō*-stem vs. an OE *i*-stem); **bonk** (an ON wk. masc. vs. an OE *i*-stem); **cost** (prob. an original ON *u*-stem vs. an OE *i*-stem); **flat** (an ON form without *i*-mutation vs. an OE *ja*-stem); **gres** ((prob.) an ON *ja*-stem vs. an OE *a*-stem); **lofte** (etc.) (an ON *a*-stem vs. an OE *i*-stem); **stange** (an ON *ō*-stem vs. an OE *i*-stem). Other items featuring contrasting declensional types are: **aghlich** (etc.) (an ON *n*-stem vs. an OE str. declension); **arwes** (an ON *wō*-stem vs. an OE *wa*-stem); **gyng** (an ON wk. neut. *ja*-stem, vs. OE wk. masc. and fem. *ja*-stems); **gloue** (an ON wk. n. vs. an OE str. n.). Some show the addition of other suffixes with a clear

---

[374] I have not attempted to fit the curious case of **vmbe-torne** into this schema. But it seems to me that it is the overall shape of this word – i.e. the presence of the *vmbe-* prefix combined with the use of *torne* as a pp. in adverbial function – which is essentially the spur to trying to connect it with ME *ummbe-trin*, and hence onwards to a (very dubious) derivation from ON.

derivational role, such as the *-t used to form nouns on a verbal stem (**draʒt,
dryftes**) and the similar *-iþō (**rawþe**); whereas in other cases the original
function of the suffix is less clear, as with **lyndes** (ON has forms with an *-īn
suffix, OE usually without) and **wast** (ON has -t only, OE -t + -m). In one
instance a different Ablaut grade is the key distinction, viz. **wykez** (the ON n.
is formed on the zero-grade rather than the pres. (e-grade) of the str. verbal root
in question).

In the remaining cases the grammatical category (part of speech) is the defining
feature. Hence the occurrence of a n. rather than an adj. for **anger** (and note that this
is an original ON es-stem n. vs. OE adjectives in u- or wja-) and **hap** (**vnhap**); a n.
rather than a v. for **froþe** (plus the proposed ON etymon shows a different Ablaut
grade from anything attested in OE) and **wandez**; a n. rather than an adj. or v. for
greme; and a n. rather than a prefix or a derived v. for **mysses**.

2. Adjectives

OE and ON adjectives are sometimes distinguished by the presence of i-
mutation; thus **brent**, **seme** (etc.) (in both cases an ON form with mutation
vs. an OE form without). The presence of a derivational suffix also frequently
plays a role in the evidence, as with **hapnest** (ON suffix -inn vs. none in
OE), **hemely** (an ON adj. extended with -ol, not affixed to this stem in OE),
heterly (prob. an *-or suffix in ON, vs. zero or *-ol in OE), **holsumly** (forms
in -samr are known in ON, but none suffixed with -sum are attested in OE),
weterly (-r suffix in ON vs. none (at least on the adj.) in OE). And in a few
other cases it is the absence of an affix which is the crucial factor, viz. for
sene (the absence of the ge- prefix expected for a native participial adj.),
wener (the simplex adj. in ON vs. attested forms only with affixes in OE).
Difference in grammatical category supplies the key contrast for: **mynne**,
sleʒe (etc.), **wrang** (adjectives rather than verbs); **mayn**, **twynne** (adjectives
rather than nouns); **derf** (etc.) (an adj. rather than a v. or a n.); and **same** (an
adj. rather than an adv.).

3. Adverbs

The operative distinction for **are** and **or** is inflexional (i.e. the existence of the
positive grade of this adv. in ON, next to the comp. (only) in OE). For **samen** it
involves the absence of affixes (ON records the simplex form, OE has -saman
only with prefixes). And for **helder** the evidence boils down essentially to a
difference of grammatical category (adv. rather than adj.).

4. Verbs

OE and ON v. forms sometimes differ in terms of basic conjugation type, wk. vs.
str. This is the primary evidence (or supposed evidence) for the following:
blande (v.) (ON has a wk. by-form, OE only the str. v.), **blende** (the derived wk.
1 v. is attested unambiguously in ON, but not in OE), **blykke** (ON attests a wk.
v. formed on the zero grade /i/, (early) OE has only the original str. v.), **bolne**

(ON has a wk. v. derived (with the *n*-suffix) on the pp. of the str. v., OE only has the latter), **fonge** (only ON has a wk. v. formed on the stem of the str. pp.), **frayn** (ON has a wk. v. formed on the pret. sg. stem of the str. v., (early) OE only attests the latter), **spene** (the derived wk. 1 v. is found in ON but not OE), **warp** (ON has a wk. 2 v. formed on the *a*-grade of the str. v., OE only has the str. v.). A difference of class within the str. conjugations is behind the case for ON input with **wouen** (ON str. IV pp. with /o/, vs. OE str. V with /e/); and a difference within the wk. conjugations holds for **henge** (wk. 1 in ON, vs. wk. 2 (or str.) in OE) and **lante** (wk. 2 in ON, vs. wk. 1 in OE). The following vary in their use of verbal derivational affixes: **glyter** (ON *-r* vs. OE *-n*); **wont** (v.) (ON has a v. formed (perh.) using a *t*-suffix, OE does not); **sware** (ON attests the v. without a prefix, OE does not).

The remaining instances once again feature a difference in grammatical category as the defining feature. Several are verbs rather than nouns: notice **leme**, **lyfte** (etc.), **piked**, and moreover **calle** (v. rather than agent n.), **chymbled** (v. with *l*-suffix rather than vbl. n.), **glemered** (v. with *r*-suffix rather than n.). Others are verbs rather than adjectives or nouns (**deȝe**, **ȝeȝe**); one is a v. (with an *r*-suffix) rather than an adj. (**waltered**).

4.1.2.2. *Probability of ON input*

As with Type B above, analysing the words gathered together under Type C reveals a wide range of different etymological profiles, and a considerable number of ancillary complications which manifest themselves when one attempts to assess the argument for ON input. The case for each item must, first and foremost, be judged on its own merits. But, as before, there are some helpful generalizations to be drawn out by examining these cases together, sub-type by sub-type. The 'probability markers' employed here have the same signification as they did for Type B above, but I repeat them here for ease of reference. As ever, they attempt to encapsulate my impressions of the quality of the evidence and the opinions of the authorities discussed in the entries.

C
The case for ON input is very plausible. There is general agreement in the scholarship, often without exception.

CC
The case for ON input is reasonable, but alternative explanations seem about equally plausible. There is usually some disagreement in the scholarship.

CCC
The case for ON input is not strong (though it still cannot be dismissed out of hand). The word's development can usually be explained more

plausibly by other means. There is some history in the scholarly tradition of attributing or at least suggesting ON input, but the weight of (especially recent) argument is against it, and/or the case for it is problematic in some fairly fundamental way.

The stems of Type C1 are divided between these probability groups as follows: C1 twenty-four stems; CC1 nineteen stems; CCC1 twenty-four stems. Items of this sub-type therefore seem to be roughly equally distributed between those where the case for ON input is strong, those where it is simply plausible, and those where it is not very probable (but notice that only twenty-four out of sixty-seven stems are of the first group, and hence are generally agreed to derive from ON).

The most plausible items, marked 'C1', are:

aghlich (etc.)
anger
bone
bonk
calle
cost
deȝe
derf (etc.)
flat
froþe
hap (etc.)
helder
lyfte (etc.)
lofte (etc.)
mynne (adj.)
or
same
seme (etc.)
sleȝe (etc.)
spene
wandez
wykez
wont (n. and v.)
wrang

A number of these items feature derivational processes or affixes which are not generally regarded as productive beyond the early OE period (at the latest). In these instances, therefore, the ME word in question seems less likely to be a novel formation within English (during late OE or ME), and hence the argument *against* ON input must fall back on the suggestion that it is a native form which has survived from an earlier period but which has previously been unattested. Especially with words which lexicalize relatively common concepts, many of these words being very frequent in ME, this counter-argument is improbable. This applies when the derivational evidence involves different n. or adj. stem-formatives in ON vs. OE (**aghlich** (etc.), **anger, bone, bonk, cost, flat, lofte** (etc.), **seme** (etc.)), when a v. is derived using the wk. 1 suffix with *i*-mutation (rather than as the wk. 2 type later more productive in OE) (**deȝe, lyfte** (etc.), **spene**), and when we have a ME word formed on an Ablaut grade of a str. verbal root which has given no other similar known derivations in OE (**froþe, sleȝe** (etc.), **wandez, wykez, wrang**). Other items which seem to me to belong here are **mynne** (adj.) (the use of a 'basic' form where only a derived usage is known in OE) and **wont** (n. and v.) (a common word formed using a different verbal suffix from that attached to this root in OE).[375]

When more commonplace types of derivation, productive in late OE and ME, are concerned (e.g. nominalization of adjectives, formation of wk. (2) verbs on nouns or adjectives, loss of affixes), some items still seem to me to merit inclusion in the 'C1' bracket when the case for ON input is reinforced by other compelling evidence. This tends to be when the concept they denote is extremely common, so that their occurrence in English only after the period of ON influence is usually taken to be an unlikely coincidence: a very good example is **calle** (a Gmc root which is moreover characteristic of this semantic domain in ON, and much less central in WGmc, inc. vanishingly rare in OE), and see also **hap** (etc.) (reinforced by the forms attested in some ME dialects) and **derf** (etc.), **helder, or, same**.

Thirteen 'C1' stems are supported by the circumstantial evidence of regional distribution (in either toponymic or general lexical usage, or both) and marked 'b' and/or 'c': **bonk, cost, derf** (etc.), **flat, helder, lyfte** (etc.), **lofte, mynne** (adj.), **same, seme/semlyly, spene, wandez, wykez**. On the other hand, eleven stems (inc. many of these same items) are labelled 'a' (in their main or subsidiary type categories), and hence show very similar forms elsewhere in WGmc; but this fact does not in itself seem to me materially to affect the likelihood of ON input. These stems are: **bonk, calle, cost, deȝe, derf** (etc.), **lyfte** (etc.), **lofte, mynne** (adj.), **same, seme** (etc.), **spene**. (For further discussion of this evidence see section 4.6 below.)

There is little significant disagreement between the major scholarly authorities over these items. Despite the occasional expression of doubt as to the Scand pedigree of some words (see notably **calle, deȝe, wrang**), the case for ON input is relatively robust and most are long-accepted examples of plausible loans. There are no major differences of opinion here between the historical dictionaries

---

[375] Plus in this case there is the strong possibility that **wont** (n.), at least, derives from an ON neut. adj. in *-t* (§14).

or the main editions;[376] and the only 'C1' stems not treated by Bj. are **spene** and **wykez**.

The less and least plausible stems, marked 'CC1' and 'CCC1', are these:

CC1
are
arwes
bolne
brent
dryftes
gyng
glemered
glyter
greme
gres
hapnest
henge
mayn
mysses
stange
sware
twynne (adj., v.)
warp
weterly

CCC1
blande (v.)
blykke
blende
chymbled
draȝt
fonge
frayn
gloue
ȝeȝe
hemely

---

[376] Amongst the less significant differences in the etymologies presented by *OED* and *MED*, notice: **anger** (possible input from Lat *angor* is referred to only by *MED*); **cost** (*MED* refers merely to 'OE', but this prob. looks back no further than late OE *cost*, usually derived from ON); **froþe** (*OED* adds possible input from ON *frauð* to the usually-cited ON etymon *froða*); **or** (*OED*'s discussion of the possible sources includes the notion of an unrecorded OE positive **ār*). *ODEE* differs from *OED* over **anger**, in treating the ME n. as having been formed on the v. ME *angren* (< the ON derived v. *angra*) rather than directly on the ON n. *angr*. Note the following minor discrepancies between TGD and GDS: **flat** (TG(D) derive direct from the ON n., GDS from the ME adj. < the ON adj.); **wont** (v.) (TG(D) suggest that this was formed on **wont** (n.) rather than direct from the ON v., as preferred by GDS). The original edition of TG derives **wykez** from OE *wīc* 'bay, creek', but the ON etymon is introduced in the 1930 revised reprint and remains in TGD.

heterly
holsumly
lante
leme
lyndes
piked
rawþe
samen
sene
vmbe-torne
waltered
wast
wener
wouen

In some of these cases, the survival through OE of a native word-form unattested until later seems quite a plausible alternative to the claim for ON input. This is particularly so when such a word would be one of several similar types of derivation on the same commonplace root, and would represent a close by-form of derivations known in the OE record (thus for instance **arwes, blykke, brent, frayn, gyng, henge, heterly, piked, weterly**), or when it stands for a concept less commonly encountered than those dealt with under 'C' above (e.g. **stange**).

At other times, the type of derivation involved seems likely to have been productive for much of the OE and ME periods, meaning that there is a viable case to be made for the form in question having been created (or re-created) in English, in parallel to its cognate in ON. This seems to me especially true of the changes of grammatical category represented by the following, none of which is particularly implausible as an endogenous development: **gloue** (a str. n. becoming wk.); **greme** and **mysses** (a n. developing from an adj., or verbal or prefix usage); **mayn** and **twynne** (an adj. developing from a n.); **fonge, leme, piked** (the formation of a new wk. (2) v.); and **wouen** (a change of str. class alignment for a pp.). It also applies straightforwardly enough to the loss of affixes, which need not be motivated by external factors; thus **samen, sene, sware, wener**. And some types of affixation seem common enough for the following to be plausibly explicable as native in origin, at least during the OE period: (nominal) **draȝt, dryftes, rawþe**; (adjectival) **holsumly**; (verbal) **bolne, chymbled, glemered, glyter, waltered**.

In a number of cases, one or more of the foregoing assumptions is reinforced by the apparent phonology of the item, which looks as though it reflects a native rather than an ON etymon: thus **chymbled, ȝeȝe, hemely, heterly, sene, wast**, and moreover **holsumly** (which can be a loan-translation at best) and **wouen** (which must also be native in form).[377] In a few other instances the formal

---

[377] See also perhaps **hapnest** (though the vocalism here could be influenced by **hap**); and also **arwes** (the AB spelling in <ear->, at least, is best explained as a native development).

difference from a native near-cognate may be superficial, and can be accounted for by an endogenous sound change; e.g. **are, gres, lante, warp**.[378] One item **(lyndes)** is indeed attested with the requisite shape in OE, but rarely; and there is good, if ambiguous, evidence for another **(blende)** also being present in OE. In another case, the argument that the feature in question is even to be found in the word's *Gaw* occurrence seems to me to be weak; see **blande** (v.). Finally, there is the curious case of **vmbe-torne**, the only evidence for ON input into which seems to be its (passing) similarity to another ME word, where the argument for ON derivation is itself dubious (and the proposed ON etymon may be a more recent borrowing from LG).

In terms of circumstantial evidence, the 'CC1' words have a similar profile to those marked with a single 'C1': twelve CC1 stems are labelled 'c', and hence are more or less restricted to the N/EM in dial distribution, plus there are two marked 'b' only; whereas nine have close relatives showing the same feature in continental WGmc, and are labelled 'a'. For 'CCC1' items, on the other hand, the 'a' figure (fourteen stems) outstrips the 'c' figure (eight stems), adding some slight weight to the impression of the greater implausibility of the case for these stems. As ever, nonetheless, caution needs to be exercised before ascribing too much significance to these cirumstantial flags (not least because so many stems, fourteen across Type C1 of all probability levels, occur in both lists).

The contentiousness of the argument for ON input here is reflected by the proportion of 'CC1' and 'CCC1' items which have occasioned significant disagreement in the scholarly literature. *OED* and *MED* differ more or less seriously over sixteen stems, viz. **arwes, blende, brent, chymbled, frayn, gloue, heterly, holsumly, lante, mayn, piked, samen, sene, wener, weterly, wouen**.[379] *MED* is marginally more likely to promote ON input for these

---

[378] It is of course this prospect which distinguishes the probability of the case for **are** (CC1) from that for **or** (C1).

[379] **Arwes**: the original *OED* does not refer to the prospect of ON input (though *OED3* now adds this as a possibility), but *MED* seems to indicate it. **Blende**: *OED* derives from ON, *MED* does not seem to (at least not explicitly). **Brent**: *OED* gives a native etymon, *MED* derives at least partly from ON. **Chymbled**: *OED* offers no etymology, *MED* derives perh. from ON. **Frayn**: *OED* explains as native, *MED* at least partly from ON. **Gloue**: *OED* assigns only the native etymon, *MED* looks at least partly to ON. **Heterly**: *OED* derives from a native source, *MED* at least partly from ON. **Holsumly**: *OED* suggests that it was reinforced from ON (in northern ME only), *MED* derives only from OE. **Lante**: *OED* treats as native only, *MED* derives at least partly from ON. **Mayn**: *OED* derives at least party from ON, *MED* gives only the native source. **Piked**: *OED* treats as native, *MED* derives partly from ON. **Samen**: *OED* derives from OE, *MED* partly from ON. **Sene**: *OED* suggests some ON influence, *MED* gives only the native etymon. **Wener**: *OED* derives from ON, *MED* from OE only. **Weterly**: *OED* derives solely from ON, *MED* offers both OE and ON etyma. **Wouen**: *OED* refers only to native origin, *MED* allows for ON influence. Notice also the more minor differences in the dictionaries' treatment of: **are** (only *OED* explicitly notices possible input from an OE comp. variant with shortening); **blande** (v.) (*MED* files under *blēnden* v.2; but neither dictionary derives from ON); **glemered** (*OED* explains as native, *MED* gives only continental WGmc comparanda); **hapnest** (*OED* does not identify the suffix, *MED* compares ON *heppinn*); **hemely** (*OED* suggests only some relationship to OE *hām*, *MED* derives from OE *gehǽme*).

items than is *OED*, doing so for ten stems as opposed to *OED*'s six. *ODEE* differs substantially from *OED* with respect to **arwes** and **glemered**.[380] TGD and GDS disagree over nine stems, i.e. **blande** (v.), **brent, fonge, gyng, hemely, lyndes, mayn, twynne** (etc.), **warp**.[381] TGD is markedly more likely to promote ON influence here, this being true for seven stems, as opposed to just two where the reverse is true. Notice also that there are four significant differences between the original TG edition and the revised TGD, viz. **brent, rawþe, warp, wener**,[382] with TGD being less likely to support ON input across these cases; and one further noteworthy change between the first and reprinted versions of TG itself (**heterly**).[383] On the whole, TG(D) and GDS rarely agree with one another in contradistinction to both *OED* and *MED*, but there is the occasional instance (see **gres, leme, mysses**). The opinion given by Bj. usually concurs with one or more of the above, but there are a few exceptions (see **glyter, greme, stange**);[384] and twenty-four CC1 and CCC1 stems are not treated in his book at all.[385] By contrast, a few words were more likely to be regarded as ON derivations early in the scholarly tradition, and since then more allowance has generally been made for native input; see esp. **blykke, dryftes, ȝeȝe, samen, waltered, warp, wast, wener.**

---

[380] In both cases *ODEE* derives from ON, where *OED* had not. Notice also **draȝt**, for which *ODEE* is also prepared to entertain a possible ON input, as against *OED*.

[381] **Blande** (v.): TG(D) derive from ON, GDS from OE. **Brent**: TGD derive at least partly from ON, GDS from OE. **Fonge**: TG(D) explain at least partly as from ON, GDS as native. **Gyng**: TG(D) derive from ON, GDS from OE. **Hemely**: TG(D) give as a native word, GDS at least partly derives from ON. **Lyndes**: TG(D) explain as at least partly from ON, GDS from OE. **Mayn**: TG(D) partly from ON, GDS native. **Twynne** (etc.): TG(D) partly from ON, GDS from OE only. **Warp**: TGD give as native only, GDS derives from ON. And there are more minor disagreements in the case of: **are** (TG(D)'s reference to late Nhb *ar* perhaps indicates partial origin in a shortened native comp.); **hapnest** (TG(D) derive from ON *heppinn* with the vowel of ME *hap*; GDS compares both ON *heppinn* and OE *gehæp*); **leme** (TG(D) derive from ON only, GDS also refers to OE); **waltered** (TG(D) compares MLG, GDS only the OE str. pp.); **wast** (TG(D) explains as native, GDS does likewise but has a 'cp'. to ON).

[382] **Brent**: TG derives only from OE, TGD adds ON input. **Rawþe**: TG derives at least partly from ON, TGD changes this to a native source. **Warp**: TG cites ON as well as OE etyma, TGD only the OE. **Wener**: TG derives from ON, TGD also gives a 'cf.' to OE.

[383] The first TG edition claims a blend of OE and ON words, but the 1930 printing refers only to OE and MLG forms.

[384] **Glyter**: Bj. prefers a native etymon, whereas the dictionaries and main editions all suggest some ON input. **Greme**: Bj. is troubled by the native words formed on the same root, and puts it only in his 'possibly' borrowed list. **Stange**: Bj. is perturbed by the occurrence of an ō-stem n. in WGmc, and thinks the ME word is probably native.

[385] These are **blande** (v.), **blende, blykke, brent, chymbled, dryftes, fonge, gyng, glemered, gloue, hemely, heterly, holsumly, lante, leme, lyndes, mayn, mysses, piked, sene, vmbe-torne, waltered, wast, wouen**. Notice also **henge**, concerning which Bj's only discussion regards the possible diagnostic value of medial /g/; and for **rawþe**, Bj. follows Knigge's error in reading (taking it as a form of an adj. meaning 'red' < ON *rauðr*).

4.2. TYPE C2

4.2.1. *Summary list*

Category C2 consists of forty-five stems, ten with sub-entries; there are fifty-nine distinct lexical items altogether:

186. **askez**; n. (pl.); 'ashes' [CC2]
187. **blaste**; n.; 'blast (of wind)' [C2]
188. **blenk**; v.; 'to gleam' [CC2c]
189. **brenne**; v.; 'to burn; broil; (pp.) refined, bright' [C2c]
190. **breþer**; n. (pl.); 'brothers (in arms)' [CC2bc]
191. **bruny**; n.; 'mail-shirt' [C2 (C1a)]
192. **brusten**; v. (pp.); 'broken' [C2]
193. **burþe**; n.; 'birth' [CC2a]
194. **busk**; n.; 'bush' [CC2bc]
195a. **cnokez**; v. (pres. 2 sg.); 'knock, deal a blow' [CCC2a]
195b. **knokke**; n.; 'knock, blow' [CCC2a]
196. **croun**; n.; 'crown; crown of the head' [FCCC2a]
197. **fawne**; v.; 'to fondle, stroke' [CCC2a]
198a. **fest**; v. (pret. pl.); 'made fast, agreed upon' [CC2c]
198b. **festned**; v. (pp.); 'made firm, bound' [CC2c]
199. **forth**; n.; 'ford' [CCC2b]
200. **ȝol**; n.; 'Yule, Christmas' [CC2c]
201. **half-suster**; n.; 'half-sister' [CC2]
202a. **haspe**; n.; 'clasp, i.e. door-pin' [CCC2]
202b. **haspe**; v.; 'to clasp, fasten' [CCC2]
203a. **hete**; v. (infin.); 'to promise' [CCC2]
203b. **hetes**; n. (pl.); 'vows, assurances of knightly service' [CCC2c]
204. **if**; conj.; 'if' [CCC2a]
205. **lygez**; v. (pres. 3 sg.); 'lies' [CC2c]
206a. **lyke**; adj.; 'like, similar' [CCC2c]
206b. **lyk**; adv.; 'like' [CCC2c]
206c. **vnlyke**; adj.; 'unlike, different' [CCC2c]
207. **lyre**; n.; 'cheek, face; flesh, coat' [CC2c]
208. **mele**; v.; 'to speak, say' [CC2c]
209a. **mensk**; adj.; 'honoured' [C2c]
209b. **menske**; n.; 'courtesy, honour; fame' [C2 (CC1)]
209c. **mensked**; v. (pp.); 'adorned' [C2 (CC1)]
209d. **menskful**; adj.; 'of worth, noble' [C2 (CC1)]
209e. **menskly**; adv.; 'courteously, worthily' [C2c]
210a. **merk**; n.; 'mark, appointed place' [CC2]
210b. **merkkez**; v. (pres. 3 sg.); 'aims (a blow) at' [CC2 (CC1)]
211. **messe**; n.; 'mass' [CCC2a]
212. **muckel**; n.; 'size' [CC2c]

213. **nikked**; v. (pret.); 'denied, refused, said no' [CCC2c]
214a. **race**; n.; 'headlong course; stroke' [C2]
214b. **rasez**; v. (pres. 3 sg.); 'rushes' [C2]
215. **renk**; n.; 'knight, man' [CC2]
216. **renne**; v.; 'to run, slide, flow; be current' [C2c]
217. **sate**; v. (pret. sg.); 'sat' [CCC2]
218. **scrape**; v.; 'to scrape, paw the ground' [CC2]
219a. **silk**; n. (adj.); 'silk, piece of silk' [CC2]
219b. **sylkyn**; adj.; 'silk' [CC2]
220. **syluerin**; adj.; 'silver' [CC2]
221. **soþen**; v. (pp.); 'boiled' [CCC2]
222. **stryþþe**; n.; 'stance' [CC2]
223. **tulk**; n.; 'man, knight' [FC2c]
224. **þenk**; v. (pres. stem); 'to take heed, remember, be mindful of' [CCC2]
225. **þynke**; v. (pres. stem); 'to seem' [CCC2]
226. **vmbe**; prep.; 'about, round' [CC2ac]
227a. **walt**; v. (pret. pl.); 'tossed, flung' [CCC2c]
227b. **ouerwalt**; v. (pp.); 'overthrown' [CCC2c]
228. **wela**; adv.; 'very' [CCC2c]
229. **whyrlande**; v. (pres. ptcp.); 'whirling' [CC2a]
230. **worre**; adj. (as n.); 'worse' [CC2ac]

4.2.2. *Further remarks*

For items of Type C2, the crucial evidence for ON input has to do with some other aspect of form (not arising from derivational features) which is shared between the ME word in question and the proposed ON etymon.

Sub-entries with exact Scand counterparts are **lyk** (206b., adv.; 206c., **vnlyke**) and **rasez** (214b.). Items whose formal evidence is supported by additional structural evidence (and which have a subsidiary type label in brackets) are **bruny**, **menske/mensked/menskful** (209b., c., d. only), **merkkez** (210b. only) (all also 'C1').

Two C2 stems are prefixed with 'F', showing a non-Gmc form-source not attested in OE, viz. **croun** and **tulk**.[386] **Croun** derives from Fr (ult. < Lat); the issue is whether it came into English direct from Fr, or via ON.[387] The ult. form-source of **tulk** is in Slavonic or Lithuanian (albeit with an obscure further etymology); it was perh. loaned to ON via LG, hence the alternative possibility that it entered English via LG rather than ON. Notice that

---

[386] **Messe, silk** (etc.) and **syluerin** are also ult. non-Gmc in origin, but in all three cases a form of these words had already reached English by early OE. Notice that ON *messa* is usually supposed to be a loan via LG or English; and ON *silfr* has also sometimes been explained as entering ON via another Gmc language.

[387] But notice that the ON word has itself often been explained as a loan from English.

influence from a related Fr word has also been proposed in the cases of **bruny**, **merk** (etc.), **messe** and **scrape**; from medieval Lat for **busk**; from medieval Lat or Fr for **haspe** (n. and v.); and from Du or LG for **vmbe**. Relatively few of the stems treated here have etymologies which are otherwise difficult or obscure, but notice in particular: **bruny**, **busk**, **cnokez** (etc.), **ʒol**, **haspe** (n. and v.), **if**, **syluerin**, **stryþþe**.[388] Etymological uncertainties which bear directly on the evidence for ON input in ME involve:

> **burþe**: the possible existence of Gmc forms without VL adds to the case for a native origin;
>
> **stryþþe**: the prospect of a native source for OE *strīð* means that a root in PGmc /θ/ is plausible, although if so it is unexplained.

Notice also the following issues:

> **askez**: a PGmc **askōn* as usually reconstructed is prob. acceptable, despite the problematic Go *azgō*;
>
> **blenk**: prob. not a causative of a str. v., but a derivation on the adj. **blanka-* as is now usually assumed;
>
> **breþer**: the ON mutated pl. prob. originated by levelling from the dat. sg., rather than in a pl. form in *-i-* as sometimes used to be claimed (e.g. by the original *OED* entry);
>
> **fawne**: some early scholarship seems not to have appreciated that a Gmc variant with suffix Ablaut existed;
>
> **lyre**: the etymology of OE *līra* has been debated;
>
> **mele**: OE *mǣl-* forms are prob. an independent parallel to OS *mahalian*, OHG *mahalen* rather than direcly cognate, even if the exact relationship of these by-forms is uncertain;
>
> **nikked**: OIcel *neka* is best explained as showing a different origin from the other early Scand forms (derived on PGmc **ne*, **ni* rather than the ON interj. *nei*), and both these are distinct from the likelier form-source of the ME word (the negated OE pron. *nic*);
>
> **race (rasez)**: Bj's alternative etymology for ON *rás* (< **rans*) is not well founded; but he is prob. correct that ME *rasen*, Ger *rasen* 'to rage' are unconnected with the v. in question;
>
> **vmbe**: the retention of the second syllable of OE *ymbe* is in itself irregular;
>
> **walt** (etc.): the existence of a str. VII v. in WGmc is debatable, and it seems more likely that the str. type represents a late by-form;

---

[388] The Gmc root of **bruny** has often been accounted for as a loan from Celtic. For **busk**, it is not clear whether Lat or Gmc forms have etymological priority.

whyrlande: there are various ambiguous forms in OE which could be derivations on the *e*-grade, but are usually taken to be *a*-grades; and OE *hwyrftlian* could be either an *a*- or a zero-grade in origin;
worre: there is some debate as to whether a PGmc **wersiz-* or **werziz-* was the original form of the comp.

Related but more minor issues of form, or sense, or interpretation in context in *Gaw*, are various. But notice in particular: **hete** (etc.) (Morris's suggestion of influence from ON *hǣta* 'to threaten', which does not however fit the required sense); **lyre** (the whole matter of how to divide up the lexemes and their meanings; and the additional problem of the identity of 1334 *lere*); **race** (the identification of two *Gaw* instances); **renk** (the interpretation of 2206 *renk*); **stryþþe** (the interpretation of the sense). I have drawn attention to previously noticed but rarely cited issues in the case of: **merk** (etc.) (the difficulties in practice with deriving *Gaw* <erk> from an OE Angl smoothed form -*erc*); **silk** (etc.) and **syluerin** (drawing attention to the arguments in Weyhe (1906) and their relevance to the vocalism of these words); **vmbe** (the possibility of LG or Du input); **whyrlande** (the possibility of input from OE *hwyrftlian*, as cited by TG(D)). I have contributed new arguments most notably with respect to: **blaste** (the possibility of input from OE *blǣst*, perhaps with short /æ/, and regarding the etymology of such a form); **forth** (the prospect of some influence from the OE adv. *forð*); **hete** (etc.) (a counter-argument to Emerson's claim for ON input); **lyre** (I argue that we really only have the one ME lexical item here, conflating several possible etymological sources, with by-forms and senses which have come to be understood as related); **worre** (a new argument regarding levelling from -*rr*- forms of the superl., which will also explain the ME vocalism).

4.2.2.1. *Types of structural evidence at issue*

What follows is a summary classification of Type C2 stems according to the formal features upon which claims for ON input depend. The features treated fall into two broad groups. In the first, we are dealing with potential instances of the regular and recurrent phonological disinctions between OE and ON which were set out in the Introduction to Type A (Formal Criteria) above (and which are keyed into that discussion as usual with §§ numbers); for the stems treated here, of course, the force of this evidence is contested, and in no cases is it *clearly* diagnostic of ON input. In the second (and smaller) group, the formal evidence does not depend upon systematic phonological correspondence between OE or ON but reflects other differences, usually involving lexically specific developments supposed to be characteristic of the Scand languages, or which have been taken to be indicative of ON influence in some other way.

Regular phonological developments

§1 PGmc */ai/ > VAN /ɑi/, /ɛi/ (> /eː/ by OEN monophthongization)
hete (etc.)

§4 PGmc /eː/[1] > VAN /ɑː/
blaste
race (etc.)
sate

§5 PGmc */iu/ + front mutation > VAN /yː/
lyre

§6.3 PGmc *swestēr-* > ON *systir*
(half-)suster

§6.4(a) VAN /i/ (> ME /i/) rather than OE /io/ with back mutation (> ME /e/)
silk (etc.)
syluerin

§6.4(b) 'stress-shift' in (late) VAN diphthongs
ʒol

§6.4(d) VAN front mutation of */ɑst/ > /ɛst/
fest (etc.)

§7 PGmc */ð/ > VAN /ð/ medially and finally
burþe
forth
soþen
stryþþe

§8.1 PGmc */k/ without palatalization (non-initially)
blenk
lyke (etc.)
merk (etc.)
muckel
nikked
þenk
þynke

§8.2 PGmc */g/ without palatalization (non-initially)
fawne
lygez

§8.3 PGmc */sk/ without palatalization
askez
busk
mensk (etc.)
scrape

§10.4(l) ON /θl/ > /l/ (with compensatory lengthening of preceding vowel)
mele

§10.4(o) ON (esp. OEN?) /rfl/ > /rl/
whyrlande

§12.1 Metathesis, esp. of /r/ plus vowel
brenne
bruny
haspe (n., v.)
renne

Other formal features:
Vowels

breþer
The presence of a front-mutated vowel in the pl. (prob. transferred from the dat. sg.).

vmbe
The presence of a non-mutated vowel (prob. generalized from a low-stress variant).

renk
The lowering of /i/ > /e/.

cnokez (etc.)
A (prob. ideophonic) by-form of the root vocalism, with /o/ rather than /u/.

messe
A by-form in /e/ rather than the lowered /æ/ found in (some) OE reflexes.

tulk (F)
The by-form with /u/ rather than /o/ is characteristic of ON forms of this originally Slavonic or Lithuanian word.

croun (F)
The loss of the pretonic vowel from the normal Fr form of this word.

walt (etc.)
ME pret. forms in /a/ perhaps show reinforcement from the ON str. *velta*, pret. *valt*.

Consonants

worre
The presence of *-rr-* in the comp., i.e. apparently from a form **werziz-* with VL.

if
The absence of initial /j/, as in ON.[389]

wela
The simplification of the medial consonant cluster (etymologically = OE *wel lā*).

4.2.2.2. Probability of ON input

The stems of Type C2 are divided between the usual probability groups as follows: C2 eight stems; CC2 twenty-one stems; CCC2 sixteen stems. Unlike with Type C1, therefore, where the items are approximately evenly distributed amongst these groupings, only a handful (eight out of forty-five) C2 stems fall into the most plausible, persuasive set. This seems to indicate that 'formal' evidence for ON input (at least once it stops short of the systematic kind analysed under Type A above) tends to be less convincing on the whole than derivational evidence. It is most common for C2 stems to belong to the less plausible, middle group (i.e. there is some justification for claiming ON input, but it is not wholly compelling; twenty-one out of forty-five); and the least plausible kind (sixteen out of forty-five) are only a little less frequent.

The most plausible items, marked 'C2', are:

blaste
brenne
bruny
brusten
mensk (etc.)
race (etc.)
renne
tulk

In all these cases, the formal feature in question seems markedly less likely to have come about by native processes than by borrowing from ON (or less likely by direct loan from a third language, than by borrowing via ON). Thus for **blaste**, while the shortening of reflexes of PGmc /e:/[1] to a sound spelt <a> is occasionally found in the dialect of the *Gaw*-manuscript, it is very rare, and loan from ON provides a more

---

[389] Notice that I have not classed the absence of /j/ in this word as a possible instance of regular ON deletion of initial PGmc */j/ (on which see e.g. Noreen §231; Br-N. §265), since there are several variants of the 'if' word without *j*- elsewhere in Gmc (inc. Go), and the etymological relationship of the various Gmc forms is uncertain.

likely scenario (the possibility of influence from an etymologically distinct OE *blæst* is also relatively slight). **Race** (etc.) are not necessarily derived from ON /ɑ:/, but if the source is a by-form in PGmc */a/ then there are no clear OE etyma available (PGmc */a/ in this root being known only in Scand); and influence from Fr is possible but unlikely. For **brenne**, **brusten** and **renne**, non-metathesized variants are rare or non-existent in attested OE (except in a very limited semantic field, in the case of **renne**); and **brenne** and **renne** moreover lexicalize very basic concepts. For **mensk** (etc.), the evidence of non-palatalized /sk/ combines with syncope in the *-*isk* suffix (which is otherwise found in clearly native variants of this suffix only in ethnonyms). **Bruny** and some **mensk-** derivatives (209b., c., d.) are supported by additional derivational evidence (C1) (though for **bruny** there is also the prospect of Fr input). In the case of **tulk**, borrowing of this ult. Slavonic or Lithuanian word via ON is supported by its relatively unusual vocalism (with a /u/) in ME (contrast Ger and Du forms in /o/).

Circumstantial evidence from Gmc or English dial distribution provides guidance relatively infrequently here. Only **bruny** has meaningful 'a' evidence to add to the counter-argument; and only **brenne**, **mensk/menskly** (i.e. subentries 209a. and e. only), **renne** and **tulk** are labelled 'c'.

There is little significant disagreement between the major scholarly authorities over these items. The most important exception is **blaste**: surprisingly, neither *OED* nor *MED* mentions the prospect of ON input here (and neither do TG(D) or GDS), but this is corrected by *ODEE*, in keeping with the strong case for Scand origin argued by Bj. The major dictionaries otherwise show no serious differences in their etymologies; and TG(D) and GDS vary only when it comes to **brusten**.[390]

The less and least plausible stems, marked 'CC2' and 'CCC2', are these:

CC2
askez
blenk
breþer
burþe
busk
fest (etc.)
ȝol
half-suster
lygez
lyre
mele
merk (etc.)
muckel
renk

---

[390] TG(D) offer both OE and ON etyma; GDS refers only to ON. Notice also **race** (etc.), where TG(D) cite both ON *ras* and *rás*, but GDS refers only to ON *rás*. The only difference between TG and the revised TGD comes with **bruny**, where TGD adds the possibility of Fr input to the ON etymon given by TG.

scrape
silk (etc.)
syluerin
stryþþe
vmbe
whyrlande
worre

CCC2
cnokez (etc.)
croun
fawne
forth
haspe (n., v.)
hete (etc.)
if
lyke (etc.)
messe
nikked
sate
soþen
þenk
þynke
walt (etc.)
wela

For all of these items, the formal feature in question seems to me at least as likely to have come about by native phonological or analogical changes as by input from ON. Purely phonological endogenous developments are plausible in the case of: **askez, ʒol, haspe** (n. and v.), **if, renk,**[391] **scrape** (native /sk/ is held to be especially likely before /r/), **sylkyn** (219b. only), **syluerin, wela, whyrlande.** Analogical changes, inc. levelling across paradigms, could account for: **breþer, hete** (etc.), **lygez, lyke** (etc.), **muckel, silk** (219a. only), **soþen, þenk, þynke.** And one or both of these types of development may lie behind: **burþe** (there are various possible contributors to the fricative here, inc. a native variant without VL as well as later analogical changes), **fest** (etc.), **forth, mele, worre.** In addition, cross-influence from a related native word-form is very likely in the case of **blenk, burþe, merk** (etc.), **worre**; and from a related word in a third language for **busk, haspe** (n., v.), **merk** (etc.), **messe, scrape** and **vmbe.** When it comes to **lyre,** it seems very possible that two (originally distinct) native words have fallen together in ME, which would account well enough for the mixture of forms and senses without recourse to ON influence. An especially complex range

---

[391] And in this case, there are potential difficulties with assuming VAN /e/ in an ON form which retained /nk/; see the entry.

of possibilities is presented by **stryþþe**, which include influence from another OE word (like OE *stīð* or the obscure *strīð*) as well as via ON input. A native ideophonic variant seems a quite plausible source for **cnokez** (etc.). For **fawne, mele, messe** and **walt** (etc.), a variant with a suitable form is indeed already recorded in OE texts (so the case for ON input is about 'reinforcement' at best). In the case of **(half-)suster**, the ME spelling is ambiguous: it might reflect ME /y/ from late OE /y/ (and hence < ON), but it might stand simply for ME /u/ (and hence the native cognate). The same is true for **sate**, where the argument for ON input applies only if the sound meant is ME /a:/, and not if it is /a/. In some instances, the form of the ME word is far more likely to be native in origin: hence **forth** (where no close cognate is attested in the Scand languages, and so ON input could amount to no more than general sound substitution), **nikked** (the nearest Scand v. forms have different vocalism) and **worre** (the /o/ vowel at least must come from a native form). And the existence of a VAN reflex of the supposed ON etymon is questionable in the case of **croun** and **messe**.

Circumstantial evidence again applies to relatively few of the items under discussion here. Only nine stems are labelled 'a' (i.e. **burþe, cnokez** (etc.), **croun, fawne, if, messe, vmbe, whyrlande, worre**), with the feature in question known elsewhere in WGmc, which in principle weakens the case for ON input. And sixteen are marked 'c' (**blenk, brenne, breþer** (also 'b'), **busk** (also 'b'), **fest** (etc.), **ȝol, hetes** (203b. only), **lygez, lyke** (etc.), **lyre, mele, muckel, nikked, vmbe, walt** (etc.), **wela, worre**),[392] although, in the face of the other difficulties presented by these words, this is not in itself cause to raise their probability any higher than the 'CC' group.

A number of these 'CC' and 'CCC' stems have occasioned disagreement between the various scholarly authorities. *OED* and *MED* differ substantially when it comes to fourteen stems, viz. **blenk, busk, cnokez** (etc.), **forth, haspe** (n. only), **lyke** (etc.), **lyre, mele, muckel, renk, scrape, silk** (etc.), **stryþþe, wela**.[393] *MED* is markedly more likely across these items to argue for ON input, which it does in ten

---

[392] And **forth** is marked 'b' only.

[393] **Blenk:** *OED* treats this v. as native, *MED* claims at least some input from ON. **Busk:** *OED* prefers ON origin, *MED* derives from medieval Lat (and positively discounts ON input). **Cnokez** (etc.): *OED* regards it as native, *MED* adds possible ON input. **Forth:** *OED* explains as native, *MED* has possible ON input. **Haspe** (n. only): *OED* derives from OE, *MED* offers both OE and ON etyma. **Lyke** (etc.): the original *OED* treats as native, *MED* suggests some ON input (as later does *ODEE*, and now *OED3*). **Lyre:** *OED* does not refer to any possibility of ON input, *MED* makes mention of both prospective ON sources. **Mele:** *OED* derives from OE only, *MED* has ON input. **Muckel:** the original *OED* explains as native only, *MED* allows for ON input (as also now does *OED3*). **Renk:** *OED* native only, *MED* has a 'cp'. to ON. **Scrape:** *OED* derives from OE with the possibility of ON input, *MED* does not mention OE (ON with possible Fr influence). **Silk** (etc.): *OED* derives from OE only, *MED* has a 'cp'. to ON. **Stryþþe:** *OED* suggests ON-influenced sound substitution, *MED* suggests the influence of OE *stīð*. **Wela:** *OED* suggests partial confusion with OE *wā lā, weg lā*, *MED* does not. Notice also the more minor differences with respect to **breþer** (*OED3* adds the possibility of some reinforcement from ON to the original *OED*'s (and *MED*'s) claim for native origin), **burþe** (*OED* refers to the possible absence of VL in a native variant as well as the analogy with the þ-suffix cited by *MED*), **fest** (*OED* thinks that ON input is likely, *MED* gives only a 'cp'. to the ON form), **ȝol** (*OED* explains as native only, *MED* adds a 'cp.' (only) to the ON form).

instances (as opposed to only three where *OED* has a stronger preference for Scand origin). TGD and GDS disagree significantly over nine stems: **burþe, croun, festned** (198b. only), **half-suster, lygez, messe, muckel, wela, whyrlande**.[394] The etymologies in GDS for these words are more likely to feature ON input: its labels have a more strongly Scand element than those of TG(D) in six cases, next to just two of the reverse. TG differs from the revised TGD when it comes to **breþer**.[395] TG(D) and GDS rarely agree with one another in the face of a different etymology in both *OED* and *MED*, but this is true for **ʒol** (where both editions refer to ON as well as OE) and **soþen** (both claim ON influence). Bj. usually agrees with one or more of the above, except with respect to **fawne** (where he allows for ON reinforcement) and **fest** (where he finds ON input very doubtful). But nineteen 'CC2' and 'CCC2' stems are not treated at all in Bj's book, viz. **blenk, breþer, cnokez** (etc.), **croun, haspe** (n., v.), **hete** (etc.), **if, lygez, messe, nikked, renk, sate, silk** (etc.), **soþen, þenk, þynke, walt** (etc.), **wela**,[396] **whyrlande**. Some items were often attributed an ON origin early in the scholarly tradition, and are now more generally explained as native, viz. **fawne, hete** (etc.), **nikked, stryþþe, walt** (etc.), **wela**. On the other hand there are also items whose potential ON pedigree has come to be stressed only in more recent work, such as **if** (Miller 2012 only), **þenk, þynke** (see esp. Krygier 2000).

4.3. TYPE C3

4.3.1. *Summary list*

Category C3 consists of forty stems, four with sub-entries; there are forty-six distinct lexical items altogether.

231.   **angardez**; n. (gen. sg., as adj.); 'i.e. excessive, arrogant' [FCCC3c]
232.   **at**; prep.; 'at (etc.)' [CCC3]
233.   **baret**; n.; 'strife, fighting; trouble, sorrow' [FCCC3bc]
234.   **bit**; n.; 'blade, cutting edge' [CC3]
235a. **borde**; n.; 'table' [CCC3]
235b. **sid-bordez**; n. (pl.); 'side tables' [CCC3]
236.   **boun**; adj.; 'ready; bound, setting out' [C3c]
237.   **bred**; n.; 'bread' [CCC3a]

---

[394] **Burþe**: TG(D) derive from OE, GDS from ON. **Croun**: TG(D) cite ON and Fr forms, GDS only the Fr. **Festned** (198b. only): TG(D) explain as native only, GDS cites OE and ON. **Half-suster**: TG (D) derive from OE, GDS from ON. **Lygez**: TG(D) derive from ON, GDS from OE. **Messe**: TG(D) regard as native, GDS suggests some ON input. **Muckel**: TG(D) derive from OE, GDS offers some ON input. **Wela**: TG(D) regard as native, GDS has input from ON (via late OE *weg lā*). **Whyrlande**: TG(D) cite OE *hwyrftlian* as well as ON, GDS gives ON only. Note also **merk** (where TG(D)'s native etymon is OE *gemerce*, but GDS's is OE *mearc*), **scrape** (GDS gives no etymology), **worre** (TG(D)) account for the vocalism by the influence of ME *wors*).

[395] TGD adds a reference to an OE form with a mutated pl., alongside ON, where TG (and GDS) refer only to ON.

[396] Though Bj. does discuss the possibility of ON influence on late OE *weg lā* itself.

238. **breue**; v.; 'to declare, announce; write down' [FCCC3c]
239. **britten**; v.; 'to break up, destroy; cut (up)' [CC3c]
240. **bur**; n.; 'onslaught, blow; strength; violence' [CC3c]
241. **caryez**; v. (pres. 3 sg.); 'rides, goes' [FC3]
242. **dowelle**; v.; 'to remain' [CC3]
243. **dreme**; n.; 'dreaming' [C3ac]
244. **dreped**; v. (pp.); 'slain, killed' [CCC3c]
245a. **dryȝe**; adj.; 'unmoved, enduring; incessant, heavy' [CC3ac (CC1a)]
245b. **dreȝ**; adv.; 'forcibly' [CC3ac (CC1a)]
245c. **dreȝly**; adv.; 'unceasingly' [CC3ac (CC1a)]
246. **fyked**; v. (pret.); 'flinched' [CC3a]
247. **fnast**; v. (pret.); 'snorted, panted' [CCC3c]
248. **forlondez**; n. (pl.); 'forelands, promontories' / 'low-lying lands' [CC3 (CC4a)]
249. **forne**; adv.; 'of old' [CCC3b]
250. **garysoun**; n.; 'keepsake, treasure' [FCC3 (FCC4)]
251. **ȝayned**; v. (pret. sg.); 'met, greeted' [CCC3a]
252. **ȝeres-ȝiftes**; n. (pl.); 'New Year's gifts' [CC3a]
253. **yrnes**; n. (pl.); 'pieces of armour' [CCC3]
254. **knape**; n.; 'man, fellow' [CCC3b]
255. **layne**; v.; 'to conceal' [C3c (C5)]
256. **lawe**; n.; 'law; style' [C3d]
257. **lete (as)**; v.; 'to behave (as if); utter' [CC3ac (CC4)]
258. **mon**; v. (pres. 3 sg.); 'must' [C3c]
259. **mosse**; n.; 'moss, lichen' [CCC3ab]
260. **ner(e), nerre**; adv./prep.; 'near, nearer' [CC3a]
261a. **seme**; v.; 'to beseem, suit, seem fitting; seem, appear' [C3]
261b. **biseme**; v.; 'to befit, become, suit' [C3]
262. **sete**; adj.; 'fitting, excellent' [CCC3 (CCC1)]
263. **sponez**; n. (pl.); 'spoons' [CC3a]
264. **steuen**; n.; 'appointment, tryst, appointed day' [CC3b]
265. **þrast**; n.; 'thrust' [CC3]
266. **ware**; v.; 'to deal, deliver; spend, employ' [CC3c]
267. **warþe**; n.; '?ford, shore' [CC3c]
268. **wynne**; v.; 'to get with effort (to), reach (intrans.); come, go' [CC3ac]
269a. **with**; prep.; 'with (etc.)' [CCC3]
269b. **withalle**; adv.; 'entirely, altogether' [CCC3]
269c. **þerwyth**; adv.; '(together) with it, thereupon' [CCC3]
270. **wondered**; v. (pret. sg.); 'made wonder, surprised (impers.)' [CC3]

4.3.2. *Further remarks*

For items of Type C3, the argument for ON input is based on a difference between the meaning of the ME word in question and the meaning we would otherwise expect to attach to the form-source (whether this is a Gmc root as it came down to OE, or a third language).

There is only one sub-entry here with an exactly parallel derived form in the Scand languages, viz. **dreȝly** (245c.).[397] Items whose semantic evidence is supported by additional structural evidence (and which have a subsidiary type label in brackets) are **dryȝe** (etc.) (C1), **forlondez** (C4), **garysoun** (C4), **layne** (C5), **lete (as)** (C4), **sete** (C1).[398]

Five C3 stems show an 'F' prefix, and hence have a non-Gmc form-source which is not attested in (early) OE: **angardez, baret, breue, caryez, garysoun**. The immediate source for all these is Fr (ult. < Gmc for **angardez** and **garysoun**), with the exception of **breue** (< Lat). The ulterior etymology of the Fr etymon of **baret** is disputed, as is that of the potential ON contributor (as in OIcel *barátta*), and borrowings in both directions have been supposed. The proposed ON etyma for **breue** and **knape** are usually taken to be loans via or from LG (though the earlier history of Gmc **knap-* and related forms is also debatable). Other C3 items whose ulterior etymologies present difficulties of one sort or another are: **britten, dreme, fyked, knape, þrast, ware**.[399] Etymological uncertainties which bear directly on the evidence for ON input in ME involve:

> **bur**: notice the arguments concerning some perh. connected OE words (OE *ambyre* etc.), which (if they really are related) would give additional support for the existence of an OE form in the right sense area;
>
> **dreme**: if the two sense branches ('dream' and 'joy, noise') are etymologically distinct, then the ME word meaning 'dream' can prob. be explained as native only if an OE word in this sense existed but went unattested (which seems unlikely); but it is also possible that the two sense branches share an origin, and in that case the independent development of the meaning 'dream' in English is more plausible;
>
> **fyked**: OE *fic-* words are often regarded as etymologically distinct from the Scand v. posited as etymon here; but the two may be related, and in that case there is a more plausible basis for an endogenous development (prob. an OE v. surviving in an unattested concrete sense); and
>
> **forne**: OE *forn(e)* is usually derived from *foran-*, but occasionally taken to be cognate with ON *forn* 'old'; and if the latter is true, then this would weaken still further the case for ON input here.

Notice also the following issues:

> **angardez**: the possibility is often raised of input from the etymologically-obscure ME *overgart* (and related forms), and/or from the various

---

[397] Notice also **withalle**, which TG(D) compare to the OIcel phrase *með ǫllu*.

[398] And notice also the correspondences between OE and ON alliterative collocations remarked upon by Olszewska for **britten** and **dreped**.

[399] In the case of **þrast**, the histories of both the OE form-source and the purported source of ON input are obscure.

supposed ON etyma of these words, in which case multiple complexities
ensue;

borde (etc.): the Gmc words meaning 'board, plank' and 'side (of a ship),
shield' have sometimes been distinguished etymologically (though they
are more usually now regarded as identical);

ȝayned: late OE *gegegnian* is formally ambiguous (we could have root-
initial /j/ here, or it could represent an early reflex of ME **gayn** (v.) with
/g/);

mon: the spelling is again ambiguous, but the weight of the broader ME
evidence favours a /u/ form (which adds to the case for ON input);

mosse: OE only had a str. n.; the ME word could in principle show input
either from the ON wk. by-form or from the Scand str. n. represented by
Sw, Dan *mos*; and

sponez: the Gmc variant in /o:/ sometimes posited is not necessary in
order to account for /o:/ forms in any of the older Gmc languages.

Related but more minor issues of form, or sense, or interpretation in context
in *Gaw*, are various. But notice the following in particular: **caryez** (the form
at *Gaw* 734 has sometimes been emended away); **fyked** (Magoun's alternative
but very unconvincing derivation); **fnast** (Savage's argument about the sense
in context, which is necessary if ON input is to be posited); **forlondez** (the
possibility of ON input again depends on the reading of the meaning in
context, this time argued by GDS); **forne** (once again, the case here depends
upon the reading of the sense, as proposed by Emerson); **ȝayned** (Morris's
apparent confusion with **ȝeȝe**); **ȝeres-ȝiftes** (the proposed emendation noted
by Rynell); **lawe** (the possible influence from OFr *loi*, Anglo-Fr *lei*, on the
sense 'style, manner'); **lete (as)** (the emendation at *Gaw* 1281); **mon** (the
identification of *Gaw* 2354); **ner(e), nerre** (most occurrences are ambiguously
positive or comp. in context); **seme** (etc.) (ON *sœma* is usually assumed to be
the source, but *sóma* is nearer in sense, as TG(D) notice); **sete** (the prospect
of ON input rests mainly on *MED*'s suggested interpretation of the sense);
warþe (the possibility of ON input depends on reading the sense 'ford',
which has become quite common but is not the universal intepretation here). I
have drawn attention to rarely cited difficulties in the case of: **angardez**
(drawing out the full range of complexities invoked especially by Brett and
McGee); **bur** (discussing the possible OE cognates, often missed in the
standard accounts); **dreme** (exploring the wealth of issues pertaining to the
etymology of this word); **sete** (disputing *MED*'s case for influence from ON
sœtr, on the basis of the vocalism of the ME forms indicated by rhyme
evidence). And I have mounted new arguments in particular for: **borde** (etc.)
(pointing out the possible indications in the 'inkhorn' *Riddles* and the OE
Bede that OE *bord* could be understood as referring to a table); **dryȝe** (etc.)
(noticing that a sense similar to that attested in OE is the only one recorded
beyond the N/EM in ME texts); **ware** (arguing that the senses found in ME

might have resulted from native semantic developments, and setting out possible etymologies for OE *warian* (II); and also noticing the markedly different distribution of *MED*'s sense (d), which is arguably a straightforward descendant of the native word).

4.3.2.1. Types of structural evidence at issue

Type C3, where the focus of the discussion is on semantic rather than formal features, demonstrates particularly well how approaching the evidence for ON input *etymologically* may cut across or complicate the categories traditionally employed in treatments of lexical borrowing – in this case, it blurs the distinction between the 'loanword proper' and input which is not morphemic, especially the 'semantic loan'.[400] At any rate, if what we are primarily interested in is the comparative, structural evidence on which we base the etymological identification of influence from one (especially closely related) language upon another, then trying to draw distinctions between some of these categories is in practice less pressing than (and can indeed sometimes be a distraction from) considering together all the items for which the argument for foreign input is fundamentally of the same type. This is not to deny that there are some C3 stems where, if ON input is to be attributed, we *must* be dealing with semantic loans as conventionally understood. In all the following cases, the form of the ME word must descend from OE,[401] but one or more of the senses attested in ME appears to be closer to a meaning not known (or known only rarely) in the OE corpus but recorded for the equivalent word (which may be its direct cognate) in ON: thus **borde** (etc.), **bred, dreme, fnast, ʒayned, (ʒeres-)ʒiftes, yrnes, lete (as), wondered**.[402] And there are several others whose shape does not guarantee a native form-source, but where this is possible,[403] and where semantic influence could again have been felt from an etymologically-related word in ON. All these could therefore in principle also represent instances of semantic loans, as traditionally conceived: **at, bit, boun, breue, bur, dowelle, dreped, dryʒe** (etc.), **forlondez, knape, layne, lawe, mon, mosse, ner(e)/nerre, seme** (etc.), **sponez, steuen, wynne, with** (etc.). Notice that there is overlap between the recorded senses of the OE and Scand reflexes in the case of **borde** (etc.), **bred, yrnes, lete (as)** and **wondered**, and similarly for **at, bit, britten, dreped, sponez, wynne** and **with** (etc.), and perh. also for **bur** and **dowelle**; there are

---

[400] For these categories, and for general discussion of the roles of semantic evidence in assessing the outcomes of contact situations, see the references cited in the Introductory Remarks at note 18 above, and further e.g. Haugen (1950: 214, 219–20), Gneuss (1955: esp. 20–37), Hock 1(991: 397–400, who refers to semantic loans as 'loan shifts'), Kastovsky (1992: 299–300, 309–12), Dance (2003: esp. 74, 93–4) and Durkin (2009: 136–7; 2014: 8–10).

[401] Unless we assume sound-substitution; see the remarks by Durkin cited under **dreme**.

[402] **Britten** ought prob. also to be grouped here, since no comparable form with the *n*-suffix is attested in the Scand languages.

[403] Or, in the case of **breue**, where we could be dealing with an earlier loan from Lat into OE.

therefore good grounds on which to base an argument for semantic loan of the 'analogical' type (i.e. the meanings of the OE word were extended by comparison with the existing range of senses of its ON counterpart).

In some other comparable instances the meaning of the ME word arguably descends from an ON etymon which is superficially similar to a word in OE, with this formal similarity motivating the possible association of the two during the contact process; but the two words might not be, or are certainly not, etymologically connected. Thus **fyked**, **forne** and **ware** (where the OE and ON words are perh., but not necessarily, related etymologically), and also **sete**, **þrast** and **warþe** (where they are definitely not related). Note that the last three are prob. native in form;[404] and further that, in the case of **sete** and **warþe** at least, the semantic difference between the native form-source and the putative ON etymon is relatively large. We must therefore assume that the conflation or confusion of two semantically quite distinct words is at work, for reasons as much of form-association as anything else, rather than these being instances of semantic loan of the more common type. For **þrast** the OE and ON etyma do at least overlap in meaning (though the nearest OE senses are only attested in relatively late glosses).

In several cases, of course, the form of the word seems to rule out an origin in OE, and instead derives from Fr: **angardez**, **baret**, **caryez**, **garysoun**. With respect to **caryez** and **garysoun**, we are prob. dealing with two originally distinct loans into English (one from ON, one from Fr), followed by subsequent cross-influence between the resultant already formally and semantically similar outcomes in ME.[405] Nonetheless, the argument for ON input here is fundamentally of exactly the same type as it is for all the stems cited above: that is, it is something about the *meaning* of the ME word in question which points the finger at some influence, somewhere along the line of its evolution, from a Scand language; and all these items therefore belong together under Type C3. A related practical and hermeneutic advantage of this grouping is that, though it is often possible to distinguish words where *only* the sense may have descended from ON from words showing the results of other kinds of morphemic relationship between the languages in contact, in not all cases can we do so. At times, that is, it simply is not possible to be sure whether (if we do assume some ON input) we have a loanword 'proper', or a semantic loan, or some combination of inputs, mutually reinforcing one another. In all the following instances, the meaning of the ME output could owe something to ON, but the form could derive either from OE (or a third language) or from ON or from both: **baret**, **bit**, **boun**, **breue**, **bur**, **dowelle**, **dreped**, **dryȝe** (etc.), **fyked**, **forne**, **knape**, **layne**, **lawe**, **mon**, **mosse**, **ner(e)/nerre**, **seme** (etc.), **steuen**,

---

[404] See the discussion of the ME rhyme evidence at **sete**.

[405] The same may also be true of **angardez**, although in this instance the precise ON word (or loanword into ME) which is the eventual source of the Scand input is unclear, and the case for ON influence is less robust altogether.

sponez, ware, wynne, with (etc.). Notice that several of these items are not conventionally described by the etymological authorities as if they could be semantic loans at all. A good example is **layne**, which is habitually labelled as if it is a straightforward loan of the ON v. represented by OIcel *leyna*; nevertheless, its rare OE cognate in an Angl form (**lēgnan*) could lie formally behind ME *layne* just as well as could this supposed ON etymon, and it is therefore the difference between their recorded meanings which is really the crucial factor in the argument for ON input, even if we are not sure whether to call what results a semantic loan, or a loanword, or both. The same is true of **boun, bur, dryʒe** (etc.), **lawe, mon, seme** and **ware**, all of which are usually analysed as loanwords proper.[406]

4.3.2.2. *Probability of ON input*

Gauging the plausibility of Scand input for Type C3 items depends upon assessing the relative likelihoods that the sense development found in ME is the result of a Norse-derived innovation versus the alternatives – i.e. usually an independent, endogenous change within English (or sometimes the survival into ME from Gmc of a branch of meaning not attested in the OE record). It is infamously difficult to generalize about semantic change, and in particular to predict the likely outcome of change in a given case, since the number of variables at work is so large – not least because the meanings of any one word are subtly interrelated with those of many others in the dynamic system of a lexicon.[407] Some kinds of semantic change nonetheless seem relatively common, and hence likely to have happened independently (esp. in closely-related words) in more than one language (see further below); whereas by comparison some other outcomes appear less likely.

Weighing up all the evidence in each case, it seems to me that the Type C3 stems may be divided between the three usual probability groupings as follows: C3 seven stems; CC3 eighteen stems; CCC3 fifteen stems. The proportions for this sub-type are therefore closely comparable to those for Type C2 discussed above (8:21:16), once again giving a relatively small proportion of stems for which the argument for ON input is convincing. These most plausible items, marked 'C3', are:

> **boun**
> **caryez**
> **dreme**
> **layne**

---

[406] The standard description of **dryʒe** (etc.) as a loanword is perh. because the existence of a late OE adj. derivation has been missed (as it seems to have been by *OED*).

[407] For the now classic statement of the problems, see Durkin (2009: 259–60); and see further the remarks at e.g. Lass (1997: 138), and the careful discussion of the ramifications of these issues for the etymologist in Hoad (1993).

lawe
mon
seme (etc.)

For these most compelling stems, where the case for ON input is most widely accepted, we tend to have a ME word which lexicalizes a relatively basic and frequently occurring concept, and moreover we have to deal with a sense which is markedly different from anything recorded for the same or a related stem in OE (hence rendering more or less implausible either an unattested OE retention of this sense or an independent endogenous generation of it) or in a third language. This seems to me to be true for **boun**, **dreme**, **lawe**, **mon** and **seme**, and also (from a Fr starting point) **caryez**. Significant support is added if the meaning in question is very characteristic of this root in the Scand languages, but not elsewhere in Gmc. For C3 words, this most obviously applies with **lawe**: only in NGmc (and in English, from the late OE period) is the PGmc *lag-* root used of the laying down of legal edict; the WGmc languages otherwise most often employ a form of *sat-* in this role. A typically ON usage is also evident in the case of **mon**, which is grammaticalized as a future auxiliary only in the Scand languages and (esp. northern/eastern) English. I have also labelled **layne** with a single 'C', since the corresponding OE word is very rare (and hence the additional C5 marker).

Four out of these seven stems are supported by the circumstantial evidence of dialect distribution within English ('c'), viz. **boun**, **dreme**, **layne**, **mon**; and **lawe** is labelled with a 'd', since its earliest attestations are strongly associated with Scand cultural influence. **Dreme** is marked 'a', since the sense 'dream' is also known in continental WGmc; but this fact does not seem to me significantly to raise the probability that the same meaning was available in OE but went unrecorded.

There is relatively little disagreement in the scholarly authorities over the C3 items in this sub-group. But *OED* and *MED* differ regarding **caryez** and **dreme** (with *MED* in both cases preferring ON input);[408] and TG(D) and GDS also diverge in their etymologies for **dreme**.[409] *Cayrez* is not treated as such by Bj. (who deals only with the more straightforward ON loanword **kayre**).

The less and least plausible stems, marked 'CC3' and 'CCC3', are as follows:

CC3
bit
britten
bur
dowelle
dryʒe (etc.)

---

[408] **Caryez**: *OED* derives from Fr only, *MED* explains this sense as showing ON input. **Dreme**: *OED* regards as native (though notice that *ODEE* refers to the possibility of ON input), *MED* derives this sense from ON.

[409] TG(D) claim ON input, GDS derives from OE only. Notice also **caryez** (GDS emends to *cayrez*, i.e. seeing ON influence on form as well as sense) and **seme** (etc.) (TG(D) derive from ON *sóma* rather than the usually cited Scand etymon, i.e. ON *sœma*).

fyked
forlondez
garysoun
ʒeres-ʒiftes
lete (as)
ner(e), nerre
sponez
steuen
þrast
ware
warþe
wynne
wondered

CCC3
angardez
at
baret
borde (etc.)
bred
breue
dreped
fnast
forne
ʒayned
yrnes
knape
mosse
sete
with (etc.)

Invoking ON input seems less necessary when the alternative is to propose a semantic development which a native word (or a word deriving from a third source) could plausibly have undergone independently. When we have a relatively commonplace type of semantic change, for which it is easy to cite parallels, then the case for an endogenous development seems especially strong.[410] Hence widening (generalization) is arguably at work in **bred**, **breue**, **(ʒeres-)ʒiftes**, **knape** and **wynne**.[411] Narrowing

---

[410] For recent discussions of broad tendencies in meaning change, and ways of classifying these, see e.g. Minkova & Stockwell (2009: 168–80), Durkin (2009: esp. 235–53), Geeraerts (2010: 25–41), Kay & Allan (2015: 70–91), and references there cited; and for reviews of scholarly approaches to semantic (and pragmatic) change see further e.g. Traugott & Dasher (2002: esp. 51–104) and Fitzmaurice (2016).

[411] For **wynne**, it is very easy to imagine generalization via an absolute usage of OE *gewinnan*; and compare later English *get*. Semantic generalizations are especially common in the language of alliterative verse (see e.g. Turville-Petre 1977: 80–1), and notice that the broader meaning ('to tell' (etc.)) of **breue** is attested only in that context.

(specialization) may be seen in **dreped** and **sete**,[412] and also in **lete (as)** and perh. **bit** and **garysoun**.[413] There are moreover some very plausible examples of narrowing by metonymy, viz. **borde** (etc.), **yrnes**, **sponez**; all these may be argued to instantiate metonymic extensions of a very common type, i.e. MATERIAL FOR OBJECT.[414] And further items in the lists above may represent other common enough types of semantic extension, such as by metaphor (e.g. **angardez**),[415] or other self-evidently likely developments in meaning and usage (e.g. **ner(e)/nerre**, the comp. 'nearer' used absolutely and hence positively; **wondered**, the development of an impersonal from a personal use, perh. by analogy with other verbs of impression in ME where both construction types were available). Appealing to ON influence appears to have least to recommend it when the distance between the two 'different' senses in question is not in effect all that great; see in particular **at**, **baret**, **fnast**, **forne**, **with** (etc.).

When it comes to **fyked** and **mosse**, there is a good case to be made for an unattested OE retention of what is (arguably) the etymologically earlier sense.[416] Sometimes the relevant meaning may already be present in the OE record, depending on how one interprets certain ambiguous instances, as with **borde** (etc.), **bred** and perhaps **bur**.[417] And in some instances it is undeniably to be found in OE, making the argument more about the spread and increase in frequency of this sense than its introduction *per se*; thus **(ȝeres-)ȝiftes**, **knape**. In some cases influence from another formally (or semantically) proximate native word seems at least as likely as ON input, viz. **britten**, **steuen**, **with**; and with **mosse** there is the prospect of input from the Fr (or medieval Lat) version of the same word. Sometimes the meanings recorded in the Scand languages do not correspond entirely to the 'new' sense shown by the ME item, and hence assuming ON input will only get us some of the way towards the sense development required. This is true of **bur** (a further metaphorical extension is required to bridge the gap from 'strong wind' to the meaning 'onslaught, strength' known in ME), **knape** (the ON cognate does not simply mean 'man' as such, requiring additional generalization, and some of the meanings attested in OE are actually nearer to what we find in ME) and **ware** (the ON v. is recorded

---

[412] With **dreped**, compare the exactly parallel evolution of the meanings of English *slay*.

[413] The development of **lete (as)** may be understood as a narrowing from 'allow' (generally) to 'allow (an impression of), behave (as if)' and 'allow (out), utter' (i.e. words). For **bit**, the development is perh. from a general idea of 'cutting' to 'something that cuts'; for **garysoun**, from a general idea of income to reference to valuable objects more specifically.

[414] The sense development of **yrnes** is easy to parallel; cp. the use of OE *īren* in verse to mean 'sword'. Another possible instance of metonymic extension is **mosse** (perhaps 'bog' > 'a plant especially associated with bogs, moss'); but see further below.

[415] With **angardez**, cp. the metaphorical senses of Fr *hauteur*.

[416] Notice also **ȝayned**: if the relevant meaning is native in origin, then either the survival of a sense not attested in OE texts or (perh. more plausibly) a new verbal derivation on the OE adj. *gegn* seem more likely than a shift in the meaning of the existing wk. 1 v. (whose sense 'to drive' is quite distant from the 'to meet' recorded elsewhere in Gmc). Similar things may be true of **(ȝeres-)ȝiftes**, if one follows *OED*'s suggestion of a new nominal derivation on the related v.

[417] The recorded OE senses of **dowelle** and **þrast** may also (arguably) come nearer to those found in ME than is often appreciated.

with the meanings 'to invest money, lay out; exert oneself', but we still need to get to the slightly different emphases found in ME, viz. 'to deal, deliver; spend, employ'). In the case of **sete** the sense supposedly influenced by ON is debated, and may not in fact be evidenced in ME; and it is also doubtful for **fnast, forlondez, forne** and **warþe**.[418] With **breue** and **knape**, the existence of the supposed ON etymon during the VAN period is doubtful.

In terms of circumstantial evidence, eleven stems belonging to CC3 and CCC3 are labelled 'a' (in the proportion 8:3), and hence for these items the existence of close semantic comparanda in continental WGmc contributes to the impression that the meaning in question might have developed in English independently of ON input. Sixteen stems are marked 'b' or 'c' or both (eight CC3, eight CCC3), but the evidence of English dial distribution is not, in the face of the various other difficulties presented by these items, enough to raise above the 'possible' category the likelihood with which Scand influence seems to me to be attributable.[419]

Many of these thirty-three stems have, unsurprisingly, been the objects of disagreement between the standard scholarly authorities. *OED* and *MED* differ substantially in their views on eleven of them, viz. **angardez, baret, dryȝe** (etc.), **fyked, knape, lete (as), sete, steuen, þrast, wynne, with** (etc.).[420] Honours are about even here, with *OED* preferring Scand input in six cases, next to five where it is advanced by *MED*. *ODEE* claims some ON input for **dowelle** and some (semantic) influence on **mosse**, where *OED* had not.[421] Fourteen stems receive significantly different treatments in TG(D) vs GDS, i.e. **bit, breue, dreped, fyked, forlondez, garysoun, ȝayned, lete (as), ner(e)/nerre, sponez,**

---

[418] And for **breue** the required meaning is not clearly attested in ON.

[419] For **knape**, the argument for any ON input (weak as it is) seems to me to be founded largely on the distribution of this element in the toponymic record.

[420] **Angardez**: *OED* relates the word to ON *ágjarn* (etc.), *MED* derives from Fr only. **Baret**: *OED*'s account refers to the possibility of ON input, *MED* derives only from Fr. **Dryȝe** (etc.): *OED* regards as native, *MED* derives from ON. **Fyked**: *OED* allows for some ON input, *MED* derives only from OE. **Knape**: *OED* derives from OE only, *MED* adds the possibility of ON input. **Lete (as)**: *OED* gives only a native origin, *MED* allows for some ON input (for the 'behave' sense). **Sete**: *OED* derives from OE, *MED* adds ON input. **Steuen**: *OED* gives a native etymon, *MED* suggests ON input. **Þrast**: *OED* involves ON input, *MED* derives from OE only. **Wynne**: *OED* derives partly from ON, *MED* only from OE. **With** (etc.): *OED* includes ON input, *MED* gives only the native etymon. Notice also: **borde** (etc.) (*OED* specifies possible input from ON, *MED* simply has a 'cp.'); **ȝeres-ȝiftes** (*OED* explains ME /j/- forms meaning 'gift' as new derivations on the v., *MED* makes nothing of the sense); **mosse** (*OED* suggests ON influence on the form of the twelfth-century <mose>; *MED* cites both OE and ON etyma, without specifing the role of ON input); **ner(e)**, **nerre** (*OED* allows for some ON input; *MED* does not refer to it s.v. *nēr* adv.2, but does suggest it s.v. *nēr(re* adv.); **ware** (*OED* derives from ON only, *MED* from ON with a 'cp'. to OE).

[421] *ODEE* is also explicit about the case for ON semantic input for **sponez**, where *OED* had been less clear.

steuen, ware, **wynne, wondered**.[422] TG(D) are markedly more likely here to claim ON input, which they do for ten stems (as opposed to only four where the argument is stronger in GDS). TGD substantially revises the opinion of TG with respect to **warþe**.[423] TG(D) and GDS rarely agree with one another in contradistinction to both *OED* and *MED*, but notice **borde** (etc.) (neither edition mentions the possibility of ON influence), **britten** (the same) and **ȝeres-ȝiftes** (both editions cite ON input, but the dictionaries do not). Twenty-five of these thirty-three stems are not treated at all by Bj.;[424] in the remaining cases, Bj. generally concurs with one or more of the above authorities (but notice **dowelle**, where his claim of ON influence is matched only by *ODEE*). Arguments for ON input are isolated and outside the scholarly mainstream for **at** (only Price 1947), **fnast** (only Savage 1930) and **forne, yrnes** (both Emerson 1922a). Other instances where the key arguments are presented outside the principal etymological authorities are **bred** (the tradition of claiming Scand influence descends from Jespersen) and **knape** (*EPNE*, albeit apparently picked up by *MED*).

4.4. TYPE C4

4.4.1. *Summary list*

Category C4 consists of twelve stems, three with sub-entries; there are fifteen distinct lexical items altogether.

271. **blande**; n.; 'mingling' (in the phrase *in blande* '(mingled) together') [CC4c (CC5)]
272. **boþe**; adj., pron., adv.; 'both' [C4a]
273. **chaffer**; n.; 'trade, merchandise' [CCC4]
274a. **felaȝes**; n. (pl.); 'companions (i.e. hounds)' [C4 (C3)]
274b. **felaȝschyp**; n.; 'love of fellow men; company' [C4 (C3)]
275a. **herber**; n.; 'lodging' [CCC4a]
275b. **herber**; v.; 'to lodge' [CCC4a]

---

[422] **Bit**: TG(D) derive from ON, GDS from OE. **Breue**: TG(D) give OE and Lat etyma, GDS adds ON. **Dreped**: TG(D) allow for ON input, GDS derives from OE only. **Fyked**: TG(D) give only an OE etymon, GDS offers some ON input. **Forlondez**: TG(D) derive only from OE, GDS suggests ON influence (based on its reading of the meaning). **Garysoun**: TG(D) cite ON input, GDS derives only from Fr. **ȝayned**: TG(D) cite OE and ON etyma, GDS only OE. **Lete (as)**: TG(D) claim ON influence on the *lete as* idiom, GDS derives only from OE. **Ner(e), nerre**: TG(D) suggest ON input, GDS derives only from OE. **Sponez**: TG(D) cite ON input, GDS regards as native. **Steuen**: TG(D) give ON input, GDS derives from OE. **Ware**: TG(D) derive from OE only, GDS from ON only. **Wynne**: TG(D) allow for ON input, GDS derives from OE only. **Wondered**: TG(D) cite ON input, GDS gives only the OE etymon.

[423] TG derives from OE only (as had GDS), but TGD adds the possibility of ON input (following Haworth 1967). Notice also **ȝayned**, for which TG does not cite ON input in the glossary, but does include the word in its list of 'blend-words' (at 126), whereas TGD has a glossary reference to ON (but has deleted the discussion).

[424] He deals only with ME *gersum*, and not with **garysoun**; and he refers to **ȝayned** only to cite it as the native cognate of **gayn** v. And notice also that his treatment of **britten** comes only in the context of his general discussion of the *n*-suffix in ME verbs.

276. **hondeselle**; n.; 'gift (at New Year)' [CC4]
277. **layde**; v. (pret.); 'uttered' (in the phrase *layde ... þyse wordez* 'spoke these words; urged') [CCC4c]
278. **sake**; n.; 'sake' (in the phrase *for (. . .) sake* 'for (someone's) sake') [CC4a]
279. **sunder**; adj. as n.; 'sunder, separation' (in the phrase *in sunder* 'asunder') [CCC4ac]
280. **twelmonyth**; n.; 'twelvemonth, year' [CCC4]
281. **vpon**; prep. and adv.; 'upon, on, etc'. [CCC4c]
282a. **welcum**; adj.; 'welcome' [CCC4a]
282b. **welcum**; v.; 'to welcome' [CCC4]

4.4.2. *Further remarks*

For the few stems of Type C4, the argument for ON input rests on the existence of a ME compound or phrase which is paralleled in the Scand languages but not known in (early) OE.

Two sub-entries contain derived forms which are exactly matched in the Scand languages; thus **felaȝschyp, herber** (v.). Stems where the existence of an ON compound/phrase is supported by subsidiary structural criteria are **blande** (C5) and **felaȝes** (etc.) (C3).

No C4 stems have a non-Gmc form-source which is not already attested in OE.[425] Input from the equivalent phrase in Fr and Lat is possible for **welcum** (adj. and v.). The ON etymon proposed for **herber** (n. and v.) has often (though not always) been supposed to be a loan from LG.

Minor issues of interpretation in *Gaw* apply only in the case of **boþe** (the reading at *Gaw* 144) and **layde** (the differing interpretations of the precise meaning in context).

4.4.2.1. *Types of structural evidence at issue*

Eight of the stems belonging to Type C4 are (etymologically) compounds,[426] and owe their claim to ON input to their similarity to compound forms attested in the Scand languages: thus **boþe, chaffer, felaȝes** (etc.), **herber** (n. and v.), **hondeselle, twelmonyth, vpon, welcum** (adj. and v.).[427] The forms of **chaffer** and **twelmonyth** are clearly native, and so (if we assume that they are based

---

[425] Though the ulterior source of the first element of **chaffer**, PGmc **kaupaz* > OE *cēap*, is in Lat.

[426] For discussions of the formation and functions of compounds in the early Gmc languages (in addition to the general references on word-formation given above, at note 9) see esp. Carr (1939); and on compound formation more generally see e.g. the essays in Lieber & Štekauer (2009).

[427] **Boþe** has been grammaticalized in ME (as has its ON counterpart) and is used as a simplex determiner (with adjectival, pronominal and adverbial functions). **Vpon** has also been grammaticalized as a (compound) preposition, and *OED*'s case for ON input moreover depends upon the word-accent falling on the second element, as in PDE.

directly on ON models) they must be categorized as 'loan-translations', with the Scand compound having been re-created in each case using the OE cognates of the original ON elements.[428] The same is prob. true for **herber** (the late OE equivalent *herebeorg* certainly has native word-forms for both elements) and **hondeselle** (the second element is not an exact match for the form of the attested ON analogues), and in **welcum** both components precisely match commonplace English word-forms. The recorded late OE and early ME forms of **fela3es** (etc.) indicate that the first element of the ON compound (cp. OIcel *félagi*) had been substituted by the native cognate (OE *fēo-*); but though it is possible that the second element had also been 'translated' in this way, the OE cognate of ON *-lagi* is attested only with quite a different sense, and so it is prob. better to assume that this ON compound entered English as a loanword, with the first element assimilated to English, rather than as a 'full' loan-translation. The borrowing of **boþe** could have involved the straightforward transfer of ON *báðir* as a loanword, perh. perceived as a single morpheme (it is doubtful whether the ON word was morphologically transparent as a compound by VAN); or alternatively the ON form could have acted as the model for the creation of a new, late OE compound from existing OE *bā* plus *þā*, as is sometimes supposed; or some combination of the two processes may have occurred.

For the remaining four Type C4 stems (**blande** (n.), **layde**, **sake**, **sunder**), the argument for ON input rests on the occurrence of the ME word in a phrase which parallels a construction in one or more Scand languages. In each case, the ME idiom has therefore been explained as modelled upon that found in ON, as a 'translation' of the ON elements analogous to the loan-translation of a compound. Three of the four involve the creation of prepositional phrases (ME *in blande, for ... sake, in sunder*), and the other is the idiomatic construction *layde ... wordez* 'spoke words; ?urged'.

4.4.2.2. Probability of ON input

Type C4 items seem to me to divide between the standard threefold probability categories as follows: C4 two stems; CC4 three stems; CCC4 seven stems. We therefore have here a markedly higher proportion of stems in the least probable set than we saw for previous C sub-types; and so the case for ON input seems on the face of it less likely to be convincing for Type C4, and more liable to involve uncompelling speculation, than hitherto. This should not be altogether surprising, since by definition C4 stems feature a lexical item whose derivational and other formal features, and whose basic sense, are already recorded in (early) OE; and in the majority of instances the development of a compound or a phrase

---

[428] On the role of compounding in the outcomes of language contact, especially loan-translation and related phenomena, see the references cited in the Introductory Remarks, at note 18 above, and further esp. Haugen (1950: 214, 220), Gneuss (1955: 31–7), and the remarks in e.g. Hock (1991: 399–400), Kastovsky (1992: 313–17), Durkin (2009: 135–6; 2014: e.g. 164–6).

involving these forms and senses will quite plausibly be something that could have taken place endogenously.

The two strongest instances (**boþe** and **felaȝes** (etc.)) lexicalize very common ideas, and therefore it seems relatively improbable that they should have been in existence in early OE and gone unattested; though they might still in theory have been created in the late OE period by wholly native processes. **Boþe** has already by early ME become a commonplace lexeme, and has evidently been grammaticalized quite quickly as a simplex determiner, lending credibility to the idea that it was loaned from ON and slotted into the English system with this ready-made function; notice nonetheless the exact parallels in continental WGmc languages (it is labelled with an 'a'). While the original *OED* prefers to derive this word from ON (though *OED3* is somewhat more cautious), *MED* cites only an OE etymon. The case for **felaȝes** (etc.) is strengthened by the fact this compound is known nowhere else in Gmc beyond ON, and moreover by the use of the **lag-* root in a sense ('to fix/agree a price') very characteristic of the Scand languages and not normal in WGmc (hence the additional C3 label).

The less and least plausible stems, marked 'CC4' and 'CCC4', are:

CC4
blande
hondeselle
sake

CCC4
chaffer
herber (n., v.)
layde
sunder
twelmonyth
vpon
welcum (adj., v.)

In these cases, the phrases and compounds are constituted of (very) common-place native lexical items (thus especially **layde**, **sake**, **sunder**, **twelmonyth**, **vpon**, **welcum** (adj. and v.)), and it seems plausible that they could have been coined endogenously.[429] For **chaffer** and **hondeselle**, notice that the senses recorded for the supposed ON models are not precisely the same as those of the ME compounds. For **herber** and **welcum**, there is the additional difficulty that the proposed ON etyma have often been explained as loans from LG (or OE), and hence their availability in VAN is dubious; and Fr and/or Lat input might also have contributed to the development of **welcum**. And for **vpon**, notice that

---

[429] ME *in sunder* is very close to the existing OE *on sundran*, and so the role of ON input prob. extends no further than the modification of a native idiom, at best. And **welcum** (adj., v.) are likewise very similar to already extant OE compounds in *wil-* and forms of the *cum-* root.

OED's case for Scand influence depends at least partly on the accenting of the second element, and the *Gaw* spelling is of course ambiguous in this respect.

Four of these stems have precise parallels in continental WGmc and are labelled 'a' in one or more sub-entries (**herber** (n., v.), **sake, sunder, welcum** (adj. only)). A further four are dialectally restricted in the ME lexicon and marked 'c' (**blande, layde, sunder, vpon**).

OED and *MED* disagree over four of these stems, viz. **herber** (n. and v.), **twelmonyth, vpon, welcum** (adj. and v.),[430] with *OED* more likely to claim ON input (3:1). TG(D) and GDS differ only over **twelmonyth**.[431] The two major editions agree in opposition to both dictionaries with respect to **chaffer** (TG(D) and GDS both offer at least a comparison to the ON compound, but neither *OED* nor *MED* refers to it), **hondeselle** (neither edition mentions ON) and **sunder** (both editions cite ON input). Eight of the ten 'CC4' and 'CCC4' stems do not appear in Bj.'s book at all; he deals only with **blande** and **hondeselle**. **Herber** (n. and v.) tend to be cited as ON derivations early in the scholarly literature, but are now more generally explained as native. And notice that **layde** is an isolated claim for Scand influence, being referred to only by Olszewska (1933).

4.5. TYPE C5

4.5.1. *Summary list*

Category C5 consists of seventeen stems, two with sub-entries; there are nineteen distinct lexical items altogether:

283. **ayquere**; adv.; 'everywhere' [CC5c]
284a. **ar**; v. (pres. pl.); 'are' [CCC5]
284b. **nar**; v. (pres. pl.); 'are not' [CCC5]
285. **bale**; n.; 'destruction, death; misery' [CCC5a]
286. **berʒ**; n.; 'mound' [CCC5a]
287. **borne**; n.; 'stream' [CCC5]
288. **bullez**; n. (pl.); '(wild) bulls' [CCC5a]
289. **burde**; v. (pret. sg. (subj.)); '(it) behoved (impers.)' [CCC5ac]
290. **caple**; n.; 'horse' [FCC5b]
291. **clyff**; n.; 'cliff, (high) rock' [CCC5a]
292. **cros**; n.; 'cross' [FC5b]
293. **dale**; n.; '(bottom of) valley' [CC5ab]

---

[430] **Herber**: *OED* suggests ON derivation, *MED* gives only the native etymon. **Twelmonyth**: *OED* derives from OE only, *MED* gives a 'cp.' to the ON compound. **Vpon**: *OED* partly derives from ON, *MED* from OE only. **Welcum**: *OED* allows for the possibility of ON input, *MED* does not mention it. Notice also the more minor differences regarding **hondeselle** (*MED* seems to derive from both OE and ON, but (the original) *OED* simply states that the 'form corresponds to' either the OE or ON compounds) and **sake** (*OED* tentatively accepts ON input, *MED* lists ON as one of several comparanda, without comment).

[431] TG(D) derive from OE, GDS also has a 'cp.' to ON.

294. **ernde**; n.; 'business, mission, errand' [CCC5ac]
295. **may**; n.; 'woman' [CC5b]
296. **ryd**; v.; 'to relieve; separate; clear' [CCC5]
297a. **til**; prep., conj.; 'to; until' [C5ac]
297b. **þertylle**; adv.; 'to it' [C5c]
298. **tor**; adj.; 'hard, difficult' [CC5ac (CC4)]
299. **wayne**; v.; 'to bring, send; urge, challenge' [CCC5c (CCC1)]

4.5.2. Further remarks

For items of Type C5, there are no aspects of form or sense which cannot be explained by derivation from an already existing native word (or from one in a third language). The case for ON input therefore rests usually on the new-found frequency with which the item appears in ME.

There are no sub-entries showing a derived form which is an exact match for a corresponding word in ON. **Tor** has an additional category label (C4), because of its collocation with ME *telle* in a phrase that is similar to one known in OIcel (but the word's frequency in ME compared to OE remains the main grounds for claiming ON input); and similarly **wayne** has a subsidiary C1 label, since OE *wægn-* is not attested in a precisely corresponding v.-form (only with a prefix).[432]

Two C5 items are prefixed with an 'F', and have a form-source beyond Gmc (which is not found already in early OE).[433] The form of **caple** indicates that it has come at some stage via Ir (ult. < Lat). The ult. form-source of **cros** is also in Lat, though there is considerable debate about the route by which it reached English (it could have come via Fr or Ir as well as via ON, and a similar range of explanations attends the immediate source of ON *kross*). Other C5 stems whose etymologies are obscure or difficult in some way are **bullez**, **burde**, **ernde** and **may**. Related but more minor issues, inc. the interpretation of one or more occurrences in *Gaw*, pertain with: **ayquere** (the reading at *Gaw* 660); **ryd** (the suggestion by PS of a formally distinct by-form at *Gaw* 1344, for which I suggest an etymology); **til** (the interpretation of OE <til> at *PPs* 116, claimed as an occurrence of the prep. by Krygier); **wayne** (the difficulties of distinguishing forms of this word from those of **wayue** in the *Gaw*-manuscript). I have drawn attention to rarely cited complexities in the cases of **cros** (the sheer range of possible immediate sources that have been claimed, esp. for ON *kross*) and **ernde** (a new suggestion that SW ME spellings in <e> might add support to the argument for ON input).

---

[432] **Bale** also features in corresponding alliterative phrases in both ME and ON, but these are not found in *Gaw*.

[433] For the FC5 items, the case for ON input is of course not quite the same as for those C5 stems of Gmc origin, since it is not the 'frequency' of the item in late OE or ME which acts as the evidence – the issue is simply whether **caple** and **cros** came into English via ON, or directly from one or more of the other possible sources. But since there is no structural evidence (no particular aspect of form, sense etc.) which marks these items out as potentially showing ON input, C5 is the only appropriate category for them.

4.5.2.1. Types of structural evidence at issue

The frequency of a C5 item in ME, next to a much more limited distribution in the OE record, is usually the main grounds for claiming ON input. The proposed ON etymon is generally the direct cognate of the native form, and is therefore regarded as having either 'reinforced' or replaced it; but notice **may**, where the OE and ON words involved do not appear to be related (and see also the remarks on **ayquere** below).

Of the OE words concerned, the potential native etyma of **bale**, **may** and **wayne** are confined largely or entirely to OE verse;[434] that of **bullez** is found (infrequently) in charter material only;[435] that of **til** (etc.) is restricted to a few occurrences in early Nhb; and those of **ryd** and **tor** are also attested only a handful of times.[436] For some items, the case for ON input is supported by the circumstantial evidence of regional distribution in ME (sometimes, indeed, this seems to be the principal evidence cited for Scand derivation); notice esp. **burde**, **dale**, **ernde**, **til** (etc.), **tor**, **wayne**.[437] But occasionally the 'evidence' for ON input seems to consist merely of the existence of an ON cognate, which could in principle have made an (undefined) contribution to the history of the ME item; see esp. the toponymic elements **ber3** and **clyff**, where the lexical items were perh. partially reinforced by back-derivation from the onomasticon.

In one case, **borne**, the form of the ME word *must* be native, and any ON input is limited to a supporting role. In most others, the item could have been loaned direct from ON, form and all, and could in principle have replaced its (rare) OE counterpart altogether. For **ayquere**, however, the immediate source of the potential reinforcement is not an ON cognate of its OE etymon (OE *ǣghwǣr*), but instead a different ME word (ME **ay** < ON *ei*) which came to be homophonous with its first element, and as which this element may have been reinterpreted. The same is prob. true of **wayne**, since ON input (if any) came via the different ME v. *wainen* (intrans., 'to go, depart'), perh. of ON origin (the supposed ON etymon has quite a different sense from our **wayne** in its trans. usage). And as well as the putative influence of ON *ar-*, *ar* (etc.) may have been reinforced by the presence in ME of the more clearly ON-derived variant *er*.

For Type FC5 items **caple** and **cros**, the argument is that the word came into English via ON, rather than direct from one or more of the alternative possible sources.

---

[434] OE *-wǣgned* is attested only once, in *Beo*.

[435] Though neither Bj. nor *OED* seem to be aware of OE *bul(l)-* forms.

[436] Though earlier scholarship, inc. the original *OED*, does not seem to know the evidence for the OE cognate.

[437] Notice also the possible formal evidence which supports the cases for **may** (at least in Orrm) and **ernde** (at least in SW ME texts).

4.5.2.2. *Probability of ON input*

The distribution of the few C5 stems amongst the three usual probability groupings is this: C5 two stems, CC5 five stems, CCC5 ten stems. This is very reminiscent of the pattern we saw for Type C4 above, in that C5 items are once again dominated by the 'CCC' set: it is relatively unlikely that the case for ON input will be compelling, and for the majority of C5 stems it is positively unconvincing. Again, this is perh. to be expected, since by definition there is nothing about the form or sense of the items in question which points directly to a Scand origin.

The strongest cases seem to me to be those for **til** (etc.) and **cros**. **Til** is in many ways the *locus classicus* of the argument for 'reinforcement' from ON: given the very 'basic' role played by this word as a prep. and conj., and its rarity in early OE, the probability of at least some input from ON *til* (whether in enabling the revival and diffusion of an existing OE form, or as a wholly new importation which replaced a by-then defunct native cognate) is high; and it is supported by the strong evidence of regional distribution in ME.[438] A good argument can also be made that **cros** entered English via ON, in turn prob. via Ir; this is buoyed up by the distribution of the word in early place-name evidence ('b'), and is generally accepted, even if the possibility of additional input direct from Ir (and even via Fr and/or Lat) is hard to rule out.[439]

The less and least plausible items, labelled 'CC5' and 'CCC5' respectively, are:

CC5
ayquere
caple
dale
may
tor

CCC5
ar (etc.)
bale
berȝ
borne
bullez
burde
clyff

[438] It is also labelled with an 'a', on account of the (perh.) independent cognate in OFris. But for Type C5 the circumstantial evidence of WGmc attestation is not an especially useful indicator, since by definition we already know that there was a cognate in OE with the same form and function.

[439] Notice that *OED* derives **cros** from ON (< Ir), but *MED* lists ON input alongside other possible sources (direct from Ir into OE, and perh. also Fr or Lat influence). TG(D) derives from ON < Ir; GDS does not mention Ir.

ernde
ryd
wayne

In all these cases the argument for ON input seems less compelling. **Bale** and **may** *are* known in the OE record, just mostly (though not entirely) in verse. **Burde** and **ernde** are also frequent enough in OE texts, and the only grounds for ON input seems to be their regional distribution in ME. The supposed OE etyma for **bullez** and **ryd** are rarely attested, but their existence is reasonably secure – and, crucially, at least some of the (earlier) claims for ON input do not seem to be aware of the evidence for them. The possible native source of **wayne** is indeed rare in OE, but the case for ON input is weakened by the rarity of the corresponding Scand form, too, whose existence in VAN cannot be assumed. **Berʒ**, **clyff** and **dale** have perhaps been reinforced by the ON cognate via its presence in place-names (and the case for **dale**, at least, is bolstered by regional distribution), but there is no way to be sure of this; as there similarly is not for the notion that the first element of **ayquere** became associated with ME **ay**. Claims that **ar** (etc.) is an ON derivation have tended to appear in general handbooks, but this is perh. at least partly due to a misapprehension of the evidence (conflating this word with ME *ere* < ON *er-*?), and it is not to be found in any of the major authorities. There is also no very serious basis for ON input into **borne**, whose form must at any rate be native. The FC5 item **caple** is perfectly possible as a loan via ON, but it may just as well have been loaned direct from Ir.

Eight 'CC5' and 'CCC5' stems have an 'a' label;[440] and on the other hand three are marked 'b', and five 'c'.

OED and *MED* show substantial differences in their treatments of nine of these stems, viz. **ayquere, bale, berʒ, bullez, burde, caple, clyff, may, ryd**;[441] honours are about even in the favouring of ON input (with *OED* advancing it more strongly for five stems, and *MED* for four). TG(D) and GDS disagree over just three, **bullez, ernde, ryd**, with TG(D) slightly more likely to opt for some Scand derivation (in the ratio 2:1).[442] Notice further **dale**, where neither edition mentions ON input, despite this featuring in both *OED* and *MED*. The only CC5/CCC5 stems dealt with at all by Bj. are **bullez, dale, may** and **til**. Isolated claims are **borne** (*EPNE*, followed by Elliott) and **wayne** (McGee only).

---

[440] But see note 438 above.

[441] **Ayquere**: *OED* derives partly from ON, *MED* from OE only. **Bale**: *OED* cites partial ON input, *MED* gives only the native etymon. **Berʒ**: *OED* derives from OE only, *MED* partly from ON. **Bullez**: *OED* gives a partial ON source, *MED* derives only from OE. **Burde**: *OED* derives from OE, *MED* partly from ON. **Caple**: *OED* is not sure of the immediate source, *MED* thinks it entered English via ON. **Clyff**: *OED* derives only from OE, *MED* partly from ON. **May**: *OED* gives OE and ON etyma, *MED* cites OE only. **Ryd**: the original *OED* derives from ON (but *OED3* now regards it as native), *MED* derives from OE (though with a 'cp'. to ON). Notice also **wayne** (*OED* explains it as a ME derivation on OE *wægn*, *MED* gives this theory but also suggests an OE wk. trans. **wægnan*).

[442] **Bullez**: TG(D) derive from OE and ON, GDS from OE only. **Ernde**: TG(D) again cite both OE and ON etyma, GDS derives from OE only. **Ryd**: TG(D) derive from OE, GDS from ON. Notice also **may** (TG(D) cite OE and ON etyma, GDS just ON) and **tor** (TG(D) derive only from ON, GDS gives both OE and ON options).

4.6. TYPE C: CIRCUMSTANTIAL EVIDENCE

4.6.1. Germanic distribution

Apart from the ten items prefixed with an 'F', which have a (certain or probable) form-source beyond Gmc,[443] all other Type C stems are by definition related to words attested in (early) OE.

It is worth noticing here that a few stems have closely-related forms only in OE and the Scand languages, and no unambiguous cognates or near-cognates elsewhere in Gmc, viz.: (C1) **bone, brent, froþe, gloue, hap (vnhap)** and **hapnest**; (C2) **silk (sylkyn)**; (C3) **britten**.[444]

There are unambiguous cognates or near-cognates in continental WGmc, *displaying the feature of form/sense/usage at issue*, for at least one sub-entry belonging to sixty-nine different stems, which as usual have been marked with an 'a'.[445] This is the case for thirty-three stems of sub-type C1,[446] plus **lofte** (159a. only) which is marked 'a' only for its secondary (C3) category;[447] nine in

---

[443] See the general preamble to this Introduction to Type C above, and the remarks under the various sub-types. Notice that the immediate Fr form-sources proposed for **angardez** and **garysoun** themselves ultimately have Gmc origins, but both must in their current shapes have come into ME via Fr.

[444] A possible cognate in OHG is occasionally claimed for **silk** (etc.). Notice also: **yrnes** (C3), OE *īren* and the Scand variant represented by OIcel *járn* are the only forms of words for 'iron' in Gmc without medial -*s*-; **blande** (n.) (C4), only the Scand languages and OE attest a str. neut. n. formed on the root of the v. *blandan-; **ar** (**nar**) (C5), only Angl dialects of OE and the Scand languages show -*r*- forms of the pres. ind. pl. of the v. 'to be'. And see further **arwes** (C1), whose root is known only in OE, the Scand languages and Go; and **til** (etc.) (C5), which is found as a prep. only in OE, Scand and Fris (the latter not certainly independently of ON).

[445] But notice that I have been relatively strict in the application of the 'a' label to Type C words. For it to be a helpful indicator here, it is assigned only when there is evidence in continental WGmc for the particular feature (of form, meaning, etc.) which ON input is being entertained in order to explain in English. So 'a' is *not* employed when there is simply a cognate in another WGmc language which shows the same features as the reflex in early OE, since in that case the WGmc cognate does not provide a parallel for the specific new development seen in ME. For the same reasons, and after some deliberation, I have also not affixed an 'a' label to Type C2 items whose continental WGmc reflexes show the 'right' sound merely by dint of this being the normal cognate development which would be expected in those languages; thus e.g. **askez**, **lygez** or **muckel** (whose WGmc cognates naturally show lack of palatalization/assibilation), or **blaste**, **race** (where they regularly have /aː/), or **brenne**, **brusten** (where they regularly lack metathesis). In none of these cases does the presence of the given sound in continental WGmc provide any supporting evidence for the argument that this feature might have developed in OE independently of ON input (which is the main purpose of the 'a' flag).

[446] Note that the OS and OFris cognates of **derf** (**deruely**) have sometimes been explained as deriving from a different Ablaut grade (the *a*-grade), but are usually now taken to represent the *e*-grade. An adj. form corresponding exactly to **mynne** is found in WGmc only in OFris, but related adv. forms are more widespread. Notice also the following (not marked 'a'): **flat**, which has WGmc cognates for the adj., but not for the ON nominal derivatives which may be the source of the ME word; **gyng**, where there are formally identical neut. *ja*-stem derivatives on *gang- in WGmc, but these are very different in sense; **wandez**, where OHG, MLG and MDu forms are often (though not universally) cited as cognates, but their meaning ('wall') is markedly dissimilar; **wont** (n. and v.), where the seemingly cognate NFris forms are always explained as loans from ON; **wrang**, which has perh. cognate MLG and MDu adjectives, but these are not found with the same sense as the ME and Scand words.

[447] The sense 'upper room', which provides subsidiary semantic evidence for ON input, is paralleled in WGmc (though not attached to the same derivational form); hence the combined label C1b (CC3ab).

C2, plus **bruny** which is labelled 'a' for its secondary (C1) category;[448] nine in C3, plus **dryʒe** (etc.) which has an 'a' label also for its subsidiary evidence (C1), and **forlondez** which is marked 'a' only there (C4);[449] five in C4; and nine in C5.[450]

The purported ON sources of nine stems have been characterized as belonging to one or the other main regional branch of the Scand languages. The vocalism of **boun** (C3) is generally regarded as marking it out as OWN; **lyre** (C2) has also been associated with OWN on formal grounds (Bj.), and Bj. regards **bone** (C1) as distinctive of the western branch; and notice also **caple** and **cros** (C5), which perh. came into ON via Ir and which have therefore been explained as reaching England with OWN speakers (Gordon).[451] On the other hand, **bullez** (C5) seems to have a vowel characteristic of OEN, and **gres** (C1) (Bj. and others) and **busk** (C2) (Gordon) have also been assigned to the eastern branch.[452]

4.6.2. *Distribution in England*

Sixteen Type C stems show at least one sub-entry which is more or less confined to the N/EM in the toponymic record; these items are marked 'b'. They are: (C1) **bonk, flat, lofte** (only), **stange**; (C2) **breþer, busk, forth**; (C3) **baret, forne, knape, mosse, steuen**; (C5) **caple, cros, dale, may**.[453] Six of these (**bonk, flat, stange, breþer, busk, baret**) are also mainly to be found in this region in the ME lexicon (see below), but the others are more widespread in general lexical use.

There are seventy-eight stems in Type C (thirty-two C1, twenty C2, sixteen C3, four C4 and six C5) which are labelled with a 'c' in one or more sub-entries,[454] i.e. they are restricted to a greater or lesser extent to the N/EM in the

---

[448] For **burþe**, notice esp. the OFris form apparently without VL. There are WGmc parallels to **fawne** which confirm the type of suffix Ablaut suspected for OE *fagnian*. For **whyrlande**, there are related OHG words apparently formed on both the *e*- and zero-grades of this root, both of which lend support to the possibility of OE derivations on these grades. Regarding **worre**, there are several apparent descendents of PGmc **werziz-* as a superl. or comp. in continental WGmc, the closest being the OFris form with -*rr*- in the comp. Notice also **mele**, which is not marked 'a' because OS and OHG forms in -*h*- do not seem to be precisely cognate.

[449] **Dryʒe** (etc.): the use of **dreug-* as an adj. stem is paralleled elsewhere in WGmc, and in the right sense. **Forlondez**: the compound formation has analogues in WGmc, but not in this precise (supposed) meaning.

[450] The OFris cognate of **til** is perh. an endogenous development, but may itself also be derived from ON. **Borne** also has cognates in WGmc, but only in the sense 'spring, fountain'.

[451] Notice also **spone** (C3), where the only Scand languages to attest the crucial sense ('spoon') are Icel and NNo.

[452] And notice that the only clear parallel to the cluster simplification in **whyrlande** (C2) is attested in Dan; and the closest Scand analogues to **glemered** are v. forms in Sw and Dan.

[453] Notice that only **lofte** (and not the prefixed **alofte**) shows this distribution. There is just one possible attestation of **baret** in place-names, in Cheshire. Toponymic reflexes of **forne** are hard to distinguish from the Scand personal name *Forni*. See also **brusten** (C2) and **lawe** (C3), closely related elements to whose proposed ON etyma also occur only in N/EM names.

[454] Those not showing this restriction in all sub-entries are: **lyfte** (i.e. 157a. **lyfte** only); **seme**, **semlyly** (168a. and d. only); **twynne** (174a. the adj. only); **hetes** (203b. only); **mensk** (adj.), **menskly** (209a. and e. only).

lexical record.[455] Twenty of these are included by Kaiser (1937) in his list of 'northern' words.[456] Only thirteen are unambiguously northern and/or eastern stems which are entirely or almost entirely confined to this region throughout their recorded history: (C1) **brent, flat, greme, spene, stange;**[457] (C2) **tulk, vmbe, worre;**[458] (C3) **angardez, dreped, dryȝe** (etc.), **warþe;**[459] (C5) **burde.**[460] Of the remainder, two are *hapax legomena* in *Gaw*, viz. **chymbled** and **layde** (in this phrase, '~ wordez'). Twelve are attested very rarely, and little can be ascertained about their distribution (beyond the fact that the few texts in which they do occur are mainly N/EM): thus (C1) **blande** (v.), **hapnest, seme** (and **semlyly**), **sware, vmbe-torne, wykez;**[461] (C2) **hetes** (203b. only), **mensk** (209a. the adj. only), **ouerwalt** (227b. only), **wela;**[462] (C3) **fnast**; (C4) **blande** (n.). Six items seem to have become (more or less) restricted to the N/EM by late ME, but to have been more widely used earlier in their recorded histories, viz. (C1) **cost, gyng, heterly,** (C2) **mele, menskly** (209e. only), (C5) **ayquere.** On the other hand, nine stems show one or more sub-entries which are attested mainly from the N/EM to begin with, but which have become widespread later (usually by the late ME period): (C1) **blende, bonk, lyfte** (157a. only), **same, wandez;**[463] (C2) **brenne, renne;**[464] (C3) **dreme**; (C4) **vpon.**[465] A further nine

---

[455] Notice also: **weterly** (C1), which is not dialectally marked as an adv., but the simplex ME *witter* is a mainly N/EM word by later ME; **fyked** (C3), which is not obviously dialectally marked in ME, but whose modern reflex is found only in northern English dial (and in Scots and Irish English); and **forlondez** (C3), which would be unique to *Gaw* in this precise supposed sense, but that sense is debated, and the compound itself is more widespread. Arguments which compare the distribution of the supposed ON-derived variant to that of its native counterpart have also been mounted for **if** (C2) and **þenk** (C2), but in each case the *Gaw* form is itself widespread in ME.

[456] They are: (C1) **bolne, brent, derf (deruely), mynne** (adj.), **samen, stange, wandez;** (C2) **mele, nikked, worre;** (C3) **angardez, britten, bur, dreped, dryȝe** (the adj. only, and only in the adv. phrase 'on ~'), **mon, ware;** (C5) **burde, til (þertylle), tor.** Kaiser's list also features **race** (C2), which does not seem to me obviously to be confined to the N/EM; and **mensked** (C2), for which the same is true (though some other members of the **mensk-** word-group, which he does not treat, *are* dialectally restricted).

[457] Possible later dial reflexes of **flat** are difficult to separate from later derivations on the related adj.

[458] But notice also *MED*'s citation of **tulk** as a surname element from Somerset (and see Hanks et al. 2016: s.v. *Tulk* for further SW attestations as a name). The possible twelfth- and early thirteenth-century citations of **vmbe** in *MED* are all ambiguous forms also found in the SWM; but forms whose spelling clearly indicates ME /u/ are confined to the N/EM.

[459] The dial restriction of **dryȝe** (etc.) and **warþe** applies only to the meaning as found in *Gaw*.

[460] **Burde** is found only in the N/EM in the post-OE period.

[461] Though regarding **hapnest**, notice that the similar word *heppen* is northern in MnE dial. **Wykez** is uncommon in ME, but modern dial evidence points to a N/EM distribution at least later. **Aghlich** (**aȝlez**) are not included in this list, since they are not primarily N/EM, though they are rare; but notice that the simplex ME *aue* is dialectally restricted in early ME, if widespread later.

[462] The later dial evidence indicates that **mensk** was by that stage clearly a northern word.

[463] **Blende** is mainly N/EM throughout ME, but has a broader attestation in later English. Note that **same** appears only in Orrm in early ME.

[464] **Brenne** is widespread in place-names, moreover.

[465] For **vpon**, however, the apparently restricted distribution is true only of the very earliest ME texts to prefer <-on> spellings, and these forms are in any case ambiguous in terms of the placement of word-accent they might indicate.

stems are recorded mainly from N/EM texts (for at least part of the ME period), but seem to have been used more widely in the vocabulary of alliterative verse (during that same time): (C1) **frayn, gyng, heterly, mynne** (adj.), **samen**; (C2) **mele**; (C3) **britten, lete (as)**;[466] (C5) **tor**. Lastly, the following stems (in at least one sub-entry) are generally N/EM words throughout ME, but not exclusively so, having some attestations further afield which indicate a broader usage: (C1) **bolne, derf (deruely), fonge, frayn, gres, helder, henge, leme, twynne** (174a. the adj. only), **warp**;[467] (C2) **blenk, breþer, busk, fest (festned), ʒol, lygez, lyke** (etc.), **lyre, muckel, nikked, walt** (227a. only); (C3) **baret, boun, breue, bur, layne, mon, ware, wynne**;[468] (C4) **sunder**; (C5) **ernde, til (þertylle), wayne**.[469]

4.6.3. *Other circumstantial evidence*

Type C provides us with our single example in this survey of an item labelled 'd', viz. **lawe** (C3), whose earliest attestations (in late OE) are strongly associated with Scand cultural influence.

---

[466] **Lete (as)** shows this distribution only in the 'behave' sense; when it means 'utter' it is found solely in the N/EM.

[467] And notice also **are** (adv.), which is esp. frequently cited from northern texts in *MED* but more widespread according to *LALME*.

[468] Note that, in the sense 'to report, tell', **breue** is known in ME only from *Gaw* and closely related N/NM alliterative poems. **Ware** is only a N/EM word in the meanings found in *Gaw*; *MED*'s sense (d) is more widespread, and perh. a more straightforward development from OE.

[469] **Til** in the sense 'until' is widespread from the fourteenth century; only when it means 'to' does it remain more or less restricted to the N/EM. The non-N/EM attestations of **wayne** are mostly of *MED*'s distinct sense (c), i.e. not the meanings found in *Gaw*.

5

TYPE D

The words treated under Types B and C above often present etymological difficulties and room for debate, the plausibility of the case for ON input varying considerably from item to item. Nonetheless, a readily identifiable form-source (usually a Gmc root, but occasionally a form of different origin) can generally be agreed. By contrast, the items reserved for this final section of the survey, **Type D**, are those for which this is not the case – these are the words where (for several possible different reasons, sometimes in combination) a single, generally accepted form-source is not available. The *Gaw* items dealt with here therefore tend to be classed as 'difficult' in the etymological and/or editorial authorities, whether in terms of their occurrences in English as a whole or specifically in their contexts in this poem. In all cases, input has been suggested from one or more comparable ON words, but these explanations have not met with general acceptance and they compete in each instance with one or more alternative derivations.

The key division amongst Type D words is between the following:

> **D1**, where the form and sense of the stem in question can be established (relatively) straightforwardly, and are usually agreed; but where there is no generally accepted etymology.

> **D2**, where the interpretation in its *Gaw* context of the ME word, and hence its most plausible etymon, is debated.

For these two sub-types, the focus of the argumentation is therefore prototyp-ically different (though in practice they may overlap). Type D1 items are words whose meanings can be given relatively uncontroversially, and which (unless they occur only in *Gaw*) can be readily identified with a stem found elsewhere in ME and/or in later English. But they have no generally agreed source, and sometimes no compelling etymology at all. This is therefore where words with an 'obscure' history are filed, and there are some well-known items here, much discussed and debated in the etymological literature, including **big**, **kylled** and **scho**.[470] Items of Type D2, on the other hand, need not be so hard to label with a specifiable form-source (and hence with input from a potential ON etymon) owing to etymological obscurity *per se*, but because in these cases it is not generally agreed which word the *Gaw* form in question actually represents, and hence which word-stem elsewhere in English we should identify it with. To take a relatively straightforward example, the debate concerning **forȝ** is whether it is an occurrence of ME *fors* 'waterfall' (in which case its most plausible source is

---

[470] For some general discussions of 'obscure' etymologies and the typical reasons for their opacity, see for instance Liberman (1994; 2002b; 2008: xiii–xvi).

ON *fors*) or ME *forwe* 'furrow, i.e. channel, bed' (in which case it clearly derives from OE).[471] In such cases, the principal subject of argument is not etymological at all, but primarily textual and interpretive, albeit often informed by linguistic evidence (such as, for **forʒ**, the most likely signification of word-final <ʒ> in the orthography of the *Gaw* scribe).[472] Having said this, it is surprising how rarely the choice for D2 items turns out to be between two possible identifications each of whose etymologies is entirely straightforward: for the majority, one or more of the available alternatives in themselves prove to be difficult, and the etymology of several is no less obscure than for items of Type D1; an example is **rak**, where both theories present complex problems, in each case involving possible ON input alongside derivation from other suggested sources.[473]

---

[471] Notice that items are usually catalogued under Type D2 only when all possible *Gaw* instances of a word are in doubt, and subject to more than one possible identification. When there is at least one unambiguous and uncontroversial occurrence of a word in the poem, any tenuous or debated possible examples are dealt with as part of the main entry for that word in Types A – D1 above, with possible alternative interpretations and reasons for disagreement always taken into account (for some examples see under **hitte**, **sene** and **won 2**). An exception is **wande** (*Gaw* 1161), since – while this may be understood as another instance of the word treated under **wandez** (C1) – the alternative theory involves reading it as a different ME word which may be derived from a different ON source, and hence it requires an entry of its own. Notice too that, in order for an item to qualify as a Type D2, the disagreement must be about the identity of the word, not simply about which sense of one and the same word attaches to a given *Gaw* occurrence (and whether that sense, perh. influenced by ON, ever existed). In the latter case the item is treated under Type C3, although the debate over interpretation is of course recorded as part of the discussion; see e.g. **forlondez**, **warþe**.

[472] For an interesting discussion of how modern readers (inc. editors and lexicographers) go about identifying words and construing their meanings in ME texts, and the kinds of disagreements which can result, see further Sylvester (2010).

[473] It should be added that problems with identifying ME forms also sometimes pertain when it comes to items I have classified as Type D1, and in some instances these arguments are not cleanly to be separated from the kinds of issues dealt with for D2 words. See for instance **mynne** (v.) (D1), where it is noticed that the dictionaries tend to struggle to decide under which head to put formally similar or ambiguous ME words (i.e. a given ME form *minnen* could be a reflex of what *OED* gives as *min* v.1 'to purpose, intend' (etc.) or *min* v.2 'to remind, remember' (etc.), depending on the exact interpretation of its sense in context, and *Gaw* 982 <mynned> has been the subject of such disagreement in editions and dictionaries); but where this confusion or conflation is in principle true of ME as a whole, and indeed forms part of the etymological difficulties of the wider word-group under discussion (in the case of **mynne**, it may indeed be most sensible to assume that late ME speakers would have identified only a single v. *minnen*, which collapses two (or more) historically distinct words). In cases like this, then, the essential problem is not fundamentally about identifying a particular *Gaw* word-form with this or that *obviously distinct* ME lexical item, but about identifying the roles of two or more different etymological origins for a set of words in the ME record more generally; hence the history of the word-form in ME at large is the source of the obscurity, and **mynne** is best classed as a Type D1. Similar things apply in the case of **ronez**, **rous** and **sprit**, the issues with which all to some extent arise from problems in explaining a (potentially inter-connected) group of ME words. Another good example of the division between Types D1 and D2 is **child-gered** versus **gere**: the former is given as a D1, since all the ME instances of this form *-gere*, however we interpret it, are at issue here (they could all represent the same stem, and so it is not really a question of identifying the *-gered* in **child-gered** with this or that other lexeme with a definite identity of its own); but **gere** is classed as a D2, since (in addition) there is the suggestion that the *Gaw* instance under discussion could be an occurrence of a different word altogether, and not the same stem as the *gere* in **(child-)gered** at all.

In each Survey entry for Types D1 and D2, the major competing theories are numbered (labelled (1), (2) etc.) in the body of the Etymology section, and etymological references for each theory are also distinguished using these labels in the reference section at the foot of the entry. (In several cases there are also more marginal suggestions, which will be noticed in passing in the main body of the entry with representative references only.) Notice that, for Type D2 only, because the meaning (and sometimes the grammar) of the item is usually a matter of debate, and its occurrences and possible referents in context in *Gaw* are central to the discussion, the format of the opening of each entry is slightly different from those in previous sections of the Survey: the headword is here followed, in the next line, by a set of numbered alternative meanings (and where necessary different proposed readings and grammatical analyses); and the Text section gives a quotation of the immediate *Gaw* context(s) as well as the standard reference to the line numbers where the word occurs.

Given the different kinds of arguments which may and tend to pertain for the two sub-types, I shall summarize and discuss the evidence for words of Types D1 and D2 separately in what follows. Following the usual summary lists of items, I shall introduce the characteristic features of and approaches to each sub-type. I shall then attempt to distil the significant information about the ON words which have variously been proposed as etyma (including their Gmc filiations), and about the regional distribution of the English stems in question. Each section then concludes with a survey of the more and less probable cases that have been made for ON input across the group, and of the differences between the opinions of the main scholarly authorities.

5.1. TYPE D1

5.1.1. *Summary list*

Category D1 comprises forty-eight stems, nine with sub-entries; there are sixty-three distinct lexical items altogether:

300.   **balʒ**; adj.; 'swelling with round, smooth surface' [DD1c]
301a. **bene**; adj.; 'pleasing, fair' [DD1c]
301b. **bene**; adv.; 'pleasantly' [DD1c]
301c. **vnbene**; adj.; 'inhospitable, dreary' [DD1c]
302a. **big**; adj.; 'strong' [D1c]
302b. **bigly**; adv.; 'mightily' [D1c]
303.   **blunder**; n.; 'turmoil, trouble' [D1c]
304.   **bost**; n.; 'outcry, clamour' [DD1]
305.   **child-gered**; ppl. adj.; 'boyish, merry' [DD1]
306.   **dare**; v.; 'to cower, shrink' [DD1]
307.   **enker-grene**; n.; 'bright (green)' [D1c]
308.   **faltered**; v. (pret.); 'staggered' [D1c]

309. **farand**; adj.; 'splendid' [D1c]

310a. **ferly**; adj.; 'extraordinary, unusual' [DD1]

310b. **ferly**; n.; 'marvel, wonder' [DD1c]

310c. **ferly**; adv.; 'wondrously, exceedingly' [DD1c]

310d. **ferlyly**; adv.; 'wondrously, exceedingly; of marvellous things' [DD1c]

311. **fyskez**; v. (pres. 3 sg.); ?'scampers' [D1]

312. **flosche**; n.; 'pool' [DD1bc]

313. **glyfte**; v. (pret.); 'glanced (sidelong)' [DD1c]

314. **glyȝt**; v. (pret.); 'glanced, looked' [DD1c]

315. **glode**; n.; 'open space, patch' [DD1bc]

316. **gryed**; v. (pret.); 'shuddered' [DD1c]

317a. **gryndel**; adj.; 'fierce' [DD1c]

317b. ***gryndellayk**; n.; 'fierceness' [DD1c]

317c. **gryndelly**; adv.; 'fiercely, wrathfully' [DD1c]

318. **grome**; n.; 'lackey, servant; man' [DD1]

319. **happe**; v.; 'to wrap, clasp, fasten' [DD1c]

320. **irked**; v. (pret.); 'wearied, irked (impers.)' [DD1c]

321. **kylled**; v. (pp.); 'killed' [DD1]

322. **loupe**; n.; 'loop' [DD1c]

323. **mynne**; v.; 'to declare; exhort; remember, think of' [D1c]

324. **neked**; n.; '(a) little, a small amount' [D1c]

325. **noke**; n.; 'angle, point' [DD1c]

326. **rake**; n.; 'path' [DD1c]

327. **raþeled**; v. (pp.); ?'entwined' [DD1c]

328. **ryue**; adv.; 'abundantly, much' [D1]

329. **rof-sore**; n.; 'gash, wound' [D1c]

330. **rokked**; v. (pp.); 'burnished, made clean by rolling under pressure' [DD1]

331. **ronez**; n. (pl.); 'bushes, brushwood' [D1c]

332. **rous**; n.; 'fame, talk' [D1c]

333a. **runisch**; adj.; ?'rough, violent' [DD1c]

333b. **runischly**; adv.; 'fiercely' [DD1c]

334. **ruþes**; v. (pres. 3 sg.); 'bestirs' [D1c]

335. **scho**; pers. pron., fem. 3 sg. subject; 'she' [DD1c]

336a. **schunt**; v. (pret.); 'swerved; flinched' [DD1c]

336b. **schunt**; n.; 'sudden jerk and swerve' [DD1c]

337. **snitered**; v.; ?'came shivering down' [DD1c]

338. **sprit**; v. (pret. sg.); 'sprang, started' [DD1c]

339. **staf-ful**; adj.; 'cram-full' [D1c]

340. **stayned**; v. (pp.); 'coloured' [D1]

341. **strothe**; n.; ?'small wood' [D1bc]

342. **sweȝe**; v.; 'to sink, stoop; fall, rush, swing' [DD1c]

343. **taysed**; v.; 'harassed, driven' [D1c]

344. **teuelyng**; n.; 'labour, deeds' [D1c]

345a. **traunt**; n.; '(cunning) practice' [DD1c]

345b. **trantes**; v. (pres. 3 sg.); 'practices cunning, dodges' [DD1c]
346a. **wapped**; v. (pret. sg.); 'rushed, blew (in gusts)' [DD1c]
346b. **atwaped**; v. (pret. sg.); 'escaped' [DD1c]
346c. **wap**; n.; 'blow' [DD1c]
347a. **wyles**; n. (pl.); 'wiles' [DD1c]
347b. **wyly**; adj.; 'wily' [DD1]
347c. **biwyled**; v. (pp.); 'deluded' [DD1]

Sub-entries with parallel forms in the early Scand languages are **ferly** (adv.), **schunt** (n.), **trantes**, **biwyled**.

5.1.2. *Further remarks*

The etymologies of all these stems are in some way difficult, and they have no generally agreed source. A few are infamous cruces, extensively discussed in the scholarship: thus especially **big** (etc.), **kylled, loupe, scho**, and to a lesser extent **irked, noke, wyles** (etc.). The issues surrounding some of these have been pretty comprehensively aired, but they retain the power to attract quite distinct competing explanations, notably **big**;[474] whereas in some instances the reasons why scholarly favour has apparently shifted from one theory to another stand to be better probed and understood (e.g. **wyles**). But most of the words grouped under D1 in this survey have seen rather less attention, in particular those which are restricted to *Gaw* or related texts or which are relatively infrequent in ME at large, such as **balȝ, bene** (etc.), **glyfte, glyȝt, neked, traunt** (etc.); some have nonetheless attracted a number of comments in work on the poems of the *Gaw*-manuscript (see most notably **fyskez** and **runisch** (etc.), and notice also **child-gered, faltered, sweȝe, strothe**).

In many cases, the competing explanations have never been properly collected and considered next to one another before, and the reasoning behind some of them (especially some of the shorter etymological labels in the editions) has never been drawn out and made explicit. For these words the Survey entries below undertake this discussion for the first time, comparing the merits of the different arguments and pursuing the connections and ulterior histories of the proposed etyma in as much detail as seems helpful and possible in the space available. I have drawn attention to older and/or neglected theories especially for the following:

> **bene** (etc.): an old suggestion by Holthausen (1923) (theory 3);
> **dare**: Kullnick's neglected derivation from ON (2);
> **gryndel** (etc.): pursuing an alternative ON source given in *OED* (2);
> **happe**: considering the neglected idea followed especially by McGee (3);
> **loupe**: returning to the old (albeit still problematic) suggestion that this word might be etymologically connected to *loop(-hole)*, and hence perhaps derived from Du (4);

---

[474] Contrast the very different emphases in the recent accounts in *OED3* and Liberman (2003; 2009).

rous: noticing Emerson's alternative (3) and suggesting an etymology;
runisch (etc.): drawing attention to the more marginal and apparently forgotten theory (3) from Knigge and Mätzner;
sprit: pursuing Knigge's long neglected alternative derivation < ON *sprita* (4);
taysed: making the case for the plausibility of the ON source given by Bj and Emerson (2);
teuelyng: exploring further another possible Scand analogue, as offered by OED (2).

I have introduced new arguments in particular for:

fyskez: exploring a hypothetical source **fis-k-* related to PGmc **fisan-* (following Torp's suggested etymological trail for NNo *fjaska*), and drawing attention to a possible imitative origin in ME;
gryndel (etc.): suggesting a link to (and possible back-derivation from) ME *gryndel-ston*;
neked: introducing the idea that this word was associated with OE *nacod*, which perh. influenced the form of the ending;
ryue adv.: exploring the problematic late OE forms and their relationships, inc. suggesting an etymology for the *hr-* forms;[475]
rof-sore: offering two further comparanda (even if these do not improve on the standard derivation from ON);
snitered: pursuing the etymologies of the various comparanda in more detail, and hence problematizing the influential TG(D) derivation from an ON *snitra and arguing instead for a formation ult. on PGmc **snūþ-*;
traunt (etc.): presenting two new possible etymologies for a word family which has been little discussed previously.

And notice also:

big (etc.): pursuing the possibility that the simplex adj. was back-derived on **bigly** adv.;
bost: drawing attention to the problems with the Anglo-Fr n. now sometimes cited as etymon;
faltered: taking Simpson's discussion a little further;
grome: considering together all the theories for the first time, and pursuing in particular the slender evidence for an ON *grómr* 'man' and its possible relationship with a suggested Fr etymon;[476]
irked: pursuing the etymology of some HG comparanda, and suggesting ME imitative origin as another option;
mynne v.: exploring the possible conflation of originally distinct verbs;

---

[475] This builds on Dance (2002b: 12–15).
[476] And see further Dance (2018: 119–23).

teuelyng: drawing attention to the phonological problems with obtaining the *Gaw* vowel <e> from the attested OE v., and to the better semantic analogue provided by the known Scand verbs;

wyles (etc.): considering a particularly complex set of issues, inc. explaining the evidence behind the now largely discarded 'OE *wīl*' and *MED*'s use of it, and the formal problems with assuming an ON **wihl-* as etymon.

More so than for the words of Types B and C discussed above, it is difficult to divide D1 items into groupings which encapsulate distinct kinds of etymological problems encountered or arguments employed, since these problems and arguments are simply so various here. It might be remarked at this point, nonetheless, that a few are alike in showing the characteristics of 'ideophones' (otherwise known as affective or sound-symbolic formations), and/or denote actions the expression of which is especially prone to (re)generation along ideophonic lines:[477] notice particularly **fyskez, flosche, glyfte, glyȝt, happe, irked, snitered, wapped** (etc.).[478] Such stems are particularly liable to lack 'orthodox' etymologies (and to have comparable forms in several closely and less closely related languages at the same time), and hence they inevitably tend to appear in lists of words with 'obscure' histories. But this should not necessarily prevent us from exploring their broader connections and trying to explain their development, since even an ideophonic origin need not of course be recent.

The words treated under D1 differ greatly from one another in terms of the complexity of the evidence which pertains to them. In some instances it seems to me especially challenging or convoluted, and several items have required unusually involved and detailed discussion in their Survey entries; see notably **big, child-gered, glode, grome, rake, ryue** (adv.), **ronez, runisch** (etc.), **snitered, teuelyng, wyles** (etc.). For a number of words, it is quite possible that a combination of two (or more) of the different potential inputs described has contributed to the outcomes we meet in ME, but none of the said inputs (I have judged) can be regarded as the most readily identifiable form-source, viz.: **ferly** (etc.), **flosche, loupe, mynne** (v.), **rak, rake, ryue** (adv.), **ronez, runisch** (etc.), **sprit, staf-ful, stayned, strothe, taysed, wyles** (etc.). In some other cases there is a single cluster of possibly related etyma, but the fact and nature of any relationship between them are uncertain (**big** (etc.), **bost, glyfte, wapped** (etc.)). By contrast, there are some items where one explanation has come to dominate accounts in the scholarship, and which also seems to me far more plausible than the alternatives. This is so most especially for **neked**, where only one concrete proposal for an etymon has been made (but whose formal correspondence to the ME word is not so close as to put its origin beyond doubt, and so most authorities voice it only tentatively); but it is also true of **flosche, glyfte, gryed,**

---

[477] For discussions of this topic see the references cited in the Introduction to Type B above, at note 356.

[478] And perhaps also **big** (etc.), which has sometimes been connected to a group of words which might be taken to be affective in origin and phonaesthematically related.

rof-sore, rokked, ruþes, schunt (n. and v.), for each of which one theory has appealed markedly more than others to recent commentators, even if other options cannot definitively be ruled out.[479]

It seems to me most helpful to categorize D1 items in terms of the number of (main) theories which have been proposed for them, and then according to the languages of the immediate etyma cited under those theories. Apart from **neked** (see above), all have two or more distinct explanations; and numerically they divide almost equally into one group with just two theories and another with more than two.

Two main theories (24 stems):
In a handful of cases, both theories involve some possibility of ON input: **gryndel** (etc.), **rof-sore, rokked, ruþes, teuelyng**.[480]

Most stems have one explanation which features at least the prospect of ON input, and another etymon with a different source: hence **balʒ, blunder, bost, dare, enker-grene, faltered, farand, flosche, glyfte, glyʒt, gryed, kylled, mynne** (v.), **raþeled, ryue** (adv.), **schunt** (n. and v.), **staf-ful, stayned, wapped** (etc.). For the majority of these items the none-Scand source is native; but in the case of four it is (or at least comes via) Fr (**bost, enker-grene, flosche, stayned**), and in one it is Celtic (**farand**).

More than two main theories (23 stems):
Three of these stems (**ferly** (etc.), **rake, sweʒe**) show possible ON input in one theory, and two alternative derivations where the source is native.

But most have a richer array of putative etyma. For eleven stems there are two or more (perh.) distinct ON inputs: **big** (etc.), **fyskez, glode, noke, ronez, rous, runisch, scho, snitered, sprit, traunt** (etc.).[481] Seven involve Fr (and/or Lat) as one of the possible options: **bene** (etc.), **child-gered, grome, happe, taysed, traunt** (etc.), **wyles** (etc.).[482] And in six cases one (or more) of the explanations derives from

---

[479] More minor disagreements especially as regards the interpretation of form or sense in *Gaw* are various, and it does not seem helpful to itemize them all here. But notice the following as amongst the more significant or interesting: **balʒ** (the emendation of MS <bay> at 967); **fyskez** (some commentators (notably GDS) think that one's preferred etymology depends upon the interpretation of the word in context, i.e. which animal in this scene it refers to); **grome** (the emendation suggested by PS for 1006); **rake** (the exact denotation at *Gaw* 2144, 2160, which might bear on the etymology); **raþeled** (the reading of the sense of this word here, which is unique in ME); **ronez** (the most likely phonology of the word in *Gaw*, and in other ME texts); **rous** (does the *Gaw* spelling <ou> stand for /uː/, or something else?); **runisch** (etc.) (the exact interpretation of the sense in its contexts); **snitered** (where the TG(D) rendering of the meaning is notably led by their proposed etymon); and **teuelyng** (the different ideas about its meaning).

[480] I have added yet further Scand comparanda for **rof-sore** which have not been adduced before (theories 3a, 3b), but these are of limited value. The main etymological strand for **rokked** (theory 1) is usually taken to be of native origin, with only Kullnick appearing to derive from ON. In the case of **teuelyng**, theory (1) derives from an ON word ult. from Lat.

[481] Of the various alternative explanations for **scho**, notice that three involve either direct borrowing from ON or a Scand-influenced pronunciation.

[482] The claimed Fr input behind **wyles** is probably ult. < Gmc.

another source: for **irked, noke** and **strothe** this source is Celtic; for **child-gered** and **grome** it is Dutch; and **loupe** has possible etyma in both Celtic and Dutch.

Notice that there are twenty-two D1 stems for which formal criteria for Scand loan might apply if we derive from one or more of the proposed ON etyma:[483]

> **bene** (etc.) (§1)
> **big** (etc.) (§§8.2, 9)
> **(child-)gered** (§8.2)
> **enker(-grene)** (§§1, 13.2)
> **fyskez** (§15)
> **gly3t** (§12.3)
> **happe** (§10.4)
> **irked** (§§8.1, 12.2)
> **loupe** (§2)
> **mynne** (v.) (§10.4)
> **neked** (§10.4)
> **rake** (§§4, 10.3)
> **raþeled** (§7)
> **rokked** (§10.4)
> **rous** (§§2, 10.4)
> **ruþes** (§7)
> **scho** (§6.4)
> **sprit** (§10.4)
> **staf-ful** (§10.4)
> **stayned** (§1)
> **strothe** (§7)
> **taysed** (§1)

5.1.2.1. *Proposed ON etyma and their Germanic filiations*

In what follows I append some further remarks on the Scand words proposed as sources of ON input for stems of Type D1, and on their relationship with Gmc vocabulary more broadly. (Where a ME stem has two or more different suggested ON etyma, these are distinguished here according to the number of the theory which features them (in round brackets), as per the relevant Survey entry.)

The ulterior etymology is more or less obscure or in some way disputed for the suggested ON etymon in the case of **bene** (etc.), **faltered, glyfte, grome, kylled, rake, raþeled, ryue** adv., **schunt** (n. and v.), **wapped** (etc.), **wyles** (etc.);[484] and this is also the case for one of the proposed Scand sources for **big** (etc.) (2),

---

[483] With §§ references back to the guide to these changes in the Introduction to Type A (Formal Criteria) above.

[484] Note that the putative ON source of **rake** (ON *rák*) has two possible ulterior etymologies (it is perh. historically a blend of these two distinct words), as does that of **wyles** (etc.) (ON *vél*). Notice also **stayned**, where the sense development of the proposed Scand etymon has attracted debate.

fyskez (1), **glode** (2, Shetl Norn *gloderek* etc.), **ronez** (3), **runisch** (etc.) (1a), **snitered** (2), **teuelyng** (2), and for both potential ON etyma for **rous**.

A handful of ON words show features associated mainly with, or which have otherwise been characterized as belonging to, a particular regional branch of the Scand languages. Hence the etyma proposed for **rokked** (2), **sprit** (3) and **staf-ful** (2) exhibit consonant assimilation of types usually restricted to OWN, and **farand** (Bj.) and **strothe** (Gordon & Onions 1932) have been claimed as loans specifically from OWN. A number of other theories are explained with reference to (more or less obscure) Scand comparanda cited only from WN languages, viz. **balȝ**, **big** (2), **bost, faltered, glode** (2), **gryndel** (etc.) (1), **grome** (1), **kylled** (1), **noke** (1), **ronez** (1), **snitered** (1), **sprit** (4), **teuelyng** (2), **traunt** (etc.) (3). Fewer suggested ON source words are characteristic of the EN branch, but notice that: the potential Scand etyma of **taysed** and **traunt** (etc.) are represented by forms attested only in Sw and Dan, as is Kullnick's claimed source for **glyfte** (2) (Sw); that for **rokked** (1) was prob. originally found only in OEN; and only in Dan is the appropriate meaning ('shallow creek') found for the proposed ON source of **flosche**.[485]

For the various suggested ON etyma, the following relationships with the wider Gmc word stock may be summarized:

Sixteen have no (clearly) related forms anywhere else in Gmc, viz. **bene, dare, fyskez** (1), **glyfte, grome, kylled, noke** (1 and 2), **rokked** (2), **ronez** (3), **runisch** (etc.) (1a), **strothe, sweȝe, teuelyng** (2), **traunt** (etc.) (3), **wyles** (etc.). In other words, if these Gmc roots were the only form-sources which had been proposed for these ME items and they had been treated in earlier parts of the Survey, they would all have been classed as sub-type B1 – with the exception of **bene** and **strothe**, which would be A1 on the grounds of form.[486]

Another sixteen potential etyma can be connected to words attested elsewhere in Gmc with at least some plausibility, but have no (clearly) derivationally related forms in OE: **bost, flosche, glyȝt, glode** (2, NNo *glott*), **gryed, mynne** (v.), **raþeled, ryue** (adv.), **rof-sore, rous** (2), **snitered** (1 and 2), **sprit** (3 and 4), **traunt** (etc.) (2), **wapped** (etc.). These theories would all individually have been labelled B2, therefore, or A1 in the case of **mynne** v. and **sprit** (3).

The putative ON sources featuring in the remaining thirty-one theories show attested forms in OE which are either directly cognate or derivationally related to the same Gmc root. All these would therefore on their own be Type C items of various sorts, or Type A when formal tests apply, as follows:

---

[485] It is also worth pointing out here that, amongst the various difficulties presented by the case for ON derivation for **bene** (etc.), ON *beinn* is sometimes described as a specifically OWN word, whereas the vocalism of its ME output appears to require typically OEN monophthongization.

[486] In this section, and in the corresponding discussion under D2 below, note that I have not attempted to affix probability markers to these notional type labels given for the proposed ON etyma (i.e. to distinguish B from BB and BBB, etc.). To do so would, it seems to me, be to add an unnecessary layer of interpretation (and annotation); and moreover any sense of the 'probability' of ON input here is of course complicated by the presence of the other competing theories which exist for Type D stems, and hence difficult to assess for each individual ON etymon in isolation.

balʒ (C1)
big (etc.) (1) (A1*)
blunder (C1)
(child-)gered (A1*)
enker(-grene) (A3)
faltered (C1)
farand (C3)
ferly (etc.) (C1)
fyskez (2b) (A2*)
glode (1, 3) (C1)
gryndel (etc.) (1, 2) (C1)
happe (A1*)
irked (A1*)
loupe (A1*)
neked (A1*)
rake (2) (A1*)[487]
rof-sore (1) (C1)
rokked (1) (C1)
ronez (2) (C3 (C1))
rous (1) (A1*)
runisch (etc.) (3) (C3)
ruþes (1) (A1*), (2) (C2)[488]
scho (1)
schunt (n. and v.) (C1)
staf-ful (A1*)
stayned (A1*)
taysed (A1*)
teuelyng (1b) (C1 (C3))

By definition, items of Type D1 do not have a readily identifiable Gmc root, and so no words in this section of the Survey have been labelled 'a'. But, taking each theory and its supposed ON etymon individually, eight would have been given an 'a' label had they featured in an earlier section of the Survey, viz.: **enker-grene**, **glyʒt**, **ryue** adv., **rokked** (1), **ruþes** (1), **snitered** (1), **traunt** (etc.) (2), **wapped** (etc.).

5.1.2.2. Distribution in England

Only three stems of Type D1 are confined in the main to the N/EM in the toponymic record, and marked 'b': thus **flosche**, **glode** and **strothe** (all of which are also mainly found in the same regions in the lexicon more broadly).

---

[487] For either of the possible ulterior etymologies of ON *rák* (see the entry).

[488] Assuming that ON *hryðja* does indeed have cognates in OE (see the entry).

Thirty-nine stems are more or less restricted to the N/EM in the lexical record in at least one sub-entry, and are thus labelled 'c'.[489] This is a remarkably high proportion of the total of forty-eight D1 stems, and it suggests (*inter alia*) just how often an attempted argument for ON input behind an 'obscure' word might have been prompted by or based on its English dial distribution. Only eight stems are recognized by Kaiser (1937) in his list of 'northern' ME vocabulary items (**farand, happe** (v.), **irked, rake, ronez, rous, traunt, wapped** (and **wap**)). Eleven are unambiguously northern and/or eastern words or word groups which are entirely or almost entirely confined to this region throughout their recorded history, viz. **balʒ, bene** (etc.), **flosche, glyʒt, glode, gryed, happe** (v.), **rake, sprit, staf-ful, traunt** (n.) (the n. only, not the related v. **trantes**).[490] Of the remainder, four are found uniquely in *Gaw* (**enker-grene, raþeled, rof-sore, trantes** (v.) (only the v.)),[491] and four only in the texts of the *Gaw*-manuscript (**gryndel** (etc.), **ruþes, strothe, teuelyng** (in this sense));[492] there is also **runisch** (etc.), which is recorded only in this manuscript and the closely-related *Erk*.[493] Five are attested only rarely, and it is difficult to draw concrete conclusions about their distribution in ME (beyond that they are known mainly from N/EM texts): **faltered, loupe, neked, snitered, taysed**.[494] Two seem to have had a dialectally restricted distribution in early ME, but to have become more widespread later (**scho, wyles** (the n. only)); and notice also **blunder** and **irked**, which are mainly or only N/EM throughout ME but became much more widely used in the modern period.[495] Generally N/EM words throughout the ME period, but not entirely, having some attestations further afield which hint at a wider usage, are **big** (etc.), **glyfte, mynne** (v.), **noke, ronez, rous, schunt** (v.) (only the v.), **sweʒe, wapped** (and **wap** n., only).[496]

---

[489] There are few discrepancies amongst the sub-entries for a single stem, but this is true of: **ferly**, where all sub-entries are classed as 'c' except for **ferly** adj. (310a.) itself; and **wyles**, where only the n. (sub-entry 347a.) is marked 'c' (being N/EM in its earlier attestations), but the other forms (347b. and c.) are not.

[490] For **gryed**, this assumes that *EDD*'s *gry* v., sb. does indeed represent the same stem; and notice that the *Gaw* occurrence is the only secure instance in ME. **Rake** is more widespread in place-names. **Sprit** is only attested in ME in *Gaw*.

[491] Though note that the adv. *enkerli*, perh. related to *Gaw* **enker-**, is found elsewhere. Amongst the derived forms in the sub-entries there is also **vnbene** (301c.), which is known only in *Gaw*. And **child-gered** is a *hapax legomenon* as a compound, but the related n. *gere* is relatively widespread (see under 360. **gere** in D2 below) and so this item has not been counted here (or labelled 'c').

[492] **Strothe** is also found in place-names. As a vbl. n. **teuelyng** is unique to *Gaw*, but the v. in this sense is attested in the other texts of the MS. Of the derived forms treated in sub-entries, notice also **atwaped** (346b.).

[493] Though notice also the (possible) nineteenth-century dial occurrences cited by *OED*.

[494] Amongst the sub-entries, the same is true of **ferlyly** (310d.) and **schunt** (n.) (336b.), the latter being found only in *Gaw* before the nineteenth century.

[495] There is also **farand**, which is always northern in ME but apparently more widespread in modern dial usage; and comparable forms with an evaluative adv. are indeed found in ME without dialectal restriction (see the entry).

[496] Though note that **noke** and **ronez** are more widespread in field-names and place-names, respectively. It is also worth commenting on **ferly**, the n. and adv. (i.e. sub-entries 310b. and c.) only, which are chiefly N/EM but found in other dialect areas in the vocabulary of alliterative verse.

5.1.2.3. Probability of ON input

Still more so than for the items dealt with under Types B and C above, it is very difficult to generalize about the variables relevant to one's assessment of the probability of ON input when it comes to words whose etymological discussions involve multiple different theories (one or more of which may present complex problems of their own). But in the hope of summing up at least some of the factors which tend to bear on weighing up the relative merits of these etymological strands, I offer some further discussion in what follows. As before, I have labelled Type D words with 'probability markers', in an attempt to give an (inevitably crude) impression of the quality of the evidence and the balance of the opinions of the scholarly authorities discussed in the Survey entries. By definition, no items treated under Type D1 show a very strong case for ON input, and all attract at least some disagreement in the scholarship; so the probability markers here work on just two levels, D versus DD:[497]

> D1 (18 stems)
> The case for ON input is reasonable, and (in most cases) has often been made in the scholarly tradition; but plausible alternative explanations are usually available.
>
> DD1 (30 stems)
> The case for ON input is not strong (though it still cannot be dismissed out of hand). The word's development can usually be explained more plausibly by other means. There is some history of attributing or at least suggesting ON input in the scholarly tradition, but the weight of (especially recent) argument is against it, and/or the case for it is problematic in some fairly fundamental way.

As will be immediately apparent from these figures, a far smaller proportion of D1 items may (in my judgement) be argued to show some ON input with at least reasonable plausibility than was the case for any of the sub-types considered under B or C. Thus the ratio of D1:DD1 items of 18:30 is tilted far more strongly towards the least probable group than was true even for sub-types C4 (where the ratio was 2:3:7) and C5 (2:5:10) above.

In the following remarks I take D1 and DD1 stems in turn, arranging them into (very approximate) sets according to the profiles they present in the scholarly tradition, and summarizing in each case the grounds on which that profile has built up.

1. The stronger cases (D1)

(i) The majority of D1 stems (ten) are those for which a modern consensus has (in the main) developed for at least some ON input. This is ordinarily because the

---

[497] D and DD may be thought of respectively as roughly equivalent to the double- and triple-letter prefixes applied to Type B and C items (i.e. a D suggests a similar probability level to a BB or a CC; a DD more or less equates to a BBB or a CCC).

suggested ON etyma will account for the ME forms in question (and often other key aspects of their sense and usage, too) at least as well as will the alternative theories, without presenting any insuperable difficulties in terms of formal or semantic development. Hence the proposed ON sources are usually now assumed to have played at least some role in the evolution of these ME words (even if, in some cases, it is likely that they did so in combination with words of other origins):

big (etc.)
The closest comparanda in terms of form are all in the Scand languages, and none is unfeasibly distant in sense, whether we derive from the ON v. as in OIcel *byggva* (theory 1) or from an adj. related to Norw *bugge* (theory 2).

faltered
Again the only close analogues are in the Scand languages (see theory 2, even if one of the consequences of Simpson's problematizing of OIcel *faltrask* is to make native derivation slightly more attractive than it had seemed hitherto).

farand
The sense development found with ON *fara* is very close (1), and often regarded as compelling evidence of some Scand input.

mynne (v.)
Some input from ON *minna* is almost always assumed (1), even if its ME reflex might well have been conflated with a formally similar native word of different origin.

neked
Even if the supposed ON etymon is not so close formally as to make the case unimpeachable, no other solid theories have been offered.

rof-sore
Consensus has developed as to a derivation from ON *rof* 'breach' (1); the earlier alternative suggestion (that ME *rof-* is related to **ryue** (v.)) is unconvincing, and other possible comparanda are relatively remote in sense or usage.

ronez
Most accounts assume some input from an ON n. represented by NNo *rune* or *rone* (2), in order to explain at least the sense of the ME word.

rous
Derivation from ON *hrós* is ordinarily accepted (1); the phonology of the ON word is not a perfect fit for (the usual implications of) the *Gaw*

scribe's orthography, but the alternative ON etymon (ON *raus*) is in itself mildly problematic formally, and Emerson's other option is less persuasive still.

ruþes

The source is generally understood to be ON *hryðja* (2) (although the medial fricative cannot be used as a robust test of loan); Kullnick's alternative ON etymon is less apposite semantically.

stayned

The sense development of the English word suggests some input from ON *steina* (2) (a borrowing of which must, nonetheless, have been conflated with a ME loan of early Fr *desteindre*).

(ii)   In two further instances there is consensus over derivation from a particular Gmc root, but no agreement as to whether the ME word descends via OE or ON. But the case for at least some ON input is plausible.

blunder

The nearest comparanda are in the Scand languages (1) and, despite the lack of enthusiasm evinced by some commentators, the case for a semantic connection between these and the ME word seems reasonable.

teuelyng

Some authorities cite only a native line of descent from the most plausible Gmc root (ult. < Lat); but derivation from ON actually accounts better for the ME form, and the attested Scand words also come nearer to the ME word in meaning (1b).

(iii)   In one case, the main modern consensus is for native derivation, but I have argued that an (at least partial) ON origin is also quite plausible (and that the theory is unjustly neglected).

ryue (adv.)

ON input has not been much considered since Skeat (other than in *ODEE*), but the supposed OE cognates of the likely ON etymon are more problematic than is usually appreciated (1).

(iv)   For the five remaining D1 stems, no clear consensus exists in recent scholarship. But the case for some ON input is sensible, and will account for the ME result at least as well as will the available alternatives (even if, again, input from another, additional source is in some instances also plausible).

enker-grene

The suggested ON etymon (1) is close both formally and semantically.

fyskez

The Norw and Sw dial verbs cited under theory (1) are the nearest known words in terms of form (even if their vocalism is not a precise match to the ME word); the other possible ON etymon (2b, ON *fÿsask*) may also have played a role.

staf-ful

A formal association with OE *stæf* is likely at some stage in the history of this compound, but the apparent sense development makes some ON input (2) look very plausible.

strothe

It is hard to rule out some input from ON *storð* (1), and several modern authorities allow for a blend of this word with OE *strōd*.

taysed

The old argument for ON input as in Bj. etc. (2) merits reconsideration, and the Scand comparanda are no more distant semantically from the ME word than is its supposed OE source.

Note that all of the above bar three (**fyskez, ryue, stayned**) are supported by the circumstantial evidence of regional distribution in the English lexicon (and thus are labelled 'c'; **strothe** is also a 'b').

As will be plain from these potted summaries, these difficult Type D1 words inevitably involve a great deal of disagreement amongst the scholarly authorities, to a far greater extent than was seen for stems of previous Types; and this is true even for those labelled with a 'D1' probability, where a consensus of sorts has nonetheless generally emerged. Indexical of this is the degree to which *OED* (in one or more of its versions) and *MED* differ, which they do in more or less significant ways over their etymologies for eight 'D1' stems, viz. **blunder, enker-grene, faltered, fyskez, ronez, ruþes, strothe, teuelyng**.[498] *MED* is slightly more likely to opt for ON input (or to forward it more strongly) than is *OED*, which it does in five cases (as compared to *OED*'s three). And notice that

---

[498] **Blunder**: *OED* derives from PGmc **blandan-* as well as ON *blunda*, *MED* compares the ON word only. **Enker-grene**: *OED* derives from Fr, *MED* from ON. **Faltered**: *OED* explains this as a native word (a development of OE *fealdan*), *MED* derives from ON. **Fyskez**: *OED* derives from a native source, *MED* compares Sw *fjäska*. **Ronez**: *OED* derives from ON (though the possibility of input from OE *rān* is added in *OED3*), *MED* from OE only. **Ruþes**: *OED* labels the etymology of this word as 'obscure' (though *OED3* derives from ON *hryðja*), *MED* derives from ON. **Strothe**: *OED* derives from the OE or ON options, *MED* from OE only. **Teuelyng**: *OED* links to *tave* v.1 (perh. < ON), *MED* derives from OE *tæflian*. And notice also the more minor differences of opinion over the following: **big** (etc.) (the original *OED* offers no clear etymology (but suspects a Scand origin), *MED* derives from the ON word represented by Norw *bugge* (which *OED3* now also includes as a possibility)); **farand** (*OED* makes a comparison to the ON sense development, *MED* does not); and **taysed** (*OED* is less certain about derivation from either of the OE or Fr possibilities than is *MED*, which puts the *Gaw* form under its entry for the native word). **Rof-sore** is apparently not treated by *OED*.

ODEE diverges markedly from both *OED* and *MED* as regards **blunder** and **ryue** (adv.).[499] TG(D) and GDS disagree seriously over five stems, i.e. **blunder, enker-grene, fyskez, ruþes, staf-ful.**[500] TG(D) make a stronger case for ON origin in four out of these five, GDS in only one. These two editions rarely agree with one another in contradistinction to both *OED* and *MED*, but notice **farand** (where both are more willing than the dictionaries to derive from ON). Only nine out of all forty-eight Type D1 and DD1 stems are treated by Bj. at all, the majority (six) of these belonging to this most plausible D1 probability category, viz. **big** (etc.), **farand, fyskez, mynne** v., **rous, taysed.**[501] Bj. is usually in accord with one or more of the other authorities referred to in this paragraph, but not always; notice in particular **taysed**, to which he attributes an ON etymon not mentioned by the others.

2. The weaker cases (DD1)

For the majority of stems treated in the Type D1 section of the Survey, however, the case for ON input is less plausible.

(i) Very often (nine stems) the main modern consensus is for native derivation (or in one case for a Fr source), and this seems to me a defensible position: these other origins will account for the forms and meanings of the ME outputs at least as well as will the posited ON etyma, which make for a less convincing match and are sometimes problematic in other ways:

balȝ
The supposed ON etymon (2) is not very close either formally or semantically, and the now generally assumed derivation from an OE (Angl) **balg* is far more compelling.

bost
The suggested ON input (1) is not a good explanation for the form of the ME word; an Anglo-Fr etymon (perh. ult. < Gmc) is better, even if the evidence for the existence of such an Anglo-Fr word is weaker than sometimes assumed.

---

[499] *ODEE* is reluctant to derive **blunder** from ON, where both *OED* and *MED* suggest it. For **ryue**, *ODEE* favours an ON origin, whereas both other dictionaries prefer a native etymon.

[500] **Blunder**: TG(D) compare ON *blunda*, GDS refers only to OE *blandan*. **Enker-grene**: TG(D) derive from ON, GDS from Fr (though it entertains the idea of ON influence). **Fyskez**: TG(D) suggest a borrowing from ON *fjaska* (though notice that the original printing of TG had derived from ON *fýsask*, with this changed to follow Bj'.s loan of ON *fjaska* with the revised 1930 reprint), GDS prefers to derive from OE (albeit with the possibility of ON input, depending on the subject of the v. in context). **Ruþes**: TG(D) derive from ON *hryðja*, GDS calls the etymology 'unknown'. **Staf-ful**: TG(D) refer only to OE *stæf*, GDS adds a comparison to Norw *stappfull*. There are also less substantial differences regarding: **ronez** (TG(D) derive only from ON (as in NNo *rune*), GDS refers both to this theory and to the possible origin in an OE form in /ɑ:/ (though without specifying an etymology)); **rous** (TG(D) cite both ON *hrós* and *raus* as potential inputs, GDS only the first option); **stayned** (TG(D) derive only from ON, GDS also from Fr); and **teuelyng** (both editions derive from ON, though TG(D) also refer to *OED* with its alternative explanation).

[501] He also has an entry for ME *enkerli*, which is perh. related to **enker-grene**, but not for the *Gaw* form itself.

flosche
Native imitative origin is usually preferred, though some input from Fr is also often raised as a possibility; the proposed ON etymon (2) is not a good match for the form of the *Gaw* word (though it may lie partly behind ME variants in /sk/).

glyfte
Native imitative origin (with the nearest comparanda in Du) is again the most plausible explanation, with theory (2) involving Scand input very much an outlier (proposed by Kullnick only, and the Sw word he cites is obscure).

glode
Best derived < an OE *glād-*, with the related or other ON forms that have been suggested (theories 1, 2 and 3) being much less helpful formally.

gryed
Generally derived from a native form related to MnE dial *grue*; only Emerson suggests a Scand source (1) (but the later Scand verbs are usually in fact derived from LG).

raþeled
Some connection with English *raddle* 'to weave or twist' is usually accepted, even if the ulterior etymology is obscure; Emerson's proposed ON etymon (2) does not seem very close to the meaning required by the *Gaw* context.

rokked
This v. is usually understood as a native word (with Scand cognates), despite Kullnick's early attempt to derive it direct from Scand (1); the alternative in TG (theory 2, also < ON) is implausible formally and semantically.

schunt (n. and v.)
The proposed ON etymon (1) is unconvincing formally, and a (different) native source is a better explanation (even if there are no close analogues recorded in OE).

(ii)   In three cases ON input is not so problematic, and can be entertained as an (outside) possibility; but a native origin will still account for what we find in ME well enough, and again most authorities agree on it:

dare
There is a neglected but interesting theory by Kullnick (2) for ON input; but a native etymon seems sufficient and is generally accepted now.

ferly (etc.)
One or both of the suggested native etyma will explain the ME words very well, even if input from ON (2) can be brought in as additional (though not especially necessary) justification for their meanings.

kylled
NNo *kylla* (1) is a good formal parallel, but the sense development starting from such an ON etymon is more of a stretch than from the generally accepted native alternative.

(iii)   In one case, the main modern consensus is for a particular Gmc root, with descent via ON an often advanced but not especially convincing argument.

noke
The ME word is generally compared to Norw *nōk* (1), but this is relatively distant in date of attestation and not an ideal match semantically, and so may only be a cognate; the other alternatives, including another ON comparandum (2), are still less compelling.

(iv)   In the majority of instances labelled DD1 (seventeen stems), which can be thought of as 'obscure' with perhaps the best justification, there is no clear modern consensus as to etymology at all – and indeed for several of these items, none of the various sources which have been proposed will account very well for the required ME output. Nonetheless, as for the other stems above, the suggested alternatives to ON input will normally explain the ME form and sense at least as well, and so it is hard to rule confidently in favour of Scand derivation as likely to have played some role; and in some cases, once again, the potential ON etyma present difficulties of their own:

bene (etc.)
The proposed ON etymon (1) is problematic phonologically, and is not very close semantically. The main suggested alternative is to derive from Fr and/or Lat, but this is also unappealing; and the most attractive option seems to me to be a now rarely cited native etymon (theory 3).

child-gered
There are reasonable grounds to draw on all three theories, but the case for ON input (1) is no stronger than the others.

glyȝt
A native (perh. imitative) origin is the best alternative to derivation from a supposed ON etymon which does not seem very close formally (2).

gryndel (etc.)
ON *grindill* is frequently brought into discussions (1), though often as a cognate rather than as a direct source; and both this and *OED*'s alternative ON derivation require conversion of a n. to an adj.

grome
An ON *grómr* (1a) in the right sense is much less securely attested than is sometimes assumed, and the supposed Fr alternative may not be independent of the ME word, leading others (e.g. *OED*) to propose a (weakly supported) native derivation.

happe
Possibly < Fr (or Gmc), although the sense development is an issue; other theories are harder to substantiate, including McGee's suggested ON etymon (3), which presents formal problems.

irked
The semantic distance between the Scand and ME usages prevents the possible ON etymon (1) from being entirely attractive, and the alternatives are all more or less problematic (the Ger comparanda are of unclear etymology, and not necessarily compatible with a Gmc source for ME *irken*; the Celtic comparanda do not look very close formally).

loupe
Derivation from ON (1) presents phonological problems (which are not always appreciated), as does loan from Celtic; and there is the added issue of a possible relationship with PDE *loop(-hole)*, perh. < Du.

rake
ON input (2) is plausible enough, but there is no clear evidence for a ME form in the right sense showing /ɑː/, /ɔː/, which would make its claim more solid; and there are two other reasonable possible sources, both from OE.

runisch (etc.)
Formally the now preferred source is OE *rūn-*; further input (especially on the grounds of meaning) is often also assumed, but there is no clear consensus as to whether this is from ON *hrjónn* (1a) or OE *hrēoh*.

scho
Direct ON input (< ON *sjá*) is now generally discounted. The starting point is usually understood as either OE *hīo* or *sīo*, but the case for ON influence on their pronunciation is only sometimes advanced (2, 3), and other explanations are credible.

snitered

Although TG(D)'s comparison to Norw *snitra* has been influential (1), it is problematic semantically. The most persuasive relationship is rather with PGmc **snīþ-*, which plausibly lies behind the sense of the ME word (with metaphorical extension), and in that case the argument for ON derivation rests mainly on dial distribution; a native ideophonic development is also hard to rule out.

sprit

Some role for OE *spryttan* (via sense extension) is very plausible, even if input from ON *spretta* (3) is reasonable, too; and Knigge's derivation from ON *sprita* (4) also merits reconsideration.

sweʒe

ON *sveigja* is often cited as a likely input (2), but OE *swēgan* makes for a reasonable enough source on its own, and *OED*'s **swegan* has also found some support.

traunt (etc.)

MDu *trant* is the most often cited comparandum, and occasionally the prob. related Sw *trant* (2); but other possibilities can be suggested, inc. most compellingly (I argue) a derivation from Anglo-Fr.

wapped (etc.)

One can look to ON *vappa* (1) or (given the WGmc comparanda) a native cognate as etymon, or explain this stem as a recent imitative creation.

wyles (etc.)

The most plausible sources are OE *wīgle* and an Anglo-Fr **wile* (= OFr *guile*); ON input (4) is also possible, but phonologically less persuasive than is often assumed.

All of these DD1 stems bar six (**bost, (child-)gered, dare, grome, kylled, rokked**) are more or less restricted to the N/EM in their distribution, and are labelled 'c' in at least one member of the word-group (and **flosche** and **glode** are also 'b'). Nonetheless, it should be stressed that this circumstantial evidence offers only very limited support for ON derivation in the face of the various problems and uncertainties in the structural cases outlined above. Even though in some DD1 instances English dial distribution is explicitly invoked as a justification for seeking an ON etymon (as for example by *OED* for **happe** and **wyles** (etc.)), on its own it is not sufficient to make the argument for ON input more compelling.

Disagreement between the principal scholarly authorities is even more pervasive for items labelled DD1 than it is for the D1 sub-type discussed above. *OED* and *MED* diverge more or less significantly over fourteen stems, viz. **bene** (etc.), **flosche, glyʒt, gryndel** (etc.), **happe, irked, loupe, rake, runisch** (etc.), **scho, snitered, sprit, sweʒe, wapped** (etc.).[502] *MED* is once again slightly more likely to promote ON input than is *OED*, which is true for seven stems, whereas (one of more versions of) *OED* only does so four times. *ODEE* differs substantially from *OED* with regard to **sweʒe** and **wyles** (etc.).[503] TGD and GDS disagree over thirteen stems, i.e. **balʒ, bene** (etc.), **child-gered, glyʒt, glode, happe, irked, loupe, runisch** (etc.), **snitered, sprit, strothe, sweʒe**.[504] TGD promotes more ON input than GDS in five cases, whereas the reverse is true in another four. And notice that there are several interesting differences too between the original TG and Davis's

---

[502] **Bene** (etc.): *OED* is not satisfied by any of the proposed etymologies, *MED* derives from Fr and/or Lat. **Flosche**: *OED* regards this as native, *MED* compares only Fr. **Glyʒt**: *OED* tentatively explains this word as native, *MED* derives from ON. **Gryndel** (etc.): *OED* compares ON *grimd*, *MED* ON *grindill* and OE *Grendel*. **Happe**: the original *OED* suggests ON origin, *MED* prefers a blend of OFr *happer* and ME *lappen*. **Irked**: *OED* discusses ON and OHG forms, *MED* derives from Celtic. **Loupe**: *OED* looks to Celtic forms and discounts ON, *MED* prefers a blend of Celtic and ON origin. **Rake**: *OED* originally refers only to ON *rák* (*OED3* adds other possibilities), *MED* only to OE *racu* and *hraca*. **Runisch** (etc.): *OED* originally calls the etymology 'unknown' (*OED3* now adduces ON *hrjónn* beside OE *rūn-*), *MED* derives from ON *hrjónn* or OE *hrēoh* plus OE *rūn-*. **Scho**: *OED* entertains ON influence on the pronunciation of either OE *hīo* or *sīo*, *MED* does not mention Scand input at all. **Snitered**: *OED* compares only early MnE *snite* and WFris *snijt, snitte*, *MED* offers MnE *snite* but also Yorks dial *snitter* and Norw dial *snitra* and claims 'Prob. ON'. **Spirt**: *OED* compares only other obscure English words, *MED* derives partly from OE *spryttan* and partly from ON *spretta*. **Sweʒe**: *OED* derives from OE **swegan*, *MED* from ON. **Wapped** (etc.): *OED* explains this stem as echoic, *MED* combines this with possible loan from ON. Notice also more minor differences in the dictionaries' treatment of **wyles** (etc.) (both *OED* and *MED* cite the full range of prospective etyma, though only *MED* gives OE *wīl* 'chain' and *OED* expresses a preference for ON derivation); and **child-gered**, whose etymology is not dealt with by *OED* (it features in the list of compounds at the foot of the entry for *child* n., but the identity of the second element is not discussed).

[503] In both cases *ODEE* refers only to ON etyma, as against *OED* which prefers native derivation for **sweʒe** and cites a much fuller range of theories for **wyles**.

[504] **Balʒ**: TG(D) explain this word as native, GDS derives from ON. **Bene** (etc.): TG(D) tentatively derive from Fr and/or Lat, GDS is not content with any proposed etymology. **Child-gered**: TG(D) connect *-gered* with ON or MDu words, GDS derives from Fr. **Glyʒt**: TG(D) give a 'cf.' to ON, GDS has 'derivation unknown'. **Glode**: TG(D) label this word simply 'obscure', GDS attempts various, especially Scand, comparanda. **Happe**: TG(D) relate this to ME *haspen*, GDS compares LG and Fris words. **Irked**: TG(D) offer no etymology, GDS compares OHG words. **Loupe**: TG(D) have no etymology, GDS derives from ON. **Runisch** (etc.): TG(D) refer to ON *hrjónn* or OE *hrēoh*, GDS to the latter but also to OE *rūn*. **Snitered**: TG(D) compare Norw dial *snitra*, GDS compares WFris *snijt, snitte*. **Sprit**: TG(D) derive from OE *spryttan*, GDS follows *OED* (i.e. neither refers to ON input). **Strothe**: TGD derive from OE and/or ON, GDS from Celtic. **Sweʒe**: TG(D) derive from OE **swegan* (as in *OED*), GDS from ON. Notice also the more minor disagreements in the case of: **glyfte** (TG(D) relate this obscurely to similar imitative ME verbs, GDS has only 'derivation unknown'); **gryed** (TGD compares MnE dial *grue*, GDS refers to this and also probable cognates in Sw and Dan); **gryndel** (etc.) (TG(D) derive from ON *grindill*, GDS compares this with a 'cp.' only (and also ON *grenja*)); **grome** (TG(D) compare OFr and MDu words, GDS only the Fr); **rake** (both editions cite OE *racu* and ON *rák*, but TGD prefers the latter); **raþeled** (TG(D) refer to MnE *raddle*, GDS to *OED*'s suggested etyma for this in Fr).

revised edition (see **child-gered, ferly** (etc.), **gryed, rake, rokked, scho, strothe**),[505] which amount to a net reduction in claims for ON input in three stems in TGD. Only three out of thirty DD1 stems (**bost, irked, sweʒe**) are dealt with by Bj. at all. This is strongly indicative of just how few of the stems treated in this section were regarded as possible Norse loans in need of (serious) analysis as such when Bj. was writing; and of the degree to which putative ON etyma for them have been generated by subsequent work seeking to explain the obscurer elements of ME vocabulary. But Bj. is therefore missing some key items which have been staples of later discussion of ON input into English, and/or which have very often been cited as of Scand origin, including **kylled, loupe, noke, scho, snitered** and **wyles**. By contrast, some of the items included under category DD1 owe their arguments for ON derivation largely or entirely to the earlier stages of the etymological tradition covered by this book (the late nineteenth to the early twentieth century), and have since fallen resoundingly out of favour as possible Norse borrowings (or indeed these earlier arguments have simply been forgotten). See most notably: **balʒ, bene** (etc.), **bost, dare, glyfte, gryed, grom, irked, kylled, loupe, raþeled, rokked, schunt** (n. and v.), **taysed, traunt** (etc.), **wapped** (etc.). Some of these have seen only very occasional treatment as Scand derivations; thus **dare** and **glyfte** (so far as I can see) only by Kullnick, **gryed** and **raþeled** only by Emerson, and **schunt** only by Skeat and Knigge.[506]

5.2. TYPE D2

5.2.1. *Summary list*

Category D2 consists of fifty-two lexical items (none has sub-entries):

348.   ***barne**; n.; (1) (**barne*) 'child'; (2) (*burne*) 'warrior, knight, man' [DD2]
349.   **bate**; n.; (1) 'strife, fighting'; (2) 'baiting' [DD2]
350.   **byled**; v. (pret.); (1) 'boiled, bubbled'; (2) 'resounded'; (3) 'swelled, rose' [DD2]

---

[505] **Child-gered**: TG refers to *OED*'s *gere* 'manners' (< ON), TGD to MDu *gere* (following Luttrell). **Ferly** (etc.): TG derives from OE *fǣrlic* plus ON *ferligr*, TGD replaces *fǣrlic* with OE **feorlic*. **Gryed**: TG has just 'not known', TGD compares MnE dial *grue*. **Rake**: TG cites only OE *racu*, TGD prefers ON *rák* (retaining a 'cf.' to the OE word). **Rokked**: TG derives from ON *hrukka*, TGD from late OE *roccian*. **Scho**: TG refers to *OED* (where ON input is regarded as possible), TGD derives only from OE *hēo* (with no mention of ON influence). **Strothe**: TG cites only the possible ON etymon, TGD adds a reference to OE *strōd* in its note (though this has not made it into the glossary etymology).

[506] Notice also **runisch** (etc.), for which only Knigge and Mätzner propose an alternative ON etymon (theory 3) to that otherwise generally adduced; and similarly **ruþes** (Kullnick, theory 1) and **sprit** (Knigge, theory 4).

351. ***bulk**; n.; (1) (*bluk*) and (2) (**bulk*) '(headless) trunk (of the body)'; (3) (**blenk*) 'gaze' [D2]

352. **clambere**; v.; (1) 'to cluster'; (2) 'to clamber' [DD2]

353. **costez**; v. (pres. 3 sg.); (1) 'coasts, passes by the side of'; (2) 'gives (full bright) quality to'; (3) 'drives' [DD2]

354. **daylyeden**; v. (pret. pl.); (1) 'trifled, made (courtly) love; conversed'; (2) 'bandied pleasantries' [DD2]

355. ***dyngez**; v. (pres. 3 sg.); (1) (**dyngez*) 'smites'; (2) (*dymnez*) 'condemns' [D2]

356. **draueled**; v. (pret.); (1) 'muttered (in sleep)'; (2) 'drawled' [DD2]

357. **fere**; adj.; (1) 'proud, bold'; (2) 'hale, healthy' [DD2]

358. **forȝ**; n.; (1) 'waterfall'; (2) 'channel, bed' [DD2]

359. **gayne**; n.; (1) 'gain, what you obtained'; (2) 'advantage, benefit, what has accrued' [D2]

360. **gere**; n.; (1) 'gear, apparatus, equipment'; (2) 'doings, behaviour' [DD2]

361. **glaum**; (1) (a) (reading *glaum (ande . . .)*, n.) 'noise of merrymaking'; (b) (reading *glaumande*, pres. ptcp.) 'noisy'; (2) (reading **glamm (ande . . .)*, n.) 'din, noise of merrymaking' [D2]

362. ***glopnyng**; vbl. n.; (1) (*gopnyng*) 'staring'; (2) (**glopnyng*) 'dismay' [D2]

363. **grwe**; n.; (1) 'grain, jot' (i.e. *no grwe* 'not at all'); (2) 'horror, dread, fear' [DD2]

364. **heme**; (1) (adj.) 'suitable, neat'; (2) (n.) 'hem, skirt' [DD2]

365. **knot**; n.; (1) (a) 'knot, cluster', (b) (**kerre*) 'thicket on marshy ground'; (2) 'rocky (wooded) knoll' [DD2]

366. **lagmon**; n.; (1) (**bi-laggid men*) 'men spattered with dirt'; (2) 'last or hindmost person' (*lad . . . bi lagmon* = 'led astray'); (3) 'lawyer' (*lad . . . bi lagmon* = 'cunningly led astray (as if by a lawyer)' [D2]

367. **laucyng**; (1) (*forlancyng*) 'throwing out' (pres. ptcp.); (2) (*laucyng*) 'loosening' (vbl. n.) [D2]

368. **lenge**; (1) (*lenge*) and (2) (**longe*) adv., 'a long while, for a long time'; (3) (*lenge*) v. infin. 'to remain' [DD2]

369. **list**; n.; (1) (**list vpon lif*) 'joy'; (2) 'the ear, hearing' [DD2]

370. **lyte**; (1) (n.) 'expectation' (i.e. 'back (in fear) 1463; *on lyte* 'in delay', 2303); (2) (a) (pron.) 'few' (*on lyte droȝen* 'few advanced', 1463); (b) (n.) 'fault' (*on lyte* 'at fault, faultily, improperly') [D2]

371. **messequyle**; n.; (1) 'time for mass'; (2) 'dinner time' [DD2]

372. **neme**; v.; (1) (a) 'took' (pret. pl.), (b) 'take' (pres. pl.); (2) 'name' (pres. pl.; *neme for*, 'name as') [DD2]

373. **quethe**; n.; (1) (reading *quethe*) 'utterance'; (2) (reading *queche*) 'advance' [DD2]

374. **raged**; ppl. adj.; (1) 'ragged, shaggy'; (2) 'hoar-frosted' [D2]

375. **rak**; n.; (1) 'drifting clouds'; (2) 'path' [DD2]

376. **rasse**; n.; (1) 'level; ?ledge of rock'; (2) 'rounded projection of a rock or mountain'; (3) 'rising or perpendicular slope'; (4) 'watercourse, channel, ditch' [D2]

377. **rykande**; v. (pres. ptcp.); (1) 'commanding'; (2) 'noisy'; (3) (*raykande*) 'loud, strong'; (4) (*rynkande*) 'ringing' [DD2]

378. **rimed**; v. (pret.), reflex., in phrase *rimed hym*: (1) 'cleared his throat'; (2) 'drew himself up' [DD2]

379. **rout**; n.; (1) 'violent movement, jerk'; (2) 'roar' [DD2]

380. ***schifted***; v. (pret.); (1) (*schifted*) 'shifted, declined'; (2) (MS *schafted*) (a) 'beamed, shone forth', (b) 'set' [DD2]

381. **scholes**; (1) (adj.) 'shoeless'; (2) (n. pl.) 'shoes with long pointed toes'; (3) (n. pl.) 'thin plates (part of the horse's armour)'; (4) (n. pl.) 'protections under and inside the thighs'; (5) (n. pl.) 'supports covering the sole of the foot' [DD2]

382. **skayned**; v. (pp.); (1) (reading *skayned*) 'grazed'; (2) (reading *skayued*) (a) 'wild, desolate', (b) 'precipitously overhanging, threatening', (c) 'twisted' [D2]

383. **skwez**; n. (pl.); (1) 'shadows'; (2) 'precipitous banks; jagged faces'; (3) 'clouds' [D2]

384. **slokes**; (1) (a) (v., imp. pl.) 'stop, enough!', (b) (v., pres. 2 sg.) 'you are dawdling', (c) (n., pl.) 'stops' (*bot* ~, 'without stops, continuously'); (2) (v., pres. 2 sg.) 'thou remainest idle, inactive' [D2]

385. ***sparred***; v. (pret.); (1) (*sparred*) 'sprang'; (2) (*sped(e) (him)*) 'hastened' [DD2]

386. **spenne (1)**; n.; (1) (a) 'space, interval'; (b) 'struggle, strife'; (c) 'enclosed ground' (*in* ~ 'there, in that place'); (2) 'ground, space of turf' (*in* ~ 'there'); (3) 'thorn bush, thorn hedge, thorn thicket' [D2]

387. **spenne (2)**; n.; (1) 'fence, hedge'; (2) (a) 'thorn-hedge'; (b) 'thorn bush, thorn hedge, thorn thicket' [D2]

388. **spenne-fote**; adv.; (1) (a) ?'with feet apart'; (b) 'with feet together'; (2) 'striking out with the feet'; (3) 'as if taking a spring with a kick'; (4) 'quickly' [D2]

389. **stemmed**; v. (pret.); (1) 'debated (with himself/themselves)'; (2) 'stopped, halted; stood about, hesitated' [DD2]

390. **toruayle**; n.; (1) (*trauayle*) 'hard task'; (2) (*toruayle*) 'hard task', 'difficulty' [DD2]

391. **twynnen**; v.; (1) (pp.) 'twined, plaited'; (2) (pres. pl.) 'match' [D2]

392. ***þwarte-knot***; n.; (1) (*þwarte-knot*) 'cross knot'; (2) (*þwarle knot*) 'tight knot', 'intricate knot', 'twirled knot' [DD2]

393. **vnhap**; (1) (n.) 'misfortune'; (2) (v., infin.) 'to unfasten' [DD2]

394. ***vntyl***; prep.; 'until'; (1) (*vntyl*) 'until'; (2) (*vntyȝtel*) 'unrestraint, lightheartedness' (*dalten* ~ 'revelled') or 'trifling talk' [DD2]

395. **vphalt**; v. (pp.)/adj.; (1) 'lifted up'; (2) 'raised, i.e. high' [DD2]

396. **waytez**; v. (pres. 3 sg.); (1) 'looks'; (2) 'treats (him) with anger, i.e. behaves angrily' [DD2]
397. **wande**; n.; (1) 'branch' (*under* ~ 'in the wood'); (2) 'difficulty, hesitation' (*under* ~ 'under difficulty, in hesitation') [D2]
398. **weue**; v.; (1) 'to offer, show (honour); give'; (2) 'to weave, i.e. contrive' [D2]
399. **wylyde**; adj.; (1) (a) 'wild, i.e. licentious, amorous', (b) 'cruel' (~ *werke* 'cruel act'); (2) 'choice' (~ *werke* 'choice handiwork'); (3) (a) 'guileful' (~ *werke* 'intrigue'), (b) 'skilful' [DD2]

5.2.2. *Further remarks*

As described in the headnote to this Type D introductory essay, all the items treated under Type D2 have been subject to more or less significant disagreement regarding how they should be interpreted in their *Gaw* contexts, and hence as to the identity of the ME word whose etymology is to be used in explaining them.[507]

Several of these items are familiar cruces in the scholarship on *Gaw*, much discussed in editions and associated reviews and notes since the nineteenth century. Notice in particular ***bulk, forʒ, lagmon, list, raged, rasse, scholes, skwez, slokes, spenne 1, spenne 2** and **spenne-fote**,[508] and to a lesser extent **knot, lyte, rykande, rimed, rout, *schifted** (mostly regarding theory (2), reading *schafted*), **skayned** (especially theory (2), reading *skayued*), ***þwarte-knot, vnhap, *vntyl** (but only until Emerson 1922a), **wylyde**. Some of these have provoked an especially large number of different theories, as high as four main alternatives for **rasse, rykande** and **spenne-fote** and five for **scholes**. (Note that in the discussion that follows, the main theories for each item are distinguished by a numbered reference in round brackets, specifying a word form if a different reading or an emendation is involved.) Nonetheless, by no means all subsequent accounts seem to be aware of all previous ones, and especially to know of the explanations offered in some earlier articles; this reinforces the value of the review of scholarly literature I attempt in this book. A particular case in point is **rasse**, where to my mind the most compelling

---

[507] There are various more minor disagreements, especially with respect to the precise form or sense in *Gaw*. See in particular under the following theories: **costez** (1), **glaum** (1), **list** (2), **lyte** (1), **neme** (1a), **rimed** (2), **rout** (1), ***schifted** (2, *schafted*), **skayned** (2, *skayued*), **slokes** (1), **twynnen** (1), ***þwarte-knot** (2, *þwarle-*), **vnhap** (2), **wylyde** (1) and (3). Most of these discussions revolve around the exact understanding of a word's sense or grammar in context, though sometimes there are additional issues, viz.: **glaum** (1) (do we have a n., or the stem of a v. in the pres. ptcp.?); **list** (2) (does the MS read <lif> or <lof> in this line?); **lyte** (2) (the alliterative stress falls on the *on* of <on lyte> at 1463, and so this is sometimes interpreted as a compound); **neme** (1a) (the different possible origins of a pret. pl. in <e> in the *Gaw*-manuscript); **skayned** (2, *skayued*) (the various possible MnE dial comparanda); **slokes** (1) (whether the derivation is direct from ON *slokinn* or a secondary formation on ME *sloknen* < ON *slokna*); **vnhap** (2) (the reading of the rest of this line).

[508] Note that **spenne 1, spenne 2** and **spenne-fote** form a set of interconnected items, perhaps related etymologically but posing distinct problems, and which it has proven more convenient to give separate entries in the Survey.

theory (2) has been little mentioned since it appeared in an article by Sundén in 1930.

There are several D2 items where one of the competing theories is now generally agreed to be right, and where one or more of the alternatives seem markedly weaker or less helpful to the argument: notice in particular **costez, daylyeden, *dyngez, forȝ, grwe, heme, lagmon, laucyng, lenge, lyte, quethe, rak, rout, *schifted, scholes, *sparred, stemmed, *vntyl, vphalt, waytez, wande, weue**. I have nevertheless given all these words entries in the Survey, and paid due attention to each theory, since none can definitively be ruled out (contrast the items in the Appendix (section 1)). But there are other words where, although a similar modern consensus has built up around one of the options, one or more of the other theories (those numbered in the following list) in reality remain plausible, and to my mind deserve more attention than they are usually given: thus **byled** (2), **clambere** (2), **daylyeden** (2) (especially given the possibility of cross-influence between the word-forms belonging to the two theories), **draueled** (1b) (again, with possible cross-influence), **fere** (2), ***glopnyng** (1b, a new suggestion), **messequyle** (2), **neme** (1a, 1b), **raged** (2), **rykande** (1), **skayned** (2, *skayued*), **skwez** (2), **slokes** (2b), **spenne 1** (1b), **spenne-fote** (3).

In the majority of instances, the argument is about the possible identifications of what is read as fundamentally the same word-form in each case. But some items involve emendation of the manuscript as part of one or more theories, viz. ***barne, *bulk, costez, *dyngez, glaum, *glopnyng, knot, lagmon, lenge, list, rykande, *schifted, *sparred, *þwarte-knot, *vntyl**.[509] And for a few the opposing theories depend on quite different interpretations of the letter-forms or their orthographic significance in the manuscript: **draueled, forȝ, glaum, laucyng, quethe, skayned, toruayle**.

Several theories identify a D2 item with a stem already treated earlier in the Survey (or explain it as influenced by one): thus **costez** (3, **castez*) (see **kest** (v.) A1); **gayne** (2) (see **gayn** (adj.) A1); **gere** (1 and 2) (see **gere** (n.) A1 and **child-gered** D1); **glaum** (2, **glamm*) (see **glam** B1); **heme** (1) (see **hemely** C1); **lagmon** (3) (see **lawe** C3); **laucyng** (2) (see **lausen** A1); **messequyle** (1) (see **messe** C2); **rak** (2) (see **rake** D1); **rasse** (2) (see **race** C2); **spenne 1** (1a) = **spenne-fote** (1) (see **spene** C1); **toruayle** (2) (see **tor** C5); **twynnen** (2) (see **twynnen** C1); ***þwarte-knot** (1) (see **ouerþwert** A3); **vnhap** (1 and 2) (see both **hap** C1 and **happe** D1); ***vntyl** (1) (see **til** C5); **vphalt** (2) (see **hale** B2); **wande** (1) (see **wandez** C1); **weue** (1) (see **wayue** A1); and **wylyde** (3) (see **wyles** D1). And some items would, according to one theory, be closely related to a stem

---

[509] Three possible different readings are involved for ***bulk** and **rykande**. For ***sparred** the generally accepted reading involves a reconstruction based on the off-set. Emendation is required to produce one or more of the possible ON inputs in the case of the following theories: ***barne** (1), ***bulk** (2) and (3, **blenk*), **costez** (3, **castez*), ***dyngez** (1), **glaum** (2), ***glopnyng** (2), **knot** (1b, **kerre*), **list** (1) (though the word *list* is itself retained), **rykande** (3, **raykande*), ***schifted** (1), ***sparred** (1), ***þwarte-knot** (1), ***vntyl**.

with an earlier entry: viz. **grwe** (2) (see **gryed** D1), ***schifted** (1) (see **skyfted** A1); **spenne 1** (1b, 1c) = **spenne 2** (1) (see **spene** C1). But the majority of the ON etyma suggested in order to account for D2 items are new possible Scand inputs which have not been dealt with previously in this book.

As with Type D1 above, the words treated in this section differ greatly from one another in terms of the complexity of the evidence discussed. A few D2 items present a choice between two or more identifications all with fairly straightforward etymologies; see for instance **skayned** (where both options are ON derivations of Type A1), **glaum, lenge** (where all the alternatives belong to the same Gmc root) and **waytez**. But in the great majority of cases, it happens that the histories of one or more of the options present difficulties or additional complications of various sorts. As before, I have pursued etymological backgrounds and scholarly arguments in detail whenever it has seemed helpful, in many cases gathering the relevant information in one place for the first time, and discussing it in more depth than has been done before in treatments of the English stems in question. I have drawn attention to older and/or neglected theories for:

> **daylyeden** (2): pursuing Emerson's alternative derivation from ON *deila*, and noticing its possible role (despite the phonological problems that ensue);
>
> **lyte** (2b): exploring the evidence for a ME loan of ON *lýti* cited in some earlier scholarship, and the reasons why this has now disappeared from the dictionaries;
>
> **rasse** (2): reviving Sundén's theory, largely neglected since McGee;[510]
>
> **skayned** (2, *skayued*): drawing attention to Sundén's interesting etymological account, inc. an alternative possible ON source (as in NNo dial *skøyva*);
>
> **spenne-fote** (3): pointing out the plausibility of Sundén's neglected alternative ON etymon;
>
> **toruayle** (1, *trauayle*): drawing attention to this neglected early reading of the MS form.

I have introduced new arguments for the following items in particular:

> **draueled** (1b): bringing ME *drevelen* and its variants to bear on the discussion (suggesting the possibility that two originally distinct verbs influenced one another, and indeed that *dravelen* 'to mumble' simply originated as a form of *drevelen*);
>
> ***glopnyng** (1b, *gopnyng*): a new theory, comparing the MS form with ON words in *gop-*;
>
> **list** (1): drawing attention to possible input from OE *list* 'art, skill';[511]

---

[510] On this word, see also Dance (2018: 123–5).

[511] Drawing on Dance (2003: 450).

slokes (2): following up theory (2b) properly for the first time, and noticing how apposite it is as a match for the likely sense in *Gaw* in particular;

sparred (1): exploring the difficult etymologies of Gmc **spar-* words, inc. a new suggestion that ME *sparren* 'to go quickly' (etc.) and *sparren* 'to lock' (etc.) might be etymologically identical.

And notice also the following, where I have pursued some specific etymological and related issues in more detail:

byled (2): analysing the formal problems pertaining to an attempted identification with OE *bylgan*;

*dyngez (1): exploring the possible attestations of an OE *dencgan*;

lagmon (1): pursuing the possible etymologies of late OE *lacge-*;

raged (1): investigating the various etymological strands for PDE *rag* and perh. related words; and (2): exploring the little-discussed etymology of MnE dial *rag* 'hoarfrost';

rak (1b.ii): exploring Scand **rak-* words having to do with moisture;

rasse (1): noticing the disparity between the attested senses of Anglo-Fr *ras* and the ME word; and (4): improving Elliott's claim for derivation from ON *rás* by introducing its Scand by-forms with a short vowel (and see **race** above);

rykande (2): exploring the etymological connections of MnE dial *rick*, inc. identifying possible ON input; and (3): noticing the not previously remarked miscopying of **raykande* as *rykande* in another ME text;

rout (1): pursuing the difficult evidence for the attestation of an OE cognate of ON *hrjóta* 'to rebound, fall' (etc.), and the possibility of a suitable endogenous sense development of OE *hrūtan* 'to snore'; and (2): discussing the problems of ME *routen* 'to cry out', especially distinguishing it from the further homophone *rout-*;

skwez (2): following the possible sources for MnE dial *skew* 'precipitous bank';

slokes (2): examining what semantic developments might give the right meaning for theory (2a);

spenne 2 (2b): considering the phonological problems with Elliott's proposed etymology;

spenne-fote (2): exploring the attestations of OE *spinnan* in a perh. compatible sense, and the possible mutual influence of forms of ME *spene* and *spinnen*;

stemmed (1): pursuing the form history and etymology of the supposed ON source, and moreover the problematic evidence for any attestation of such an ON loan in ME (which I problematize still further);

toruayle (2): noticing that a VAN reflex of ON *torveldi* would have been less close to ME *toruayle* than generally seems to be assumed;

*þwarte-knot (2, *þwarle-*): examining the perhaps related *thwerl* and its possible etymologies, in two cases making new suggestions about derivation on the *a*-grade of their prospective etyma;

wylyde (1): exploring similar phrases in ME, especially the Vernon spelling <wyled>.

As for D1 above, it seems to me most helpful to break Type D2 words down according to the number of (principal) theories which have been proposed for them, and the languages of the immediate etyma involved in each case. For the majority of items of this type there are just two main alternatives under consideration; but a significant minority has more than two options.[512]

Two main theories (31 stems):

In ten cases, both theories involve at least the possibility of some ON input. For **skayned**, both options produce unambiguous derivation from an ON etymon (both would be Type A1, each being guaranteed by two formal criteria); for **glaum**, one reading (theory 1) has an ON source similarly demonstrable on phonological grounds, and the other (theory 2, reading **glamm*) gives a ME word always derived from Scand; and for **stemmed**, both possible ME identifications are also usually explained as loans from ON. Scand input is also fairly plausible for both theories behind **raged**, **rak**, **rout** and **twynnen**, where in each case both options apparently show Gmc origin, but where both present difficulties, and native as well as ON descent can be considered. Otherwise, the argument for one of the possible ON inputs is stronger than it is for the other; hence **wande** (where the identification under theory (1) is usually derived from ON, but that for theory (2) could have come down via ON or OE), and **gere** and **vnhap** (for both of these, option (1) clearly or very probably derives from ON, but option (2) is of obscure origin, each involving perh. ON and Fr amongst the various possible sources (also Du in the case of **gere**)).[513]

---

[512] Some additional alternatives, where these are more obviously marginal (and often palpably implausible), have been relegated to a brief mention or to a note. Notice for instance **bate** (Morris's reference to an 'AS *bate*'), ***bulk** (Madden's *blunk*), **forȝ** (Madden and Morris's identification with **forth**), **lagmon** (Morris's identification of the first element with **loȝe**), **list** (the M(G) reading *lift*), **rimed** (Morris and Mätzner's derivation from OE *hrīeman*), **rout** (Mätzner's derivation from ON *rót* 'tossing, pitching'), ***schifted** (Morris's **sattled*), **slokes** (Madden's gloss 'blows', Morris's identification with ME *slaken*), ***þwarte-knot** (2, *þwarle-*) (Kullnick's comparison to Du *dral*), ***vntyl** (various early attempts to understand MS <vntyȝtel>), **waytez** (the additional suggested emendation to **wlytez* in GDS). And see also under **skayned** (2, *skayued*) for Sundén's suggested alternative ON etymon which he goes on to reject.

[513] As it happens, for **gere** both competing interpretations involve input (certainly or possibly, respectively) from the same ON etymon; and the same is true of **twynnen** (where ON input is no more than possible in both cases).

For ten other items, one theory clearly or very probably involves a native origin, next to one other where the case is for ON input with varying degrees of plausibility: thus ***barne, clambere, heme, list, neme, *schifted, *sparred, *vntyl, vphalt, weue**.[514] The remaining eleven present a choice between one identification which certainly or possibly derives from ON, versus another with a different ME word which is clearly from Fr:[515] hence **daylyeden, gayne, laucying, waytez**, for all of which the evidence for ON input under the relevant theory is unambiguous (all would be Type A1 items if the competing suggestion were not on the table); and also **bate, *dyngez, fere, grwe, messequyle, spenne 2** and **toruayle**, where in all cases ON has less demonstrably or plausibly played a part in accounting for the identified ME form in question.

More than two main theories (21 stems):

In two instances, one of the options involves possible ON input, next to two or more other theories where native descent may be assumed: thus **draueled, lenge**.

But usually the picture is a more complex one. The following items offer two or three distinct theories (numbered) which each features the prospect of ON input: ***bulk** (2, 3), **costez** (2, 3), ***glopnyng** (1a, 1b, 2), **knot** (1b, 2b), **lagmon** (2a, 3), **lyte** (1, 2a, 2b), **quethe** (1a, 1b), **rasse** (2, 4b), **rykande** (1, 2, 3), **rimed** (1a, 1b), **scholes** (1, 4), **skwez** (1, 3), **slokes** (1, 2a, 2b), **spenne 1** (1a, 1b, 1c), **spenne-fote** (1, 3, 4), ***þwarte-knot** (1, 2c), **wylyde** (2, 3).[516]

In these cases, one or more of the alternatives (numbered) involves the possibility of Fr derivation: **byled** (1), **costez** (1), ***bulk** (1, *bluk*), **rasse** (1a, 1b, 4a), **scholes** (2), **skwez** (2), **spenne 1** (3), **wylyde** (3).[517] And lastly notice **spenne-fote** (2), conceivably a loan-translation from Du or LG.

There are twenty-six ME stems treated under theories belonging to Type D2 items for which formal criteria might apply as tests of loan from one or more proposed ON etyma. These theories are (with the usual §§ references):

> **byled** (2) (§12.4)
> **costez** (3, **castez*) (§8.1)
> ***dyngez** (1) (§8.2)
> **daylyeden** (2) (§1)

---

[514] For ***sparred** (1), there is also the prospect of some input from a Fr word of Gmc origin. For **vphalt**, theory (2) identifies the second element with **hale**, prob. from Fr but with the slighter possibility of ON input. For **weue**, the form is evidently native under either theory, but option (1) may show influence from **wayue** of ON origin.

[515] The Fr etymon is ult. from Gmc in the case of **gayne, grwe** and **waytez**.

[516] Though notice that for **quethe** the two theories in question both feature putative ON etyma derived on the same Gmc verbal root; and for **spenne 1** there are three distinct but similarly etymologically-related strands.

[517] For ***bulk** (1) and **skwez** (2) the Fr etymon is prob. ult. from Gmc. For **rasse** there are (perh.) two distinct Fr etyma, (1a) and (1b), plus the prospect of Fr input under theory (4a).

*bulk (3, **blenk*) (§8.1)
gayne (2) (§8.2)
gere (1, 2a) (§8.2)
glaum (1) (§2)
knot (1b, **kerre*) (§8.1), (2b) (§6.4)
lagmon (2a) (§8.2)
laucyng (2) (§2)
lyte (2b) (§5)
quethe (1a) (§7)
raged (1a) (§9)
rak (1a) (§10.3), (2) (§§4, 10.3)
rasse (4b) (§4)
rykande (1) (§8.1), (2) (§8.1), (3) (§1)
rout (2) (§2)
scholes (4) (§4)
skayned (1) and (2, *skayued*) (both §§1, 8.3)
skwez (1) and (3) (both §8.3)
spenne-fote (3) and (4) (both §10.4)
twynnen (1) (§10.4)
*þwarte(-knot) (1) (§§11.2, 14)
vnhap (2) (§10.4)
waytez (2) (§1)

5.2.2.1. *Proposed ON etyma and their Germanic filiations*

As with Type D1 above, it seems helpful to offer here a few further remarks on the Scand words variously proposed as sources of ON input for D2 items, and about their relationships with Gmc vocabulary at large. The different theories involving potential ON etyma are, as ever, distinguished by a number in round brackets (bearing in mind that some D2 items have more than one distinct alternative argument featuring a suggested Scand input).

Amongst these proposed ON source words, notice that the ulterior etymology is more or less obscure or difficult for: ***bulk** (2), **glaum** (2, **glamm*), **raged** (1a; 2), **rak** (2), **rimed** (1b), **rykande** (3, **raykande*), **skwez** (1), ***sparred** (1a.ii), **spenne-fote** (3), **stemmed** (1), **wylyde** (2; 3).[518]

A handful may be characterized as belonging to a particular regional branch of the Scand languages. Hence **knot** (2b), whose prospective ON etymon shows *u*-mutation, and is thus perh. more likely to descend from an OWN variant (as pointed out by McGee); and **rasse** (2), since metathesized

---

[518] And see also **clambere** (1), where there is some disagreement as to the relationship of Gmc *-mb-* and *-mm-* forms.

by-forms of the proposed Scand source are also known mainly in WN. The supposed Scand inputs for **glaum** (1) and **spenne 1** (1b) are also suggested as specifically OWN by Gordon and Sundén respectively; and **clambere** (1), **draueled** (1), ***glopnyng** (1b, *gopnyng*) and (2, **glopnyng*), **rykande** (2), **rout** (1) and (2) are all theories explained with reference to (more or less obscure) Scand comparanda cited in the right form only from the WN languages. On the OEN side, notice also **rimed** (1a), where the nearest attested Scand sense is that of the Dan phrase *rømme sig* ('to hem, to clear one's throat').

For the various suggested ON etyma, the following relationships with the wider Gmc word stock may be summarized: twelve have (clearly) related forms nowhere else in Gmc: **costez** (3, **castez*), ***bulk** (2), **forȝ** (1), **glaum** (2, **glamm*), **knot** (1b, **kerre*), **raged** (1a; 2), **rykande** (2; 3, **raykande*), **rimed** (1b), **slokes** (2b), **wylyde** (3). All these would accordingly have been classcd as sub-type B1 if this were the only theory available, with the exception of the (emended) options treated under **costez** (3, **castez*), **knot** (1b, **kerre*) and **rykande** (3, **raykande*), which would all have been A1 on the grounds of form.

A further twelve may be connected with at least some plausibility to words attested elsewhere in Gmc, but have no (unambiguously) derivationally related forms in OE: **clambere** (1), ***dyngez** (1), ***glopnyng** (1a, *gopnyng*; 1b, *gopnyng*; 1c, **glopnyng*), **grwe** (2), **knot** (2b), **lyte** (1), ***schifted** (1), **slokes** (2a), the first element (< ON **und*) in ***vntyl** (1), **vphalt** (2).[519] All these would otherwise be classed as B2, therefore.

The remainder of the putative ON etyma (fifty-nine theories) all show attested forms in OE which are either directly cognate or derivationally related to the same Gmc root. All these would therefore on their own be Type C items of various sorts, or Type A when formal tests apply, as follows:

> ***barne** (1) (C5)
> **bate** (2) (C1)
> **byled** (2) (C1 (C2))
> ***bulk** (3, **blenk*) (C2)
> **costez** (2) (C1)
> **daylyeden** (2) (A1*)
> **draueled** (1a) (C1)
> **fere** (2) (C3)
> **gayne** (2) (A1*)
> **gere** (1) (A1*); (2a) (A1*)
> **glaum** (1) (A1*)[520]
> **heme** (1) (C1)

---

[519] But notice that the supposed ON etymon of **clambere** (1) is prob. ult. related to the Gmc root of OE *clam*, *clæmman* etc.; and that of ***glopnyng** (1b, *gopnyng*) is prob. connected to OE *gēap*, though without a clear derivational relationship.

[520] Cognates are known only in OE and the Scand languages.

lagmon (2a) (C2); (3) (C3)
laucyng (2) (A1*)
lenge (1) (C1)
list (1) (C1)
lyte (2a) (C5); (2b) (A1)
messequyle (1) (C2)
neme (1b) (C2)
quethe (1a) (A1*); (1b) (C1)
rak (1a) (A1*); (2) (A1*)
rasse (2) (C2); (4b) (C2)
rykande (1) (C1)
rimed (1a) (C4)[521]
rout (1) (C3);[522] (2) (A1*)
scholes (1) (C4); (4) (C2)
skayned (1) (A1*); (2, *skayued*) (A1*)
skwez (1) (A1*); (3) (A1*)
slokes (1) (C1)
***sparred** (1) (C3)[523]
spenne 1 (1a) (C1) (= **spenne-fote** (1)); (1b) (C1); (1c) (C1) (= **spenne 2** (1))
spenne-fote (3) (C1 (C2)); (4) (A1*)
stemmed (1) (C1); (2) (C1)
toruayle (2) (C5) (*tor-* only)[524]
twynnen (1) (C2 (C1)); (2) (C1)
***þwarte(-knot)** (1) (A3*); (2, *þwarle-*) (C2)
vnhap (1) (C1); (2) (A1*)
***vntyl** (1) (*-tyl* only) (C5)
waytez (2) (A1*)
wande (2) (C5)
weue (1) (C3)
wylyde (2) (C1)

As for Type D1 above, none of the words grouped under D2 has a readily identifiable Gmc root, and so no items in this section have been marked 'a'. But nineteen word-elements figuring in D2 theories would have been given an 'a' label had they featured in earlier parts of the catalogue, viz.: ***barne** (1), **bate** (2), **byled** (2), **costez** (2), ***dyngez** (1), ***glopnyng** (1a, *gopnyng*), **neme** (1b), **rykande** (1), ***schifted**

---

[521] The main point in favour of ON input is the existence of the reflex. construction in (modern) Dan.

[522] It is debatable whether an OE cognate of ON *hrjóta* in the right sense existed, but this is generally assumed; the main evidence for ON input is in any case semantic.

[523] Assuming that ON *sperra* is related to OE *spear-*, *spær-* in place-names and to OE verbs in *spar-*.

[524] There is no clear evidence for input from the second element of ON *torveldi*, but this would be a C1.

(1), **spenne 1** (1a) (= **spenne-fote** (1)), **spenne 1** (1b), **stemmed** (2), **toruayle** (2) (*tor-*), **twynnen** (1) and (2), ***vntyl** (1) (both *vn-* and *-tyl*), **vphalt** (2), **waytez** (2).

5.2.2.2. Distribution in England

Unlike for items appearing under all the previous sub-types in the Survey, it is not possible to indicate a broader English distribution for words of Type D2 simply by attaching 'b' or 'c' labels to their entry – since, by definition, every D2 item may be identified with two or more different ME words, each with its own characteristic regional attestation. But I take the opportunity in this section to summarize the distribution of the various ME identifications belonging to those theories which involve possible ON input.

Of these theories, three feature English forms which occur mainly or entirely in the N/EM in the toponymic record, viz. **forȝ** (1), **knot** (2b) and **spenne 1** (1c) (= **spenne 2** (1)); all these are similarly restricted in the lexical record.

Moreover, a very large number of D2 interpretations involving possible ON input (fifty-three different theories altogether) give ME identifications which are (more or less) confined to the N/EM in the ME lexicon, and which would have been marked 'c' if they had featured in earlier sections of the Survey (though notice the remarks below about the number of *hapax legomena*). The relevant theories are:

> ***barne** (1)
> **bate** (2)
> ***bulk** (3, **blenk*)
> **byled** (2)
> **clambere** (1)
> **costez** (2)
> **daylyeden** (2)
> ***dyngez** (1)
> **draueled** (1)
> **forȝ** (1)
> **glaum** (1); (2, **glamm*)
> ***glopnyng** (1b, *gopnyng*); (2, **glopnyng*)
> **grwe** (2)
> **lenge** (1)
> **lyte** (1); (2a); (2b)
> **raged** (2)
> **rasse** (2)
> **rykande** (1); (2); (3)
> **rimed** (1)
> **rout** (1); (2)
> **scholes** (3)
> **skayned** (1); (2, *skayued*)
> **skwez** (1)
> **slokes** (1); (2a); (2b)

sparred (1)
spenne 1 (1a); (1b); (1c) = **spenne 2** (1)
spenne-fote (1); (3); (4)
stemmed (1); (2)
toruayle (2)
***þwarte-knot** (1); (2, *þwarle-*)
vnhap (2)
vntyl (1)
waytez (2)
wande (1); (2)
wylyde (2); (3)

Unambiguously N/EM words or word groups which seem to me entirely or almost entirely confined to this region throughout their recorded history are: ***bulk** (3, **blenk*), **forȝ** (1), ***glopnyng** (2), **knot** (2b), **lyte** (1) and (2b), **raged** (2), **rak** (2), **rykande** (2), **rout** (1), **slokes** (1), **spenne 1** (1c) (= **spenne 2** (1)), **stemmed** (2), **vnhap** (2), **wande** (2); though notice that only three of these (***glopnyng** (2), **lyte** (1), **vnhap** (2)) are given by Kaiser (1937) in his list of 'northern' words.[525] A significant proportion of would-be 'c' items belonging to D2 theories (twenty-four out of fifty-three) are, however, limited to these putative *Gaw* occurrences. (*Inter alia*, this is of course indicative of the tenuous nature of many of these proposed theories, which rely on the hypothesizing of a ME word for whose existence there is no independent evidence.) These *hapax legomena* are: **bate** (2), **byled** (2), **clambere** (1), **costez** (2), **glaum** (1), ***glopnyng** (1b, *gopnyng*), **grwe** (2), **lenge** (1), **rimed** (1), **scholes** (3), **skayned** (1) and (2, *skayued*), **skwez** (1), **slokes** (2a) and (2b), **spenne 1** (1a) and (1b), **spenne-fote** (3) and (4), **toruayle** (2), **þwarte-knot** (1) and (2, *þwarle-*), **wylyde** (2) and (3); and perh. also **twynnen** (2) (since the one other possible instance is doubtful).[526] Another word, **rasse** (2), is found elsewhere only in the *Gaw*-manuscript. There are eight other theories which produce words attested only quite rarely, and for which it is difficult to draw conclusions about their ME distribution

---

[525] **Raged** (2) and **rykande** (2) would be found only in *Gaw* in the ME period, and **forȝ** (1) only once elsewhere in ME texts. ***Bulk** (3, **blenk*) is (otherwise) attested only in Scots as a n. in the right sense, but other *blenk-* forms in ME are all N/EM. **Knot** (2b) would be making its only appearance outside toponymic usage in *Gaw*. **Rak** (2) is more widespread regionally in place-names.

[526] Notice that: **bate** (2) would be a *hapax legomenon* in this form, unless *OED*'s seventeenth-century instance is really the same word; **costez** (2) would be unique as a v., though the related ME n. is well attested (mainly N/EM by later ME); **grwe** (2) would occur only here as a n., but the related v. is found elsewhere in ME (mainly N/EM); **skayned** (1) is perh. the same word as Yorkshire dial *skane*, and (2, *skayued*) is perh. related to Shetl *skave* adj.; **spenne 1** (1a) has a related v., which is N/EM only, and **spenne 1** (1b) would be a *hapax legomenon* unless it is to be equated with <spene> in *WA*; ***þwarte-knot** (1) would be unique as a compound, though the adj. *þwert* is of course commonplace in itself, and (2, **þwarle-*) would be found only in *Gaw* in this form but is perh. the same as Lancashire dial *wharl-knot*; and **wylyde** (3) would be unique as a derived form in *-ed*, but the related n. *wile* (**wyles**) is common in ME (mainly N/EM).

beyond that they seem on this evidence mainly to be N/EM: **daylyeden** (2), **draueled** (1), **glaum** (2, **glamm*), **rykande** (1), **rout** (2), **sparred** (1), **spenne-fote** (1), **stemmed** (1).[527] The ME words identified with **barne* (1) and **lyte** (2a) appear to be restricted mainly to N/EM texts by later ME (although **barne* (1) occurs more widely in alliterative verse), but to have a wider attestation earlier in the period; on the other hand, **vntyl* (1) and **wande** (1) have a narrower N/EM distribution early in ME, but are more widespread later. Generally N/EM words throughout the ME period, but not entirely, having some attestations further afield which hint at wider usage, are **dyngez* (1), **rykande** (3), **waytez** (2).

5.2.2.3. Probability of ON input

As with Type D1 above, I have divided D2 items into two loose groups according to my impression of the relative probability with which ON input may be claimed in each case. Nineteen items belong to category 'D2', where (it seems to me) a reasonable argument has been or can be made for ON input; and thirty-three to category 'DD2', for which the plausibility of the case is weaker. Hence the ratio of more to less probable items is almost identical to that for Type D1 above (where it was 18:30).

In what follows I discuss D2 and DD2 items in turn, arranging them into (very rough) sets by the profiles they present in the scholarly tradition, and summarizing in each case the grounds on which that profile has built up.

1. The stronger cases (D2)

(i) The majority of D2 stems are those for which at least some ON input is generally claimed in the scholarly tradition. Because of the nature of Type D2, this usually means *both* that one of the theories featuring the prospect of ON input may be regarded as a convincing explanation of the word in its *Gaw* context(s), *and also* that the etymology of the identification made under this theory may be accounted for at least fairly plausibly by proposing some ON input. Both these requirements are met by all of the following:[528]

*bulk
Theory (2) offers a plausible emendation which fits the sense here well, and very likely shows some ON input. By contrast, retaining the MS

---

[527] **Draueled** (1) is attested only twice in ME, although *OED*'s later citations are all from Douglas. For **glaum** (2, **glamm*) there are hints of wider distribution in modern dial usage. **Sparred** (1) is not necessarily to be equated with later instances given under the same head in *OED*. And all other supposed examples of **stemmed** (1) are open to other possible interpretations.

[528] Notice that some of these items also feature other, less compelling theories which involve the possibility of ON input, too; and which in themselves might therefore be regarded as DD2 options. They are (with these less plausible ON input theories numbered): **bulk* (3, **blenk*), **glopnyng* (1a *gopnyng*; 1b *gopnyng*), **lagmon** (3), **lyte** (2a, 2b), **rasse** (4b), **skwez** (1).

reading (1) produces a ME word which is less apposite in terms of form and sense; and McGillivray's recent alternative (3) is another possibility (and also has possible ON input), but gives a form which is less close to the MS reading (and there is no clearly attested ME *blenk* in the right sense).

*dyngez
ON input is plausible for the majority theory (1), and Vant's alternative (2, *dymnez*) seems much less likely.

gayne
There is little to choose between the two options in terms of the (very similar) sense they make in context; but ON derivation (2) is mildly to be preferred over that from Fr (1), there being no clear instances of the Fr loan in English before the late fifteenth century.

*glopnyng
Theory (2) is that usually now adopted, and the case for some input from ON is plausible (albeit no precise match in the Scand languages is attested showing both the /o/ vowel and the *-n* suffix). Of the alternatives, option (1a, *gopnyng*) (= ME *gapen*) is a poor fit to the *Gaw* spelling, and my new suggestion (1b, *gopnyng*) would produce a word not otherwise known in English.

lagmon
Theory (2), relating the *Gaw* form to MnE *lag*, is usually now accepted; derivation from ON is a reasonable etymological explanation, although there are others available (inc. a native affective formation). Of the other theories, option (1, *bi-laggid*) relies on emendation and (3) on a rather impressionistic interpretation forwarded by Matthews (1975) only.

laucying
Theory (2) is that normally now accepted, and unambiguously derives from ON. Alternative (1, *forlancyng*) produces a plausible form and sense, but gives what would be a unique ME v. *forlancen*.

lyte
The standard consensus favours theory (1), a strong contender for ON input. The other options require strained readings in context, viz. (2a) with a marginal case for some ON input, and (2b) which identifies the word with a different supposed ON loan of which there are now no generally accepted occurrences in English.

rasse

Theory (2) (< ON *ras*) seems to me the best explanation for the *Gaw* word, and a strong case can therefore be made for ON input (the metathesized by-form is distinctively Scand). Theories (1) and (4) are also fairly plausible (inc. a different prospective ON input behind 4b) and far more often cited, but both suffer difficulties of one sort or another.

skwez

Theory (3) (< ON **skiw-*) is that usually now accepted, and fits the form and sense very well. It is clearly preferable to (1) (also perh. with ON input, but there are no other occurrences of such a word in ME), but not necessarily by much to (2), from Fr (though this word is only otherwise known in the MnE dial evidence, and there are no attestations in ME).

spenne 1

Theory (1c) is the generally preferred interpretation (here and in treatments of the place-name evidence), and makes good sense; it can be derived from ON with some justification (though an unattested native cognate is also viable). Theory (1b), deriving from an alternative but related ON source (Sundén), is also plausible enough, but seems to me to fit the *Gaw* context slightly less well; the other options are less apposite (e.g. (2) derives from an obscure English word only clearly attested otherwise from the late eighteenth century).

spenne 2

Theory (1) (= **spenne 1** (1c) above) is again the normal preference; the alternative interpretations (2) (both < Fr) account markedly less well for the *Gaw* form.

twynnen

Theory (1) is that usually followed, and the case for ON input is reasonable (being a good way of explaining *-nn-* and the short vowel). Theory (2) also works fairly well for the *Gaw* context, but the argument for ON input here does not seem to me quite as strong (see **twynne** adj. above).

wande

Consensus has built up over theory (1), for which the case for ON input is good (as with **wandez** (C1) above). Theory (2) also features the prospect of Scand derivation, but it is both much less persuasive as an interpretation of the *Gaw* context and the argument for ON input is relatively weak in the face of the known OE cognates.

weue
Theory (1) is the generally accepted identification, and influence from ME
wayue (< ON) is the best explanation for the sense (though others are
sometimes attempted). Emerson's alternative (2) is less persuasive, inc. as
an explanation of the *Gaw* form.

(ii) There is also a small number of D2 items where two of the available
options both seem reasonably apposite as identifications in the *Gaw* context, and
where a plausible argument for ON input can be mounted for both:

glaum
The standard interpretation is theory (1), which gives a ME word
demonstrably ON in origin on formal grounds,[529] but unique to this
Gaw occurrence. Option (2, **glamm*) is therefore an attractive
alternative, not least because it produces an identical phrase to the
other known occurrence of **glam** (B1) in *Gaw*; and this too is a good
candidate for ON input.

raged
General consensus now favours theory (1), for which the assumption of
some Scand input is reasonable, though not essential (given alternative
(1b), which may be independent of the ON *ragg-* words). But theory (2)
also produces a plausible enough identification, and again there are good
grounds to argue for ON input.

skayned
The majority of editions now favour theory (1) (mainly owing to their
interpretation of **skwez** earlier in the line); but both identifications will
work well enough for this particular item in itself, and both are guaranteed
as ON derivations by phonological criteria.

slokes
Identification (1) is usually now agreed: it makes for reasonable sense in
context, and produces a well-attested ME word family, with a fair case for
ON input. But the neglected theory (2b) also seems to me a very plausible
explanation, if anything fitting the *Gaw* context better still, and Scand
input again looks likely. By contrast, theory (2a), from a different ON
etymon, is more of a stretch.

---

[529] And notice also the near-parallel of the OIcel phrase *glaumr ok gleði* to the collocation in *Gaw*.

spenne-fote

Theory (1b) is normally preferred; it offers a plausible explanation of the sense, and ON derivation is also reasonable. But Sundén's neglected theory (3) (likely from a different ON source, though perh. with cross-influence on its form from the ON etymon of theory (1b)) also works well enough in the *Gaw* context. Of the other alternatives, (2) has good comparanda in WGmc but is less apposite formally, and the outlier (4) is very unconvincing.

Notice further that sixteen out of these twenty-four leading theories with ON input are supported by the circumstantial evidence of regional distribution in the English lexicon (see under 'Distribution in England' above). These theories are ***dyngez** (1), **glaum** (1) and (2, **glamm*), ***glopnyng** (2), **lyte** (1), **raged** (2), **rasse** (2), **skayned** (1) and (2, *skayued*), **slokes** (1) and (2b), **spenne 1** (1c) (= **spenne 2** (1)), **spenne-fote** (1b) and (3), **wande** (1).[530]

Unsurprisingly, disagreement is often to be found in the principal scholarly authorities even over these more plausible D2 items. Amongst the words cited in one or more of their *Gaw* occurrences by both *OED* and *MED*, nine show significant differences of interpretation and/or etymology, viz. **gayne, laucyng, rasse, skayned, skwez, spenne 1, spenne 2, twynnen, weue**.[531] *MED* is more likely here to offer an ON etymon; it more strongly prefers ON input in four cases, compared to just one where *OED* does so. TGD and GDS differ in more or less substantial ways over four D2 items, **raged, rasse, slokes, spenne 2**, and **weue**.[532]

---

[530] **Spenne 1** (1c) (= **spenne 2** (1)) is also mainly N/EM in the toponymic record.

[531] **Gayne**: *OED* derives from ON (2); *MED* treats both etymological origins under the same head, but its gloss implies derivation from Fr (1). **Laucyng**: *OED* derives from Fr (1, *forlancyng*); *MED* originally made the same identification, but latterly changed to theory (2), *laucyng*) from ON. **Rasse**: the original *OED* offers no theory, and *OED3* derives from Fr (1b); *MED* derives from a (perh. different) Fr source (1a). **Skayned**: the original *OED* follows early editors in reading (2) (though later revised this to theory (1)), both from ON; *MED* has theory (1), from ON. **Skwez**: *OED* agrees with early editions regarding (1), with possible ON input; *MED* takes (3), from a different (and clear) ON source. **Spenne 1**: *OED* says 'meaning obscure', and offers no etymology; *MED* opts for theory (1c), from ON. **Spenne 2**: *OED* has (2a), = PDE *spinney* from Fr; *MED* has (1), from ON. **Twynnen**: *OED* offers (1), from OE only; *MED* also has (1), but includes a comparison to ON. **Weue**: *OED* derives from a native cognate of ON *veifa* (1); *MED* also has (1), which it derives from OE *wǣfan* or *wefan*. Notice also the following: ***bulk** (*OED* has no entry citing the *Gaw* word; *MED* opts for (1, *bluk*), comparing MDu and OFr); ***dyngez** (neither dictionary cites the *Gaw* occurrence, but under their entries for ME *dingen* (1) *OED* tentatively derives from ON but *MED* from OE **dingan*); ***glopnyng** (*OED* has no citation of the *Gaw* word; *MED* derives from ON (2)); **lagmon** (*OED* does not treat the *Gaw* form; *MED* tentatively derives from ON (2a)); **lyte** (*OED* does not cite the *Gaw* instances; *MED* treats one under theory (1); both dictionaries derive the ME word under theory (1) from ON; whereas for theory (2a), *OED* suggests ON input and *MED* derives from OE only). Neither dictionary treats **glaum** at all.

[532] **Raged**: TG(D) cite both ON *raggaðr* and OE *raggig* (1a); GDS refers to MnE dial *rag* 'hoarfrost' (2). **Rasse**: TG(D) prefer theory (1) with Fr derivation; GDS offers no etymology. **Slokes**: TG(D) derive from ON under (1); GDS offers two different sets of ON comparanda (2). **Spenne 2**: TGD gives (1), from ON; GDS prefers (2a), = PDE *spinney* from Fr (as TG). **Weue**: TG(D) cite theory (1), from OE plus some ON input; GDS follows *OED* in deriving from the OE cognate of ON *veifa* (1). Notice also the more minor differences with: ***bulk** (TG agrees with GDS for (1, *bluk*), although GDS also notices (2) in its note, and suggests a possible blend of the two words; TGD then emends to **bulk* (2)); **glaum** (both editions derive from the same ON word, but TG(D) follow (1a, n.) and GDS (1b, pres. ptcp.)).

TGD argues more strongly for ON input in three of these instances, GDS in none. There are also five items for which TGD significantly revises the interpretation and etymology in TG, hence *bulk, laucyng, spenne 1, spenne 2, spenne-fote.[533] In all five cases, Davis introduces an ON derivation which had not been there in TG. There is also one change from the original printing of TG in its 1930 revision, viz. lagmon.[534] In his great study, Bj. treats seventeen of the ME words used as identifications in D2 theories and which perh. show ON input (whether or not he lists *Gaw* as one of the texts in which they occur), i.e. *bulk (2), *dyngez (1), gayne (1), glaum (1) and (2, *glamm), *glopnyng (1a) and (2), lagmon (3), laucyng (2), lyte (2b), raged (1a), rasse (4b), skwez (1) and (3), slokes (1), wande (1) and (2). Lastly, a number of interpretations and consequent etymologies may be noticed as outliers when seen against the main picture presented by the scholarly tradition. In all cases, the following produce an alternative theory with possible ON input, as against the more common identification with a different putative Scand loan; *inter alia*, they suggest the sheer range of possible competing suggestions lurking in (especially the older) scholarship:

> *bulk (3, *blenk) (McGillivray)
> glaum (2, *glamm) (McGillivray and PS)
> *glopnyng (1a, gopnyng) (Vant)
> lagmon (3) (Matthews)
> lyte (2a) (Emerson); (2b) (Emerson)
> rasse (2) (Sundén, Hug)
> rykande (1) (Emerson, Vant); (2) (Wright); (3, *raykande) (Morris, Knott)
> skwez (1) (*OED*, Bj.)
> slokes (2) (GDS)
> spenne 1 (1a) (Kullnick, Strat.-Brad., Emerson); (1b) (Sundén)
> spenne-fote (3) (Sundén); (4) (Emerson)
> wande (2) (Emerson)

2. The weaker cases (DD2)

As was true of D1 above, however, for the majority of Type D2 items the case for ON input is less plausible.

---

[533] *Bulk: TG retains the MS reading (1, *bluk*) and derives from Fr; TGD has (2, *bluk*), from ON. Laucyng: TG has theory (1, *forlancyng*), from Fr; TGD changes this to (2, *laucyng*), from ON. Spenne 1: TG has a native origin under (2); TGD prefers (1c), from ON. Spenne 2: TG identifies with PDE *spinney* from Fr (2a); TGD has (1), from ON. Spenne-fote: TG gives theory (2), < OE *spinnan*; TGD prefers (1b), from ON. See also skwez, where TG derives from ON *ský* and TGD amends this to the closer etymon ON *skiw-.

[534] The original TG takes theory (1) and emends to *<bilagged men>; the 1930 reprint (followed by TGD) prefers theory (2a), from ON.

(i) In several instances, theories which do not feature purported ON input will account better for key aspects of the form, sense and/or usage of the word in its *Gaw* context(s), and there is usually consensus over these theories in the commentators. Quite often, the potential ON-derived option (numbered in what follows) is in itself problematic, and/or the case for Scand input is not compelling:

*barne (1)
Retaining the MS reading gives a perfectly plausible (and unproblematically native) word *burne*, and almost all editors have been content with this (2). Even if one emends to **barne* (1), the case for 'reinforcement' from ON is circumstantial and the word's history can be explained well enough without it.

bate (2)
There is no very good evidence for a word elsewhere in English with the form and sense required for theory (2), and accordingly derivation from Fr (1) is normally preferred.

daylyeden (2)
Neither the form (in particular the medial syllable) nor the meaning of the *Gaw* word match well the attested ME *deilen* < ON *deila* (2), and identification with the Fr loan treated under (1) has found more favour.

grwe (2)
It is doubtful that a VAN reflex existed of the Scand words cited under theory (2), and these are ordinarily now explained as later loans from LG. Option (1) (derived from Fr) is far more sensible.

lenge (1)
There is no other evidence for a ME *leng(e)* adv. (other than as the native comp.) (1), and the generally preferred theory (3, reading **longe*) will account for the *Gaw* form more economically.

*schifted (1)
ON input is of dubious help in accounting for the emended form **schifted* (1), which must at least show sound substitution of initial /sk/ > /ʃ/, and is more likely native. Theory (2, reading *schafted* as in the MS) is, in any event, rightly preferred.

*vntyl (1)
To produce an ON derivation here requires drastic emendation; but since Emerson (1922a) and TG's explanation of the MS reading (2, *vntyʒtel*), the latter has universally been accepted.

waytez (2)
The meaning required by the *Gaw* context is not a good fit for the other attested senses of ME *waiten* < ON *veita* (2), and option (1) (from Fr) is much more apposite.

(ii) In a couple of cases, the theory with prospective Scand input seems to me more plausible than it has often been given credit for; but it is still no stronger than is the more often cited alternative explanation:

fere (2)
Either reading makes sense in context, but (1) is much more often assumed; and under (2), ON input is semantic at best.

rykande (1)
Theory (1) makes for a decent defence of the MS reading, and it is certainly more plausible than the alternative ON input options, viz. (2) which is not very close in sense, and (3) which requires emendation to **raykande*. But (1) would give a rare ME word, and there has been little enthusiasm for this theory next to the emendation given under (4, **rynkande*), now generally accepted.

(iii) In a few instances, there is no general consensus in the scholarship as to which theory is more or most compelling; but the grounds to prefer the option(s) featuring ON input are not especially strong, and the alternatives are at least as well supported:

byled (2)
Theory (2) (< ON *bylja*) would fit the *Gaw* form and sense well enough (and certainly better than does option (3), < OE *bȳl*). But it would be the only known occurrence of such an ON loan in English, next to the much commoner Fr derivation preferred under theory (1) (even if the precise by-form required here is otherwise unknown in ME).

costez (2), (3, **castez*)
The main possible ON derivation (2) demands a strained interpretation of the sense in context. Loan from Fr (1) is the majority view, and requires no emendation of the MS form such as is required by the other chief alternative (3, **castez*).

forʒ (1)
The interpretation with likely ON input (1) is problematic formally in terms of *Gaw*-manuscript spelling, and identification (2, < OE) is generally now preferred.

list (1)
The reading produced by theory (1) used to be preferred (and in that case
ON input is plausible but not essential). But a recent consensus seems to
be emerging for option (2) (including by both PS and McGillivray),
where the line can be read without requiring emendation.

neme (1b)
Theory (2) (< OE) is that most often encountered now. Of the alternatives,
(1b) in particular still has some followers; but the case for ON input under
this interpretation is tenuous.

rimed (1a), (1b)
Theory (2) (< OE) is usually preferred, and it will explain form and sense
well enough. Interpretation (1) is also still encountered, and the (1a) ON
input option (etymologically identical to (2), in fact) is plausible enough;
but early evidence for the reflex. usage in ON is lacking.

(iv) In one case, general agreement attends the theory which features ON input; but in fact the other possible explanation is more plausible
than is ordinarily assumed, and seems to me to merit equally strong
consideration:

clambere (1)
The usual assumption of ON input under theory (1) evaporates if we
instead identify these *Gaw* occurrences with forms of PDE *clamber* (2).

(v) But in many other instances, it is the etymological arguments which
produce the primary stumbling block – i.e. a theory featuring possible ON input
is the best identification of the *Gaw* item, but Scand derivation does not seem
very plausible or necessary to explain the word's etymology:

draueled (1)
Theory (1) is dominant in the scholarship (alternative (2) being a less
good identification of the likely form of the *Gaw* word). But a native
by-form of the related OE *dreflian* looks quite plausible as the source
(and perh. for the whole family of words discussed under (1)), in
which case the extent of ON input is unclear, even if some remains
possible.

gere (2a)
Both main options perh. involve ON input, but (2) (the more often cited)
has a difficult etymology, and ON derivation is only one potential
explanation.

heme (1)
Theory (2) makes less good sense of the *Gaw* form, and is much less often supported by commentators. But native origin is more plausible phonologically than derivation from the ON near-cognate for theory (1).

knot (2)
Theory (2) is a reasonable explanation, and in that case some ON input is possible, although the word in this sense *can* be explained adequately enough without it. By contrast, alternative (1) will only work for one of the two *Gaw* instances, and the other then requires relatively heavy-handed emendation (to another ON derivation; 1b, **kerre*).

messequyle (1)
Interpretation (1) is generally agreed (though the rarer (2) is in fact hard to rule out, too); but the case for ON input (as for **messe** (C2) above) is not compelling.

quethe (1)
Theory (1) has been the standard reading, but in that case the argument for ON input is not particularly strong (a formation on the stem of the related ME v. will account for *quethe* well enough). McGillivray's new alternative (2, reading *queche*) produces a ME n. which would otherwise be unattested.

rak (1)
Option (1) is the normal identification of this form, but in that case it can be explained plausibly as a reflex of OE *racu*. Theory (2) is less apposite in context (and ON input is one of several options in its difficult etymology).

scholes (1)
Theory (1) is the explanation now most often encountered, but it can be explained adequately as of native descent without recourse to the influence of the ON compound. All other theories are variously problematic, including the ON-derived alternative (4), where the form is not ideal (necessitating sound substitution in English) and the sense development would be unexplained.

*sparred (1)
Reading (1) is the usual explanation of the MS form (the older idea (2) now essentially having been dispensed with); but this can be accounted for well enough with reference to native words (inc. my new suggestion of identity with the *spar* words) and without bringing in the putative ON etymon (though this is near in sense).

stemmed (2)
Theory (2) is usually accepted, and an ON etymon generally cited for it; but derivation from a native cognate is plausible (and may lie behind the late Nhb *forestemman*). Alternative (1), also perh. from ON, is less persuasive semantically and there are no other secure attestations of such a v. in ME.

toruayle (2)
Reading (2) is always now assumed, in which case ON input is possible, but not essential. But *toruayle* would be a *hapax legomenon*, and so it is hard to rule out the idea that this is simply a ghost word, and that we really only have another instance of ME *trauayle* here (1).

*þwarte-knot (2)
Theory (2) retaining the MS reading *þwarle-* is now almost always accepted, but this element is etymologically very obscure; a connection with PDE *whirl*, perhaps itself with ON input (see **whyrlande** (C2)), is only one possibility. The alternative (1, emendation to **þwarte-*, certainly from ON) has not really convinced anyone (even GDS, which proposes it), and in itself the vocalism here does not match that expected for this form in *Gaw* spelling.

vphalt (2)
Option (2) is that ordinarily now followed (and makes the best sense of the morphology of the v.); but the case for ON input in **hale** (v.) (see B2) is thin, and the ON etymon in question is usually now derived from LG.

wylyde (3)
Theory (3) is generally now the favourite (and makes for the best explanation of the *Gaw* form); but this is to connect it with **wyles** (D1), where the argument for ON input is difficult (and OE and perhaps Fr origins are better). The other options explain the form less well, and (2) would give a loan from ON which is otherwise unknown in ME.

(vi) There is one further item where both of the two possible interpretations seem fairly plausible, and both feature an argument for ON input, but in only one of these is the case for a Scand etymon strong:

vnhap (1), (2)

Both competing readings of the line have attracted followers, and it is difficult in practice to choose between them. But while (1) presents good grounds for ON input (= **vnhap** (n.) (C1)), the other (2) identifies the second element with a word of obscure etymology (= **happe** (v.) (D1)), for which an ON ingredient is only a remote prospect.

Disagreement between the principal scholarly authorities is again frequent for DD2 words. *OED* differs from *MED* in marked ways for eight items, viz. **knot, rak, rout, stemmed, *þwarte-knot, *vntyl, vphalt, wylyde.**[535] *MED* argues for more ON input on three occasions, *OED* on just one. TGD and GDS diverge when it comes to the interpretation of some eighteen items: **bate, costez, fere, forȝ, heme, knot, messequyle, neme, quethe, rimed, scholes, *sparred,**

---

[535] **Knot**: *OED* apparently puts both instances under its entry for theory (1), from OE; *MED* separates them, taking *Gaw* 1431 as from OE in the 'knot' sense, and 1434 as the toponym, with partial ON input. **Rak**: the original *OED* derives from ON (1a) (*OED3* considers both options 1a and 1b); *MED* derives from OE (1b) only. **Rout**: the original *OED* and *MED* both favour theory (1) (though *OED3* now also notices (2) as an alternative), but only *MED* indicates the possibility of ON input. **Stemmed**: *OED* follows (1), < ON *stemna*; *MED* takes (2), < ON *stemma*. ***þwarte-knot**: *OED* gives reading (2, *þwarle-*), with no attempt at an etymology; *MED* compares Lancashire dial *wharl-knot* (2). ***Vntyl**: *OED* suggests emendation to ***vnstyȝtel*; *MED* follows (2, *vntyȝtel*), from OE. **Vphalt**: *OED* has (1), from OE; *MED* has (2), with the possibility of ON input. **Wylyde**: *OED* derives from OE under theory (1); *MED* gives all three possibilities (though glosses according to (3)). Notice also: **bate** (*OED* has the *Gaw* form in its entry for the Fr loan (1), but is unsure about a possible connection with *bait*; *MED* is similarly uncertain, but treats the *Gaw* word in an entry of its own); **byled** (*OED* does not cite the *Gaw* form under any head; *MED* derives from OE (3) or Fr (1)); **fere** (*OED* does not cite the *Gaw* instance; *MED* identifies it with the Fr loan (1)); **forȝ** (*OED* does not cite this occurrence, though it gives a spelling <forȝ> in its form list under *furrow* (2); *MED* derives from ON (1)); **heme** (*OED* is not clear about the etymology beyond a connection with OE *hām*; *MED* derives from OE *gehǣme* (1)); **neme** (*OED* does not treat the *Gaw* word; *MED* has it under (1b), though does not claim any ON influence); **rykande** (the original *OED* does not cite the *Gaw* instance, but it is implicit in the list of forms in *OED3* for theory (4, ***rynkande*); *MED* has the same explanation); **scholes** (*OED* does not deal with this word; *MED* has it under (1), without reference to the ON compound); ***sparred** (neither dictionary treats the *Gaw* form; but for ME *sparren* (as theory 1) *OED* calls the etymology simply 'obscure' (contrast *ODEE*'s derivation from OE *sperran, spyrran*), while *MED* derives from Fr and OE); **toruayle** (not in *OED*; *MED* derives from ON *torveldi* and OFr *travail* (2)); **waytez** (*OED* does not cite the *Gaw* word; *MED* derives from Fr (1)). Neither dictionary deals with the *Gaw* instances of ***barne, gere, lenge, list** or **vnhap**.

twynnen, ***þwarte-knot***, **vnhap**, **vphalt**, **waytez**, **wylyde**.[536] Interestingly, for DD2 words GDS is significantly more likely to favour ON input: there are twelve cases where this edition argues more strongly for Scand derivation than does TGD, next to just two of the other way around. Notice that TGD and GDS rarely agree in contradistinction to both *OED* and *MED*, but there is the occasional instance, e.g. **byled**, **list**.[537] The TGD revision changes the TG interpretation/etymology in a major way in four instances, viz. **forȝ**, **neme**, **rout**, **scholes**.[538] TGD therefore removes two claims for ON input from the TG glossary (though adds a 'cp.' to an ON form under **scholes**). The original version of TG differs from the revised 1930 reprint in their treatment of *sparred.[539] In his survey, Bj. deals with eighteen of the ME words (or their immediate ME sources) perh. derived from ON and which appear as identifications under D2 theories (whether or not he lists *Gaw* as one of the occurrences): ***barne*** (1), **bate** (2), **costez** (2), **daylyeden** (2), **fere** (2), **gere** (1) and (2a), **grwe** (2), **knot** (1b, *kerre*), **quethe** (1), **rykande** (3, *raykande*), **rout** (2), *schifted (1), **scholes** (4), ***þwarte-knot*** (1), **vnhap** (1), *vntyl (1), **weue** (1). Items which are sometimes explained as Scand loans early in the scholarly tradition, but which have since generally been given a native or some other source are: **byled**, **daylyeden**, **grwe**, **neme**, **rykande**, *schifted. As with category D2 above, a

---

[536] **Bate**: TG(D) derive from Fr (1); GDS from OE or ON (2). **Costez**: TG(D) take theory (1), from Fr; GDS has (3, *castez*), from ON. **Fere**: TG(D) derive from Fr (1); GDS from ON (2). **Forȝ**: TGD has option (2), from OE; GDS reads (1), from ON (as TG). **Heme**: both follow identification (1), but TG(D) derive from OE and GDS at least partly from ON. **Knot**: TG(D) read both instances under (2), including ON input; GDS takes the first from OE (1a), and emends the second (1b, *kerre*) and derives from ON. **Messequyle**: Both follow theory (1), but TG(D) regard **messe** as native whereas GDS accepts some ON input. **Neme**: TGD derives from OE *nemnan* (2); GDS from OE *niman* (1b), but does not mention ON input. **Quethe**: both read (1), but TG(D) regard it as native, and GDS derives from ON *kviðr*. **Rimed**: TG(D) follow theory (2), from OE; GDS offers (1a) and (1b), from ON. **Scholes**: TGD follows (1), with a comparison to ON; GDS opts for (5), of obscure origin. ***Sparred**: TG(D) take theory (1) (though give no etymology); GDS (and the first printing of TG) read (2, *spede), from OE. **Twynnen**: TG(D) derive from OE *twīn* (1); GDS from OE *twinn* (2). ***þwarte-knot**: TG(D) prefer theory (2, *þwarle*-), which they relate to OE *þweorh*; GDS cites (2) as perh. identified with *OED*'s *thwerl* v., but also entertains (1, *þwarte*-) from ON. **Vnhap**: TG(D) give (2), = **happe** (v.) (which they explain as native); GDS has (1), from ON. **Vphalt**: TG(D) offer theory (2), with possible ON input; GDS has (1), from OE. **Waytez**: TG(D) follow identification (1), from Fr; GDS has (2), from ON. **Wylyde**: TG(D) have theory (3), = **wyles** (which they derive from OE and/or Fr); GDS has option (2), from ON. Notice also **gere**, which both editions derive from the same ON source, but TG(D) gloss as under interpretation (2) and GDS as under (1).

[537] For **byled**, both editions derive from Fr (theory 1); *MED* entertains this as an option, but also regards OE *bȳl* as a possible input. For **list**, TGD and GDS both derive from ON (1); for the ME word identified with this theory, the dictionaries derive from the related OE v., with a 'cp.' only to ON.

[538] **Forȝ**: TG has reading (1), from ON; TGD amends this to (2), from OE. **Neme**: TG has theory (1a), < OE *niman*; TGD prefers (2), < OE *nemnan*. **Rout**: TG gives option (2), from ON; TGD has (1), which it derives from OE. **Scholes**: TG takes (2), from Fr; TGD follows (1), with a 'cp.' to ON. Notice also **wylyde**, where TG glosses 'guileful' (3a) and TGD 'skilful' (3b).

[539] The first printing reads *<sped [him]> (2), but this is changed in 1930 (retained in TGD) to theory (1, *sparred).

significant number of theories claiming ON input into DD2 words are met only as isolated alternatives in the occasional commentator, and have not made it into the main stream of accounts:[540]

byled (2) (Knigge)
costez (2) (Wright)
daylyeden (2) (Emerson, McGee)
grwe (2) (Emerson)
knot (1b, *kerre*) (GDS, Burrow)
lenge (1) (Emerson)
neme (1b) (Knigge)
quethe (1a) (Knigge, GDS); (1b) (Emerson)
rak (2) (Vant)
rykande (1) (Emerson, Vant); (2) (Wright); (3, *raykande*) (Morris, Knott)
rout (2) (TG)
***schifted** (1) (M(G))
scholes (4) (Brett)
***sparred** (1) (McGee)
stemmed (1) (*OED*)
***þwarte(-knot)** (1) (GDS)
***vntyl** (1) (Morris)
waytez (2) (GDS, Moorman)
wylyde (2) (GDS)

Knigge and Emerson are, as ever, well represented in this list; but so too (more surprisingly, perhaps) is GDS.

---

[540] In the case of **costez, knot, rak, rout, scholes, stemmed** and **wylyde,** these identifications produce different ON etyma for words which have seen better supported claims for input from another ON source.

6

CONCLUDING REMARKS

Writing in the Preface to his great *Etymological Dictionary* (1882: xi), Skeat is disarmingly frank about the pragmatic approach to time management which must attend the investigation of any large body of lexical material. 'In very difficult cases,' he admits, 'my usual rule has been not to spend more than three hours over one word. During that time, I made the best I could of it, and then let it go'. There are of course far fewer items treated in the Survey in this book than Skeat had to reckon with, and I have been able to give much more time to each of them than he was; in many cases, I must have spent longer pursuing and considering their etymologies than anyone before me. But this is not to say that I could not have taken longer still, if time and space had permitted. In this and other important respects, the study presented in this book remains a preliminary, and there will inevitably be inadequacies about it. Despite my best efforts to catch as many claims as possible for ON input into words occurring in *Gaw*, it is not impossible that I have missed some, simply because scholarship on the poem is so extensive. Readers interested in the histories of particular words amongst those dealt with here will doubtless wish that I had been able to go a little further in examining them, perhaps in pursuing an ulterior etymology, or in tracing the attestation of cognates in the Gmc languages, or in exploring the details of occurrences in other ME texts. Needless to say, much work has gone into the etymological discussions in the Survey, not least in reconstructing the thinking behind the attributions in those authorities where the arguments are only implicit; and I have both made many refinements to existing accounts and introduced new theories of my own. But, like Skeat, I eventually had to stop and let my words loose again. There is ultimately only so much one can do with each item in a corpus of this size, and I have absolutely no doubt that the etymologies of many of them, especially those belonging to the complex and difficult Type D, may fruitfully be reopened and approached from still other directions. In reflecting upon the task undertaken in this book, I find that I can put it no better than Björkman did in 1900: 'To solve the innumerable problems involved in these investigations would be the work of a lifetime; but I trust that my attempts in this direction will prove of assistance to those who wish to pursue the subject' (Bj. v).

This book has presented and analysed the 496 different lexical items in *Gaw*, grouped into 399 stems, for which some ON input has been claimed with at least a degree of plausibility somewhere in the scholarship. On the basis of a detailed consideration of the etymological evidence for Scand derivation (discussed at length in the Introductory Remarks above), I have arranged the items in the Survey into four principal categories, Types A to D (and further sub-types), for each of which the fundamental nature of the argument is different. In the Introductory Essay for each Type above, I have commented upon the key characteristics of the items belonging to these categories, including the nature of the etymological argumentation, and the supporting evidence of distribution in the Gmc languages and in English dialect contexts. I have also assessed the relative strength of the claims for ON input found in each group, keeping track of instances where the principal scholarly authorities have disagreed over the origin they have attributed. In the brief closing remarks which follow, I shall draw together some of these findings, collate a few of the figures I find most interesting, and make some concluding observations. I shall then consider some of the various possible avenues for further exploration of the *Gaw* data, and of other similar sets of words which will be established by future research, beginning with 'The *Gersum* Project'.

6.1. SOME IMPRESSIONS

It seems helpful to begin by presenting some figures pertaining to the main categories defined in this book. For the four structural Types, Tables 1 to 4 below give the total number of stems recorded by sub-type (A1, A2 etc.), and the numbers of these marked with one of the circumstantial flags 'a', 'b' and 'c' (in one or more sub-entries).[541] Types B, C and D are also broken down by probability marker (B, BB, BBB etc.). Totals (in italics) are given beneath each sub-type, and for the whole Type at the foot of each table.[542] Notice that the figures in these tables represent, as usual, stems rather than individual lexical items: for the reasons set out in the Introductory Remarks (at pp. 65–6) above, it is generally most helpful when summarizing etymological findings to refer to stems, treating together items for which the etymological case is essentially identical (and which are or may be recent sub-derivations on the same base).

Table 1. Summary figures for Type A

Sub-type	Total stems	*	a	b	c
A1	62	40	5	12	50
A2	5	4	0	0	5
A3	2	2	0	1	1
Total A	*69*	*46*	*5*	*13*	*56*

[541] For the applicability and precise significance of these labels in the case of each Type (and also the '*' for Type A), see the various Introductory Essays (under 'Germanic distribution' and 'Distribution in England') above. Notice that I have omitted the 'd' flag from these tables, since it applies in the *Gaw* corpus to only one item, viz. **lawe** (C3).
[542] Dashes indicate that the feature in question is not applicable to that category. See further the Introductory Essay to each Type above.

Table 2. Summary figures for Type B

Sub-type	Total stems	a	b	c
B1	12	–	0	9
BB1	7	–	1	5
BBB1	2	–	0	1
Total B1	*21*	*–*	*1*	*15*
B2	10	6	1	4
BB2	10	7	1	7
BBB2	8	7	0	2
Total B2	*28*	*20*	*2*	*13*
Total B	*49*	*20*	*3*	*28*

Table 3. Summary figures for Type C

Sub-type	Total stems	a	b	c
C1	24	11	3	12
CC1	19	9	1	12
CCC1	24	14	0	8
Total C1	*67*	*34*	*4*	*32*
C2	8	1	0	4
CC2	21	4	2	11
CCC2	16	5	1	5
Total C2	*45*	*10*	*3*	*20*
C3	7	1	0	4
CC3	18	8	1	7
CCC3	15	3	4	5
Total C3	*40*	*12*	*5*	*16*
C4	2	1	0	0
CC4	3	1	0	1
CCC4	7	3	0	3
Total C4	*12*	*5*	*0*	*4*
C5	2	1	1	1
CC5	5	2	3	2
CCC5	10	6	0	3
Total C5	*17*	*9*	*4*	*6*
Total C	*181*	*70*	*16*	*78*

There are 100 different lexical items in Type A, 62 in Type B, 219 in Type C and 115 in Type D.

Of the 399 stems in the Survey, sixty-nine (17.3%) belong to Type A, forty-nine (12.3%) to Type B, 181 (45.4%) to Type C and 100 (25.1%) to Type D.[543]

[543] All percentages here and below are given to one decimal place.

Table 4. Summary figures for Type D

Sub-type	Total stems	a	b	c
D1	18	–	1	15
DD1	30	–	2	24
Total D1	48	–	3	39
D2	19	–	–	–
DD2	33	–	–	–
Total D2	52	–	–	–
Total D	100	–	3	39

It is immediately striking, then, what a relatively small proportion of the possible Norse-derived stems in *Gaw* belongs to the most secure category, Type A, for which there is systematic, formal evidence of the most reliable sort for Scand input. Another small group, perhaps surprisingly so, is Type B, where the case is based on the fact that the Gmc root in question is not known in early OE. By some distance the most populous category, in which nearly half of all the stems with suggested ON input are to be found, is Type C; for all these stems, the Gmc root is already represented in early OE (or there is an unambiguous form-source in a third language), and hence the case for some Norse derivation or influence rests on the more or less questionable grounds of some feature of form, sense or usage supposed to be better paralleled in the Scand languages. Finally, a quarter of the claims belong to the inherently still less secure Type D, for which no generally accepted form-source is available. Even in themselves, these bare numbers suggest that many of the stems in the Survey have been derived from ON on the basis of arguments which are, at the very least, open to doubt. And this impression is reinforced if we divide up the stems under each Type according to the loose 'probability markers' I have attached to them. Altogether, some 120 stems (30.1%) belong to the BB, CC or D level, i.e. where the case for ON input is reasonable, but where alternative explanations seem to me about equally plausible (and hence where we often find disagreement in the scholarship). And a still higher 145 stems (36.3%) have been classed under the least plausible category (BBB, CCC, DD), where the evidence for Scand involvement is relatively weak, and an item's history can be accounted for more credibly by other means (and where the weight especially of recent scholarly argument is against ON derivation). On the other hand, if we take Type A as a whole, plus items labelled with a single B and C, to represent the group where the case for ON input is very plausible, and generally agreed, this leaves us with a 'solid' set of relatively uncontroversial stems of only 134 (33.6%). In the course of the Introductory Essays above, we have kept an eye on the relative proportions of stems of each Type and sub-type which belong to these three probability levels (or two levels, in the case of Type D). But it is worth repeating that the ratio increasingly favours the less and least plausible levels as one progresses through the categories of structural evidence from Types B to D; and therefore that, prototypically at least (and as observed in the Introductory Remarks), the quality of the case for Scand input tends to decline from Type to Type in the order in which these are presented in this book. Hence we move from a general preponderance of the most persuasive level for Type B, where the ratio for B:BB:BBB stems is 22:17:10;[544] to a steady decline in the course of the five C sub-types (C1 24:19:24; C2 8:21:16; C3 7:18:15; C4 2:3:7; C5 2:5:10); to a point for Type D where the least plausible cases even further outnumber the others (D1:DD1 = 18:30; D2:DD2 = 19:33).

Another very telling set of figures generated by the discussions of each Type in the Essays above, and which reinforces the impression that the etymological arguments for ON input are so often open to debate, is the tally for the differences of opinion between the chief scholarly authorities. The most interesting discrepancies come when one compares the verdicts of the two great historical dictionaries, *OED* and *MED*, and similarly those of the two major editions containing glossaries with consistent etymological labels, TGD and GDS. *OED* and *MED* disagree substantially in their explanations of 108 stems, i.e. 27.1 per cent of the stems in the Survey. Notice that the proportion of stems in the various structural categories showing this disagreement steadily increases from Types A to C: the dictionaries differ over no stems in Type A, then over eleven out of forty-eight stems in Type B as a whole (22.9%), then 16/67 stems for C1 (23.9%), 14/45 for C2 (31.1%), 13/40 for C3 (32.5%), 5/12 for C4 (41.7%) and 10/17 for C5 (58.8%). Divergence is also relatively high for Types D1, at twenty-two out of forty-eight stems (45.8%), and D2, at seventeen out of fifty-two (32.7%), both of which show a greater rate of disagreement than all categories bar C4 and C5 (where the proportions are no doubt skewed by the small absolute numbers involved). These figures therefore cement the sense that we have already obtained of a decline in the quality of the case for ON input from Types A to D, with an increasing likelihood that the different authorities will interpret the etymological evidence in different ways. *MED* is marginally more likely overall to favour ON input; it does so in fifty-four instances, next to the forty-two for which *OED* argues more strongly for Scand derivation. But these figures conceal much more uneven relative preferences in some category types: *MED* is especially keen on ON input for Types C2 (the ratio of Scand etyma preferred in *MED* next to *OED* being 10:3) and D2 (7:2), and somewhat more than *OED* for Types C1 (10:6) and D1 (12:7); whereas only for Type C3 are the dictionaries approximately equal (7:6), and *OED* is actually somewhat more likely to prefer ON input when it comes to Types B (*MED:OED* = 3:8), C4 (1:4) and C5 (4:6).

TGD and GDS differ less frequently overall than do the dictionaries, showing significant disagreement over eighty-three stems, i.e. 20.8 per cent of the total. Again, there is no discrepancy at all in their verdicts for Type A items; the

---

[544] Albeit that the cases under B1 are on the whole stronger than those under B2; compare the B1 ratio of 12:7:2 with that for B2 of 10:10:8.

editions then disagree markedly less than do *OED* and *MED* for Types B (5 out of 48 stems, 10.4%), C1 (9/67, 13.4%), C2 (10/45, 22.2%), C4 (1/12, 8.3%) and C5 (3/17, 17.6%), and slightly less for D1 (18/48, 37.5%). Interestingly, however, TGD and GDS come to different conclusions somewhat more often than do the dictionaries for Type C3 (15/40, 37.5%), and especially for Type D2 (22/52, 42.3%), where there is a noticeable spike in divergence. As with *OED* versus *MED*, there is a general increase in the proportion of disagreements as we move down the structural categories from Types A to C3, followed in this case by a dip for C4 and C5, and then the figure increases again for both D1 and D2. The relative preference for ON input is virtually identical overall in the two editions, which cite it more strongly in the ratio of 38:35 in TGD next to GDS. But when we look at the individual categories distinguished in the Essays above, this approximate parity is evident only for Types B (2:3), C4 (0:1), C5 (2:1) and DD1 (5:4). Otherwise, TGD notably prefers explanations favouring Scand input for Types C1 (7:2), C3 (11:4), 'D1' (i.e. the more plausible, single 'D' label only) (4:1) and 'D2' (again, the single 'D' label only) (3:0); whereas GDS favours an ON etymon in the case of C2 (2:7) and in particular 'DD2' (2:12). Amongst the Type D stems, then, TGD is more likely to cite ON input only when the argument seems on balance (and, in the broader scholarly context, has generally seemed) to be persuasive; but, interestingly, GDS appears to be much quicker to try its hand at an ON derivation for the more difficult D2 items, even though the case is rather less compelling. In this connexion, it is also worth noticing that the differences between the original TG edition and Davis's revision (TGD) are not inconsiderable, affecting twenty-two stems in total, the majority (sixteen) of these belonging to Type D.[545]

Finally, we have also been keeping track of the stems not treated at all in the pioneering study of Scand borrowings in Bj. Once again, and this time particularly markedly, the proportion of stems concerned in each Type and sub-type increases very much in line with the declining quality of the evidence for ON input. So there are no meaningful omissions for Type A; Bj. deals with all bar ten of the forty-nine Type B stems (20.4%); but he does not include 26/67 (38.8%) for Type C1, 19/45 (42.2%) for C2, 26/40 (65.0%) for C3, 8/12 (66.7%) for C4 and 13/17 (76.5%) for C5; and these figures culminate in a massive rate of 39/48 (81.3%) omissions for Type D1.[546] In other words, this is an especially clear index of the relative attention given in the foundational scholarship on ON

[545] Overall honours are about even, with TG preferring an ON etymon for ten stems, next to TGD's eight. But in most structural categories Davis is more likely to delete an earlier claim for ON input than to add one, the major exception being Type 'D2' (single 'D' level only), where his revision gives ON etyma for five stems which were otherwise explained in TG.

[546] Notice that it is more difficult to arrive at a meaningful figure for Type D2, since the identification of a D2 item with this or that ME word is by definition one of the problems here; and more than one of the ME words in question may in themselves be treated by Bj., whether or not he refers to a supposed occurrence in *Gaw*. But it may be remarked that Bj. has an entry for a ME word applicable to one or more potential identifications of a D2 item in thirty instances, i.e. he omits anything for twenty-two out of fifty-two items (42.3%).

loans to the kinds of structural evidence belonging to each Type; and it demonstrates just how many of the items belonging to Types C and D in particular have had purported Scand etyma generated by work since Bj.'s day.

6.2. FURTHER STUDY

The data that I have routinely gathered about the words in the Survey, and the analyses of them undertaken so far, are of course those that have seemed to me most germane to the objects of this book – that is, the principal focus has always been etymological. But it goes without saying that there are many and various further, more detailed studies of this material that can be made, even confining ourselves to *Gaw* alone. To take an obvious example, the account given in the Survey entries of English regional distribution is inevitably summary and impressionistic, drawing mostly on what can be deduced from *MED*; this impression is then condensed still further to produce a crudely generalized sense of the items which are restricted (to one extent or another) to the N/EM during the ME period, these items being marked by the circumstantial 'c' flag (see further the Introductory Remarks at pp. 62–3 above). Two hundred and one stems are labelled 'c' in one or more of their sub-entries, which at first glance looks like a massive number. But from the remarks on dialect distribution made in the Introductory Essays above, it should already be plain how much complexity lurks behind this label. If we combine the findings for the various structural Types,[547] it is clear that only forty-two of these 201 stems (20.9% of them) are unambiguously Northern or Eastern, entirely or almost entirely restricted to one or more parts of those regions throughout their recorded histories. Many of the others show signs of wider distribution, including twenty-five which are attested mainly in the N/EM in their earliest occurrences but are more widespread by the end of the ME period, fourteen where the reverse is true, and a further sixty-six most often found in the N/EM across ME but which are also occasionally recorded in other areas. Some other 'c' stems are attested too rarely for claims that they are regionally restricted to be very meaningful, including twelve which occur only in the *Gaw*-manuscript. But though noticing these facts adds a little nuance to our findings, it of course hardly begins to touch upon the deeper issues that lie behind them. Anything approaching a detailed understanding of the distribution of our words in the ME period would of course require a dedicated study, focusing not simply on the mere attestation of these items, on what we can tell about exactly where and when they are recorded, but analysing their competition within those textual traditions with synonyms and near-synonyms of whatever etymological origin, taking account of stylistic as well as semantic contexts in order to try to get closer to what

---

[547] Not including Type D2, for the reasons set out in the Introductory Essay to Type D, at p. 212 above.

might be motivating the choice of a particular word by this or that author or redactor.[548]

It is my hope that the present book, and the methods of etymological analysis and classification that it sets out, prepare the ground for such investigations; and hence that they will enable further research affording us a better grasp of the complex, multi-faceted and extensive impact of Anglo-Norse contact on the ME lexical system. Scholars wishing to use the Survey to undertake such further analyses on *Gaw* are, of course, still faced with the matter of deciding which amongst the items I have treated they wish to count as showing ON input for the purposes of their own studies. As described at the outset, my objective here has not been, and could not be, to provide a 'definitive' list of Norse-derived words; it should by now be clearer still that no such list is possible. But by exploring and characterizing the nature of the etymological evidence for each category of item, and moreover by offering a steer as to (what I reckon to be) the relative plausibility of the argument in each case, I hope that I have enabled users of this book to extract corpora of probable or possible Scand derivations in *Gaw* according to a consistent set of criteria. Some may prefer to set the bar of etymological plausibility lower, and others higher, depending on the nature of the study they wish to undertake – whether, for example, they are interested in exploring the maximal possible extent of the ON impact on ME vocabulary, or in tracing detailed biographies only of the most securely identified items.[549] To my mind, the most robust list to use for further, in-depth analysis consists of those 134 stems for which the case for ON input is most plausible and generally accepted; that is, all of Type A, and those stems of Types B and C with the highest probability level (i.e. single-letter B and C prefixes only). This gives a working corpus of sixty-nine Type A stems, twenty-two Type B and forty-three Type C,[550] made up of 195 different lexical items altogether.

If we glance briefly at these 195 items then, *inter alia*, we gain an immediate impression of the diverse destinations of originally ON material in the ME lexicon. To begin with, it is obvious that this material has penetrated every part of the grammar of the scribal dialect of *Gaw*. Fifty-eight of these 195 words are classed in the Survey as nouns (including one vbl. n.), fifty-five as verbs, thirty-seven as adjectives,[551] thirty-two as adverbs,[552] three as pronouns, two as prepositions, three as conjunctions and one as an interjection.[553] Needless to say,

---

[548] For provisional remarks about these matters as regards Norse-derived lexis in *Gaw*, see Dance (2013); and further the Introductory Remarks at pp. 56–8 above.

[549] And see also my remarks at Dance (2011: 93).

[550] These stems are supported, incidentally, by 18 'b' and 90 'c' circumstantial flags.

[551] Including two past participial adjectives, perhaps still interpretable as the past participles of verbs (**stad, þryuen**); two present participial adjectives (**þryuande, vnþryuande**); and one adj. which can also function pronominally (**same**).

[552] Including two which are dubiously so parsed: see **gayn** (12b.), **wiȝt** (67b.).

[553] There are also a handful of others which cannot be fitted easily into traditional 'parts of speech' categories, viz. one prep./conj. (**til**), one adv./prep. (**alofte**), one adj./pron./adv. (**boþe**) and one num. (adj./n.) (**hundreth**).

examining the grammatical categories to which these forms belong in *Gaw* is first and foremost a window onto the English word-formation processes in which Norse-derived lexical elements have participated since their adoption, as witnessed indeed by the great array of other elements affixed to them or combined with them to make compounds. This is especially evident with the thirty-two adverbs in our list, only ten of which are formed on stems which occur only as adverbs in *Gaw* (**agayn, ay, helder, heþen, mekely, skete, snart, tite, as-tit, wheþen**); and two even of these (**mekely, skete**) were probably or certainly sub-derived on some other ME category. It would naturally require a finer-grained etymological analysis, and some speculation, to recover in each case the grammatical category which was initially borrowed or influenced by ON lexical material during the period of Anglo-Norse contact itself; although this would of course be a very interesting subject to pursue, and it is obvious even at first blush that the original forms derived from ON must have consisted of items belonging to every part of speech, including closed-class items like pronouns and prepositions.

The wide range of semantic domains in which our list of most plausible items participates is also very much apparent. Even if we take just the fifty-eight nouns, for instance, we find several denoting some aspect of the physical world: terms for parts of the landscape are especially prominent (**bonk, felle, flat, gate, ker, myre, scowtes, wro**), but we also have words for other elements of the natural world, including weather (**blaste**), plants (**rotez**), animals (to be hunted) (**wayth**) and the bodies of humans and other creatures (**leggez, swange, wykez; dok**), and words for other substances (**froþe**), alongside terms for buildings/ locations (**kyrk, won (1)**) and architectural features (**lofte, wyndow**); there is also a more general word for a relative spatial location (**melle**, found in ME only in the prepositional/adverbial phrase *inn melle*). A number of items mainly denote objects, especially those with military roles (**bruny, gere, stele-gere, grayn, sparþe**), but also others (**sete, skyrtez, wandez**); while several describe actions (literal or figurative), including motion (**kest, race**), or refer to the results of actions (**anger, get, scaþe**). There is also a considerable group referring to human social and cultural matters (and the rules governing them): this includes relationships between people (**felaȝes, felaȝschyp, gest, sister-sunes**) and other roles (**tulk**), as well as religious symbols (**cros**), the law (**lawe**), and a range of terms which can broadly be thought of as denoting social activities or relations of one sort or another, including communication and entertainment (**bone, carp, layk, laykyng, lote**). Finally, there is a miscellaneous set lexicalizing abstract phenomena, from (mental) faculties or abilities (**skyl, sleȝt**) and internal experiences (**dreme**) to an array which may loosely be classed as relating to emotion, opinion or evaluation (**cost, hap, ille, menske, vnhap, won (2), wont, woþe**). Some of these findings are things that we would strongly have suspected at the outset; it is hardly surprising, for example, that the domains of the landscape and military accoutrements are relatively well populated, by words of whatever origin, in a quest romance two of whose outstanding features are descriptions of the natural world on the one hand and of the tools and trappings of warfare on the other. But the main impression garnered from this briefest of conceptual surveys is, again, simply one of the diversity of the destinations of originally ON lexical material in ME – something which is entirely to be expected by this period, but which is strongly confirmed by our data.[554] As emphasized above, reaching beyond immediate and impressionistic conclusions like these, to appreciate the full extent of the roles played by these ME words both in *Gaw* itself and more broadly in the ME lexicon, will require far more detailed, sensitive analyses of their usage, with a focus on the semantic and stylistic contexts associated with the members of particular word-fields.

6.3. Coda: The *Gersum* Project

One of the main contexts in which further study is currently being carried out, and one which aims to take forward both the work of the present book and research into the ON influence on the English lexicon more broadly, is 'The *Gersum* Project'. This is a collaborative venture involving a research team in Cambridge (myself and Dr Brittany Schorn) and Cardiff (Dr Sara Pons-Sanz), with digital support from the Digital Humanities Institute in Sheffield. We are funded by the Arts and Humanities Research Council of the United Kingdom for three years, beginning in January 2016.[555] Like this book, the principal research focus of *Gersum* is etymological. Its intention is to continue and deepen the work begun here via the collection and analysis of a larger corpus of late ME words for which ON input has been claimed; it will apply to other ME alliterative verse the same methodological principles (and the same etymological typology and labels) as those established in this book, beginning with the full contents of the *Gaw*-manuscript and progressing to other key poems from the North and North Midlands, including *St Erkenwald* and *The Wars of Alexander*. The findings of this research will be presented in a fully searchable electronic catalogue, freely available on the web from the conclusion of the project. The catalogue will describe the crucial etymological issues for each lexical item, alongside information about its variant forms, meanings, occurrences, distribution, and so on, with reference to the major dictionaries, handbooks and other scholarly authorities, including links to the *HTOED*. The *Gersum* catalogue will therefore contain entries for all the words treated in the present book, but it will not simply repeat the analyses made here: its etymological remarks will consist of briefer summaries of the discussions in the *Gaw* Survey (with reference to them), but the key information will be searchable in additional and more sophisticated ways; and of course data on the occurrences of the items in *Gaw* will form only one element in a much fuller guide to their attestations, forms and usage in a broader corpus of

---

[554] For the range of concepts expressed by ON loans in earlier phases of English, see the conclusions esp. by SPS (149–244), Dance (2003: esp. 212–13); and more generally Durkin (2014: 213–17).

[555] See the project's website at <https://www.gersum.org>.

alliterative verse. Moreover, further investigation of the items in the *Gersum* catalogue will take place under the aegis of the project, whose outputs will include detailed case studies of words belonging to particular lexical fields and their semantic and stylistic contexts.[556]

The *Gersum* project is just one example of the work that can and, I very much hope, will be done to build on the foundations of the Survey presented in this book, and in all kinds of other ways to pursue the Scand role in the evolution of English vocabulary. If nothing else, the huge myriad of scholarly claims for ON input reviewed here, with regard to the lexis of just one poem, must demonstrate beyond doubt that this is a subject with enormous and enduring appeal: it has massive significance for our understanding of the development of the English language, in a whole range of ways, from late OE right through the medieval period; and it still has important repercussions today, being a key element in the potent idea of 'the Viking legacy' which still resonates so strongly in modern constructions of British identity and heritage, especially in the North of England. But there remains an immense amount of research to do on this subject before we can claim thoroughly to understand it, and that work must always be grounded, it seems to me, in the detailed, contextually-sensitive analysis of the words themselves in the particular texts and traditions where they are found. As I hope to have shown throughout this book, the etymological identification of ON input is no mere preliminary to that analysis, but a crucial part of comprehending the extent and ramifications of the Scand influence on English, and a vital object of research in its own right. Tracing how and why ON etyma have been attributed to the words in the Survey is a complex and fascinating task, not only because the linguistic and textual evidence itself presents so many challenges, but because of what the conclusions reached by generations of scholars reveal about the methods, attitudes and goals which underlie the interpretation of that evidence. I began these Introductory Essays by likening the etymological elucidation of the words in *Gaw* to a foray into a dangerous wilderness. But I hope that this book suggests some of the respects in which the hazards of this 'adventure' are not simply a distraction or a diversion in the study of word history, something that we have to get out of the way first; the hermeneutic processes which our etymological investigations involve us in tracing, the hows and whys of deriving a word from Norse, must in fact be one of the focuses of our study, since these ways of thinking are crucially important to the whole basis on which we judge Scand influence to have happened, to whatever results we and anybody else have ever got. Or, to put it another way, and as Sir Gawain himself becomes painfully aware, the experience of getting there sometimes turns out to be the most important thing about a quest.

---

[556] This research is being led by Dr Pons-Sanz, and will appear in a series of separate publications (starting with Pons-Sanz forthcoming).

Printed and bound by CPI Group (UK) Ltd, Croydon, CR0 4YY

09/06/2025

14685988-0001